by the same author

★

PROPHET AND POET:

The Bible and the Growth of Romanticism

BIBLICAL DRAMA
IN ENGLAND

BIBLICAL DRAMA
IN ENGLAND

From the Middle Ages to the Present Day

by

MURRAY ROSTON

NORTHWESTERN UNIVERSITY PRESS
Evanston
1968

Cover illustration by Aubrey Beardsley.
From Salome *(London, 1894; Elkin Mathews & John Lane)*
Courtesy of The Newberry Library, Chicago

Library of Congress Catalogue Card Number 68-20202

In memory of
my brother
JERROLD

ACKNOWLEDGEMENTS

The preparation of this book has included two visits to the United States, and I am most grateful to the English departments of Brown and Stanford universities for the warm hospitality extended to me during the periods I taught there. I am also indebted to a number of individuals for helpful comments and suggestions. They include Professors Arthur Brown and Norman Callan of London University, Leicester Bradner, Barbara K. Lewalski, and Millicent Bell at Brown, Harold Fisch of Bar-Ilan University (who has followed the book's progress with his usual interest and sympathy) and, more recently, V. A. Kolve and A. G. Rigg of Stanford. Their advice has been most valuable to me, and I welcome this opportunity of expressing my thanks.

M.R.

Bar-Ilan University
Israel

CONTENTS

11

Contents

INTRODUCTION

Inscribed above the entrance to the Delphic oracle was the challenging injunction *Know Thyself*, and drama, born within that cultural context, has in its finest form continued to offer an exploration of man's inner self, an enquiry into the human predicament. The biblical ethos, on the other hand, encouraged obedience rather than self-exploration, an obedience epitomized in the words of Micah: *What doth the Lord ask of thee but to do justice, love mercy, and walk humbly with thy God?* For the Greek, then, an unfettered investigation of man's nature and destiny; for the Christian, a humble acceptance of divine order and the performance of good deeds on earth.

The very phrase 'biblical drama' would thus seem a contradiction in terms, offering the bleak prospect of dramatized sermons on moral rectitude with casts drawn from the saints and sinners. Such, indeed, it has been at its worst – in the kind of simplistic Sunday-school play either ignored or only glanced at in this present study. But at its best, scriptural drama is set not within the millennial Jerusalem to which Micah points but in the craggy terrain that lies before it where men may stumble and fall. If the prophet demanded justice in the name of a righteous God, Job's uncompromising insistence upon truth impelled him to question the example of that justice afforded by heaven; and even Peter, the most faithful of New Testament disciples, denied his Master three times before the crowing of the cock. It was within this spiritual struggle of men committed to an ideal yet torn from it by their human weaknesses and strengths that such writers as Milton, Byron, and Fry found the themes for their biblical plays.

13

Introduction

In adapting these stories to the stage, the playwright was hampered both by the sanctity of the Bible and by the audience's familiarity with its text, but the stylistic compression of biblical narrative offered him some compensation. The scriptural account suggests no reason for the rejection of Cain's sacrifice. The medieval dramatist ascribed it, with patent homiletical intent, to Cain's refusal to pay his tithes; but the later dramatist, particularly in a Protestant country, was free to supply his own conjectural reason without fearing a charge of blasphemy. Moreover, the very act of transposing these characters from narrative to drama demanded from the playwright some degree of personal identification, an attempt to visualize the scriptural scene from within. Motive assumed a new importance in rounding out a character of whom we catch only a glimpse in the Scriptures. Frequently the dramatist would select a biblical figure into whom he could project his own spiritual dilemma without wrenching the original account too drastically out of shape; and in more iconoclastic periods of history, a dramatist might deliberately wrench that account out of shape in order to expose what he termed the falsity of biblical narrative.

The choice of biblical themes in each era, as well as their treatment, was therefore dictated not only by the individual taste of the English dramatist, but also by fluctuations in his religious and social milieux. Perhaps the greatest danger in studies of this kind has been the temptation to speak of the Bible as an indivisible entity, a body of writings which together rose and fell in the respect accorded to it by each generation. In fact, I have argued here that the status of the Old Testament fluctuated almost independently of the New, and that within each Testament there existed numerous hierarchical subdivisions repeatedly exchanging their places on the ladder of sanctity in response to subtle movements within the English cultural scene. This history of biblical drama has, therefore, a twofold aim: to provide a critical evaluation of the plays themselves in the context of the periods in which they were written, and at the same time to suggest the insights they afford into the religious and cultural history of the English people.

CHAPTER I

THE MEDIEVAL STAGE

(i) REALISM AND EXPRESSIONISM

Medieval drama has, until very recently, been the ugly duckling of dramatic history, studied more for its quaintness than for its dramatic power. Even E. K. Chambers, to whose *Medieval Stage* we are so indebted for our knowledge of the background to the plays, admits in the preface that he produced the work solely as a stepping-stone for his later study of the Elizabethan theatre; and it was not fortuitous that the three anthologists primarily responsible for introducing these plays to a wider audience – A. W. Pollard, J. M. Manly, and J. Q. Adams – all used the term 'pre-Shakespearean' or 'pre-Elizabethan' in the titles of their collections, as if the plays' only value lay in their antedating the Elizabethan era. By applying the criteria of the more naturalistic Elizabethan theatre to an art-form which was essentially non-naturalistic, critics such as Tucker Brooke praised the livelier scenes of clowning and fisticuffs as harbingers of the full-blooded Renaissance stage, while the more solemn pageants were often dismissed as stiff and awkward.[1]

There was, in fact, some justification for their view. The York Passion play, for example, seems to contain an incongruous mingling of naturalism and dramatic clumsiness. On the one hand the Pinmakers who helped produce the pageant used their craftsmanship to make the torture grimly effective in its authenticity, the soldiers hammering nails into Christ's body with nauseating professionalism; but the climax of the play –

[1] C. F. Tucker Brooke, *The Tudor Drama* (Cambridge, Mass., 1911), p. 13.

15

Christ's speech as he hangs in agony from the Cross – seems singularly undramatic in its calm didacticism:

> *Al men þat walkis by waye or strete,*
> *Takes tente ʒe schalle no trauayle tyne,*
> *By-holdes myn heede, myn handis, and my feete,*
> *And fully feele nowe or ʒe fyne,*
> *If any mournyng may be meete*
> *Or myscheue mesured vnto myne.*
> *My Fadir, þat alle bales may bete,*
> *For-giffis þes men þat dois me pyne.*
> *What þai wirke wotte þai noght,*
> *Therfore my Fadir I craue*
> *Latte neuere þer synnys be sought,*
> *But see þer saules to saue.* [1]

Drama is one of the most evanescent of arts, and the text of an ancient play alone offers little more than the raw material. Without corroborative evidence from the era, the original methods of production must remain conjectural, and in fact only the sketchiest accounts of performances have survived. There is, however, one source of evidence which can, I think, provide us with an invaluable clue – the pictorial art of the Middle Ages; not so much in its depiction of performances as in its parallel treatment of the same themes. In the famous *Martyrdom of St. Erasmus* at St. Peter's, Louvain, Dirk Bouts, for example, portrays the martyr as gazing at his own disembowelment with almost

---

[1] *The York Plays*, ed. L. Toulmin Smith (Oxford, 1885), p. 357. In the footnotes I have offered translations of the more difficult Latin and medieval quotations. This passage might be rendered:
> All men that walk by way or street
> Take care lest you neglect this grief.
> Behold my head, my hands, my feet,
> And fully feel now while there's time
> If any mourning may be meet
> Or mischief measured unto mine.
> Father, that can torn flesh renew,
> Forgive these men that cause me pain.
> They know not what they do.
> Therefore, my Father, I crave
> Keep not their sins in view
> But seek their souls to save.

undisturbed tranquillity. As in the York Crucifixion, the physical torture itself is depicted with vivid realism, the saint's entrails being slowly extracted on a spit; but there is no attempt to provide any realistic coherence between the gruesome scene and the victim's calm, almost detached response. For the artist here is stylistically superimposing the spiritual content of the scene upon the physically realistic setting, so that by transcending the limits of chronology he permits us an advance glimpse of the saint's joyful acceptance into heaven. The failure of earlier critics to perceive this distinction is the more remarkable as the theatre at the turn of this century was already experimenting with an expressionism which sought to transcend the surface realism of the phenomenal world in order to explore the truer reality that lay beyond. In such plays as Strindberg's *Ghost Sonata*, chronological sequence collapsed, the inner workings of the mind became the new focus of interest, and scene designers rejected the conventional stage-settings of room interiors in favour of empty stages or startlingly symbolic backcloths. When O'Neill removed the house-façade in *Desire Under the Elms* to expose the inhabitants moving in supposed privacy from room to room, drama critics were duly impressed; but when the rubric of a medieval play instructed Joseph in Egypt to stand a few feet away from his brethren in Palestine, they smiled at the dramatist's ineptitude.

This medieval penchant for mingling expressionism with realism by superimposing the spiritual significance of a scene upon its physical representation became a hallmark of martyrological art; and there is an even closer parallel to the York Crucifixion play in Antonio Pollaiuolo's *Martyrdom of St. Sebastian*. There the saint's serene, if slightly troubled countenance dominates from above the anatomically detailed depiction of the muscular archers bending to prime their crossbows or leaning back to take their deadly aim. The concern with sadistic torture both here and in the Crucifixion play is part of the medieval attempt (of which Hieronymus Bosch forms the Renaissance climax) to impress the Christian with a sense of horror which should lead him both to compassion and repentance. By association he was to recall the tortures of Hell which awaited him if he failed to respond in time to the implications of Christ's suffering. But above all, the juxtaposition of physical cruelty and spiritual transcendence of the flesh was intended to reflect the central Christian message that this world was merely an anteroom to the world to come. It was a form of expressionism inherited from the art of the later Roman period, with its attempt to suggest the inner tension and soulfulness of its figures,[1] but was incorporated into Christian art as ideally suited to the adumbrative philosophy of the Middle Ages. Between twentieth-century Expressionism and that of the Middle Ages there was, perhaps, this difference which may have misled the critics – that the former deliberately startled audiences by the novelty of ignoring the limitations of time and space, while the medieval playwright wrote for an age already imbued with a disregard for these merely temporal criteria. Essentially, however, the techniques were the same.

Since the appearance of Hardin Craig's *English Religious Drama*, with its salutary warning against exaggerated interest in clowns and sheep-stealing, there has been less danger of our regarding the mystery cycles solely as precursors of the secular Elizabethan stage, and V. A. Kolve's recent study has underscored the formality of the 'play-game' elements of the drama exemplified in the term *ludus*.[2] We are becoming increasingly aware of the powerful dramatic effect these plays must have produced on an audience responsive to artistic and liturgical stylization. To a devout Christian, the Mass was less a re-enactment than a reliving of the central Christian scenes, and the doctrine of transubstantiation, as yet unchallenged by the Protestants, confirmed the feeling that here was a truer reality than mere dramatic verisimilitude could offer.[3] However, as critical fashions swing back and forth we are now, perhaps, in equal danger of erring in the opposite direction. Miss Eleanor Prosser has recently carried Craig's warning much further. In an eloquent plea for a reassessment of medieval drama in terms of the dramatic unity of the plays, of their effectiveness in achieving

[1] Arnold Hauser, *The Social History of Art*, tr. S. Godman (New York, 1951), i, 122.

[2] Hardin Craig, *English Religious Drama of the Middle Ages* (Oxford, 1955), pp. 6–7, and V. A. Kolve, *The Play Called Corpus Christi* (Stanford, 1966). See also Glynne Wickham, *Early English Stages*, vol. i (London, 1959).

[3] See O. B. Hardison Jr., *Christian Rite and Christian Drama in the Middle Ages* (Baltimore, 1965), pp. 35 f.

their ultimate purpose as religious art, she condemns
hand the brawling and coarseness of the so-called '
scenes as destroying the carefully wrought dramatic eff
whole. While she is prepared to accept the comic scene
Shakespeare's *Lear* as contributing to the overall dramatic effect,
for her the Towneley Cain provides an instance of '. . . an over-
grown gargoyle who almost totally obscures the cathedral, the
religious purpose'.[1] Where earlier critics were urging us to
wade through the duller scenes of medieval drama for the sake
of the livelier comedy, Miss Prosser would have us, in effect,
omit the Wakefield Cain and Noah scenes as offending against
the dramatic solemnity of the religious pageant, and concentrate
solely on the graver theme.

The truth probably lies between these two extremer views
which are not, I would suggest, mutually exclusive. For the
medieval drama should be seen not as a hotch-potch of buffoonery
and solemnity but, like martyrological art, as a deliberate
blending of the spirit and the flesh, of mundane realism and
expressionist stylization within the confines of a unified cycle.
Like the comic scenes of *King Lear*, the slapstick of the mystery
plays served to reinforce the graver message, however divorced
the two may appear on the surface. Noah's recalcitrant wife is
not a secular importation into the religious drama but a dramatization of the oft-recurring Shrew of the medieval sermon, who
was luridly described from the pulpit in language echoing Proverbs vii. She was attacked in the sermons, for 'over muche
spekynge', for 'curiouse and bold tellynge of talis' and, in the
tradition of Eve, for disobedience to her lawful spouse–all of
which form the leading traits of Noah's wife in the various comic
versions that have survived.[2] To suggest, then, that she dis-
tracted from the dramatic solemnity of the cycle is to miss the
homiletical significance to which a medieval audience would
immediately have responded.

However, if there was no dichotomy between the solemn and
the comic elements in the cycles, and, as in Pollaiuolo's painting,
realism and surrealism could fruitfully coexist within one frame,

[1] Eleanor Prosser, *Drama and Religion in the English Mystery Plays*
(Stanford, 1961), especially pp. 82–86.
[2] G. R. Owst, *Literature and Pulpit in Medieval England* (Oxford,
1961), pp. 388 and 492.

there was nonetheless a certain compartmentalization determining which biblical figures were by their very nature eligible for realistic exploitation and which for stylization. Clearly, the gargoyle could not appear in the centre of the high altar, nor the Crucifixion scene on the guttering. I propose to argue, however, that the distinction was far more subtle, and that there existed within the mystery plays a carefully graduated hierarchy of sanctity predetermining the degree of realism which the playwright was at liberty to introduce.

In tracing the growth of this realism, we have not returned to the earlier critics' search for signs of pre-Elizabethan naturalism within a somewhat crude drama. For if we begin from the assumption that the more sacred scenes, so far from being dramatically crude, were at their best profoundly moving stylizations—paralleling fourteenth-century Sienese paintings with their haloed figures set like jewels against a background of rich gold[1]—then the growth of the comic scenes within the plays becomes a matter of scholarly interest and not of literary justification. We shall, in other words, be watching a movement from expressionism to naturalism without partisan preference of the one over the other.

(ii) THE SACRED AND THE PROFANE

The more formal presentation of those plays centring on Jesus arose naturally from the greater reverence they evoked and from their more intimate connection with the Mass out of which they had grown. But this greater formality was, I believe, fortified by a historical precedent; for behind the Nativity plays and, by association, the plays of the Passion, may be perceived the tradition of the *praesepe* or crèche. As early as the third century, it had become customary to decorate the Grotto in Bethlehem with a model of the Nativity scene lavishly executed in gold, silver, and precious jewels. From Palestine the practice spread across Catholic Europe until before long, at the Christmas season, every church and chapel had its own, often

[1] Cf. *The Deposition* by Ugolino di Nerio, originally from the altarpiece of Santa Croce in Florence and now in the National Gallery, London.

lifesize, model of the manger, and the earliest shepherd plays were probably an outgrowth of the liturgical office performed at this *praesepe*.[1] The debt of art to the medieval play has recently been noted – Emile Mâle has drawn our attention to the statues at Saint-Trophime in Arles in which the shepherd's scrip accords with a rubric in the Rouen play of Emmaus, and Miss Anderson has remarked that medieval bosses and windows in England were frequently modelled on scenes from the liturgical drama.[2] But the reverse process must have been even stronger, for medieval art was well established before the rebirth of the drama. It requires little conjecture to realize that no medieval audience would be impressed by a Nativity play which fell short of the annual *praesepe* model in visual impact. The play provided, in a sense, a live version of a model familiar to every spectator, in which haloed figures in gorgeous robes offered and received the gifts of the Magi in a setting glittering with jewels and glowing with richly coloured tapestry. We know, for example, that in the thirteenth century St. Francis of Assisi made a live model of the *praesepe* at his altar in the forest with men and women impersonating the main figures and with a live ox and ass to complete the scene. It was this *praesepe* tradition, coupled with the supreme sanctity of the theme for the Christian spectator which lent a ceremonial and almost static quality to the plays of the Epiphany, with the emphasis upon dazzling spectacle rather than emotional realism. The haloes crowning the holy figures on medieval triptychs and in the *praesepe* itself were a form of insignia which discouraged that identification of audience with character so necessary to naturalistic drama, but which served to enhance, by the distance they created between mortal and divine figures, the solemnity of the semi-liturgical scene represented. It is significant that during the period of the more fully developed cycles, the *Adoration of the Magi* was assigned at Newcastle to the guild of goldsmiths, who could ensure the lavishness of the décor.

[1] E. K. Chambers, *Medieval Stage* (Oxford, 1903), ii, 42–43.
[2] Emile Mâle, *Religious Art from the Twelfth to the Eighteenth Century* (New York, 1949), pp. 26–28, and M. D. Anderson, *Drama and Imagery in the English Medieval Churches* (Cambridge, 1963); also W. L. Hildburgh, *English Alabaster Carvings as Records of the Medieval Religious Drama* (Oxford, 1949).

One of the earliest extant plays of the Magi, the *Officium Stellae* of Rouen, shows how early this emphasis on spectacle existed within the Nativity plays. Three members of the clergy accompanied by servants bearing the gifts followed a moving star towards the altar, where a curtain, suddenly drawn aside, dramatically revealed the posed figures of the Madonna and Child.[1] As in pictorial art, they are caught at a moment sacred in Christian history, embodying both the past and future of humanity. And to emphasize the point, an image of the Virgin and Child is there substituted for human actors.

In the *Shearmen and Taylors' Pageant* at Coventry (not to be confused with the *Ludus Coventriae* whose home was probably Lincoln) there was an additional reason for presenting the Nativity scene in a more static form; for the seal of that guild represented 'the Virgin Mary seated and crowned with the infant Christ in her lap, receiving gifts from the Magi.'[2] With that mingling of commerce and religion peculiar to the medieval guilds, the pageant thus constituted not only a thanksgiving to the patron Mother and Child but also a trade emblem for the public; and there is a distinctly ceremonial quality in the king's reverent offering of their gifts:

I. REX. *Hayle, Lorde thatt all this worlde hathe wroght!*
      Hale, God and man to-gedur in fere!
      For thow hast made all thyng of noght,
      Albe-yt thatt thow lyist porely here;

[1] Karl Young, *The Drama of the Medieval Church* (Oxford, 1933), ii. 45.
[2] *Two Coventry Corpus Christi Plays*, EETS e.s., ed. Hardin Craig (London, 1957):

    1st King: Hail, Lord, that all this world hath wrought!
              Hail, God and man combined in one!
          For thou hast made all things of nought,
              Although thou liest poorly here;
         A cup full of gold I have thee brought,
              In token thou art without peer.
    2nd King: Hail be thou, Lord, of high magnificence!
         In token of priesthood and dignity of office,
         To thee I offer a cup full of incense,
              For it becomes thee to have such sacrifice.
    3rd King: Hail be thou, Lord long-looked-for!
         I have brought thee myrrh for mortality,
         In token thou shalt mankind restore
              To life by thy death upon a tree.

The Sacred and the Profane

A cupe-full ⌈of⌉ golde here I haue the broght,
In toconyng thow art with-out pere.

II. REX. *Hayle be thow, Lord of hy magnyffecens!*
In toconyng of preste⌈h⌉od and dyngnete of offece,
To the I offur a cupe-full off in-sence,
For yt be-hovith the to haue soche sacrefyce.

III. REX. *Hayle be thow, Lorde longe lokid fore!*
I haue broght the myre for mortalete,
In to-cunyng thow schalt mankynd restore
To lyff be thy deyth apon a tre.

But in all cycles, these central scenes retain, not surprisingly, a marked formality and richness of ceremony. In our own day, it is frequently difficult, if not impossible, to distinguish between dramatically impressive formalism in such scenes and mere woodenness of presentation. But since the main stress must have been placed on the solemnity of the acting and the magnificence of the décor, we should beware of underestimating their effectiveness as the climactic scenes of the mystery cycles.

The stylized solemnity of the more sacred scenes, although reinforced by the tradition of the static *praesepe*, was in itself so suited to the liturgical and didactic purposes of the early drama that explanations of its growth are almost superfluous. The lively realism of the comic scenes, however, still surprises us, as does their very inclusion in the religious cycles. For if the cycle moved with the Church's blessing[1] out of the cathedral into the charge of the guilds, it still depended for its existence upon the approval of the clergy. Under ecclesiastical rule, comedy would in all probability never have been tolerated and certainly not encouraged as a separate genre, as it was, for example, in ancient Greece. Consequently, its growth within the cycles themselves and as an integral part of them had of necessity to be gradual and almost unnoticed lest it arouse the ire of the authorities. Inevitably, therefore, its beginnings are to be found at the

[1] See Grace Frank, 'The Genesis and Staging of the Jeu d'Adam', *PMLA lix* (1944) and her *Mediaeval French Drama* (Oxford, 1954), p. 74. Her theory that the Church approved of its egress is based on the rubric *Tunc vadat Figura ad ecclesiam* which suggests a performance near the church door.

opposite end of the sacred hierarchy, where no one could object on the grounds of blasphemy.

It has long been noted that much of the comic elaboration and realism of these plays is to be found among the supernumeraries, the characters like Cain's servant Garcio and the Roman executioners who either do not appear in the Scriptures at all or are only cursorily mentioned there. With them the playwright felt free to indulge his comic or naturalistic bent without fear of sacrilege. If, however, we extrapolate the theory, we shall find that, not only in the mystery plays but in the development of biblical drama as a whole, realism, whether comic or empathic, advanced slowly up the rungs of the sacred hierarchy, retreating whenever theological or social changes increased the sanctity of this or that biblical figure. In a sense, therefore, our study of the dramatic realism within these plays will serve as a graph recording fluctuations in the reverence accorded in each period to the various parts of the Bible, as well as to the Bible as a whole. Conversely, an awareness of the current sanctity of certain biblical figures will help to explain why they achieved fuller dramatic elaboration in some periods while in others they remained at best stylized or, at worst, dull and wooden.

The first, and perhaps most obvious group of characters available for more lively dramatization consisted of the enemies of Christ, the 'goats' of New Testament narrative. The most priggish of clerics could not object to the ridiculing of evil, and it was through these 'goats' that a more boisterous and often secular note first entered the plays. Before a performance began, it was the unholy trinity of Herod, Pilate, and the devil which served the useful purpose of quieting the crowd, sometimes by running among the bystanders and striking them over the head with inflated bladders, while the more sacred characters kept their distance from the mob. The former, by their greater kinship with mortals, could afford to mingle with them and in the plays themselves their more human qualities were soon exploited. Although the evidence adduced for Herod as a comic figure is, I think, unconvincing,[1] as a ranting, bombastic tyrant he became a lively and at times even troublesome figure of medieval drama

[1] Miss O. E. Wilson, *Low Comedy as a Structural Element in English Drama* (Chicago, 1926), p. 21, argues unconvincingly that the ranting is comic in effect.

whose overacting had become proverbial by the time of Shak speare. But here too the process was gradual, as if the dramatis were afraid of causing offence. Despite the description of Herod in the Vulgate as exceedingly angry (*iratus est valde*), in what is probably his first appearance in Latin drama, a play from the Cathedral of Nevers, he is a mild and inoffensive creature.[1] But before long he was depicted as irascibly casting a book to the floor, and was soon the tyrant with which we are more familiar, raging and pouring out a torrent of abuse. It has even been argued that he was largely responsible for the egress of drama from the church. The ecclesiastical authorities encouraged, on the one hand, this lively and unsympathetic depiction of the forces of evil, but on the other hand his blasphemous roaring seemed unseemly within the walls of a holy building, particularly when, as at Padua, he invaded the liturgy itself, beating the officiants with that favoured weapon, the inflated bladder, and reading the ninth lesson *cum tanto furore*.[2] Once outside the church, he could roar as much as he pleased without causing offence, as in the Coventry play:

> . . . *owt! owt! owtt!*
> *Hath those fawls traytvrs done me this ded?*
> *I stampe! I stare! I loke all abowtt!*
> *Myght I take them, I schuld them bren at a glede!*
> *I rent! I rawe! and now run I wode!*
> *A! thatt these velen trayturs hath mard this my mode!*
> *The schalbe hangid yf I ma cum them to!*
>
> *Here Erode ragis in the pagond and in the strete also.*[3]

As in the New Testament, the Pilate of the mystery plays was less markedly villainous than Herod. The Gospels had depicted

---

[1] Young, ii, 50. The source is Matt. ii. 15.
[2] Young, ii, 100.
[3] . . . out, out, out!
Have those false traitors done this deed?
I stamp! I stare! I look all about!
If I catch them, I'll burn them alive!
I rant! I rave! and now I run mad!
Ah! these villainous traitors have ruined my plan!
They shall be hanged if I find them!
Here Herod rages on the pageant-car and also in the street.

him as submitting to Pharisaical pressure with reluctance, and authorizing the Crucifixion solely in order 'to satisfy the people' (Mark xv. 15). In many of the pageant plays this more sympathetic tradition was preserved; but if Pilate was not invariably among the damned, he was certainly not to be classed with the sacrosanct, and was thus available for more lively dramatization. We know that at Coventry in 1490 Pilate was assigned a club and took a leading part in the play, being paid four shillings for his performance as against Herod's three shillings and fourpence and God's two shillings. The club, made of green material, is mentioned a few times in the records of the Coventry trading companies and must have been used energetically as it required extensive repair.[1] Moreover, if Herod was proverbial in Shakespeare's day as the ranting tyrant, it was to 'Pilates voys' that Chaucer compared the raucous swearing of his Miller. In the Towneley *Talents*, he is the central figure in a scene of buffoonery over the division of Christ's garment. The three torturers bring the garment to Pilate, who at once claims it as his own. There ensues a lengthy scene in which he makes various attempts to outwit them, such as dividing it to leave himself with the best portion and the others with shreds. They insist upon throwing dice, and Pilate loses. Complaining that the winner had blown on the dice before throwing, he suggests that it might be wiser for them to present the winnings to him as a gift. The play concludes on a didactic note with the usual warnings against gambling, but the conclusion smacks of an attempt to justify the presence of some lively realism in the religious cycle, introduced once again by means of the villains and supernumeraries.

Judas Iscariot is a perfect instance of the restraints imposed on comic elaboration by the sanctity of the setting. As the betrayer of Jesus, he stands very obviously with the 'goats' of the New Testament; but as an intimate of Jesus in the climactic scenes of the cycle, his comic development never passes beyond the embryonic. He wears the red wig associated with the devils, but that is all. The moment, however, that he is removed from this proximity to Jesus and transferred to the morality play where he

---

[1] Appendix II of the EETS edition of the Coventry plays. See also Arnold Williams, *The Characterization of Pilate in the Towneley Plays* (East Lansing, 1950).

coalesces with the Devil himself, he becomes the comic butt of his Vice. In fact, L. W. Cushman has noted that in the mystery plays as a whole the Devil was rarely treated as a comic figure; [1] like Judas, his didactic function and his participation in the central New Testament scenes precluded frivolity. But the under-devils developed his comic potentialities vicariously within the cycles, notably Tutivillus in the Towneley *Judgment* amusingly parodying the extravagant fashions of the day.

A second group whose lesser sanctity encouraged dramatic realism–a group not normally isolated by critics–consisted of the Old Testament figures. If Cain was classed with the 'goats' of Scriptural narrative, Noah, Abraham, and Isaac belonged to the brotherhood of saints traditionally haloed on the stained-glass windows. Yet instead of remaining stylized, they became before long among the most human and realistic of medieval *dramatis personae*. This change was the more remarkable since the highly developed prefigurative tradition of the Middle Ages had, of course, seen in the Hebraic section of the Bible a series of cyclical prophecies of the Christian Messiah; and such typological exegesis which perceived in Noah an adumbration of the Redeemer of the World saving mankind from perdition served to enhance his sanctity even further. Not only was he in his own right the most perfect of his generation but he was depicted on the pillars of the Doge's Palace posed against the vine like Jesus against the Cross or, nearer home at Canterbury, as paralleling in the Flood the Baptism of Jesus. [2] The laminated interpretation of the Bible on the four exegetical levels of literal, allegorical, moral, and anagogical had become little more than a formality as far as the Old Testament was concerned, and it was typology which became the almost exclusive concern of medieval commentators and preachers. Homily did indeed occupy a central position, particularly in the pulpit. Master Robert Rypon, for example, the sub-prior of Durham, insisted on the homiletical reading in a sermon delivered about 1400. There he argued with some subtlety that the Gospel story

[1] L. W. Cushman, *The Devil and the Vice in English Dramatic Literature Before Shakespeare* (Halle, 1900), p. 16.
[2] Helen Gardner, *The Business of Criticism* (Oxford, 1963), p. 92, and Jean Danielou, *From Shadows to Reality: Studies in the Biblical Typology of the Fathers* (London, 1960), pp. 69 f.

of the loaves and the fishes teaches allegorically a contempt for the literal meaning of the Pentateuch:

'By the five loaves, doctors understand the five Books of Moses which are aptly compared to a barley loaf; for a barley loaf on its outside is rough, in part, and harsh, yet within it is full of the purest flour. Likewise, the Books of Moses, too, are rude when considered literally; nevertheless within they are full of moral senses and doctrines, useful alike to the preacher and his audience.'[1]

But the sermons employing the Old Testament figures as homiletical models for good and evil saw them largely in terms of Christological antetypes. Moreover, medieval prefiguration was capable not merely of perceiving general foreshadowings of the Gospels in the Old Testament, but of pursuing the parallels into the minutiae of the text. Augustine, writing in his *Contra Faustum* of Noah the Redeemer of mankind, was troubled by the apparently degrading incident of drunkenness, until he found in it an antetype of Jesus drinking the cup of the Passion. In Noah's nakedness he discerned a symbol of the mortality of the flesh whereby the Crucifixion confirmed the piety of the righteous (Shem and Japheth) and provoked the scorn of the mockers (Ham). No medieval spectator bred on this typological tradition could miss the Crucifixion parallel in Cain's murder of the innocent Abel, or the sacrifice of the Father's only begotten Son in the binding of Isaac.

One of the few independent dramatizations of Old Testament themes to survive – the twelfth-century *Ordo de Ysaac et Rebecca et Filiis Eorum* – exemplifies this antetypal concern. A chorus interrupts the tale of Jacob and Esau after almost every speech in order to explain the prefigurative significance of the preceding passage, both with regard to the story at large and to the smallest details of the scene. And again the most elaborate parallels are worried out of the text. The overall allegory portrays Esau as representing the Pharisaical Jews, and Jacob the faithful Christians, even though Jacob is here involved in an action of doubtful morality.[2]

---

[1] Quoted in G. R. Owst, *Literature and Pulpit*, p. 58.
[2] The Bible itself recognizes the immorality by pointing out the Hebrew pun in the name Jacob with its connotation of 'trickery' (Gen. xxvii. 36).

The Sacred and the Profane

> *Quod natus maior uocatvr*
> *synagoga designatvr,*
> *prior pressa sub onere*
> *non spiritus sed littere.*
> *Maior lege procedentem,*
> *minor fide subsequentem*
> *populum notat uocatum*
> *et in Christo adunatvm.*
> *Ysaac Seyr amauit,*
> *se uenatu cuius pauit;*
> *sic Devs primo Iudevm,*
> *hostiis dum colit eum.* [1]

The clothes left behind by Esau and donned by Jacob signify the decalogue neglected by the Jews and now adopted by the Christians. In such an allegorized setting, there could be little room for dramatic realism.

All this allegorizing might seem to disqualify the Old Testament as a candidate for realistic elaboration, since prefiguration continually stressed that it foreshadowed the sacred scenes of the New. Nevertheless, there was a world of difference between the central Gospel scenes themselves and the preceding stories which, even according to typological interpretation, merely *mirrored* the climactic events. They were inevitably less sacrosanct than the events they were believed to adumbrate. Moreover, even the most respected figures of Old Testament narrative were, to the medieval Christian, somewhat suspect. True, at the Harrowing of Hell Jesus had, according to the Gospel of Nicodemus, endowed the patriarchs with heavenly bliss, but the

---

[1] Young, ii, 260:
> Named the elder of the two
> Esau is the ancient Jew
> Burdened by the legal fetter
> Not of spirit, but of letter.
> Like the Hebrew race he fights
> For his legal firstborn rights.
> But the Christian will inherit –
> As the younger child – by merit.
> Isaac loved his elder son
> For his tasty venison,
> Just as God the Hebrews favoured
> When their offerings he savoured.

spiritual status of the Hebrew patriarchs and prophets remained ill-defined in the medieval hierarchy. In the twelfth-century *Jeu d'Adam*, the prophets are solemnly escorted back to hell after the delivery of their testimony like prisoners on parole who need to be watched with the greatest care, and the earliest Prophet Plays introduce a marked reluctance into their Christological testimony. Isaiah is sharply reprimanded in one of the earliest extant texts of this kind:

> *Isayas uerum qui scis,*
> *ueritatem cur non dicis?*[1]

The reprimand betrayed an uneasy suspicion that the Old Testament, so far from being an integral part of and prologue to the New, was in a sense a Pharisaical document which, like Balaam, yielded its Christological utterances with reluctance.

Despite the prefigurative reading of the Old Testament, then, it ranked in medieval Christianity considerably lower in sanctity than the New; and its characters, although to be regarded with some reverence, were still thought of as creatures of flesh and blood. There are, of course, no saints in the Old Testament. Abraham lied about his wife, Moses struck the rock in anger, David committed adultery; and their fallibility made them more human and hence more amenable to dramatic realism. Since both tragedy and comedy focus upon blemishes and eccentricities of character, the need for such materials sometimes drove the medieval writer to examine the New Testament sheep before their messianic 'dipping', as in the almost lascivious description in the *Carmina Burana* of Mary Magdalen before her conversion:

> *Mundi delectatio dulcis est et grata*
> *Cuius conversatio suavis et ornata.*[2]

or her depiction in the Digby play as sighing longingly for her lovers:

> *A! god be with my valentynes,*
> *My byrd swetyng, my lovys so dere!*

---

[1] In the version from St. Martial at Limoges, Young ii, 139:
> Isaiah, you who know the truth,
> Why do you not tell the truth?

[2] The world's delights are sweet and charming
And its pleasures gratifying.

The Sacred and the Profane

for þey be bote for a blossum of blysse;
me mervellyt sore þey be nat here,
but I woll restyn in þis erbyr
A-mons thes bamys precyus of prysse,
Tyll som lover wol apere,
That me is wont to halse and kysse.[1]

All this formed part of the same process as turned the attention of dramatists to the pre-Nativity world of the clownish shepherds and, more broadly, to the pre-Christian world of the Old Testament; for within the sacred scenes themselves there was little room for liveliness and none for comedy.

For instance, in *The Salutation and Nativity* of the Chester cycle, *The Pewtereres and Foundours Play* of the York cycle, and the parallel scene from the Hegge cycle, Joseph is portrayed as a weak old man, ashamed of having wedded a young wife, jumping to the obvious conclusion when the Virgin conceives during his three-month absence from home, and understandably refusing to believe the assurances of his wife or her servants until God or an angel appears in order to convince him. The scene is perfect for the appropriate bawdy jokes so beloved by popular drama; yet the sanctity of the matter and of the character involved precludes even the faintest suggestion of humour or indecency. In the lengthy York play, although some two hundred and fifty lines are devoted to Joseph's concern, his emotions are of sadness and self-accusation tinged with melancholy love, in place of the conventional fury of an outraged husband. In the Chester play, where the scene is shorter, the most he permits himself is the general observation:

God lette never an oulde man
Take hym a yonge woman,

---

[1] *Digby Plays*, EETS e.s., ed. F. J. Furnivall (London, 1896), p. 76:
Ah God! be with my valentines,
My sweetheart, my loves so dear!
For they console a flower like me.
I marvel that they are not here.
But I will rest within this grove
This sweetly scented place,
Until some lover will appear
To kiss me and embrace.

31

Nay sette his harte her uppon,
Leste he begilde be.[1]

and in the Hegge play he simply laments the fact that men will
call him cuckold. Thus the situation, though ideally suited to
indecent exploitation, remains highly proper, while in the Cain
play of the Wakefield Master, merely on the biblical hint of
Cain's brusque reply to God, his language becomes so obscene
that for the general reader Adams could only bring himself to
publish a bowdlerized version.[2] Similarly, of no central character
in the New Testament could such a scene be conceived as that
of Noah indulging in a bout of fisticuffs with his wife – and we
should recall that the latter even lacked a biblical foundation
which might have excused it.

(iii) THE OLD TESTAMENT PLAYS

The two main theories concerning the origin of the Old Testament plays in the cycles, different though they are, have this in
common – that they both begin from the unavoidable assumption
that these plays developed as a didactic corroboration of the
Gospels and hence were at all times subordinated to them.
Marius Sepet's *Les Prophètes du Christ* (Paris, 1878) had argued
that the mystery cycle burgeoned out of a pseudo-Augustinian
sermon from the fifth or sixth century entitled *Contra Iudaeos,
Paganos, et Arianos Sermo de Symbolo* whose purpose was to convert unbelievers by means of quotations from their own sacred
texts. These quotations were soon declaimed by a second reader,
and eventually dramatized into the *Ordo Prophetarum* or Prophet
Play. The theory was widely accepted until Hardin Craig
challenged it in 1913, maintaining that the medieval desire for

---

[1] *Chester Plays*, ed. Thomas Wright for the Shakespeare Society (London,
1843), i. 99:

> O God, never let an old man
> Take himself a young woman
> Nor set his heart upon her,
> Lest he be beguiled.

[2] J. Q. Adams, *Chief Pre-Shakespearean Dramas* (Cambridge, Mass.,
1924).

completeness was sufficient to explain the extension backwards into the Old Testament of scenes from the life of Jesus, particularly since certain Old Testament plays had existed independently as outgrowths from the liturgical readings.[1] Even the sole mystery cycle devoted exclusively to the Old Testament, the lengthy *Mistère du Viel Testament* which dramatized Old Testament stories up to the period of Solomon and the Queen of Sheba, shows numerous traces of an original intention to reach eventually to the Gospels. As Craig puts it, it is in its present anomalous form 'a violation of the liturgical basis of the religious drama, since Old Testament subjects are merely beginnings'; and V. A. Kolve's persuasive theory that their selection was based partly on the medieval division of history into Seven Ages is offered only as a supplement to the prefigurative selection in order to explain why some relevant Old Testament stories were never included.[2]

To stress the subordinate character of the Old Testament plays may appear like pushing at an open door; for no scholar would seriously dispute the point. My purpose, however, is to suggest that they achieved their dramatic realism both in spite of and, paradoxically, because of that subordinate position, and the point once made has validity for much of biblical drama subsequent to the medieval period. Had the central figures of the Passion plays been remarkable for their dramatic realism, the explanation would have been ready to hand – that they formed the *raison d'être* of the cycle and hence aroused a deep feeling of identification. Instead, they were presented like beautiful frescoes preserving for eternity the most sacred moments in Christian history. On the other hand, the dramatic liveliness of the Old Testament scenes is self-evident. In the three best-known anthologies of medieval drama, whose purpose was primarily to interest the modern reader in the dramatic quality of these ancient cycles, the Old Testament plays exceeded

---

[1] See Craig's 'The Origin of the Old Testament Plays', *MP x* (1913) and his *English Religious Drama*, pp. 66 f. Also A. M. Jenney, 'A Further Word as to the Origin of the Old Testament Plays', *MP xii* (1915–16). Oscar Cargill's *Drama and Liturgy* (New York, 1930) also rejects Sepet's theory, but is apparently unaware of the above articles.

[2] Kolve, pp. 86 f.

those from the New in number even though they constitute less than one-fifth of the cycles themselves.[1]

The development of the *Ordo Prophetarum*, whether or not it was the source of the cycles, provides the earliest dramatic example of the expansion and elaboration of the Old Testament stories at the expense of those from the New. The portion of the sermon that found its way into the liturgy was a lengthy prose passage addressed to the recalcitrant Jews and introducing the testimony of Isaiah, Jeremiah, Daniel, Moses, David, and Habakkuk, followed by the New Testament witnesses Simeon, Zacharias, Elizabeth, and John, and concluding with the pagan testimonies of Virgil, Nebuchadnezzar, and the Erythraean Sybil. Such was the form in which it entered the cycles; but even before the cycles were transferred to the vernacular, two Old Testament plays had budded off from it to form independent units.

In the various texts of the *Ordo* which have survived, there is a gradual transition from prose sermonizing to poetic dramatization. But without any laboriously detailed examination of the texts, we may glance forward to two of the most highly developed dramas of the Latin liturgy – the two twelfth-century Daniel plays by Hilarius and by the students of Beauvais.[2] Karl Young has shown beyond doubt that the wording of the final prophecy in both these plays is indebted not to the Vulgate, but to the text of the *Ordo*, and hence they must be regarded not as independent compositions, but as elaborations of the more primitive Nebuchadnezzar scenes in the earlier versions. These two plays form the most elaborate examples of staging within the framework of the liturgy. As Belshazzar enters '*cum ponpa sua*' his soldiers burst into a chorus accompanied by musical instruments, and the words alone convey the vigour of the scene:

---

[1] The anthologies of J. M. Manly, A. W. Pollard and J. Q. Adams contain a total of twenty Old Testament plays as against eighteen from the New.

[2] Young, ii, 276 f. The Daniel playlet arose naturally out of the Nebuchadnezzar scene of the *Ordo* because of the similarity between Nebuchadnezzar's throwing three Hebrews into the furnace and Darius's casting Daniel to the lions, as well as their juxtaposition in the same book of the Scriptures.

The Old Testament Plays

Resonent unanimes cum plausu populari
Et decantent principis potenciam preclari![1]

But this does not have the static quality of a 'stained-glass' pageant. There is a battle in which Darius kills Belshazzar, writing appears miraculously on the wall, lions consume Daniel's detractors and there is a liveliness of psychological realism when Daniel chats to the courtiers who have been sent to summon him. The musical setting, as the New York Pro Musica performances have shown, tends to stylize the work, but there can be no doubt that the author of the text itself was working towards a liveliness not always exploited by the musical score. The text constitutes only embryonic drama, but it possesses the marks of that realism which distinguishes the later dramas on the Old Testament.

The most striking development in the *Ordo*, however, and one preserved right through into the mystery cycles themselves was the inclusion of a parallel to the pagan ass festivities by means of a Balaam scene. It is strange that the author of the original sermon had omitted Balaam from the list of witnesses, since his testimony 'There shall come forth a star out of Jacob, and a sceptre shall rise out of Israel' had always been interpreted Christologically by the Church. But the list of witnesses had in any case been greatly expanded in later versions, and once Balaam entered that list, he and his ass were ensured a valued place and introduced a piece of theatricality with which audiences were loath to part. In these versions (as later) he appears seated upon a hobby-horse with a boy concealed beneath. The latter, as the rubric tells us, delivered a brief speech when prodded by the prophet:

Hic veniat Angelus cum gladio, Balaam tangit Asinam, et illa non precedente, dicit iratus:

> *Quid moraris, asina,*
> *obstinata bestia?*
> *Iam scindent calcaria*
> *costas et precordia.*

Puer sub asina respondet:

> *Angelus cum gladio,*
> *quem adstare uideo,*

[1] Let the multitude cheer together,
And chant the praise of our mighty king!

35

The Medieval Stage

prohibet ne transeam;
timeo ne peream.[1]

It has been argued that there is little in this passage to suggest buffoonery, and that there may be deep religious implications in the use of the ass which witnessed the Nativity and patiently bore both the Virgin Mary and Jesus upon its back, while the Balaam scene was in any case regarded as paralleling typologically the offerings of the Magi.[2] But our knowledge of the *asinaria festa* and of the Feast of Fools with which they became associated suggests that, whatever the play's original implications, the opportunity for a little comedy was not ignored. The Feast of the Ass at Beauvais on January 14, for example, contained an extraordinary mass in which the responses took the form of communal braying. According to the rubric, the priest was to pronounce the Latin equivalent of 'Hee-haw!' in place of *Ita missa est*, and the people to respond three times in the same fashion. A similar practice is recorded at Sens, from which it becomes clear that the associations with the ass were not entirely devotional. Indeed, in the Balaam scene we have a striking instance of the degrees of sanctity at work. For with all the secular pressures for the introduction of an ass playlet, the obvious opportunities of exploiting the ass in the manger and the ass on which Jesus rode into Jerusalem were totally ignored, while the Old Testament playlet was instinctively selected as the more appropriate setting.

Moreover, we return here to a point made earlier – that for all the slapstick, humour, and even blasphemy that grew up

[1] Young, ii. 150:
Here an Angel enters with a sword. Balaam touches the ass and, when it refuses to move, says angrily:
Why, you stubborn animal,
Do you thus delay?
Soon my spurs will slash your flanks
If you don't obey.
A boy answers from beneath the ass:
I see an angel standing there.
With sword he guards the lane.
And if I try to pass him by
I fear I shall be slain.
[2] E. K. Chambers, *Medieval Stage*, i, 330 f. and M. D. Anderson, *Drama and Imagery*, pp. 23–24.

within the framework of the less sacred portions of the cycles, the playwright never lost sight of the ultimately religious purpose of his drama. The Boy Bishop revelry within the Church did occasionally get out of hand and the Feast of Fools more often; for although the day for these celebrations was fixed beforehand, the specific form of revelry was often spontaneous and hence exceeded the bounds of propriety. These plays, on the other hand, were carefully rehearsed months ahead and, what is more, developed accretively from year to year. Thus even in the latest form of the Balaam scene as it is preserved in the Chester cycle, the Christological testimony remains paramount. The players are directed to 'sett yt out liuely', so that there must have been a tradition of sprightly presentation; but the gargoyle, so far from obscuring the cathedral, is serving to enliven the more solemn architectural structure. In much the same way as the Catholic church often overcame the counter-attraction of paganism by transforming local pagan deities into saints, so by incorporating aspects of the Feast of the Ass into the liturgical drama in a manner subordinated to the religious ethos, the ultimate effect of the ecclesiastical plays was firmly buttressed.

If the fallibility of the Old Testament characters heightened their potential realism, it also introduced a very human fear of death into the plays. The martyr owed his blissful expression to the certainty that the angels were, at that moment, trumpeting a new saint into heaven. But Noah and Abraham, apart from being maculate in their lives, were, as we have seen, not quite assured of their places in the heaven envisaged by the Middle Ages, partly because they predated the Christian era. This difference in attitude emerges most strikingly if we compare the Crucifixion plays (where the saintliness of the central figure is axiomatic) with their Old Testament antetype, the Binding of Isaac.

In the earliest forms of the Isaac play, the Christological element is so strong that it swamps any possibility of empathy. The term *xylophorus* is prominent, equating Isaac bearing the wooden faggots on his back with Jesus carrying the Cross to Calvary. In the York cycle, which in all probability figures among the oldest versions, Isaac is portrayed as a mature man of thirty who, on being informed of the fate in store for him, responds cheerfully:

37

> *And I sall noght grouche þer agayne*
> *To wirke his wille I am wele payed;*
> *Sen it is his desire,*
> *I sall be bayne to be*
> *Brittynd and brent in fyre,*
> *And þer-fore morne noght for me.*[1]

His only doubt is lest delay allow his flesh to overcome his spirit, and his consequent eagerness for the fulfilment of the sacrifice makes the angel's intervention savour more of frustrating interruption than of divine salvation. Similarly, the play from the Hegge cycle puts into Isaac's mouth the grateful cry of the medieval martyr:

> *Al-myghty god, of his grett mercye,*
> *Fful hertyly I thanke þe sertayne:*
> *At goddys byddyng here for to dye,*
> *I obeye me here for to be sclayne.*[2]

But in the Chester cycle, the Abraham play shows signs of a moving naturalism. Isaac, perceiving that there is no animal for the sacrifice, at once suspects the truth, and fearfully presses his father for an answer. Having wrung it from him, he pleads with childlike innocence, wondering what great sin he can have committed to deserve such punishment:

> *Yf I have treasspasede in anye degree,*
> *With a yerde you may beate me.*

[1] *York Plays*, p. 181:
> And I shall not of this complain.
> To work his will I am well pleased.
> Since it is his desire
> I am ready to be
> Carved up and burnt in fire.
> Therefore, mourn not for me.

[2] *Ludus Coventriae*, EETS e.s., ed. K. S. Block (London, 1922), p. 47:
> Almighty God, for thy great mercy,
> Full heartily I thank thee.
> At God's bidding here to die,
> I am ready to be slain.

The Old Testament Plays

Put up your sorde, yf your wil be,
For I am but a childe.[1]

The final line makes it clear that the Christ parallel (which is drawn by the Expositor at the close of the play) is only applied to the general features of the story—to the acceptance of God's will, as the Expositor specifies—and that the child Isaac is being portrayed in realistic terms as an independent being, rather than as a prefiguration. The dread of death forms the motive force of the play:

Would God, my mother were here with me!
Shee would kneele downe upon her knee,
Prainge you, father, if yt may be,
For to save my liffe.

His eventual submission to fate is no theological *tour de force.* He makes the touching plea that his eyes be bandaged lest he see the sword-stroke, and asks his father to remember him kindly to his mother and brothers whom he will see no more.

The parallel Crucifixion play of the same cycle is, as we might expect, a stylized pageant in which Jesus calmly comments on his martyrdom in language drawn almost directly from the Gospels:

Father of heaven, if thy wilbe,
Forgeve them this the do to me,
For the bene blynde, and maye not see,
How fowle the done amisse.

Similarly, in the Towneley version, after the phrase *hely, hely, lamazabatany,* Jesus formally commends his soul to God as having fulfilled its divine function on earth:

Now is my passyon broght tyll ende!
ffader of heuen, in to thyn hende
I betake my saull![2]

---

[1] *Chester Plays,* i, 68:
    If I have transgressed in any way
    With a stick you may beat me.
    But put up your sword, if you will,
    For I am but a child.

[2] *Towneley Plays,* EETS e.s., ed. G. England and A. W. Pollard (London, 1897), p. 276.

The finest of the Abraham plays, those known as the Dublin and Brome texts, derive their moving realism primarily from these Old Testament qualities of human fallibility and terror of death. The Dublin manuscript introduces Sarah solely to emphasize the pathos of the child's near-sacrifice. She welcomes her husband home from his interview with the angel, creating an atmosphere of happy family-life. When Abraham uses the subterfuge of taking Isaac to witness a sacrifice, she is reluctant to release him, only agreeing on condition that Abraham will take good care of the boy and watch that his horse is kept under good control. She concludes with the heavy dramatic irony:

> *Now good hert, god send þe home sownde*
> *þi fader & all his men.*[1]

Death becomes something fearful, the cancellation of God's decree bringing relief not only to Isaac but to the audience too; and conversely the earlier part of the play gains enormously in dramatic effectiveness by the portrayal of Isaac as a child not yet versed in the subtleties of theological dogma.

(iv) THE SECOND SHEPHERD PLAY

The theory that Old Testament drama was more amenable to dramatic realism may appear to founder on that most realistic and amusing of all medieval plays – the Second Shepherd Play of the Wakefield cycle. But some interesting research into the origins of the play published some twenty years ago provides evidence neatly dovetailing with all that has been argued here.

The *Prima Pastorum*, or the traditional Shepherd play in the

[1] *The Non-Cycle Mystery Plays*, EETS e.s., ed. O. Waterhouse (London, 1909), p. 29. Rosemary Woolf, 'The Effect of Typology on the English Medieval Plays of Abraham and Isaac', *Speculum xxxii* (1957), 805 tentatively suggests that Sarah may here prefigure the Virgin Mary in her solicitous concern for her son; but if so, the typological allusion is slight. Miss Woolf's article offers some excellent insights into the realism of these Abraham plays, but by examining them in isolation she misses the progressive shedding of typology in the Old Testament plays as a whole, attributing it instead to the authors' conviction that their audiences were so familiar with the prefigurative meaning of the scenes that any underscoring was unnecessary.

various cycles, of which the Wakefield Master's was a later
version, is in itself fully in line with the theory that the 'goats'
were the first to be humanized. Here are the 'imperfect' characters of the New Testament, the coarse, ignorant shepherds,
typifying the people who walked in darkness before they saw
the great light. Their very clumsiness, greed, and brute strength
in the humorous opening scenes throws into contrast their gentle
faith and solicitude at the Nativity and their earnest determination to reform their way of life. Each, after witnessing the Birth,
declares that he will forsake his craft and dedicate himself to his
new faith.

> *Over the sea, and I maye have grace,*
> *I will henge and aboute goe nowe,*
> *To preache this in everye place,*
> *And sheepe will I kepe non nowe.*[1]

They will henceforth be shepherds only of the Lamb of God. In
the earlier part of the play their rustic realism brings them close
to the audience, particularly when one of them claims to be the
best shepherd 'from comelye Conwaye unto Clyde'. The
wrestling match to determine whether the hireling Trowle
should receive the wages he has earned, however good-
humoured its presentation, underscores the unscrupulousness
of a world to be reformed only when all men, both overlords and
hirelings, would (as at the conclusion) accept the kingdom of
heaven. Similarly, their inability to comprehend the angel's
Latin hymn *Gloria in excelsis*—a comic device common to almost
all the earlier versions:

> *Naye, it was glory, glory, with a glo!*
> *And moche of cellsis was therto:*
> *As ever have I reste or roo,*
> *Moche he spake of glasse.*[2]

[1] *Chester Plays*, i, 44:
> Over the seas, with God's grace,
> I shall wend my way now,
> To preach this in every place,
> And sheep will I keep none now.

[2] Nay it was 'glory, glory' with a 'glow'.
> And much of 'cellsis' was there too.
> As sure as I have rest or woe,
> Much he spoke of 'glass'.

—serves to show that even the most boorish of men would be ennobled by the coming of the Saviour. There is a sharp contrast at the moment of the Nativity itself, which in effect marks the transition from this world to the elevated world of the New Testament, and the shepherds become suddenly transformed into haloed saints. Despite its proximity, then, to one of the central scenes of the Gospels, there is that degree of dramatic elaboration which we have come to associate with the 'goats' of the pre-Nativity world. The Second Shepherd Play, on the other hand, is far more than this – it is a lively, boisterous play which takes us much further into the realm both of realism and of genuine comedy.

However, E. Kölbing's discovery of the similarity between this play and the ballad entitled *Archie Armstrang's Aith* suggested that the Mak episode, so far from being a dramatic elaboration of the New Testament scene, was in fact a clever engrafting onto it of an already existing tale.[1] The ballad, published in Scott's *Minstrelsy of the Scottish Border*, relates a story remarkably similar to the Mak episode, and Kölbing argued in 1897 that the two derived from a common source. This alone might be unconvincing, but in an article published half a century later,[2] T. M. Parrott made an illuminating point. The ballad story has a roundness of plot which leaves no doubt that it either was or paralleled a form of the story antedating the Wakefield version. In the ballad, the shepherd, after stealing the sheep and disguising it as a baby in the cradle, swears that he will eat the child if he is telling a lie. The oath thus forms the pivot of the tale, as its title indicates, and after the complete success of the ruse, Archie salves his conscience by actually eating the 'baby'. The entertaining rascal has triumphed over society. In the Wakefield play, although the oath is actually pronounced, once the trick has been exposed, Mak is tossed in a blanket as a deterrent for the future, and the oath is totally forgotten.

[1] Kölbing's article appears in translated form in the EETS edition of the Towneley Plays, p. xxxi.

[2] T. M. Parrott, 'Mak and Archie Armstrang', *MLN lix* (1944), 297. Other parallels to the Mak episode have been suggested, none as close as Archie Armstrang. See, for example, A. S. Cook, 'Another Parallel to the Mak Story', *MP xiv* (1916), A. C. Baugh, 'Parallels to the Mak Story', *MP xv* (1918), and R. C. Cosbey, 'The Mak Story and its Folklore Analogues', *Speculum xx* (1945).

The Second Shepherd Play

Parrott argues that the Wakefield Master recognized the opportunity of adapting the story to the existent Shepherd Play, but was troubled by an ending morally unsuited to a religious cycle. He decided, therefore, to forgo the fulfilment of the oath and to incorporate it in its truncated form, since victory could not be accorded to a criminal even in a comic scene. We may note, for example, that in the Chester Shepherd play even the milder sin of withholding wages was duly punished. It would appear, then, that the Mak episode did not develop out of the Shepherd Play but was extraneous, secular material cleverly incorporated into it.

A further problem remains. The suggestion that the play may constitute a comic reflection of the Nativity scene itself, with the Lamb being visited by shepherds as it lies in the cradle might be interpreted as detracting from the sacrosanctity of this central New Testament scene.[1] But within the medieval setting such comic distortion, provided it remain separate from the holy scene itself, provided a polarity which heightened the sanctity of the latter. Where the Garcio-Cain slapstick forms an integral part of the biblical scene, it must serve to make Cain a more human and even comic figure. In the Second Shepherd Play, however, the two sections remain so sharply divorced that, as has often been pointed out, they almost form two separate plays, loosely linked by the presence of the same shepherds at the two events. Moreover, Nikolaus Pevsner has identified as a specifically English trait the ability to provide a comic counterpart to the most serious and sacred aspects of medieval life. In his *Englishness of English Art*, he traces the origin of the medieval *babwyneries* (or 'monkey-business') to thirteenth-century England.[2] In the margin of the richly ornamented Queen Mary's Psalter, for example, we find a Mock Funeral conducted by rabbits; and vividly drawn scenes from contemporary life

[1] Homer A. Watt, 'The Dramatic Unity of the "Secunda Pastorum" ' in *Essays and Studies in Honor of Carleton Brown* (New York, 1940), pp. 158–66; W. M. Manly, 'Shepherds, and Prophets: Religious Unity in the Towneley *Secunda Pastorum*', *PMLA lxxviii* (1963), 151; and Margery M. Morgan, ' "High Fraud": Paradox and Double-Plot in the English Shepherds' Plays', *Speculum xxxix* (1964), 676.

[2] Nikolaus Pevsner, *The Englishness of English Art* (London, 1956), p. 26.

decorated the margins of the Rutland Psalter and other religious manuscripts of the period. But they remain in the margins, never detracting from the sanctity of the manuscript itself, and usually having little bearing on the subject-matter of the page on which they appear. Drawing materials were, of course, at a premium then, and it may be that the caricaturist was driven to sketch on the margins of holy works in much the same way as the Wake-field Master was compelled to insert his extraneous comic sketch into the framework of a religious cycle.

(v) THE CAIN AND NOAH PLAYS

In contrast, the comic episodes of the Old Testament plays grew organically out of the original text and out of the legends which had accumulated around them. We have already seen that the Balaam scene, for all the outside pressures of the *asinaria festa*, was not a pagan importation but provided a counter-attraction by means of a simple elaboration of the original story. And the same is true of the Cain and Noah episodes which remained, for all their contemporary realism, essentially true to their origin. Moreover, of these two biblical figures, one is sinful, the other virtuous, which suggests no such distinction in dramatic realism as we have seen in the New Testament protagonists.

A number of painstaking researches into the Cain legends has been published, but without going into detail here it is easy to see how the main lines of the *Mactatio Abel* derive directly from the sources.[1] In most versions, it is Cain's opposition to tithing and sacrifice which transforms him from the usual puppet-like figure of the earlier mystery plays into a daring and almost Promethean challenger of divine authority. Why, he asks, should he give of his best produce when (like so many of the farmers in the audience) his endless toil had merely been rewarded with meagre harvests and blighted crops. Tithing and sacrifice, he argues, should only be offered when God has played his own part fairly and has deserved the gift:

[1] See, for example, O. F. Emerson, 'Legends of Cain', *PMLA xxi* (1906), 831.

The Cain and Noah Plays

> ffor he has euer yit beyn my fo;
> ffor had he my freynd beyn,
> Other gatis it had beyn seyn.
> When all mens corn was fayre in feld,
> Then was myne not worth a neld.
> When I shuld saw, and wantyd seyde
> And of corn had full grete neyde,
> Then gaf he me none of his,
> No more will I gif hym of this.
> hardely hold me to blame
> bot if I serue hym of the same.[1]

His identification with the Devil, and his coarse shouting and brawling in the earlier part of the play, quite apart from his subsequent fate, ensure that he remains ultimately the villain. But he is a very human villain–almost dangerously so–and all this is within the tradition. For even in the brief story as recorded in Genesis, Cain slays Abel because his own sacrifice is rejected. No reason for the rejection is given there, but ancient commentary maintained that he only offered what was left after he had satisfied his own needs, and the early Church Fathers explained: *Obtulit ex fructibus terrae, non a primis fructibus primitias Deo.*[2] Similarly, the Pikeharness and Garcio scenes are elaborations of the character suggested by Cain's impertinent reply to God 'Am I my brother's keeper?' and the servant functions as a foil for the boorish, yet strangely attractive Cain.

It is easy to forget in glancing through these mystery plays that typologically Noah's wife was regarded as an adumbration

[1] *Towneley Plays*, p. 13:
> For he has always been my foe;
> For had he used a friendly tone,
> Differently it would have shown.
> When others' corn was fair in field
> Mine would not a pin's worth yield.
> When I would sow and wanted seed
> And of corn had pressing need,
> Then he gave me none of his.
> No more will I give him of this.
> Hardly hold it to my blame
> If I give him just the same.

[2] Ambrose, *De Cain et Abel*, ii, x: 'He offered to God from the fruits of the earth, not from the firstfruits.'

of the Virgin Mary – *Noe significat Christum, uxor eius beatam Mariam.*[1] Thus her depiction here as a shrewish gossip ran directly counter to her prefigurative identification. The latter interpretation is, perhaps, preserved in the French *Mistère du Viel Testament*, where she suggests to her daughters that they retire to pray before entering the Ark and meekly obeys all her husband's behests. But in the English plays, the scene of domestic strife enjoyed universal popularity. Once again, as the typological reading weakens, the Old Testament figures come alive. Yet even in the scene of slapstick there is still a trace of typology. Prefiguration has the Janus-like quality of being able to look backwards as well as forwards, and in the Newcastle play there is a strong Eve parallel when the devil, merrily swearing by his 'crooked snout', persuades her to oppose her husband's plans and to offer him a special potion to drink. But at this stage, the dramatist is already free to choose the typological reading which suits his needs, and to blend it with the Shrew of the sermon in order to create a lively, if still morally didactic scene.

Of greater significance for the development of biblical drama is the characterization of Noah himself. For despite both his intrinsic sanctity and his prefigurative identification with Jesus, he emerges with extraordinary vividness as a creature of flesh and blood. There is no 'stained-glass' depiction here. He is a tired old man, finding it difficult to cope with the enormous tasks suddenly thrust upon him and, particularly in the York play (which is appropriately shared between the Shipwrites and the Fysshers and Maryners), he stresses the physical aspect of his labours:

> To hewe þis burde I will be-gynne,
> But first I wille lygge on my lyne,
> Now bud it be alle in like thynne,
> So put it nowthyr twynne nor twyne.
> þus sall I iune it with a gynn,
> And sadly sette it with symonde fyne,

---

[1] A. de Laborde, *La Bible Moralizée, illustrée* (Paris, 1911), i, 9, quoted in Anna Jean Mill, 'Noah's Wife Again', *PMLA* lvi (1941), 615. See also Howard H. Schless, 'The Comic Element in the Wakefield Noah', in *Studies in Medieval Literature*, ed. MacEdward Leach (Philadelphia, 1961).

The Cain and Noah Plays

Þus sall y wyrke it both more and mynne,
Thurgh techyng of god maister myne.[1]

There is a pride in craftsmanship here which shows that Noah has become imaginatively alive and human, speaking almost as a member of the guild fraternity. The lapse of centuries is immaterial; he is conceived in contemporary terms constructing just the kind of boat which the shipwright himself would build were he to carry a similar cargo. And this attempt to relive the biblical scene in contemporary terms is a primary source of the wife scenes, which symbolize the incredulity Noah would, like all prophets, encounter among the local Gossips and neighbours. After his lengthy interview with God, he returns to the mundane with the depressing realization that he must now inform his irascible wife. The Towneley version has:

> *I am agast*
> > *that we get som fray*
> *Betwixt vs both;*
> *ffor she is full tethee,*
> *ffor litill oft angre,*
> *If any thyng wrang be,*
> > *Soyne is she wroth.*[2]

Despite the hen-pecking, he is still the steersman, retaining his dignity even in the fisticuffs and evoking our sympathy for him in his struggles.

[1] *York Plays,* p. 43:
> To hew this board I will begin,
> But first I will stretch out my line.
> Now make it uniformly thin
> Lest flaws should spoil the smooth design.
> Then shall I join it sure and true,
> Cementing with the finest glue.
> Thus shall the work with skill be wrought
> Just as my Master[craftsman] taught.

[2] *Towneley Plays,* p. 28:
> I am aghast
> > lest there be some fray
> > between us both;
> For she is very touchy,
> For little, often angry.
> If anything be wrong
> > She's quickly full of wrath.

It is clear, therefore, that the reasons for dramatic elaboration in these early mystery plays are more complex than has usually been thought. True, the villains and supernumeraries are exploited for comic purposes; but at a deeper level there is discernible even at this early stage a divergence between two main trends. On the one hand, a stylized and reverent re-enactment of the holiest scenes of the Gospels with the sacred figures treated as though they were crowned with haloes; and on the other, a more realistic and almost contemporary treatment of the less sacred characters, prominent among them being those of the Old Testament, both good and evil, who gradually shed their typological significance to emerge as human creatures. At this stage, the distinction was still embryonic, but it was a distinction which, with all the varying social and religious pressures of later years, persisted in the main throughout the history of biblical drama.

CHAPTER II

THE EARLY RENAISSANCE

(i) THE COVENANT

For all the swirling currents and undercurrents within the period which we term the Renaissance, with its conflict between the humanist idealization of Reason and the Counter-Renaissance insistence upon Faith, the old definition still holds true: that essentially it marked a new awareness of the challenges and potential splendour of the physical world. Man was no longer a dim figure reduced to shadowy insignificance before the flames of Hell. He had become instead a being noble in reason, infinite in faculties; and where the medieval mind, focussed on the world to come, had accepted man's return to dust as the natural order of creation, the Elizabethan was for ever amazed that worms would one day feast upon his flesh. His body, symbolic of the temporal world, had assumed a new dignity.

There is little wonder that the interests of the sixteenth-century dramatist when he turned to biblical themes now became more obviously diverted from the saintly other-worldliness of the New Testament to the martial vigour of the Old with which he discovered a new kinship. The plays devoted to Gospel themes dwindled away within a short period after the close of the mystery cycles, and in their stead appeared a host of plays devoted to those stories from the Old Testament and its apocrypha which paralleled the excitement and stimulus of the Renaissance itself – the vindication of Susannah, the rebellion of Absalom, and the heroism of Judith prominent among them. The Renaissance concern with the world of the sword and the flesh might itself have sufficed to explain this diversion to Old Testament themes, but it was firmly buttressed, particularly in England, by the theological clash between Protestant and Catholic.

Although Calvinism somewhat paradoxically laid new emphasis on predestination and the doctrine of unearnable Grace, the Reformation paralleled the Renaissance in its yearning for spiritual emancipation and personal dignity. The Lutheran demand for a Bible translated into the vernacular (as well as Luther's own provision of such a version) was aimed primarily at circumventing the Catholic church's monopoly of Scriptural interpretation. We sometimes forget that at this period only a small proportion of the clerics themselves possessed sufficient learning to interpret the Latin Vulgate unaided. In Colet's day, the highest university degree awarded, the doctor of divinity, did not 'admit a man to the Reading of the Scriptures', and even the most educated layman relied largely on hearsay for his knowledge of the Bible.[1] It was primarily through the vernacular sermon in which the preacher retold the stories of the Bible in homiletical and allegorical terms that the layman became acquainted with the subject-matter of both the Old and the New Testaments. The unquestioned authority of the Vulgate as the basis for medieval Christian theology was challenged initially by the philological studies of Reuchlin who insisted on returning to the Hebrew and Greek originals, almost forgotten in the Middle Ages. The consequent flowering of Hebrew scholarship under the leadership of such humanists as Colet, ensured a new intimacy with the Old Testament which inevitably weakened the typological reading. The ferment of translation activity in England, which between 1535 and 1611 produced eight complete translations of the Bible apart from a number of sectional versions, not only removed the linguistic obstacle to a personal reading of the text but, what is more, encouraged the English Protestant (and, after the appearance of the Douai version, the English Catholic) to read the story of Jacob and Esau as a historical account of two real brothers rather than as an antetype allegorizing the Christian birthright. Many of these versions did, indeed, retain sectarian comment and exegesis in the margins and chapter-headings, and the stained-glass win-

[1] Samuel Knight, *The Life of John Colet* (London, 1724), p. 51. See also Beryl Smalley, *The Study of the Bible in the Middle Ages* (Oxford, 1952), p. xiv.

dows were still in the church to remind worshippers of the typological reading; but now nothing prevented the reader from focussing on the text and ignoring the commentary.

The Protestant's kinship with the Old Testament was deepened by his concern with the Covenant.[1] The individualism which the Protestant pitted against the monopolistic authoritarianism of the medieval church (an authoritarianism which he was not loath to employ within his own Geneva) needed firm theological anchoring within the Christian tradition. Triumphantly he pointed out that the covenant inherited by the Christian was initially a personal covenant established between God and Abraham and of only secondary communal significance. The doctrine of Protestant election itself grew out of the renewal of that covenant with Isaac but not Ishmael, with Jacob but not Esau; and its symbol was not, as for Noah, a rainbow visible to all mankind, but the circumcision of each individual male at the moment of his initiation. If the circumcision was now rarely observed by Protestants, the lesson it offered of the personal nature of the covenant was not missed. Calvin argued that, if the Christian church had inherited the Hebrew birthright, it had failed in its turn, and now only the few elect could inherit. The Old Testament patriarchs and their progeny thus became not only a theological sanction for the Protestant's rebellion and for his determination to dispense with the services of a priest as an intermediary between himself and God; they were also his own spiritual forebears. The Christological reading was still valid for the sixteenth-century Reformer, but the literal level achieved a new and personal vitality in his eyes as the account of the progressive revelation of his own covenant. And within the drama, the changes soon became apparent.

[1] William Perkins, for example, the spokesman for English Calvinism, wrote in his *Golden Chain, or Description of Theology* (1590) that the means to salvation '. . . are God's covenant and the seals thereof. God's covenant is his contract with man concerning life eternal, upon certain conditions. This covenant consists of two parts; God's promise to man, man's promise to God. God's promise to man is that whereby He binds Himself to man to be his God, if he break not the condition. Man's promise to God is that whereby he vows his allegiance unto his Lord and to perform the condition between them.' H. Fisch, *Jerusalem and Albion* (London, 1964), pp. 93 f. examines the place of the Hebrew covenant in Calvinism.

In the earlier part of the sixteenth century, both churches viewed the theatre with indulgence. The Catholic church, which had fostered both the liturgical drama and the mystery cycles, continued to permit plays on biblical themes with only occasional warnings against abuse and sacrilege. While it is true that the Council of Trent's strictures on superstitious worship of images were later regarded as applying to the theatre, at the time they were interpreted literally and hence had no bearing on the stage.[1] Although the recrudescence of scriptural drama was, particularly in England, predominantly Protestant in origin, Catholic writers such as Macropedius and Cornelius Crocus were in the vanguard of the continental movement.

The Protestants, despite their distrust of an art 'tainted' by Catholic usage, vacillated between a reluctant toleration of biblical drama and positive encouragement, especially when it served as an effective propaganda weapon. The fierce opposition to all forms of drama apparent in later English Puritanism formed part of the anti-humanist element of that sect, but the early reformers, under the influence of such erudite classicists as Erasmus and Colet, left ample room for the growth of drama within the new church. Luther himself had remarked that the book of *Judith* was a tragedy and *Tobias* a comedy, even specifically commending the use of the Bible as a source for stage plays, and his statements were quoted and paraphrased throughout the century as justification for the Protestant writing of scriptural drama.[2]

In the Calvinist stronghold of Geneva, the problem was a vexed one. William Farel had published a statement in 1524 that to abstain from 'disguising' was a counsel of perfection, but he had not forbidden drama completely, and Calvin had prohibited only the clergy from play-acting. In 1546 a troupe of players requested permission to perform a dramatization of the *Acts of the Apostles*. It was granted reluctantly, mainly because one of the ministers deciding the issue happened to be the author of the play (which is itself significant). This author, Abel Poupin, was made responsible for the performance, but it nonetheless evoked a public denunciation from the pulpit by a

[1] See H. C. Gardiner, *Mysteries' End* (New Haven, 1946), p. 20.

[2] Edna Purdie, *The Story of Judith in German and English Literature* (Paris, 1927), p. 41.

preacher who was at once accused, but soon acquitted, of insubordination. Tempers became frayed, particularly when Calvin was accused of playing the Pope, and, perhaps as a result of this fracas, Calvin himself, in a sermon delivered in 1556, defined the biblical prohibition against exchanges of apparel between sexes (Deut. xxii, 5) as applying particularly to dramatic performances.

On the other hand, in 1547 the Genevan council itself attended a performance by the college scholars of a Latin dialogue on the theme of Joseph, and in the following two years there are records both of a performance by a wandering player and of a complete performance of a comedy of Terence, again by the scholars. Theodore Bèze, Calvin's successor, in atonement for having published his *Juvenilia* before his religious conversion, composed his drama *Abraham Sacrifiant* which was published in Geneva in 1550, the second edition of 1560 being officially approved by the Council.[1] Thus, whatever the theoretical stand of the Calvinists, in practice they tolerated the drama even in Geneva itself, and there can be no doubt that it was often regarded with favour by Protestants elsewhere. At this crucial period in the development of biblical drama, then, both churches regarded it, if not with positive encouragement, then at least with indulgence.

(ii) Justice on Earth

Where Herford and Chambers had previously categorized the scriptural dramas of the Renaissance as a natural offspring of the medieval cycles, Miss Lily B. Campbell has shown more recently that they arose primarily out of an attempt to compete with, or even to supplant the classically inspired dramas of the Revival of Learning. She links them with that desire for a more positively Christian literature which culminated in Du Bartas' *La Muse Chrestiene* (Bordeaux, 1574).[2] We should not forget, however,

[1] E. K. Chambers, *Elizabethan Stage* (Oxford, 1923), i, 245 f., and J. E. Gillet, 'The German Dramatist of the Sixteenth Century and his Bible', *PMLA xxxiv* (1919), 465.

[2] Lily B. Campbell, *Divine Poetry and Drama in Sixteenth Century England* (Cambridge, 1959), p. 148. Also C. H. Herford, *Studies in the Literary Relations of England and Germany in the Sixteenth Century* (Cambridge, 1886), and Chambers, *Medieval Stage*, ii, 216–17.

that part of the mystery cycles too had arisen out of the sermon *Contra Judaeos, Paganos et Arianos* with its desire to convert the infidel, and that the cycles had needed to compete throughout the Middle Ages with such pagan festivities as the *festa asinaria*. The change, therefore, is less in the propaganda purpose than in the realignment of forces which it had to combat. The erudite humanists were far more challenging foes than the ignorant pagan, but the strength of the Church lay in those Christian humanists who were prepared to employ the new ammunition of the Renaissance in defence of the Church itself. Since the Bible contained no dramas of its own (with the possible exceptions of *Job* and the *Song of Songs*, neither of which was sufficiently dramatic in *form* to foster a new dramatic school), the plays written in this period as in all subsequent periods closely followed the techniques of the secular drama of the day. The classical revival of the sixteenth century thus encouraged within the religious sphere the rise of the so-called Christian Terence and Christian Seneca movements, which aimed at sugaring the didactic pill with the livelier fashions of the Renaissance stage.

Nevertheless, the pill was not forgotten, and the biblical drama of the Renaissance preserved beneath its classical exterior that concern with a religious message which had animated the medieval mysteries. The religious message was, however, a very different one: it was a new insistence upon divine justice visible in the pattern of human affairs. In the Middle Ages, the injustice of this world had been accepted as axiomatic. The Day of Judgement became the focus of medieval thought as the only explanation for the victory of the ungodly and the suffering of the righteous in this false world of mortality; and the meek of this earth were comforted with the thought that they were destined to inherit the world to come. As the Renaissance shifted its gaze from eternity to temporality, so the Protestant and, to a markedly lesser extent, the Catholic, began to search for evidence of divine participation in human affairs, for some pattern which should support their view of a theodicy. It was a search for evidence which formed part of that embryonic empiricism soon to dominate the age. Moreover, this shift in focus was paralleled in the new economic patterns. The medieval monk had rejected worldly wealth as a deception and had preached with bitter iteration against 'usury' and the amassing of property beyond what was necessary for basic subsistence. Weber and Tawney have shown that the Reformers' return to Old Testament sources and their concern with the temporal world led them, like the Hebrew patriarchs of old, to regard the amassing of flocks and herds as a mark of divine blessing, provided, of course, that no extortion or dishonesty was involved in their acquisition.[1] If in later years this new view was to lead to the Church's acquiescence in some of the worst aspects of the Industrial Revolution, at this early period it betokened little more than a concern with the physical as well as the spiritual victory of the righteous. This growing concern with physical wealth parallels, then, the urge to find divine reward in the temporal world rather than the afterlife. Where the medieval martyr had triumphed in spirit at the very moment of his physical defeat, Milton, as the later embodiment of this Protestant concern, became almost obsessed with the need to justify the ways of God to men, and to explain away to himself even more than to others the glaring injustice of his own blindness and political defeat.

It has long been noted that the most popular themes in the biblical drama of this period were Joseph, Adam, David, Esther, and Susannah, but in the light of this new concern with divine justice the reason for their preference becomes apparent. In each, the good are seen to be vindicated and the guilty to be duly punished, and a closer examination of the sections from each story which were selected for dramatization and of the treatment of those sections leaves no doubt of the theodical emphasis.

By far the most widely dramatized theme was that of Joseph. A dozen plays are known to have been written before 1560 and at least twenty-five versions appeared in French with a similar

---

[1] Max Weber's essay on *The Protestant Ethic and the Spirit of Capitalism*, developed in R. H. Tawney's *Religion and the Rise of Capitalism*, gave rise to a host of books and articles attacking and defending the validity of the thesis. Almost all disagreement centred on their definition of capitalism, or the misconception that Weber was arguing a causal connection, but the acquisitive elements in Protestantism were acknowledged. See, for example, Ephraim Fischoff, 'The Protestant Ethic and the Spirit of Capitalism: the History of a Controversy', *Social Research xi* (1944), 61, and John F. New, *Anglican and Puritan* (Stanford, 1964), pp. 96 f.

number in such languages as Italian, Spanish, Dutch, and German.[1] The colourful stories of Joseph's youth, of his boyhood dreams and the jealousy he aroused in his brothers were almost completely ignored. Instead the playwrights concentrated on the virtuous rejection of his mistress's advances (with his long and edifying sermons to her on the *rewards* of chastity), his unjust condemnation and – the point of the whole story – the divine intervention which prompts Pharaoh miraculously to deliver him from the pit and to elevate him to the highest position next to the throne itself. Cornelius Crocus's play (1536) was divided into three sections – Protasis, Epitasis, and Catastrophe – in order to underscore the reversal of fortune, and it concluded with a word to the audience on the blessings in store for the righteous. Macropedius's *Josephus* of 1544 confined itself to the same section of the story with similar purpose, laying somewhat more stress on the theme that chastity pays. These two dramatists were in fact Catholic (Crocus himself is believed to have been a crypto-Protestant), but the new theories were already in the air, and the Protestants carried the insistence on reward and punishment much further. Sixt Birck (Xystus Betuleius), for example, wrote a drama on *Susannah* (among biblical themes the *locus classicus* for the vindication of the falsely accused) first in German and then in Latin (1537), in which the scenes themselves were interspersed with songs of praise sung by a chorus and eulogizing on scriptural authority the justice of God and his concern for the faithful. On Susannah's repulsing the elders, they sing from Psalm xxx: *In Thee, O Lord, have I hoped; let me never be confounded.* The wrangling between the elders and the magistrates is concluded with a song based on Proverbs viii: *Doth not Wisdom cry aloud?* The decision to hold a trial is greeted with: *Princes have persecuted me without cause* from Psalm cxviii. And at her condemnation, the chorus echoes her faith in heavenly intervention with Psalm lxxxii which declares that God will preserve justice in the courts of law. Finally, Daniel on reversing the decision is acclaimed with the verses: *Out of the mouths of babes and sucklings thou hast perfected wisdom, because of thy enemies; that thou mayest destroy the enemy and the avenger* and the chorus adds the final touch with a song from

[1] Leicester Bradner, 'The Latin Drama of the Renaissance', *SRen iv*, (1957), 31 and Craig, *English Religious Drama*, p. 364.

The Christian Terence

Psalm i: *Blessed is the man who has not walked in the counsel of the ungodly*. It is, to say the least, a little difficult to miss the didactic message.

A glance at the other themes popular in scriptural drama reveals equal concern for the lesson of virtue rewarded. *David* taught the wages of sin, *Esther*, *Deborah* and *Judith*, the victory of the faithful over the unrighteous, and *Tobias* the blessings due to the upright. They were lessons of particular concern both to Protestants and Catholics now that the Lutheran Reformation had endangered the lives of both in the various countries in which they constituted a minority. Until now, the mystery cycles had spoken with the unquestioned authority of a united church to an audience composed of true believers needing merely to be reminded of their moral duties. But the new drama acquired a polemical tone in which each scriptural dramatist saw in the Bible the indisputable vindication of his own sect. Frequently, as in Birck's play, there is little overt polemicism—we are merely made to feel that the 'faithful' refers exclusively to the author's own religious group. But often the polemicism was more blatant. Although Naogeorgus's *Pammachius*, which was the most famous dramatic attack on Catholicism, did not employ a scriptural theme, it inspired the English martyrologist John Foxe to enter the lists with his *Christus Triumphans* (1556), which provided a comparatively non-sectarian series of scenes from church history, culminating, however, in two final acts attacking the papacy and depicting the Protestants as faithfully awaiting the messianic coming. As Foxe's play shows, the continental drama was well known in England at this time, and there was a fruitful interchange of ideas. In the predominantly Protestant England, those qualities peculiar to the Reformation gradually became more clearly marked.

(iii) THE CHRISTIAN TERENCE

The revival of classical drama at the end of the fifteenth century had reintroduced Europe to the works of the Greek tragedians and of Seneca, but Terence had never been entirely forgotten during the Middle Ages. Hroswitha's somewhat lame attempt to entertain and instruct her fellow-nuns with edifying pseudo-

Terentian playlets in the tenth-century attests to this popularity
—a popularity based largely on his success as a stylist and his
pithy epigrams—and Conrad Celtes' edition of Hroswitha in
1501 helped towards a revival of pseudo-Terentian drama.
Herford has rightly pointed out that the so-called Christian
Terence movement originated with three schoolmasters—
Macropedius, Crocus, and Gnaphaeus—who in all probability
were unhappy at the growing habit of using Terence in the
schools for teaching 'Latin without tears'.[1] The plays of Terence
themselves usually offered humorous situations in which mischievous servants outwitted their duller masters, using the
house in the master's absence as a brothel or for some similar
paying proposition. The theme was scarcely satisfactory as
moral instruction, and the three schoolmasters independently
hit upon the idea of attaching the Terentian-type play to the
story of the prodigal son. To call such drama 'biblical' is clearly
absurd. The brief passage: '. . . and wasted his substance in
riotous living' became the subject-matter of the play, in which
the young man, be he Acolastus, Asotus, or Petriscus, wallowed
happily in scenes of prostitution, gambling and trickery and,
after losing all his money, was welcomed home with the fatted
calf. They were only biblical insofar as they used divine sanction
to authorize an otherwise secular theme of more than doubtful
morality. Ostensibly such plays were to provide a sober warning
against riotous living and debauchery, but even apart from the
lively and frequently attractive pictures they presented of such
debauchery, the happy ending (which allowed such plays to be
called comedies) scarcely accorded with the principles of divine
justice which dominated the Protestant plays. If anything, it
suggested that the dissolute young man would be more joyously
received on his return home than he had ever been treated
during his days of obedience and sobriety. It is significant that
the three best-known English versions of the prodigal son play
—the anonymous *Nice Wanton* (1560), Thomas Ingelend's
The Disobedient Child and George Gascoigne's *Glass of*

---

[1] Lily Campbell challenged them in her *Divine Poetry*, pp. 148 f., on
the grounds that the movement formed part of the more general
attempt to counter the secular Renaissance. At a broader level that
may be true, but I think they are right as regards the specific
cause.

Government (1577) – all disregarded the biblical ending and saw that the youths received their due punishment. Gascoigne even went so far as to have the dissipated young men hanged or banished.

Although it is not strictly within the scope of this present enquiry, a peculiar omission in scholarship may be noted here. It is strange that the connection between these prodigal-son dramas and the rise of the picaresque has never been suggested. Gnaphaeus's *Acolastus* went through thirty-one editions between 1529 and 1577 and the high-water mark of prodigal-son dramas coincided exactly with the appearance of the first picaresque work *Lazarillo de Tormes* printed in Burgos in 1554, but probably written a few years earlier. Its title indicated that some analogy is to be drawn between the hero and the New Testament Lazarus who, though a beggar, ultimately rested in Abraham's bosom while the rich man burned in hell. Most important of all, it relates the story of a young boy cheerfully stealing, lying, and revenging himself upon an immoral and unscrupulous world. Its strong vein of anti-clericalism, which led to its being banned by the Inquisition a few years after publication, suggests that the anonymous author had noted the exploitation of Terentian scenes for ostensibly moral purposes in these prodigal-son plays and had neatly turned the tables. The parallel between the theft of food and wine in Macropedius's *Aluta* (1535) and Lazarillo's devices for stealing bread from the locked bin and wine from the beggar's flask cannot be ignored; and his repeated invocation of God to justify his pilfering is only effective if read as a satire of some contemporary religious genre. As he opens the bread-bin to commit his first theft, Lazarillo ingenuously parodies the Eucharist itself: '. . . I was so gladde, that mee thought I did see in figure (as they say) the face of God.' The fact that Utrecht (where these plays originated) was part of the Spanish empire, and the discovery of an extant prodigal-son play in Spanish make it certain that the Latin plays were known there. The one play discovered, the *Comedia Prodiga* of Luis de Miranda of Plasencia, printed at Seville in 1554 but probably written 1532, follows closely the usual outline of the continental prodigal-son play as established at Utrecht. The author, while expressly stating his didactic purpose as warning young men of the dangers of debauchery, clearly enjoys describing the boy's downfall among harlots and social parasites. Moreover, the close similarity between *Lazarillo* and a play by Sebastian de Horozco, makes its connection with the stage even more likely and it has even been argued that Horozco wrote both the play and the story.[1] This suggestion requires more serious investigation than can be given here, but if it is valid, then the novel itself owes its origin to a satire on the prodigal-son plays of the Christian Terence movement.

This sudden blossoming of continental biblical drama, of which the Christian Terence formed only a part, found a ready interest in England. The two largest collections, *Comoediae et Tragoediae aliquot et Novo et Vetere Testamento desumptae* published by Brylinger in Basel (1540) and Oporinus's collection *Dramata Sacra* published at Basel in the same year, were widely known in England. Gnaphaeus's *Acolastus*, the first and most famous of the Christian Terence plays, was translated into English by the schoolmaster John Palsgrave and published in London in 1540 (a busy year for the biblical drama) and Cornelius Schonaeus's *Terentius Christianus* published in Cologne in 1592, not only saw publication in London that same year, but became the most famous collection of foreign plays used in English schools.[2] It was prefaced in England by a few words of praise for the author who '. . . has clothed more chaste subject-matter in the pure language of Terence, in order that along with elegance of style boys may imbibe holiness and uprightness of character,' thus stressing the formula of Christian content in classical garb.

(iv) JOHN BALE

The distinction of having written the first Renaissance biblical play belongs to John Bale, bishop of Ossory. But it is a distinction to which he has only a tenuous claim, for his plays stand so close to the medieval tradition that they mark only a small, if important, advance. Born in 1495 near Dunwich in Suffolk, he received a sound Catholic training at a Carmelite convent in Norwich, from which he moved to Jesus College, at that time

[1] R. Foulché-Delbosc, 'Remarques sur Lazarillo de Tormes', in *Revue Hispanique vii* (1900), 81.

[2] Foster Watson, *The English Grammar Schools to 1660* (Cambridge, 1908), p. 322.

the most monastic of the Cambridge houses.[1] His stern up-bringing appeared to have made of him a fervent member of the Catholic faith in which he actually took holy orders, but his association with the frequenters of the White Horse Inn at Cambridge exposed him to the new humanist approach to Scripture and eventually drove him into the ranks of the Protestants. He created a scandal by renouncing his vows of chastity and taking a wife; and like most converts he became more zealous in reviling his former colleagues than were those he had joined, his splenetic outbursts earning him the name 'bilious' Bale. Without the patronage of Thomas Cromwell, who was eager to exploit his polemical flair, he would doubtless have ended his days at the stake together with some of his Cambridge friends. On Cromwell's fall from power, he was forced to flee to the Continent where, in the course of his travels, he was welcomed by Oporinus, the publisher of one of the Christian Terence collections.

Of Bale's dramatic work there survive, apart from his *King John* (which marked the beginning of the English history play), three so-called 'mystery plays' and a biblical morality; and among the works listed in his Catalogue, nine plays which have not survived are devoted to scriptural themes. The first of the mystery plays, *God's Promises*, was compiled, according to Bale, in 1538 and is extant in the original edition of 1547/8 published by Dirk Van Der Straten of Wesel. The two subsequent sections, *A Brefe Comedy or Enterlude of Johan Baptystes Preachynge in the Wyldernesse* (subtitled with typical Balean rancour as *openyng the craftye Assaults of the Hypocrytes* [i.e. friars]) and *The Temptation of Our Lord*, were published separately, but W. W. Greg has shown that together they formed a unified trilogy.[2]

God's Promises is the most interesting of the three, adopting the form of the Prophet Play from the mystery cycles and depicting in seven brief scenes the dialogue between *Pater*

---

[1] For details of Bale's life, see J. W. Harris, *John Bale* (Urbana, 1940) and Honor McCusker, *John Bale, Dramatist and Antiquary* (Bryn Mawr, 1942).

[2] W. W. Greg, 'Notes on Some Early Plays', *Library*, 4th series, xi (1930). All three plays were performed together under Bale's direction at Kilkenny on 20th August, 1553.

Coelestis and Adam, Noah, Abraham, Moses, David, Isaiah, and John the Baptist in each of which God reaffirms his covenant with man. The adoption of the medieval dramatic form is sufficiently explained both by Bale's antiquarian interests and his Catholic upbringing, but his departure from the medieval form is even more significant. For where the Prophet Play had aimed at proving from biblical sources the authenticity of Christianity in the face of heathen and, more specifically, Jewish disbelief, Bale's purpose is to use those same sources as justification for the Protestant claim of divine election on the basis of the covenant. In the controversy between the Catholics and the Reformers, the divinity of Christ was, of course, no longer an issue requiring proof, and behind much of the dialogue in Bales' play may be perceived a theological dispute concerning the place of *grace* in Christianity.

Luther had insisted that grace could not be merited by man, but depended almost exclusively on divine mercy, man's contribution being merely his own faith. Calvinism adopted the Lutheran viewpoint by and large, and in this play man's utter dependence upon that mercy and his complete unworthiness to expect it other than as a gratuitous gift occupies a central position. Adam, no longer the puppet of the medieval mysteries, proclaims with remorse:

> *Lord, now I perceyue what power is in man*
> *And strength of hymselfe, whan thy swete grace is absent.*
> *He must nedes but fall, do he the best he can.*[1]

Man deserves nothing and can claim nothing from God. Helpless he hangs upon the merciful generosity of the Heavenly Father, and in the same way that sinful Adam accepts his punishment as the very least he can expect, so the righteous Noah, redeemed and delivered by God, acknowledges that he has received far greater blessings than he deserved:

> *Whom maye we thanke lorde, for our helthe & saluacyone*
> *But thy great mercye and goodnesse undeserued?*
> *Thy promyse in faythe, is our iustyfycacyon,*
> *As it was Adams.*

To underscore even further this theme of grace towards the Chosen Seed, Bale himself appeared on the stage to read the

[1] Tudor Facsimile Text (London/Edinburgh, 1908).

prologue, in which the Protestants were clearly identified with that Chosen Seed by means of the concluding pun:

> *God wyll shewe mercye to euery generacyon.*
> *And to hys kyngedome, of hys great goodnesse call,*
> *Hys elected spouse, or faythfull congregacyon,*
> *As here shall apere, by open protestacyon.*

Nevertheless, even in so early a Protestant work as this, the central paradox of Calvinism is at once apparent. For with all the insistence on sinful man's helpless prostration before the divine throne, Bale's characters speak with the rational self-confidence of the Renaissance humanist, challenging the apparent cruelty of God and demanding justice as well as mercy. *Pater Coelestis* is portrayed as a stern and almost inexorable tyrant, exacting his full measure of retribution, and reluctantly granting man the one hope of eternal redemption in the form of the covenant. He is a projection of rigid Calvinism at its worst, concerned more with punishment than mercy and zealously stamping out all forms of human weakness. He begins by recalling Adam's sin, in punishment for which this supposedly 'merciful' Father had determined to send:

> *. . . plages of coreccyon,*
> *Most greuouse and sharpe, hys wanton lustes to slake,*
> *By water and fyre, by syckenesse and infeccyon,*
> *Of pestylent sores, molestynge hys compleccyon,*
> *By troublouse warre, by derthe and peynefull scarsenesse.*

In answer to Adam's gentle plea for forgiveness, he states brusquely:

> *Thu shalt dye for it, with all thy posteryte.*

and after further supplication from Adam, insists with inflexible cruelty:

> *I am immutable, I maye change no decre.*
> *Thu shalt dye (I saye) without anye remedye.*

This is a very different figure from the kindly, patriarchal *Deus* of the mysteries. And no less a change is discernible in the characters themselves. The timidity of the medieval figures has been replaced by a respectful dignity; they no longer cower, but firmly refuse to accept the stern decrees of God until they have wrung from him a contract in the form of a covenant sealed with an eternal symbol. The following dialogue suggests a kindly uncle reasoning sweetly with a wayward child, but the medieval situation has been reversed—for God is the obstinate child and Noah the sweet reasoner:

Noah: *All thys is true, lorde, I cannot thy words reproue,*
           Lete hys weaknesse yet thy mercyfull goodnesse moue.
Pater: *No weaknesse is it, but wylfull workynge all,*
           That reigneth in man, through mynde dyabolycall.
           He shall have therfor lyke as he hath deserued.
Noah: *Lose hym not yet lorde, though he hath depelye swerved.*
           I knowe thy mercye, is farre above hys rudenesse,
           Beynge infynyte, as all other thynges are in the.
           Hys folye therfor, now pardone of thy goodnesse,
           And measure it not, beyonde thy godlye pytie.

This supplicatory dialogue clearly echoes Abraham's plea that Sodom and Gomorrah be spared, but again the situation is reversed. In the Bible, God generously accedes to Abraham's prayer for mercy in the certain knowledge that divine justice will be vindicated. Eventually he agrees to spare the cities even if only ten righteous men be found there, but when not even that meagre number can be found, Abraham submits with humility to God's superior wisdom and admits that the original decree had been fully justified. In Bale's play, the human characters prove wiser: it is God's lack of mercy which needs to be tempered.

Bale's drama marks an important advance in humanization of characters, but it is offset by the poor structural quality of the play. Each scene is just long enough to arouse interest in the central figure but too short to develop that interest; and the repetitious nature of the seven scenes destroys much of the play's appeal. Compared with Bale's other plays, it has the advantage of being free from 'bile', since it was not intended primarily as a polemical work except insofar as it provided, in a sense, a substitute for the Catholic mysteries which were still being performed regularly throughout England.

If *Pater Coelestis* was depicted as a tyrant, his very appearance in the drama was of some interest, for it was a question which had been, and continued to be, vigorously discussed in Reformation circles. Juan Luiz Vives, the Spanish humanist who lectured at Oxford, described in his commentary on the *City of God* (undertaken at Erasmus's suggestion) the cat-calls and ribald laughter which he had witnessed at the performance of a Passion play in the Low Countries.

'And by and by this great fighter comes and for feare of a girle, denies his *Maister*, all the people laughing at her question, and hissing at his deniall; and in all these reuells and ridiculous stirres Christ onely is serious and seuere: to the great guilt, shame, and sinne both of the priestes that present this and the people that behold it.'[1]

The fear of such sacrilege prompted Luther to discourage Joachim Greff from writing a Passion play and, although Luther declared in 1530 that he would willingly see Christ represented in Latin and German school plays, in an earlier sermon he had warned that Jesus should not be portrayed as a man to be pitied and wept over, but should be presented in such a way as to provoke the audience to weep over themselves. Grimald allowed God the Father on the stage in his *Christus Redivivus* and Hans Sachs in a famous scene brought him on to question Adam's children on their catechism; but after Bale's play there were few instances of the appearance of God among the *dramatis personae*. As long as the earlier mystery plays consisted of characters speaking their lines like wooden puppets, there was no incongruity in God's appearing to question Adam and Eve; but once the human characters came to life, God himself needed to be humanized, and rather than risk the sacrilege involved (as the twentieth-century dramatist was later to do) the Renaissance playwright removed him into the wings. Christ, as God in human form, remained a little longer, but was destined before long to disappear from the stage together with God himself.

Bale's play follows the mysteries in its total disregard of the passage of time by seeking to compress the history of mankind from Adam to John the Baptist into the confines of a few brief scenes; but since the structural framework makes no attempt at continuity, the lapse of time is not felt to be strange. Again as in the mysteries, it aims at conveying the cyclical aspect of biblical

[1] Juan Luiz Vives, *St. Augustine, of the citie of god*, translated by J. H. H[ealey] (1610), p. 337.

history, each character reciting the list of his predecessors and prophesying those that are to come and Kolve's remarks on the relevance of the Seven Ages of the world help to explain the structural framework.[1] As Bale was in his *King John* the originator of the chronicle play, he helped to transmit to the new genre that sense of purposeful history which he had inherited from the mysteries and which was to reach its Renaissance climax in the monarchal plays of Shakespeare. There the sweep of English history from Richard II to Henry V is presented not as a series of isolated reigns but as part of a national destiny moving forward under divine aegis.[2]

The two remaining plays of Bale's trilogy are simpler in structure, with a substratum of mild anti-Catholic polemic. That vicious and open denunciation of sexual licence within the convents and monasteries which had pervaded his *Three Laws* is here replaced by a merely allusive anti-papalism. John the Baptist upbraids the Pharisee and Sadducee who come to scoff at him:

> *Ye generation of vipers! ye murtherers of the prophets!*
> *Ye Lucifers proud, and usurpers of high seats!*
> *Never was serpent more stinging than ye be;*
> *More full of poison, nor inward cruelty!*
> *Neither your good works, nor merits of your fathers,*
> *Your fastings, long prayers, with other holy behavers*
> *Shall you, afore God, be able to justify*
> *Your affections inward, unless ye do mortify.*

Only in the epilogue are the Pharisee and Sadducee identified as representing the monastic orders:

> *Hear neither Francis, Benedict, nor Bruno,*
> *Albert nor Dominic, for they new rulers invent;*
> *Believe neither Pope, nor priest of his consent;*
> *Follow Christ's Gospel, and therein fructify*
> *To the praise of God, and his son Jesus glory.*

Apart from Satan's assurance that 'Thy vicar at Rome, I think, will be my friend', the final play drops all sectarianism and

[1] Kolve, p. 94.

[2] Miss Catherine Dunn develops this point in her 'Medieval Cycle as History Play', *SRen vii* (1960), 76. See also T. F. Driver, *The Sense of History in Greek and Shakespearean Drama* (New York, 1960).

offers a refreshingly simple dramatization of the temptation scene. The figure of Jesus is calm and dignified; but the simplicity of the play is achieved at the expense of dramatic tension; for in the medieval tradition Jesus opens the play by recounting the lessons to be learned from the subsequent scene. There is, as yet, no possibility of bringing the play to life by suggesting an inner struggle, and the dramatic advance over the mystery plays remains minimal.[1]

Bale provides our only link with a fellow dramatist, the elusive Ralph (or Robert) Radcliff(e). In 1538, when Bale was composing *God's Promises*, Radcliffe, who was a product of Oxford and Cambridge and had adopted Protestantism at the latter university, took over an abandoned Carmelite monastery at Hitchin and converted the lower portion into a spacious theatre. He opened a school there, using this theatre for school productions to which he invited the local townspeople. Bale, who visited the school in 1552, was greatly impressed by the work being done, but despite his urging Radcliffe to publish his plays, they remained in manuscript. Although Bale quotes from the plays in perfectly metrical Latin, it is by no means certain that such was the language of the plays (Bale has an awkward habit of giving Latin titles to English plays) and the fact that they were performed before the townspeople would make English more likely. Since one of the main purposes of these school plays was to provide exercises in translation, my own view is that Radcliffe's plays probably existed in both languages, Bale quoting from the Latin texts which Radcliffe showed him. The existence of Sixt Birck's plays in both German and Latin would support such a theory.

Of the ten plays we know to have been written by him, six are biblical and all but one of the latter are devoted to Old Testament themes. They are *The Burning of Sodom, The Delivery of Susannah, Job's Afflictions, Jonah, Judith,* and *Lazarus and Dives*. Only one of these, the Job play, survived in manuscript but, like Greene's later play on the same theme, was

[1] A fragmentary manuscript of a Resurrection drama to be performed over two days is cautiously assigned by the editors of the Malone Society Reprint to Bale's authorship on the flimsy evidence that he lists a play on that theme among his works. Stylistically, it lacks Bale's directness and economy of language.

consigned to the flames by Warburton's thoughtless servant. We know of very few Job plays from this era, probably because it did not suit that emphasis on a neat divine justice which dominates these school plays. It would, therefore, have been particularly interesting to see Radcliffe's treatment of the theme, especially since the other themes he chose were so admirably suited to the theodical approach. None of his plays is now extant, despite a disappointingly false rumour to the contrary.[1]

A minor interlude, first recorded in the Stationers' Register in 1566, has been assigned to the mid-century on the basis of a reference in the prologue to the king rather than the queen. It is *The Life and Repentaunce of Marie Magdalene* by Lewis Wager, of whom little is known other than the clues provided by the text itself—that he was a 'learned clarke' apparently with a university background. The opening of the interlude, with its parody of Catholic liturgy, leaves no doubt that Wager was a staunch Protestant, and the main doctrinal lesson the work sought to teach was that Faith was demanded of man even more than Love. For all its theological intent, it would appear that Wager was interested in material returns no less than spiritual, for after a lengthy defence of the playwright's craft against some unspecified attack, he insists that the audience is receiving its full money's worth:

> *Truely, I say, whether you geue halfpence or pence,*
> *Your gayne shalbe double, before you depart hence.*
>
> *Is wisedom no more worth than a peny, trow you?*
> *Scripture calleth the price thereof incomparable.*
> *Here may you learne godly Sapience now,*
> *Which to body and soule shall be profitable.*[2]

For the historian, the main interest in this otherwise undistinguished mingling of biblical and morality figures is the lively topicality with which the early, profligate Mary is presented.

---

[1] Lily B. Campbell, *Divine Poetry*, p. 167, refers to the discovery of three manuscript plays by Radcliffe in the National Library of Wales. They are, in fact, merely translations by Radcliffe of works by Ravisius Textor, used widely as school texts in that period and no doubt intended for his own pupils.

[2] Quotations are from the edition by F. I. Carpenter (Chicago, 1902).

Although the play is, of course, set in Jerusalem at the time of Christ, the women's fashions satirized are obviously contemporary. *Infidelitie* and his cronies *Pride*, *Cupiditie* and *Carnall Concupiscence* flatter the preening Mary on her beauty, advising her how to curl her hair 'with a hotte needle' and wear it piled on her forehead 'the breadth of an hand'. Gentlemen, it appears, preferred blondes even in the sixteenth century:

> *If the colour of your haire beginneth for to fade,*
> *A craft you must haue, that yellow it may be made;*
> *With some Goldsmyth you may your selfe acquaint,*
> *Of whom you may haue water your haire for to paint.*

For a play so moral in its intent, there is an extraordinary amount of hugging and kissing on the stage itself, and the scene of 'debauchery' ends with the singing of a merry song. So much for the pre-Christian world and all its forbidden fruits. Now Christ enters (one of his last appearances on the English stage for some three hundred and fifty years[1]) and announces with more theological than dramatic force:

> *The Sonne of Manne is come to seke and saue*
> *Suche persons as perishe and go astraye;*
> *God hath promised them lyfe eternally to haue,*
> *If they repent, and turne from theyr euill way.*

In a dramatically implausible *volte face*, Mary is at once purified and ennobled. With the blossoming of naturalism on the sixteenth-century English stage, it was becoming painfully obvious that the stylized presentation of sacred figures in the medieval tradition was drawing to a close.

(v) 'Postfiguration'

At this point, a new spirit began to infuse the biblical plays of the period, and it not only betokened a change in the approach to the Scriptures, but served at the same time to lend a new vitality to their dramatic representation. It is a phenomenon for which I have coined the term *postfiguration*.

[1] John Foxe's *Christus Triumphans*, a non-biblical play concerned with contemporary morals and performed at Trinity College, Cambridge in 1562/3, introduces Christ as a member of the cast.

The Early Renaissance

We have seen how, in the gradual development of the mystery cycles and the earliest of the Renaissance scriptural plays, the haloed figures of the Bible whose lesser sanctity encouraged realistic dramatization became increasingly life-like until, at the final stage, they began to be seen almost as contemporary figures. Noah becomes a master craftsman of the local shipbuilders' guild and Abraham was 'feudalized' as *the bold earl*.[1] The dramatist bridged the gulf of years by trying to see these characters as contemporary people. However, there was also a desire, not always explicitly stated, to minimize the fact that the original characters were Jews. Sir Thomas More records an amusing anecdote which throws some light on this tendency:

'Ye be wiser, I wote well, than the gentlewoman was, which in talking once with my father, when she harde saye that our Lady was a Jew, first could not believe it, but saide, what ye mock I wis, I pray you tel trouth. And when it was so fully affermed that she at last bileued it quod she, so help me God and Halidom I shall love her the worse while I live.'[2]

It was in that mood that Luther aimed in his translation at making Moses speak in such a way that 'you would never know he was a Jew.'[3] He was to become not merely clothed in sixteenth-century garb, but a German Protestant speaking the language of the age, thinking its thoughts, and struggling with the same problems as beset the Reformers.

All this marked a withdrawal from prefigurative exegesis and a concern with the characters as creatures of flesh and blood; but it was only a transitory phase. The climax of this trend was a complete reversal of prefiguration. It will be recalled that typology functioned on the principle that the Old Testament shadowed forth the events which were due to occur in the New Testament; the commentator, therefore, looked to the Gospels in order to discover the true meaning of Abraham's sacrifice. The Protestant's growing concern with the Covenant tradition, gave the Old Testament stories a new archetypal significance. For if the covenant reaffirmed throughout the generations was contracted with the individual as well as the group, then the

[1] Owst, *Literature and Pulpit*, p. 114.
[2] *English Works* (1557), p. 136.
[3] See Roland H. Bainton, *The Reformation of the Sixteenth Century* (Boston, 1952), p. 62.

Protestant's *own life* should bear the marks of that cyclical repetition. As he read the biblical tales of the patriarchs, prophets, and kings, and of their struggle for moral probity in the midst of worldly temptation, the Protestant looked for their true meaning in his own spiritual and even political exertions. He began to see himself in biblical terms, re-enacting or 'postfiguring' in his life leading incidents from the lives of the scriptural heroes. Instead of searching in the Old Testament for stories whose validity lay in their adumbrating the New, he now searched for those which seemed to parallel his own personal history, those which he felt were being relived by him in a later generation. Sometimes, it is true, the saints had been seen retrospectively as having re-enacted the Passion of Christ and fulfilled in their deaths the requirement of *imitatio Dei*. But here was an essentially new concept, with its roots in the soil of the temporal world, whereby mortal men, not elevated into sainthood, began to see their daily struggles, both spiritual and physical, in terms of a biblical archetype. The Puritans sailing towards the New World proclaimed that they were bound for the Promised Land, for 'God's own country' not because they had found a neat rallying-call, but because their voyage was for them a seventeenth-century cyclical re-enactment of the Exodus from Egypt. Milton, the discarded champion of God longing for revenge on his enemies, instinctively saw within himself a reworking of Samson eyeless in Gaza. And implicit in this postfiguration was the encouraging conviction that the victorious destiny of the biblical hero was, by virtue of the other parallels, the destiny of the postfigurer too; so that Milton in his spiritual darkness found some comfort in the belief that his salvation must lie before him.

Throughout the biblical drama of this period we shall see this pattern repeated, with the Protestant, always of course as the Chosen Seed, reliving the Bible in his contemporary setting. Occasionally his postfiguring even rubbed off onto the Catholic, but it was in the main a Protestant tendency. Where in medieval times such intensely personal identification with scriptural heroes would have been regarded as presumptuous and was relegated to generalized homiletical parallels encouraging the Christian to emulate the virtues and shun the vices of a Noah or Esau, it now became the inspiration of the militant Protestant as he brandished his sword or pen with the fervour of his spiritual forebears.

The change was at first gradual, and the earliest instances give only a hint of what is to come. Bale's chronical play *King John* was not, of course, itself biblical in theme, but in embryonic form the author sees the English kings as repeating within their actions the pattern of Moses and Joshua:

> *This noble Kynge Johan, as a faythfull Moyses,*
> *Withstode proude Pharo for hys poore Israel,*
> *Myndynge to brynge yt owt of the lande of darkenesse,*
> *But the Egyptyanes did agaynst hym so rebell*
> *That hys poore people ded styll in the desart dwell,*
> *Tyll that duke Josue, whych was our late Kynge Henrye,*
> *Clerely brought us in-to the lande of mylke and honye.*

The implication here is that the divine right of kings is insufficient – the king must justify himself by his deeds. And by identifying the king with the righteous leaders of Israel, Bale suggests that disloyalty is tantamount to joining the ranks of Korah and the blasphemous defiers of God. It served to accentuate that sense of divine destiny in the English monarchal plays to which we have already referred.

A much deeper concern with the contemporary relevance of the Scriptures is discernible in the anonymous *New Enterlude of Godly Queene Hester* (entered in the Stationers' Register in 1560/1), although its political allusions escaped the attention of critics until the late nineteenth century. On the surface, it merely relates the story of the book of Esther, with due attention to its moral teachings:

> *Come nere vertuous matrons and women kind*
> *Here may ye learne of Hesters duty,*
> *In all comlines of vertue you shal finde*
> *How to behave your selue in humilitie.* [1]

The story, however, does not follow the original slavishly. Instead, it employs it as a setting for a debate on the humanist topic of kingly responsibility. Mordecai's part dwindles to insignificance, Vashti disappears from the list of characters, and

[1] Quotations from W. W. Greg, *Materialen zur kunde des alteren Englischen Dramas* (Louvain, 1904), vol. v.

the beauty contest becomes a test of wit. Ahasuerus, deciding after a disappointingly cursory glance that all the contestants 'be fayre and goodly eche one', proceeds to subject Esther to an examination of her views on the virtues requisite for a queen. Her answers prove eminently satisfactory, particularly, we may suspect her politic conclusion:

> . . . *as muche goodnes aye must be seene,*
> *As in the kynge to be in the Quene,*
> *And how many vertues long to a kynge,*
> *Lyke vnto your grace, I cannot make recknynge.*

Ahasuerus, understandably, commends her wisdom, and the story then follows the general pattern of the biblical tale, interspersed with scenes of Morality figures – Pride, Adulation, and Ambition – who soon retire disgruntled when they find that Haman outdoes each of them in their particular vices.

Such is the ostensible theme of the play. However, in 1873, A. B. Grosart remarked that no one who had read Froude's history could fail to recognize this play as a political satire voicing the complaints of the people against Henry VIII and his ministers. In his own edition of the play, Greg identified the principal minister attacked as Wolsey, noting the similarity in political allusion to William Roy's *Read me and be not wroth* and Skelton's *Why come ye not to Court?* Accordingly he places its date of composition before Wolsey's fall in 1530 and, since the play concerns itself with Haman's plotting against the Queen, narrows the date down to 1525–9 when Wolsey was using his influence to turn the king against Catherine.[1]

The interpretation of the play as a political parody greatly enhances its dramatic effectiveness. As it stands, it is a somewhat crude and selective version of the biblical story, but as a polemical play its otherwise turgid dialogue takes on a new life and subtlety. 'This carnifex Aman' is no longer a mere term of abuse, but a sly dig at Wolsey's obscure origin as a butcher's son; and the admission of the allegorical Vices that Haman outdoes them

---

[1] A. B. Grosart's introduction to the private edition of *Miscellanies of the Fuller Worthies' Library* (1873) and W. W. Greg in the *Athenaeum* (1900) i, 538, where he rejects Mrs. C. C. Stopes' attribution of the play, on very flimsy evidence, to William Hunnis. Greg suggests Skelton or one of his circle.

all becomes a device for political denigration. The identification of Wolsey with Haman is particularly apt in the scenes of his meteoric rise to power by royal patronage and the prediction of his equally sudden fall, and the biblical parallel at once unleashes upon him the wrath of the righteous for the ungodly.

A more specific and purposeful translation of contemporary events into a scriptural setting, Nicholas Udall's *Ezechias*, has been preserved for us only at second-hand in the form of two Latin accounts of its performance before Queen Elizabeth at King's College, Cambridge on August 8th, 1564, some eight years after the author's death. Fortunately, the accounts, particularly that of Hartwell, are sufficiently detailed to make the analogies clear and to indicate the methods used for elaborating the initial comparison of Henry VIII to Hezekiah.[1]

Udall himself, the author of *Ralph Roister Doister*, steered a dangerous course between Catholicism and Protestantism, falling into disgrace at Oxford for his Lutheran leanings, yet succeeding in being appointed tutor in the household of the Bishop of Winchester and Master of the Chapel under Mary. Despite his imprisonment for homosexuality while headmaster of Eton, he was, surprisingly enough, later appointed headmaster of Westminster, and he used the opportunity afforded by both positions to stage performances of his plays with casts drawn from his pupils.[2] It is probable that the posthumous performance of *Ezechias* before Elizabeth was at the instigation of some of his old pupils, at that time students at King's College.

The play, based upon 2 Kings xviii–xix, relates how King Hezekiah purged the country of its idolatrous practices and destroyed the brazen serpent which, having been used by Moses to heal the sick, had later become an object of superstitious

[1] The accounts are Abraham Hartwell's *Regina Literata* and Nicholas Robinson's *Commentarii Hexaemeri Rerum Cantabrigiae Actarum* printed in *Progresses of Elizabeth*, ed. J. G. Nichols (London, 1788). See also F. S. Boas, *University Drama in the Tudor Age* (Oxford, 1914), pp. 94 f.

[2] For a recent theory that he was guilty of no more than theft, see William L. Edgerton, *Nicholas Udall* (New York, 1965), p. 40. The author suggests a scribal error in the transcript of the trial – an unlikely theory but it would, at least, explain Udall's puzzling reappointment to a headmastership.

veneration. A recurrence of heathen worship provokes a prophetic warning of imminent punishment, fulfilled immediately by the appearance of an Assyrian host and the insolent demands of its leader Rabshakeh. Hezekiah's prayer for divine aid and the mysterious death of the invaders concludes the drama.

The parallel between Hezekiah's righteous zeal against image-worshippers and Henry VIII's dissolution of the 'superstitious' monasteries is sufficient to denote the anti-papist intent of the play. Elsewhere, without direct reference to this drama, Udall removes all doubts regarding the identification when he describes the king as '. . . a new Ezechias [Hezekiah] to confound al idols, to destroy all hillalters of supersticion, to roote vp al counterfeit religions, and to restore . . . the true religion and wurship of god, the syncere preachyng of gods word, and the booke of the lawe, that is to say of Christes holy testament to be read of the people in their vulgare toung.'[1]

How far the continuation of the story paralleled the current fear of foreign invasion and, indeed, what other topical references the play may have possessed, it is impossible to determine, both because of our ignorance of the exact date of composition[2] and because we possess merely an eye-witness account and not the text itself. But what has been transmitted to us through the good offices of Hartwell makes it clear that, although not himself an official member of the Protestant church, the author's Lutheran sympathies had prompted him to see in contemporary events a postfiguration of biblical narrative.[3] His use of the brazen serpent was particularly apt in an age when Protestantism was aiming at removing the medieval abuses of Catholicism, amongst which there figured prominently the 'superstitious' worship of holy images within the church. It was, incidentally, to this drama that Bale probably referred when in 1548 he spoke of a *Tragoedia de Papatu* by Udall.

Recent evidence has made the attribution to Udall of a further,

---

[1] Preface to *St. Luke* in his *The Second Tome of the Paraphrases of Erasmus* (London, 1551).

[2] A. R. Moon, 'Nicholas Udall's Lost Tragedy *Ezechias*', *TLS*, 19th April, 1928 suggests 1539 as the most likely date.

[3] In Mary's reign Udall, on his own testimony, tried to persuade the Protestant martyr Thomas Mountain to renounce his Protestantism, but that was, no doubt, for reasons of expediency.

and perhaps more significant, biblical play almost certain. *The Historie of Jacob and Esau* entered in the Stationers' Register in 1557/8 and printed by Henry Bynneman in 1568, is a delightful, boisterous comedy, closely paralleling the style and dramatic technique of *Ralph Roister Doister*; yet only in 1912 did C. W. Wallace suggest Udall as the author, and an article by Leicester Bradner in 1927 presented persuasive evidence for Udall's authorship on the basis of the play's metrical form.[1]

The play succeeds in combining almost all the qualities of biblical drama discussed so far, with comic exploitation of minor characters, a concern with the Calvinist doctrines of predestination and election, prodigal-son moralizing, and the translation of the biblical narrative into contemporary terms. It is particularly illuminating to compare it with the twelfth-century treatment of the same theme, the *Ordo de Ysaac et Rebecca et Filiis Eorum*, in order to see what changes had taken place in the intervening period.

The medieval play, it will be recalled, by identifying Esau with the Hebrews and Jacob with the Christian inheritors of the birthright, interpreted the story as prefiguring the rejection of the corrupt Pharisee in favour of the followers of Jesus; the donning of Esau's clothes signified, for example, the adoption by Christianity of the decalogue long neglected by the Jews. Typology was here fulfilling its medieval function of confirming faith in the validity of the Christian mystery. The Protestant, however, perceived in the literal story the triumphant election of the righteous Hebrew, his own spiritual ancestor. Esau now becomes for Udall not the Jewish people but the Catholic anti-Christ who claims the rights of the first-born without justifying those rights by his own moral integrity, whereas the Protestant Jacob not only qualifies by his deeds but is also blessed with the divine Grace which constitutes election. The prologue draws the audience's attention to this doctrinal point by referring to Calvin's well-known quotation from Malachi and Romans on which he had based the doctrine of predestination:

---

[1] C. W. Wallace, *The Evolution of English Drama up to Shakespeare* (Berlin, 1912), p. 101 and Leicester Bradner, 'A Test for Udall's Authorship', *MLN xlii* (1927), 378. Bradner's thesis is generally supported by J. E. Bernard, *The Prosody of the Tudor Interlude* (New Haven, 1939).

'Postfiguration'

> *As the prophete Malachie and Paule witnesse beare,*
> *Jacob was chosen, and Esau reprobate:*
> *Jacob I loue (sayde God) and Esau I hate.*
> *For it is not (sayth Paule) in mans renuing or will,*
> *But in Gods mercy who choseth whome he will.*[1]

Since the play is ultimately a comedy, Esau's 'crime' is reduced to habitual horn-blowing at unearthly hours. He is thus an obvious offshoot of the prodigal-son tradition, providing for the young a warning against inconsiderateness towards others, and the moral lesson is duly spelt out by the long-suffering neighbours:

> *Hanan:*   *Neither see I any hope that he will amende.*
> *Zethar:*   *Then let hym euen looke to come to an yvil ende.*
>   *For youth that will folow none but theyr owne bridle,*
>   *That leadeth a dissolute lyfe and an ydle,*
>   *Youth that refuseth holsome documentes,*
>   *Or to take example of theyr godly parentes,*
>   *Youth that is retchelesse and taketh no regarde*
>   *What become of them selfe, nor which ende goe forwarde,*
>   *It is great mervaile and a special grace,*
>   *If euer they come to goodnesse all theyr life space.*

The liveliness of the play derives primarily from the servants in whom the tradition of the Middle Ages meets and mingles with that of the humanist. Ragau, Esau's servant, comes straight out of the Wakefield cycle and plays Garcio to Esau's Cain, preceding his master onto the stage, and cursing him liberally before he arrives with frequent invocations to the 'dyvell'. Isaac's servant, on the other hand, the pert, mischievous Mido, is a typically Terentian slave using his intelligence to outwit his master and winning the audience's sympathy by his saucy humour. But for all the comedy, the didactic purpose is not forgotten. Rebecca's substitution of Jacob for Esau at the blessing (conveniently whitewashed in the play as 'a pretty knacke') demonstrates that the righteous are rewarded; Esau,

[1] Malone Society Reprint, ed. J. Crow and F. P. Wilson (Oxford, 1956). Since the quotations first appeared in the 1539 edition of Calvin's works, the play could not have been published earlier. See G. Scheurweghs, 'The Date of *Jacob and Esau*', *ES* xv (1933).

again in the prodigal-son tradition, repents at the last moment, and a hymn is sung eulogizing God's mercy in selecting his Chosen. The play concludes by emphasizing both the contemporary relevance of the theme and its significance for the doctrine of election:

> *Our parte therfore is first to beleue Gods worde,*
> *Not doubtyng but that he wil his elected save:*
> *Then to put full trust in the goodness of the Lorde*
> *That we be of the number which shall mercy haue:*
> *Thirdly to liue as we may his promise craue.*
> *Thus if we do, we shall Abrahams chyldren be:*
> *And come with Jacob to endlesse felicitie.*[1]

This play, illustrative – in its postfiguration, Protestant identification, and comic elaboration – of so many features of the biblical drama of the sixteenth century, provides a convenient place to pause for a brief review of the non-vernacular biblical plays of this period.

(vi) The Greek and Latin Plays

These scriptural plays written in Greek and Latin may seem scarcely classifiable as English drama; yet as the dramatic products of the English and Scottish universities, they deserve some consideration here, indicating as they do the new tendency of biblical dramatists to find their models in classical tragedy as well as comedy. The reader concerned solely with the mainstream of English biblical drama may prefer to omit this section and continue with the next chapter.

The rediscovery of classical literature by the humanist scholars had resulted in a revival of St. Jerome's nightmare – the accusation from heaven that he was not really a Christian but a Ciceronian. Erasmus, it is true, had translated Euripides'

[1] The prayer for the well-being of clergy, Queen, politicians and subjects which follows these lines (the major part devoted to the Queen's well-being) suggests a royal performance, although there is no record of such. It is unlikely that a play so obviously Protestant would have been performed before Mary, and as Udall died before Elizabeth's accession, the lines were probably added by the producer or printer.

Hecuba and *Iphigenia* with a clear conscience on the grounds that the work would assist him in mastering Greek for his translation of the New Testament. But it was also his contribution to the task shared with such men as Grocyn and Linacre, of spreading in England a new interest in Greek literature. However, when Ascham's immense popularity as a teacher at St. John's College has succeeded (as he himself put it) in making Sophocles and Euripides as famous as Plautus had been,[1] the Christian humanist began to wonder whether he was really doing the work of the devil in diverting attention from the Bible to pagan literature. The complaint: 'Would God that all schoolmasters and teachers of youth would, instead of Virgil, Ovid, Horace, Catullus, Tibullus, Propertius, &c., teach these verses of David'[2] began to be applied to Greek drama as well. Martin Bucer, who came to England from Strassburg in 1549 and associated closely with the religious dramatists of the university, insisted that tragedy should be restricted entirely to biblical themes, and even advocated that a board of censors be set up to determine the moral quality of such plays.[3] The sudden outcrop of biblical dramas in classical guise showed that he was not alone in this view. They included George Buchanan's *Jephthes* and *Baptistes*, John Christopherson's Ἰεφθάε, Thomas Watson's *Absalon*, and Nicholas Grimald's *Christus Redivivus* and *Archipropheta*.

It was no coincidence that both Buchanan and Christopherson independently chose the theme of Jephthah in their attempt to find common ground between Greek tragedy and the Bible. For the story of Jephthah sacrificing his daughter in fulfilment of a vow is closer to classical mythology – Agamemnon's sacrifice of Iphigenia – than, perhaps, any other section of the Scriptures, although we should note that the parallel only holds true according to the typological reading. In the light of the detailed Old Testament laws for financial redemption of vows which cannot or ought not to be fulfilled, Jewish commentators were at pains to prove that the abhorrent human sacrifice did not in fact take place.[4] But in the Christian context the story was seen

[1] *Epist. xii.*
[2] *The Early Works of Thomas Becon* (Cambridge, 1843), p. 267.
[3] *De Ludis Honestis* (1550).
[4] See, for example, Kimchi's commentary on the passage.

as shadowing forth God's willingness to sacrifice his only
begotten Son; and St. Paul accordingly numbered Jephthah
among the righteous.[1] For Buchanan and Christopherson,
however, the story had an added attraction—its relevance to the
urgent contemporary problem facing hundreds of Catholic
priests who had joined the Reformation. The vows of chastity
and obedience they had made on entering the priesthood now
seemed as morally unjustifiable to them as Jephthah's had
appeared in his own eyes when he saw his daughter leading the
procession from the house. Yet, they asked, were they entitled
even on those grounds to renounce an oath so solemnly, if
misguidedly, undertaken? The dramatization of Jephthah's
dilemma gave ample opportunity for grandiloquent discussion
of the theme, an opportunity of which both Buchanan and
Christopherson took full advantage. The full title of Buchanan's
play was, in fact, *Jephthes sive Votum* and its acknowledged
concern with the theme of vows was prompted not only by the
general problem but, more specifically, by the contemporary
pamphlet war on the subject led by Bucer and the Catholic
Latomus.[2]

Buchanan, Scottish by birth and educated partly in France,
spent more than fifty years of his life ostensibly as a Catholic,
although repeatedly hounded and attacked for Lutheran leanings,
even being formally charged and tried at Lisbon by the Inquisition. He preserved his life by denying such charges, earning the
reputation of a turncoat both for his official denials and for his
ambiguous attitude to Queen Mary. In the course of his wanderings, he spent three years, from 1539 to 1542, at the College
of Guienne at Bordeaux, where he composed his *Jephthes* and
Baptistes intended for performance by his pupils, amongst whom
was numbered Montaigne.[3] In fact, his *Jephthes* reached a much
wider audience, running into its fourteenth edition by the mid-
seventeenth century. For all its contemporary popularity,
however, its lengthy Senecan-type speeches on the problem of

---

[1] *Epistle to the Hebrews*, xi, 32.
[2] J. M. Atkin, *The Trial of George Buchanan before the Lisbon Inquisition* (Edinburgh, 1939), p. 13.
[3] 'My selfe (without ostentation be it spoken) was reputed, if not as a chiefe master, yet a principall Actor in them', *Essays of Montaigne*, trans. J. Florio, ed. G. Saintsbury (London, 1892), p. 186.

fulfilment of vows make it dull reading today and it lacks any real dramatic power.

His *Baptistes*, which seems to have been performed at Trinity College, Cambridge in 1562/3, is a much livelier work, reflecting Buchanan's vacillation between Luther and Rome. Its primary purpose was to voice the author's disgust at Henry VIII's execution of Sir Thomas More when the latter refused to countenance England's break with the Pope. At Lisbon, Buchanan testified:

'. . . when I escaped thence, I recorded my opinion of the English in that tragedy which deals with John the Baptist, wherein, so far as the likeness of the material would permit, I represented the death and accusation of Thomas More and set before the eyes an image of the tyranny of the time.'[1]

It was, then, a drama taking as its hero a Catholic martyr who had refused to succumb to the political and theological pressures of English Protestantism. In this respect, his sympathy with Rome is patent. Yet in a much deeper sense the play betrayed those leanings towards Protestantism with which he was charged and which later prompted him to convert officially; for both in the play itself and in his remarks about it elsewhere, Buchanan insisted that he intended it as a protest against harsh authoritarianism rather than as a sectarian polemic – an attack upon 'the torments and miseries' of tyrants. It provided, in fact, a vivid instance of that postfiguration which, we have seen, became typical of the Protestant reading of the Bible. Thomas More in his condemnation of the royal divorce and remarriage is seen as a 'type' of John the Baptist refusing to recognize the illicit marriage of Herod and Herodias, and laying down his life in the light of his moral vision. For Buchanan, here was the biblical story being cyclically repeated in his own generation. It was not surprising that in 1642 the work was translated by the Puritans (possibly by Milton himself),[2] published by order of a rebellious House of Commons as *Tyrannical-Government Anatomized or a Discourse Concerning Evil-Councillors*, and presented to the King as a solemn warning. But of course, in this

[1] Quoted in J. M. Atkin, *The Trial of George Buchanan*, p. 22.
[2] Francis Peck was the first to attribute the translation to Milton in his edition of the work published in 1740.

instance the cyclical repetition did not hold true to the biblical pattern – this time it was Herod who lost his head.

John Christopherson, who produced the second of the two Jephthah plays, was like Buchanan a Christian humanist exiled to the Continent for part of his life because of his religious convictions; but there the resemblance ends. For he combined with his humanism a militant and uncompromising faith in Catholicism which, after the delivery of a fiery sermon at St. Paul's Cross, resulted in his imprisonment and death. His reputation for cruelty towards the Protestants in his see won him the hatred of many as a man who 'though carrying much of *Christ* in his *Surname*, did bear nothing of him in his *Nature*, no meekness, mildness or mercy, being addicted wholly to cruelty and destruction, burning no fewer than *ten* in one fire in Lewes, and *seventeen* others at several Times in sundry Places.'[1] Yet, paradoxically, a dominant theme of his play is the dislike of strife, and in it he succeeded almost completely in avoiding polemical issues which, he maintained elsewhere, should be excluded from the drama.

Despite its lesser fame at the time, Christopherson's play is far superior to Buchanan's in delicacy of character-delineation, structure of plot, and beauty of language.[2] The characters are left unnamed, but the play does not lose thereby in individualization. Jephthah is shown to have been merciless to women and children in battle and must lose his own female child as fate's ironic punishment; and with some poignancy, the daughter justifies her calm submission to her fate by insisting that she can never replace her father, whereas Jephthah can always beget another daughter. But the most marked difference from Buchanan's treatment is the Catholic concern with typology; for Christopherson saw in the Jephthah story a reflection of three other biblical themes. Jephthah's rejection by his brothers in the opening scene parallels the Joseph episode, his forgiveness is

[1] Thomas Fuller, *The History of the Worthies of England* (first printed 1662), ed., J. Nichols (London, 1811), ii, 386. Christopherson opposed polemical drama in his *Exhortation to all menne to take hede and beware of rebellion* (1554).

[2] It remained in manuscript until published with a translation by F. H. Forbes (Newark, 1928). Boas, pp. 49 f. and W. O. Sypherd, *Jephthah and his Daughter: a study in comparative literature* (Newark, Delaware, 1948), p. 20, offer detailed analyses of the play.

evocative of Jesus on the Cross, and the sacrifice of his daughter is made to mirror the binding of Isaac. Without pressing the point too far, it is clear, then, that Christopherson, as a staunch Catholic inimical to Protestantism, remained untouched by that postfiguration so noticeable among the Protestant dramatists of his era, preferring the typological reading to which he had a greater affinity. And the point holds true for the next play.

Watson's *Absalon* presents primarily a problem of identification of manuscript. That Thomas Watson, Catholic bishop of Lincoln under Mary, wrote a Latin drama on the theme of Absalom is beyond doubt. As graduate, fellow, and later dean of St. John's College, Cambridge, he became a close friend of Roger Ascham who recorded Watson's extraordinary fastidiousness in matters of metre:

'M. Watson had an other maner care of perfection, with a feare and reuerence of the iudgement of the best learned: who to this day would neuer suffer yet his *Absalon* to go abroad and that onelie bicause, in *locis paribus*, *Anapestus* is twise or thrise vsed in stede of Iambus: A smal faulte, and such one as perchance would neuer be marked, no neither in *Italie* nor *France*.'[1]

One might have imagined that Watson would take the trouble to find and correct his metrical errors, but in fact the manuscript was never allowed 'abroad'. However, the manuscript of a Latin verse play on the theme of Absalom preserved in the British Museum seems likely to be Watson's.[2]

Like Christopherson, Watson was a staunch Catholic who died in custody and like him he omitted polemic from his play. This omission is particularly remarkable as the subject-matter was so ideally suited to religious propaganda. The theme of the son rebelling against his divinely anointed father and hence doomed to fail could so readily have symbolized Henry VIII

---

[1] R. Ascham, *The Scholemaster*, in *English Works*, ed. W. Aldis Wright (Cambridge, 1904), p. 284.

[2] Boas, unfairly I think, rejects the attribution on stylistic grounds, although he does admit that Renaissance tastes differed from our own and that the numerous manuscript corrections suggest the rigorous self-criticism indicated by Ascham. For a more recent study of the problem, accepting the Watson identification, see, J. H. Smith, *Thomas Watson's 'Absalom'*, an unpublished thesis at the University of Illinois (1958).

(or Luther) rebelling against the Pope, the father of the established church. But in fact, apart from one dubious reference there are no hints of political parallels.[1] Again, then, the Catholic showed less inclination for postfiguration, although it should be recalled that the exploitation of biblical drama for religious disputation (which such postfiguring would have implied) was in any case drawing to a close. The majority of biblical plays written during Elizabeth's reign, as opposed to those earlier in the century, are free from religious polemic. Strangely enough, the religious controversy continued in the secular rather than the scriptural drama. Marlowe revelled in the anti-papist activities of Faustus in Rome, and Bishop Gardiner was frequently satirized on the stage as a malicious Catholic intriguer.[2] Mostly, of course, the dramatists concurred in attacking the Puritans, the common enemy of the stage. Middleton led the anti-Puritan attack, Marston's *Dutch Courtesan* had as its main character a sanctimonious and hypocritical Puritan, and the pseudo-Shakespearean *The Puritan* with Jonson's *Bartholomew Fair* continued the skirmishing. There was some justice in the Puritan charge that the dramatists were 'professed Papists'; Lodge converted to Catholicism and Ben Jonson was drawn to Rome during his imprisonment. But there were, of course, many Protestant dramatists too who had no hesitation in attacking or replying to the attacks of the Puritans.[3] At all events, in this play the family blood-feud, beginning with the incestuous rape of Tamar by her brother Amnon, and the resulting revenge motif culminating in fratricide provided a background for the opening of the play sufficiently ghoulish even for the pseudo-Senecan drama. The plot itself, involving attempted patricide, gory murders, hacked limbs, and Absalom dangling by his hair from the boughs of a tree gave the author every opportunity for weighty epigrams, sententious stichomythia, and blood-thirsty descriptions – an opportunity which he exploited to the full.

[1] David is, in one place, described as *pater sanctissimus*.
[2] Cf. Shakespeare's *Henry VIII*.
[3] See W. Creizenach, *English Drama in the Age of Shakespeare*, trans. C. Hugon (London, 1916), pp. 107 f. and E. M. Albright, *Dramatic Publications in England 1580–1640* (New York/London, 1927), pp. 99 f.

The Greek and Latin Plays

The most remarkable of this group of dramatists was undoubtedly Nicholas Grimald who at the age of twenty produced an impressive Latin play on the theme of the Resurrection. When, as a graduate of Christ's College, Cambridge, he transferred to Brasenose College, Oxford, he occupied himself until the arrival of his books by writing his first play, *Christus Redivivus*, published in 1543 at Cologne, probably through the good offices of his friend Bale, and serving eventually as the main source for the original Oberammergau Passion Play. The play itself is written with the vigour and confidence of a mature dramatist, the lines having a fine epic ring, but Grimald's artistry is especially visible in his stagecraft. Where so many previous and contemporary dramatists used the medieval prologue to inform the audience of the events leading up to the opening scene, he allows the play itself to unfold the background in the course of a more natural dialogue. Mary Magdalene is found weeping beside the tomb and, in the midst of her lament, she describes how Jerusalem gazed unpityingly on the Crucifixion. In contrast to the stylized scenes of Eternity to which we have become accustomed in the Gospel plays, the drama at once becomes rooted in time, largely because Grimald has approached the sacred theme obliquely. We have before us a woman of flesh and blood grieving for her Master who had died some hours before, and unaware that she is soon to witness the miracle of the Resurrection. The Crucifixion is more naturalistically conceived through the tearful recollection of a mourner grieving over the body than through the direct portrayal of the Passion upon the stage, and Grimald's play, despite its use of Latin rather than the vernacular, is a rare instance at this period of a non-stylized Gospel play moving close to humanization.

Bale, who is an unreliable bibliographer, records a Nativity play by Grimald and a *Protomartyr* (probably on the death of St. Sebastian) neither of which has survived. Grimald's other extant play, the *Archipropheta* (1546) has been termed the first full-length tragedy written by an Englishman, since it preceded *Ferrex and Porrex*, the first tragedy in the English tongue, by a few years. It is in its way no less remarkable than the *Christus Redivivus*, foreshadowing much that was to be central to Elizabethan drama without deserting or even subordinating the religious message. If Buchanan, Christopherson, and Watson surrendered the biblical ethos in exchange for classical style, Grimald never allows us to forget his religious purpose. In this drama set in the court of Herod, and derived mainly from Josephus, we find one of the earliest instances of the witty court Fool enlivening the drama by a distorted reflection of the main love theme, that passionate royal love which was to animate the secular Renaissance stage, and the play is interspersed with songs and lyrics to lend it a richness and regal splendour. But through this almost Renaissance court stalks John the Baptist, burning with prophetic zeal, denouncing illicit marriage, and demanding moral purity above all. For all the apparent secularization, the plot is tightly related to the central figure of John, who continues to speak in the idiom of the Bible itself. Grimald had proved in these two dramas that the use of a classical language need smother neither the ethical content nor the didactic message of a biblical play.

CHAPTER III

THE LATER RENAISSANCE

(i) Garter's 'Godlye Susanna'

The danger of surrendering to the spell of the classics was clearly less acute in those biblical dramas written in English than in the Greek and Latin plays which had consciously modelled themselves on Euripides and Seneca. The English plays soon achieved a compromise; after a passing and frequently lively flirtation with the classics, the dramatist returned like a chastened husband to his lawful spouse, the biblical ethos. That concern with theodicy, if it no longer formed part of the sectarian conflict between Protestant and Catholic, remained to the fore as the central message of the Renaissance scriptural plays; but the pagan dallying with the classics often provided the more memorable and attractive portions of the plays.

Thomas Garter's *The Commody of the moste vertuous and Godlye Susanna*,[1] probably written before 1568 and printed in London in 1578, was known only by name until its discovery at Coleorton Hall in Leicestershire as recently as 1936, when a reprint was issued by the Malone Society.[2] The apocryphal theme had been treated on the continent as part of the Christian Terence

[1] I have omitted the negligible *King Daryus* (1565?) reproduced in the Tudor Facsimile Texts. It is a dull and unpretentious interlude with heavily didactic morality scenes of anti-papist intent.

[2] The Stationers' Register has an entry for 1568/9 'Re of Thomas colwell for his lycense for pryntynge of ye playe of susanna iiid' (Register A, fol. 176a). Since Hugh Jackson, who eventually printed Garter's play, inherited his business from his father-in-law, Thomas Colwell, it is likely that the entry refers to Garter's *Susanna*.

movement and although Garter's play shows some indebtedness to these earlier treatments, it was essentially an original work, revealing a sensitivity to those changes in biblical drama which had occurred since the beginning of the century.[1] Moreover, it had moved a step forward. A recent article has claimed that Peele's *David and Bethsabe* was the first biblical play indebted to Ovidian influence, but there can be no doubt that Garter's *Susanna* not only looked to Ovid some twenty years earlier, but also drank more deeply from the source.[2]

Ovid's *Ars Amatoris* had, in fact, been published in England in both Latin and English as early as 1513, but interest flagged until the sixties when a crop of translations appeared almost simultaneously. The years 1560–80 saw the publication in English translation of his *Narcissus*, *Hermaphroditus* and *Salmacis*, the complete *Metamorphoses*, the *Heroides*, the *Ibis*, and the *Tristia*. If we are right in identifying Garter's *Susanna* with the play of that name registered by Colwell in 1568, then it was written at the height of this new interest in Ovid and only three years after Colwell himself printed the 1565 versions of the *Hermaphroditus* and *Salmacis*. But even if the conjecture is false and Garter wrote his play just prior to its publication in 1578, the literary climate was still vibrant with Ovidian interest, the *Tristia* appearing in 1580.

Such erotic Ovidian scenes as Actaeon gazing at the unwitting Diana as she bathes naked in the crystal spring may well have first drawn Garter to the story of Susanna (who was, of course, also surprised bathing when the two elders attempted to rape her). By naming the two elders Voluptas and Sensualitas, he neatly overcame the difficulty of depicting two old men in place of the handsome young man in the parallel incidents from Ovid. For if the Morality figures were ostensibly intended to offer a didactic warning against licentiousness, in fact their names served to underscore the erotic element within the play. Like the more popular Sunday journals of today, Garter was hiding

[1] For the play's indebtedness to those by Birck (1532) and Tibortio Sacco (1537), see M. T. Herrick, 'Susanna and the Elders in 16th Century Drama', in *Studies in Honor of T. W. Baldwin*, ed. D. C. Allen (Urbana, 1958).

[2] I-S. Ekeblad, 'The Love of King David and Fair Bethsabe', *ES xxxix* (1958), 57, discussed below in connection with Peele.

his fascination with the prurient subject behind a sanctimonious moral indignation, but his Ovidian delight in the theme is nonetheless apparent.[1] In the opening of the play, Ill Reporte quotes (or rather misquotes) the relevant advice from Vergil:

Omnia vincit Amor: et nos cedamus Amori

followed almost immediately by the Ovidian line:

Res est solliciti plena timoris amor.[2]

The very association of the elders' lust with the classical *Amor* lends it a certain attractiveness and reveals that Garter has his classical sources in mind. The sensuality within this apparently biblical play soon grows from mere hints to open eroticism when Voluptas lovingly recounts Susanna's physical attractions:

Her brestes that are so round and fayre, her armes that are so long,
Her fyngers straight with vaynes beset, of blew and white among.
Her middle small, her body long, her buttockes broade and round,
Her legges so straight, her foote so small, the like treades not on
ground.[3]

There is, of course, a world of difference between this lecherous description of a married woman by an old man, and the frank, yet delicate imagery of the *Song of Songs*:

How beautiful are thy feet with shoes, O prince's daughter!
the joints of thy thighs are like jewels the work of the hands of a
cunning workman.
Thy navel is like a round goblet, which wanteth not liquor: thy
belly is like an heap of wheat set about with lilies.
Thy breasts are like two young roes that are twins.

---

[1] Here again pictorial art offers a close parallel. Sixteenth-century Neoplatonism, which interpreted Ovidian themes in terms of their Christian allegorical significance, encouraged paintings of the Rape of Europa symbolizing, a trifle incongruously, the redemption of the Christian Soul. But an undercurrent of pagan eroticism remained within this Christianized Ovid – as in Bronzino's *Venus, Cupid, Folly and Time* (1540), which excited erotic interest in its pearly nudes while allegorically condemning licentiousness.

[2] *Bucolica x*, 69 and *Heroides i*, 12 both slightly misquoted. The changes are of no significance.

[3] Malone Society Reprint, 415 f.

The Ovidian element in Garter's play is underscored both by quotation and allusion. At the moment the elders conceal themselves in the orchard to await Susanna's coming, Sensualitas sighs:

Heu mihi quod nullis amor est medicabilis herbis![1]

Whether or not Garter's audience would recognize the specific source, it is clear that Garter himself realized the similarity in situation between the Ovidian scene in which this line appears and that for which he used it. In the *Metamorphoses*, Daphne utters this lament as Phoebus Apollo is bearing down upon her in hot pursuit through the woods, and the subsequent lines describe how her naked limbs are uncovered by the winds:

nudabant corpora venti
Obviaque adversas vibrabant flamina vestes.[2]

Similarly, there are frequent references to Venus and her son as the symbols of classical love. Voluptas prays to her, with sly admission of his previous escapades:

Oh Venus that hath suffred me, to quench my youthfull fyre
With love of those from tyme to tyme, that I did most desyre[3]

and he complains of 'that blynde boy' who has smitten him with love, so that 'Cupids flame doe burne my harte'. In fact, then, Garter's debt to Ovid and his perception of the parallels between the erotic Ovidian scenes and those of his biblical subject-matter are far more clearly marked and, in a sense, acknowledged, than Peele's.

Nevertheless, the play retains a firm awareness of biblical morality and at the climax, when the elders reveal themselves to her in the garden – a climax which in Ovid would have been the *raison d'être* of the tale – the play suddenly drops all prurience, and becomes even more modest than the biblical account by leaving Susanna fully clothed throughout. The pagan flirtation was over and Garter had decided that it was time to drive home the moral lesson. Despite all the Ovidian elements recounted here, the play, therefore, as a whole remains strictly

---

[1] *Metamorphoses i*, 523 again with insignificant changes, such as *Ei mihi* . . .
[2] *Ibid.* 525–6.
[3] Malone Society Reprint, 390.

moral, for the sensual speeches are, of course, restricted to the villains of the piece. Susanna as the central character is a model of moral steadfastness, so that the didactic quality of the work is never obscured.

In this play, Garter succeeds in bringing Susanna wonderfully alive and his success is of particular significance in this study. As we have noted frequently, the sanctity of the central characters in biblical plays served to artificialize their dramatization, but in this play Susanna and her husband tease each other with the tender repartee of an affectionate married couple. Joachim, calling her a shrew for gently chiding him, teases her by pretended terror and she responds in kind. The reason for this greater ease in the treatment of the main characters lies in the change from scriptural theme to apocryphal. The books of the Apocrypha were still holy, to be treated with deference and respect, but their holiness was many degrees below that of the canonical books, and hence the dramatist felt a greater freedom in handling his material. Susanna is no idealized figure. While her husband Joachim never doubts her integrity, Susanna's parents reveal the wisdom of age in recognizing that no human is above temptation. The father, Helchia, hushes his wife's impulsive declaration of Susanna's innocence with the words:

Peace wyfe, attempt not God, thou knowest all flesh is frayle.

to which she reluctantly agrees. The haloes have been removed, and the audience can see the biblical characters as human beings rather than as demi-gods. This change forms part of the new identification with biblical characters which Protestantism and, particularly, the translation of the Bible into the vernacular had produced. Moreover, it is a humanization exploiting that fallibility of character symptomatic of Old Testament narrative.

The dénouement of the scriptural story in which Daniel (whose name means 'the judge of the Lord') exposes the false testimony of the elders and rescues the innocent prisoner, was ideally suited to the theme of divine justice which, we have noted, attracted dramatists so powerfully in this period. Ill Reporte is unceremoniously hanged, Satan discomfited, and the noble characters in turn declare their gratitude to God and their faith in his righteousness. Apparent, too, is that mixture of comedy and gravity which had now become typical of biblical

drama. The flippant exchanges between Satan and his disrespect-
ful offspring retain their humour today, transforming the play
into a tragicomedy. As the prologue of the play aptly puts it:

And though perchaunc some wanton worde, doe passe which may
*   not seeme*
Or gestures light not meete for this, your wisedomes may it deeme,
Accoumpt that nought delightes the hart of men on earth,
So much as matters graue and sad, if they be mixt with myrth.

The dramatization of biblical stories demanded a greater
appreciation of the human elements involved than did a non-
dramatic version. The playwright was forced to think himself
into the part, to see it from within and hence to present the
events more vividly upon the stage; and it is illuminating to
compare Garter's play with Greene's *A Princelie Mirrour of
Peereles Modestie* published in 1584. In this prose version,
Greene aims merely '. . . to pen out this storie of Susanna more
largelie than it is written in the Apopcripha [*sic*].' It becomes
a charming tale in elegant prose, driving home the moral lesson;
but the villains are incorrigible rascals, Susanna an impossibly
noble and virtuous young woman, and the sin of the elders is,
from the first, described as 'lascivious concupiscence' which had
overcome men 'droonken sodenlie with the dregs of filthie
desire.'[1] Its effect is that of a religious tract advocating the
paths of righteousness rather than an attempt to come to grips
with the human weaknesses and temptations which beset man
in every age. Until the later novel gave prose-writers a vehicle
for subtle delineation of character, drama was alone in allowing
both the writer and his audience to conceive of the scriptural
figures as beings of flesh and blood.

A play which lies, in a sense, outside the stream of English
drama nevertheless deserves mention here, if only to enquire
why it affected the development of drama so little. Theodore de
Bèze published his *Abraham Sacrifiant* in Geneva in 1550, but
it was not until 1577 that it was translated and published in
England. As a work by Calvin's assistant and later successor at
Geneva, it was read eagerly by Protestants on the Continent and
achieved enormous popularity, running into twenty-three

[1] *Complete Works*, ed. A. B. Grosart for the Huth Library (n.p.
1881–3), iii, 12.

editions before the end of the seventeenth century. It became, in addition, the leading model for the flood of continental scriptural dramas during the next fifty years.[1] In England, however, Arthur Golding's excellent English version produced little reaction and, in fact, was never republished until 1906. Indeed, Golding may well have been prompted to translate the work in much the same way as Bèze had begun it, in order to compensate for his own secular and somewhat pagan writings. Bèze informs us that he wrote the play as a penance for his *Juvenilia*, published shortly before his conversion, while Golding, a fervent Protestant, had been known primarily for his elegant translations of Ovid, for which he had offered the usual excuse that Ovid's poems concealed moral lessons.

> *As for example in the tales of Daphne turn'd to Bay*
> *A mirror of virginity appear unto us may.*

Similarly, after an elaborate parallel between the accounts of creation given in *Genesis* and in Ovid, he justified his translation of the fables on the same grounds as the Sunday tabloids referred to above.

> *For sure these fables are not put in writing to th'intent*
> *To further or allure to vice: but rather this is meant,*
> *That men beholding what they be when vice doth reign instead*
> *Of virtue, should not let their lewd affections have the head.*[2]

The play itself, translated with great care and considerable elegance, is, as is to be expected, strongly Calvinist in tone, and illustrates numerous features of biblical drama which typified the versions in the mid-sixteenth-century. Most clearly of all, one notes the postfigurative element. Bèze felt a special bond with Abraham since, like him, Bèze had been forced to leave his land and settle in a foreign country. The parallel between the opening words of the preface: 'It is now a two yeares, since God graunted me the grace to forsake the countrie where he is persecuted, to serue him according to his holy will' and the opening words of the play:

[1] Craig, *English Religious Drama*, p. 364.
[2] *A Tragedie of Abrahams Sacrifice*, ed. M. W. Wallace, University of Toronto Library (Toronto, 1906), p. xxx.

Abraham: *Alas my God, and was there euer any,*
                That hath endured of combrances so many
                As I haue done by fleeting too and fro,
                Since I my natiue countrie did forgo?

leaves little to conjecture. Abraham is a stern Calvinist figure, softened by affection for his son who is, in this play, a very young child and by no means the Christ figure of medieval Catholic typology. The drama takes on a patently anti-papist tone with the introduction of the figure of Satan dressed, as in Bale's *Three Lawes*, in a monk's cowl, and Bèze cannot resist the comment:

> *O cowle, o cowle, such mischef thou shalt wurk,*
> *And such abuse shall underneath thee lurke*
> *At high noon daies.*

But the figure of Satan is used to excellent effect. In the moments when Abraham is struggling with his inner self, Satan stands beside him, urging him to take the path of evil. The device serves to present Abraham as a human being torn between faith and impiety, and it points forward to the similar usage in Marlowe's *Dr. Faustus*. God does not appear throughout the play, in accordance with the new views prevalent in Geneva that the presentation of the Deity upon the stage was liable to be blasphemous. His place is taken therefore, by an angel. In this connection, and as a hint of the future battles between the Puritans and the stage, we may note Bèze's comment in the Prologue:

> *Would God we might each weeke through all the yeare*
> *See such resort in Churches as is here.*

This comment gives us the likeliest explanation of the limited appeal which this play had for English audiences; for it reached England too late to be original. In 1550, it had been an exciting extension of the mystery plays, marking an important advance from the puppet-like and haloed figures to which audiences had become accustomed. But next to Garter's *Susanna*, with the latter's sophisticated classical allusions, its humanization of character, its boisterous good humour, and its comparative freedom from religious restraint, there was little that Bèze's play could offer. The Church and the stage were drifting far apart and, whatever biblical themes might be exploited to justify drama, the stage was no longer a rival to the pulpit for the dissemination of Christian doctrine.

Since, like Bèze, the contemporary Protestant saw himself as the hero of Old Testament narrative, nobly suffering for the cause of righteousness and divine service, the absence of Job from the themes popular amongst them is particularly noticeable. In a form more readily adaptable to the stage than any other biblical story, *Job* relates the spiritual struggles of a profoundly religious man desperately searching for justification of the apparent travesties of justice in this temporal world, and hearing from God's own lips at last the message that man's faith alone can lead him to an unquestioning acceptance of a supreme justice beyond his limited comprehension. It seems ideally suited to the hand of the Protestant dramatist, yet it was almost totally ignored. Two reasons may be offered for its unpopularity as a dramatic theme. On the one hand, despite the fallibility of Job's character expressed in his religious doubts, medieval commentators had vigorously denied his sinfulness and presented him as a 'perfect' hero. Origen, St. Jerome, and Gregory the Great portrayed him as God's champion successfully overcoming the temptations offered by his wife and comforters. As an infallible character foreshadowing Christ, he was too closely akin to a Christ figure to be a popular dramatic theme.[1] On the other hand, the dramatists of the later sixteenth century who might have viewed him stripped of his medieval robes were probably disturbed by the apparent blasphemy of his challenge to God and were consequently chary of risking a charge of blasphemy from others.

It is, therefore, particularly unfortunate that the only two full-length plays on this subject to survive from this period both perished at the hand of Warburton's thoughtless servant,

---

[1] See, for example, Jerome, *Opera*, ed. J. Martanay (Paris, 1705), v, 677 and Gregory the Great, *Moralia in Job*, translated in A Library of the Fathers (Oxford, 1844), xviii, pp. 20–21, 77–78. The book of Job is discussed below in further detail in connection with Milton and MacLeish.

Betsy.[1] Like Radcliffe's *Job*, Robert Greene's play entitled *The History of Jobe* disappeared in the flames. Registered in 1594 but probably staged some years before, it may have been the same as was witnessed about 1610 by the Dutch theologian Voetius in Leyden, acted by an English company and cited by him as proof that scriptural subjects cannot be presented on the stage without profanation of the divine name.[2] But it is destroyed and we can merely lament its loss.

Its existence, however, does confirm the impression that Greene found biblical subjects attractive. His autobiographical *Groatsworth of Wit bought with a Million of Repentance*, despite its obvious exaggeration, suggests nevertheless that his biblical interests may, once again, have been a form of penance for sin (although sin somewhat more serious than that of Bèze or Golding). His *Princelie Mirrour of Peereles Modestie* had merely suggested the modesty of Susanna as a model for young ladies tempted to vice, but his work of collaboration with Thomas Lodge, *A Looking Glasse for London and England* had the more specific purpose of presenting the vices and corruptions of London as reflections of the ungodly city of Nineveh.

The idea it contained was not new – indeed it was the logical outcome of the rediscovery of Old Testament narrative, prompted, as we have seen, both by the Reformation demand for an open and translated Bible, and by the Calvinist emphasis upon covenant and hence identification with the Old Testament patriarchs. The title itself suggests that where the medieval church had seen the New Testament mirrored in the Old, the Protestant found the world around him a mirror or looking-glass of the biblical world. Latimer had declared in his sermons: 'And when should Jonas have preached against Ninive if he should have forborne for the respects of the times, or the place, or the state of things here? For what was Ninive? A noble rich and wealthy city. What is London to Ninive? Like a village, as Islington or such another, in comparison to London.' More

---

[1] Frederick Thornhill lists the destroyed manuscripts in the *Gentleman's Magazine* (Sept., 1815), pp. 217–22 and W. W. Greg in 'The Bakings of Betsy', in *The Library*, 3rd series, ii, 225–59.

[2] He refers to a *Comoedia Jobi* in his *Selectae disputationes*, iv (Amsterdam, 1667), p. 361. Cf. W. Creizenach, *English Drama in the Age of Shakespeare*, p. 161 n.

recently, in 1570, J. Brentius' *Newes from Ninive to Englande brought by the prophete Jonas* had been published in translation with its admonition:

> *Repent England in time,*
> *As Nineve that Citie did*
> *For that thy sinners before the Lorde,*
> *Are not in secret hid.*[1]

Lyly maintained that God had a care 'of England as of a new Israel, his chosen and peculier people' adding that 'the living God is only the English God,' and almost exactly contemporary with the play by Greene and Lodge was Nashe's pamphlet *Christ's Teares over Jerusalem* (1593) which had as its theme 'Now to London must I turn. Whatsoever of Jerusalem I haue written, was but to lende her a Looking Glasse.' These comparisons continued well into the next century. Jonson's *Bartholomew Fair* (1614) made the pointed comparison, 'Jerusalem was a stately thing, and so was Nineveh, and the city of Norwich, and Sodom and Gomorrah,' and in 1648 Paul Knell delivered a sermon entitled *Israel and England Paralelled in a Sermon*, in which, discoursing on the punishment suffered by the Jews whenever they rebelled against God's word, he warned his audience to avoid similar rebellion against their own divinely appointed king. The theme of *A Looking Glasse for London* contained, therefore, little that was new in conception, but it had not been presented in dramatic form.

The new trend in biblical drama, illustrated by Garter's *Susanna*, to exploit the biblical text and the moral lessons involved for sensational purposes is again apparent in the *Looking Glasse*. With sanctimonious moral admonitions, the prophet Osea, introduced as a chorus to comment on the activities of his colleague Jonah, warns the audience:

> *London, looke on, this matter nips thee neere;*
> *Leave off thy ryot, pride and sumptuous cheere:*

[1] L. B. Campbell, *Divine Poetry and Drama*, p. 249 n., suggests a connection between this work and the play by Greene and Lodge. The translator was T. Tymme.

Spend lesse at boord, and spare not at the doore,
But aide the infant and releeue the poore.[1]

The scenes of *ryot*, however, attracted the authors, and no
doubt the audience, more than the solemn advice. Incestuous
love blasted by a thunderbolt from heaven, an attempt to steal
a friend's wife resulting in the poisoning of her husband, these
were the elements which won the play its great popularity.[2]
Again we note the fusion of comedy and gravity in the clowning
of the ruffians, a fake 'devil' ignominiously exposed, and a
cheerful rascal who would rather be hanged than undergo the
five-day fast prescribed by the prophet.

But once again it would be false to imagine that the indulgence
in ribaldry and scenes of vice obscured the moral lesson of this
biblical play. In parts, it remains closer to the original text than
any contemporary play we have yet examined. Jonah's prayer
from the belly of the fish, transferred for dramatic convenience
into a song of thanksgiving after his reaching dry land, is a close
poetic paraphrase of the original:

> *Out of the belly of the deepest hell*
> *I cride, and thou didst heare my voice, O God!*
> *Tis thou hadst cast me downe into the deepe:*
> *The seas and flouds did compasse me about;*
> *I thought I had bene cast from out thy sight;*

[1] *The Plays and Poems of Robert Greene*, ed. J. C. Collins (Oxford,
1905), i, 153. No agreement has been reached concerning the sections
to be attributed to each of the joint authors, although R. A. Law's,
'*A Looking Glasse* and the Scriptures' in the University of Texas
Studies in English No. 3926 (July, 1939), maintains that since Greene
rarely quoted verbatim from the Scriptures, the biblical passages
which remain so close to the original text should be attributed to
Lodge. As the latter was busy with his translation of Josephus at about
this time (it was registered in 1591 and printed in folio in 1602), he
was probably more concerned with original texts than Greene, which
would support Law's hypothesis. Miss Campbell notes that the anti-
Romish conclusion to the play dates its composition before Lodge's
conversion to Catholicism, but since this itself can only be dated
roughly to his university period, the suggestion is not particularly
helpful. See L. B. Campbell, *Divine Poetry*, p. 247.

[2] Copies of five different editions before 1617 have survived, and
there are numerous references to performances. On this see Greg's
introduction to the Malone Society Reprint.

Garter's Godlye Susanna

The weeds were wrapt about my wretched head;
I went into the bottome of the hilles:
But thou, O Lord my God, hast brought me vp.[1]

Indeed, so close is this to the original text that it has been possible to establish with some degree of certainty that the Bishops' Bible was the version used by the author—a point which it is impossible to establish in almost all other plays of the period. Where a plot has been loosely dramatized and the theme reworded for the stage without close adherence to the biblical text, the comparatively minor differences between the various sixteenth-century versions of the Bible have no counterpart in the play, so that even the most painstaking comparison offers either an unsubstantiated conjecture or a frank admission of defeat.[2]

The combination in this play of close adherence to the original text on the one hand, and the introduction of extraneous material for sensational exploitation on the other is typical of the new school of biblical drama, and suggests that the dramatists were suffering some pangs of conscience. We are, it should be noted, no longer dealing with religious teachers using the stage for purpose of instruction nor, for that matter, with authors devoting their entire work to biblical subjects, but with Elizabethan dramatists in the hurly-burly of theatrical life. Nashe, Greene, Lodge, and Peele were men of stature in the field of secular drama who turned aside from such work to write religious tracts or scriptural plays, and we may suspect that their religious work constituted an attempt to justify either the stage as a whole or themselves as individuals. The Puritan controversy with the stage we shall soon examine more closely, but for the moment it may be sufficient to note that in his reply to Gosson's *Schoole of Abuse* Lodge admitted that the theatre was inclined to immorality and that dramatists frequently abused their art; but he felt that better than the abolition of all drama would be the reform of its vices so that, by presenting scenes of virtue, it could be a source of good rather than evil:

'I must confess . . . that it were good to bring those things on

---

[1] *ed. cit.*, p. 187.
[2] Cf. the inconclusive studies of Peele's *David and Bethsabe,* by Sampley, Blistein and others referred to below.

stage, that were altogether tending to vertue: all this I admit, and hartely wysh, but you say unless the things be taken away the vice will continue: Nay, I say, if the style were changed the practise would profit.'[1]

It is, perhaps, in that light that we must view these biblical plays. Lodge published the above plea in 1579/80, a few years before he collaborated with Greene on *The Looking Glasse*. The period of collaboration itself coincided with Greene's repentance and his determination that instead of being thought 'a patron of loue and a second Ovid' he 'may with the Ninivites shew in sackcloth [his] hearty repentance' by devoting his pen to religious or moral subjects.[2] The secularization of the stage and, more important, the attacks made upon it by such pamphleteers as Northbrooke, Gosson, and Stubbes had created an awareness among the dramatists of a contradiction between their professional work and their Christian obligations, and by combining the two in a biblical play they felt instinctively that the sacred theme excused or perhaps even justified their profession. But more of that later.

(ii) PEELE'S 'DAVID AND BETHSABE'

Peele's biblical play, *David and Bethsabe*, was registered in 1594 and published in 1599 with the note on the title-page 'As it hath been diuers times plaied on the stage'. There is, however, no evidence of its having been performed earlier, though the fact that fourteen copies of the original quarto edition survive indicates its popularity. Henslowe has the teasingly brief entry in October, 1602: 'pd for poleyes & worckmanshipp for to hange absolome . . . xiiijd.' which may refer to Peele's play, since some scaffolding is required by Peele in order to present Absalom dangling by his hair from the tree. This need for scaffolding, which, irrespective of Henslowe's entry, we know was required by the text,[3] suggests the non-Senecan character of the play, for

[1] Thomas Lodge, *A Defence of Poetry, Music, and Stage-Plays* (*1579/80*), ed. D. Laing for the Shakespeare Society (London, 1853), p. 27.

[2] *ed. cit.*, i, 137.

[3] Scene xv contains a lengthy dialogue between Ioab and the dangling Absalom.

the murder took place in full view of the audience and not offstage. In fact, there is little Senecan influence to be felt throughout the drama, and those scenes of murder, incest, and rape which
had provided Watson with this Senecan horror are here treated
with an epic sadness.

Critics have displayed a remarkable diversity in their critical
evaluation of this play, their comments ranging from contempt
to lavish praise. Bullen remarked casually that he '... did not
care two straws for it', adding that the play '... is exasperatingly
insipid – a mess of cloying sugar-plums.' Dyce and Ward regard
it beyond question as Peele's masterpiece; Creizenach sees it as
'... a crapulous morality dating from the last years of the dissolute poet's life', and Horne describes it as Peele's 'highest
dramatic achievement.'[1] Perhaps the most significant clue to
this discrepancy is that, almost invariably, the same couplet is
quoted from the play, either as a grudging admission of its
redeeming features or as proof of its magnificence:

> *Now comes my louer tripping like the Roe*
> *And brings my longings tangled in her haire.*

Miss Ekeblad has noted that the opening scene of the play, with
its beauty of imagery revealing a mingling of the *Song of Songs*
and Elizabethan blank-verse, is biblical only in its setting and
imagery. It is inspired by the classical and, more specifically, the
Ovidian attitude to love – passionate, erotic, and sensual.[2] We
may go further and note that David is unrecognizable as the
deeply religious Psalmist, succumbing despite his religious

[1] A. H. Bullen, *The Works of George Peele* (London, 1888), i, xli;
A. Dyce, *Works* (London, 1829–39), i, xxxviii and A. W. Ward,
A History of English Dramatic Literature (London, 1899), i, 376;
W. Creizenach, *English Drama in the Age of Shakespeare* (London,
1916), p. 161; and David H. Horne, *Life and Minor Works* (New
Haven, 1952), p. 93. One should note here Fleay's unlikely theory
that this play contains a political parody in which Elizabeth is represented by Bethsabe, Leicester by David, and Mary Queen of Scots by
Uriah. Apart from necessitating a pre-dating of its composition to
1588, the parallels suggested are substantiated neither by characterization nor allusion.

[2] I-S. Ekeblad, '*The Love of King David and Fair Bethsabe:* A Note
on George Peel's Biblical Drama', in *ES xxxix* (1958), 57. Under her
married name, Mrs. Ewbank has recently published an interesting
account of continental parallels to this play in *Renaissance Drama viii*
(1965), 3.

scruples, to the temptations of illicit love. With the ardour of the Elizabethan courtier he sweeps aside Cusai's gentle admonition that Bethsabe is a married woman, continuing in the same vein of luxuriant imagery:

> *Bright Bethsabe shall wash in Davids bower*
> *In water mix'd with purest Almond flower,*
> *And bath her beautie in the milke of kids,*
> *Bright Bethsabe giues earth to my desires,*
> *Verdure to earth, and to that verdure flowers,*
> *To flowers, sweet Odors, and to Odors wings,*
> *That carrie pleasures to the hearts of Kings.*

But critics have overlooked the brevity of this opening Ovidian scene. After less than two hundred lines the love is consummated, and the passion, eroticism, and pagan classicism evaporate in the more sinister atmosphere of warfare, rebellion, revenge, and divine retribution. The play, in fact, falls into two very unequal parts, of which the opening forms a brief, dazzling scene of ardent passion preceding a lengthy chronicle play of a more sombre nature. Many have noted the lack of structural unity which mars the play—the unwieldy fusion of the Bethsabe, Amnon, Solomon, and Absalom themes. For although united in the sense that the last three arise out of the first whether as punishment or consolation, dramatically they lack cohesion. However, in the light of that new Ovidian interest examined in connection with Garter's play, we can see that Peele was initially attracted to the biblical theme by its parallel to such Ovidian scenes as Actaeon watching Diana bathing naked in the crystal stream:

'And it came to pass in an eveningtide, that David arose from off his bed, and walked upon the roof of the king's house: and from the roof he saw a woman washing herself; and the woman was very beautiful to look upon' (2 Sam. xi. 2).

The title of the play, *The Love of King David and Fair Bethsabe,* misled many critics into assuming that the play's real theme was love, when in fact it served merely as the springboard for a dark tragedy of bloodshed and incest. Peele, it would seem, had discovered the modern paperback technique of attracting readers by a provocative title only tenuously related to the content of the book itself, and the critics' frequent quotation of the same couplet from the opening of the play when there are just as fine lines further on suggests that the device proved only too successful in misleading them. What is really a fine biblical tragedy has thus often been judged as a drama of Renaissance love, and been found wanting.

The title itself contains no hint of the sin so prominent in the biblical account. The epithet in 'Fair Bethsabe' evokes sympathy rather than condemnation, and the subtitle *With the Tragedie of Absalon* suggests little correlation between the two sections. A glance at a contemporary poem on the same theme reveals that the dichotomy was Peele's. Francis Sabie's epyllion *David and Beersheba* (1596) is certainly as indebted to Ovid as Peele's play, yet it at no time loses sight of the moral implications. The seduction itself is described in erotic Ovidian terms:

> *Then nimbly castes she off her Damaske frocke,*
> *Her Satten stole most curiously made:*
> *Her Partlet needle-wrought, her Cambricke smocke,*
> *And on a seat thereby them nicely laid,*
> *And so to wash her in the well assay'd.*
>   *O shut thine eies* Narcissus *come not neare,*
>   *Lest in the well a burning fire appeare.*

Yet the moment David succumbs to temptation, the poet cries:

> *What hast thou done, O Psalmist, blush for shame!*

In contrast, Peele's opening scene makes no direct reference to the retribution which is to follow: but once the love-scene has run its course, the play reverts to the biblical account in depicting the death of David's new-born son as the punishment for his adultery and murder. Absalom's revolt, however, is not overtly depicted as part of the same punishment, but rather in the Greek tradition of personal *hybris* and *nemesis*. His death, as he hangs with his hair entangled in the boughs of a tree is treated with striking symbolism, the hair by which he is trapped representing his vanity. Absalom regards his beauty, of which his hair is the crowning glory, as a mark of divine favour and a sure omen of his eventual accession to the throne. God's

> *. . . thunder is intangled in my haire,*
> *And with my beautie is his lightning quencht,*
> *I am the man he made to glorie in.*

The hair-symbolism is reiterated throughout the work, and the final taunt from Joab just before he stabs him to death serves as a choric commentary:

> *Now Absalon how doth the Lord regard*
> *The beautie wherevpon thy hope was built,*
> *And which thou thoughtst his grace did glorie in?*

The symbolic interpretation, although not appearing in the biblical source,[1] serves to underscore the theme of divine retribution – that concern with theodicy inherited from the earlier Protestant dramatists. For if the two sections of the play are apparently disconnected, is there not a subtle, allusive unity suggested by that very couplet so frequently quoted by critics as a mere random sampling – a grim hint of Absalom's end which will form the final punishment for David's illicit love:

> *Now comes my louer tripping like the Roe*
> *And brings my longings tangled in her haire.*

The unifying force of this hair-symbolism, once it is perceived, lends to the work not merely a dramatic wholeness, but an ethical force echoing that of the Bible itself, an overarching sequence of temptation, sin, and retribution.

The influences discernible in the play are so varied that they deserve some special attention. The plot is, of course, taken directly from the Bible and remains extraordinarily close to it. Nathan's speech is simply a versification of the original prose passage, and the events themselves follow the scriptural text faithfully. The opening section, we have seen, owes much to Ovid and to the classical conception of love. There are, in addition, small but significant signs of an indebtedness to Seneca both in the choice of plot (which was discussed above in connection with the manuscript attributed to Watson) and in scattered instances of particularly gruesome speeches. Cunliffe notes such strains in Joab's speech over Absalom's corpse, with its 'stinking

[1] The Bible does record that when he polled his hair at the end of each year it weighed two hundred shekels, but no direct connection is suggested between his vanity and his fall. The Jewish commentator Kimchi remarks on the passage that 'he prided himself on his hair and therefore was caught by his head', but it is doubtful whether Peele had any access to the comment since Buxtorf's *Rabbinic Bible* was not published until 1618.

bones' and 'preyes of Carrion'.[1] But these Senecan influences are small, and after the Bible itself, the main source is to be traced to Du Bartas. This indebtedness has been examined in such detail by Cheffaud and Sykes that we need only note it here, particularly since the influence is related primarily to language and imagery.[2]

Despite the close paraphrase of the biblical text in parts of the play, it has been impossible to establish the version of the Bible which Peele used in writing it. The story of the painstaking research into this is indicative of the difficulties which beset the investigator. Bruno Neitzel concluded in 1904 that no proof existed either within the text or without to make any valid judgement,[3] but in 1928, A. M. Sampley published an article in which he maintained that it was 'in the highest degree probable' that Peele used the Bishops' Bible.[4] Since he explained away problems by suggesting that Peele used a Latin Vulgate in addition, his views cannot be accepted as in any way conclusive; and, in fact, the most recent re-examination of the problem by Elmer Blistein in 1953, which again collates the text with six versions of the Bible, confirms this impression. The most Blistein can say is that the Bishops' Bible 'might have been' the source.[5]

We are left with the problem of determining Peele's motive in writing a biblical play. Certainly the subject-matter was attractive for its Ovidian and Senecan possibilities; but while this might explain the choice of this theme as opposed to others in the Bible, it does not suggest why he turned to the Bible at all. On the basis of Peele's association with Greene and of Francis Meres' assertion that he died of syphilis ('the pox'), Peele has usually been imagined as a dissolute and unredeemed scapegrace, scarcely the man to write a biblical play. But as

[1] J. W. Cunliffe, *The Influence of Seneca on Elizabethan Tragedy* (London, 1893), p. 62.

[2] P. H. Cheffaud in his *George Peele* (Paris, 1913), and H. Dugdale Sykes in *N & Q* cxlvii (1924), 349–51 and 368–9 apparently reached their conclusions independently.

[3] Bruno Neitzel, *George Peele's 'David and Bethsabe'* (Halle, 1904).

[4] A. M. Sampley, 'The Version of the Bible Used by Peele in the Composition of *David and Bethsabe*', University of Texas Studies in English viii (1928), p. 79. See also *PMLA li* (1936), 698.

[5] E. M. Blistein, *George Peele's 'David and Bethsabe'*, an unpublished Ph.D. thesis in Brown University Library (1953), p. 82.

David Horne has recently pointed out, the evidence of his profligacy is flimsy, to say the least.[1] His death from syphilis may have been the result of a wild youth later regretted (or even perhaps of a single indulgence) and is no sure indication of an 'unredeemed' life of dissipation; while his association with Greene has a double implication. On the one hand Peele may have been simply a dissolute companion, but he may also have been, as a close personal friend, influenced by Greene's own moral reformation. Indeed, this last piece of evidence suggests that Peele, as an acquaintance of Greene and Lodge, knew of their concern with religious matters and with the improvement of the moral standards of the stage; and he may well have offered his own biblical drama either for reasons of conscience or simply to mollify those who accused the dramatists of corrupting the people. The evidence is too slight for any firm assertion but we should at least be aware of this neglected possibility that his motives were religious. At all events, whatever its deficiencies and however indebted to classical sources, his play succeeded in treating the biblical story without offending religious susceptibilities and showed that a very creditable dramatic work, rivalling much that was to be seen on the contemporary stage, could be built on the foundation of a scriptural story. Its speeches rarely become turgid, and the reader is rewarded not infrequently by splendid passages, at times reminiscent of Shakespeare's *Richard II*.

> *Sin with his sevenfold crowne and purple robe,*
> *Begins his triumphs in my guiltie throne,*
> *There sits he watching with his hundred eyes,*
> *Our idle minuts, and our wanton thoughts,*
> *And with his baits made of our fraile desires,*
> *Giues vs the hooke that hales our soules to hell.*[2]

It is significant that the parallel passage in *Richard II* speaks not of sin but of death:

> *. . . for within the hollow crown*
> *That rounds the mortal temples of a king*

[1] D. H. Horne, *Life and Minor Works of George Peele* (New Haven, 1952).
[2] Malone Society Reprint, ed. W. W. Greg (Oxford, 1912), 402–7.

Peele's David and Bethsabe

Keeps Death his court and there the antic sits,
Scoffing his state and grinning at his pomp.

The biblical *sin*, with all its medieval connotations of the devil dragging the unrighteous down to hell, has here been replaced by its Renaissance counterpart, Death the Equalizer. Despite his Ovidian affinity, Peele is concerned primarily with the moral problem of sin and divine wrath, while in the secular writings of the contemporary stage the prime interest has become the temporal world and man's efforts to achieve splendour and dignity before death reduces him to dust.

The extent of the changes in biblical drama during the sixteenth century is apparent if we pause to compare Bale's *God's Promises* with Peele's *David and Bethsabe*. Bale's *Pater Coelestis* has disappeared from the list of characters not merely because God was not to be associated with the ribaldry of the stage (for there was sufficient ribaldry in the fifteenth century to ban him on those grounds) but because the greater humanization of the mortal characters demanded also a greater humanization of the figure of God – a degree of anthropomorphism which could only be regarded as blasphemous by the church. As long as God was a cardboard figure among other cardboard figures, his halo or white robe was sufficient to awaken the awe felt by a spectator before the *praesepe*; but as the human members of the *dramatis personae* began to question the justice of the world and to speak of sin and retribution in their own lives, God could not join them as a disputant. The dramatist had developed his art beyond the need of a puppet God, and had not yet attained that degree of confidence which would permit him either to justify or to condemn the ways of God to men.

There are traces in Bale's characters of the humanist's enquiring mind, but the play, chopped into seven scenes, each crowned with a symbol, remains a medieval pageant with patently theological intent. It is, in a sense, a religious polemic, concerned more with teaching the doctrine of *grace* and the validity of Protestantism than with that portrayal of the joy and suffering of man which forms the subject of all great drama. Yet this religious polemic itself guided drama into a new channel. The Protestant identification with Old Testament characters gave new impetus to the sympathetic portrayal of biblical heroes, of which we perceived some traces in the mystery cycles. This growing sympathy had received a set-back in the abstract allegorizations of the morality plays, but as the Protestant began to see himself in the characters of the Scriptures, those characters achieved a new depth and moved with a more human gait. Esau blowing his horn in the morning is a small step forward, but the ease with which Susanna converses with her husband, the gentleness with which he chides her and the doubts which assail her parents all point to a concern with biblical characters as beings of flesh and blood rather than as sacred figures.

The didactic element of the Christian Terence movement – an element present in some form in almost all biblical drama – resulted, together with this humanization and empathy, in the topical allusiveness of the biblical stage. Not only was Abraham the prototype for the Reformer hounded out of his country, but Haman now became a 'type' for Wolsey, and Hezekiah for Henry VIII. The tradition of preaching in the Jewish and then the Christian Church has inevitably concerned itself with the continual reinterpretation of the Bible for the contemporary era. When Isaiah began his prophecy with the call, 'Hear O heavens, and give ear O earth!' he was deliberately recalling the opening phrase of Moses' final prophecy in Deut. xxxii. He was, in a sense, identifying himself with the first prophet of Israel and reminding his audience that Moses' cry for righteousness and humility before God applied as much in the eighth century as it had some five centuries earlier. Christianity had transferred the Jewish habit to its own teachings, making the *imitatio Dei*, the attempt to model oneself on the life of Jesus, a central part of Christianity. There was, therefore, nothing essentially new in the sixteenth-century adaptation of biblical stories to contemporary events. The change which did occur, however, was that Protestantism and the freer access to the Scriptures produced a wealth of new models drawn from the Old Testament rather than from the New. The Protestant recognized the impossibility of imitating the Christian messiah in any but the lamest sense, and chose instead such mortal yet sacred models as Abraham, Moses, and David. The prefigurative method was largely swept aside as 'supersticion' and medieval shibboleth, and in its place arose a new respect and admiration for the ancient Hebrews struggling, often successfully, against sin and despair in their vision of the ultimate victory of righteousness.

But the stage was not to benefit from this reinvigoration for long. The sense of spiritual dedication which prompted this affinity to the biblical heroes demanded a profound seriousness —a seriousness which pervaded the pages of the Bible itself, and which left no room for humour where the fate of man was concerned. The slight traces of humour visible in the liturgical drama had been enlarged by the English mystery cycles, and the Englishman's love of combining the most serious themes with deft touches of light comedy had made the stage even more unsuited to the Calvinist temperament than it might otherwise have become. The 'secular' classics had offered to Buchanan and others the comparatively chaste models of Euripides and Seneca, but when an Ovidian delight in erotic themes resulted in the prurience of *Susanna* and the 'romantic' portrayal of David's sin in Peele's play, it became apparent that the stage and the Church must part ways.

(iii) Censorship and the Puritan Opposition

The disappearance of biblical drama from the English stage coincided almost exactly with the climax of the Puritan attack upon the contemporary theatre. But, as with the cock who thought his crowing brought the dawn, coincidence in time is no sure indication of cause and effect. It is not, of course, difficult to find specific attacks by the Puritans upon the sacrilegious elements in scriptural plays. The argument was advanced that the word of God had not been given 'to be derided and iested at, as they be in these filthie playes and enterluds on stages and scaffolds, or to be mixt and interlaced with bawdry, wanton shewes, & vncomely gestures.'[1] But the Puritan habit, visible most clearly perhaps in Prynne's *Histriomastix*, of swamping the reader with a flood of reasons or, more often, with a flood of quotations to prove a single point suggests that not too much importance should be attached to this minor element in the Puritan opposition. Indeed, a closer examination of the

---

[1] Philip Stubbes, *The Anatomie of Abuses* (1583), p. 140.

arguments adduced by Northbrooke, Gosson, and Stubbes places the problem of sacrilege far down the list of objections to contemporary drama.

Primarily the attack was directed against the immorality which had become the concomitant of drama, rather than against the drama itself. The Corporation of London, working hand-in-glove with the Puritans, justified its opposition by the prevalence at performances of 'frayes and quarrelles, eavell practizes of incontinencye in great Innes, hauinge chambers and secrete places adjoyninge to their open stagies and gallyries, inveyglynge and alleurynge of maides, speciallye orphanes';[1] and the central attack of the Puritans' leading protagonist sounded a similar note. Gosson, who knew the theatre well from his own previous connection with it, described vividly the immoral adjuncts to the stage:

'In our assemblies at playes in London, you shall see suche heaving and shooving, such ytching and shouldering to sytte by women; suche care for their garments that they be not trode on; . . . such ticking, such toying, such smiling, such winking, and such manning them home when the sportes are ended.'[2] Although the theatre encouraged vice and immorality, he admitted that the players 'seeke not to hurte, but desire to please'.

The traditional opposition of the Church to the stage had its origins in its condemnation of the Roman theatre, which the Christian martyr had stained only too often with his own blood. In 314 the Council of Arles had excommunicated all players, and a later decree from the Council of Carthage in 397 forbade churchmen from having any contact with the stage. But the Roman stage and the contemporary were so vastly different that reliance upon statements by the early churchmen could serve merely to add official sanction to an attack upon contemporary vice. Similarly, the attack upon the papist origins of the modern theatre rang hollow when one recalled the Protestant exploitation of the stage for political purposes by Bale, Bèze, and others. It was useful for rhetorical purposes to condemn drama on the grounds that 'it was twice damned, since, like the maypole, it

---

[1] Quoted in E. N. S. Thompson, *The Controversy Between the Puritans and the Stage* (New York, 1903), p. 40.

[2] Stephen Gosson, *The Schoole of Abuse* (1579), Shakespeare Society ed. (London, 1841), p. 25.

was heathen, and like the mass, popish,'[1] but if so, the Protestants had awakened to the fact somewhat late.

The reasons offered for the abolition of the theatre can be multiplied many times over from the texts of the Puritan attacks. 'The cause of plagues is sinne, if you look at it well: and the cause of sinne are playes: therefore the cause of plagues are playes'[2] ran a favourite argument, and the collapse of a scaffolding was similarly interpreted as a sign of divine retribution. The stage involved desecration of the Sabbath; it drew people away from the church and the pulpit; and, what was to become a key factor in the later years of this dispute, the impersonation of women by male actors was interpreted by Rainoldes and others as a desecration of the law in Deut. xxii concerning apparel.[3] In vain Nashe protested that this was the lesser of two evils: 'Our players are not as the players beyond the sea, a sort of squirting baudie Comedians, that have whores and common Curtizans to play womens parts and forbeare no immodest speech or unchast action',[4] and Selden later proved in vain that the prohibition did not apply to the stage.[5] When the Puritan had determined on a course of action, any argument which came to his hand was at once exploited. We may note here that when the supporters of the stage, taking the advice to heart, did allow women to act the female roles, William Prynne leapt to the attack with a cry of '*Whores!*', and lost the tips of his ears when it was found that one of the 'whores' happened to be the Queen of England.

In the attack upon the stage, then, the aspect of the playhouse which could be denounced least effectively was the religious

[1] Dover Wilson in the *Cambridge History of English Literature*, xiv, 375.

[2] Thomas White, *Sermon* (1576), p. 47, quoted by Dover Wilson on p. 376.

[3] In Oxford, John Rainoldes, the learned theologian, interpreted the law strictly in his attack on the Latin dramatist, William Gager of Christ's College. Gager replied that the law was not intended for the merely temporary donning of women's garments for stage purposes. The argument, which took place in 1591, is preserved in the pamphlet, *Th' Overthrow of Stage Playes, By the way of controversie betwixt D. Gager and D. Rainoldes* (1599).

[4] *Pierce Pennilesse* (1592), in *Works* (London, 1883/4), ii, 92.

[5] He did this at Ben Jonson's request. See Selden's *Works* (London, 1726), ii, 1690 and also E. N. S. Thompson, *Controversy*, p. 100.

drama. The biblical dramatists could answer them in much the same way as Bale had responded to the earlier law curtailing religious polemic in drama:

'So long as they played lyes and sange baudy songes, blasphemed God, and corrupted men's consciences, ye never blamed them, but were verye well contented. But sens they persuaded the people to worship theyr Lorde God aryght, accordyng to hys holie lawe and not yours, and to acknoledge Jesus Chryst for their onely redeemer and Saviour without your lowsie legerdemains, ye never were pleased with them.'[1]

The biblical dramatist at the end of the sixteenth century who, let us remember, no longer portrayed God or Jesus upon the stage, and whose worst crime was allowing some comic scenes to creep into the minor parts of the play, was justified in answering the Puritan that he would be wiser to confine his attack to the immoralities of the secular stage instead of attempting to sweep biblical drama away with the rest of the contemporary theatre. It was in this sense that Lodge objected to the Puritan view 'unless the things be taken away the vice will continue,' maintaining instead that a reform of the stage and an encouragement of religious drama would cleanse the stage of its impurities more effectively.[2]

If, then, the Puritan opposition to the stage merely included biblical drama in the general condemnation, why did the composition of biblical plays shrivel away by 1600 while the secular drama continued to flourish and, indeed, to reach its fullest flowering during the next two decades? Clearly, the end of biblical drama cannot be attributed to the Puritan controversy except in so far as the latter acted as an irritant to an already existent malady.

The theory that laws of censorship curtailed the development of biblical drama is equally invalid, for there is a fundamental distinction to be made between attacks upon the religious

[1] Bale, *Epistel Exhortatorye of an Inglyshe Christian* (1544), written under the pseudonym of Henry Stalbridge in protest against the *Act for the Advancement of True Religion* of 1543. See Chambers, *Elizabethan Stage* (Oxford, 1923), i, 242.

[2] Some years later, Lodge succumbed to the opposition and wrote in his *Wits Miserie* (1596), that 'in stage plaies to make use of Hystoricall Scripture, I hold it with the Legists odious, and as the Council of Trent did . . . I condemne it.'

polemics for which the stage was exploited and attacks upon the dramatization of scriptural themes which, at least from the mid-sixteenth century, was free from such sectarian disputes.

In discussing the disappearance of the medieval mystery cycles, Father Gardiner has argued that these cycles disappeared not through the disapproval of the Catholic Church but as a result of a deliberate act of policy by the leaders of the Protestant Reformation.[1] His book has with justice been attacked by Greg for its partiality;[2] it conveniently dismisses the condemnations of the stage by Catholic clergymen as 'unofficial' because they were not backed by papal Bulls, and leans heavily upon this absence of official disapproval to transfer the responsibility to the Protestants. But whatever the standpoint of the contemporary Catholics, Father Gardiner is undoubtedly correct in pointing out that the Protestants did take active steps to discourage and, at times, to ban the performance of the medieval mysteries.

This opposition to the mystery plays was intensified by the close association in England between the authority of Church and State. A 'papist' attack upon the Reformation was a treasonable attack on the Crown, and it is clear from an examination of the edicts issued concerning the censorship of stage plays that the motivation of such edicts was not the fear of sacrilege but of sedition. In an undated letter to a justice of the peace concerning a recent 'seditious rising in our ancient city of York' attributed to Catholic instigators, Henry VIII warned the justice to imprison 'any papists who shall, in performing interludes which are founded on any portion of the Old or New Testament, say or make use of any language which may tend to excite those who are beholding the same to any breach of the peace.'[3] Scriptural drama, in this early example of dramatic censorship, was not itself attacked, but merely its exploitation for seditious purposes. The *Act for the Advancement of True Religion* (1543) was similarly intended to discourage the use of the stage for religious polemic and included the Protestants in the ban.

[1] H. C. Gardiner, *Mysteries' End: an Investigation of the Last Days of the Medieval Religious Stage* (New Haven, 1946).

[2] See W. W. Greg's review in *MLR xlii* (1947), 260.

[3] J. O. Halliwell-Phillips' edition of *Letters of the Kings of England* (London, 1848), i, 354.

113

On the accession of Queen Mary a decade later, the restrictions were broadened to censor (through the Master of the Revels) all plays of a religious nature; but, read in its context, the edict is seen to be aimed at preserving the authority of the Crown and preventing anti-Catholic propaganda:

'And furthermore, forasmuche also as it is well knowen, that sedition and false rumours have been nouryshed and maynteyned in this realme, by the subteltye and malyce of some euell disposed persons, which take vpon them withoute sufficient auctoritie, to preache, and to interprete the worde of God, after theyr own brayne, in churches and other places, both publique and pryuate . . . her highnes therefore strayghtly chargeth and commandeth all and every her sayde subiectes . . . that none of them presume from henceforth to preache . . . or to interprete or teache any scriptures or any mane poyntes of doctryne concernynge religion . . . nor to play any interlude except that haue her graces speciall licence in writynge for the same vpon to incurre her highnesse indignation and displeasure.'[1]

Udall, we recall, was in high favour with the Queen despite the Protestant bias of his plays.

Queen Elizabeth's proclamation of 16th May, 1559 ordered officials to ban all plays 'wherein either matters of religion or of the governance of the estate of the common weale shalbe handled or treated,' adding that these subjects were 'no meete matters to be wrytten or treated vpon but by menne of aucthoritie, learning and wisdome.' This coupling of religion with the authority of the State was echoed in the letter of 1589 issued from the Star Chamber to the Archbishop of Canterbury which complained of the plays and interludes in the area of the City of London whose players 'take uppon them to handle in their plaies certen matters of Diuinytie and of State unfitt to be suffred.'[2] Again it was prompted by concern lest a weakening of the authority of the Church might lessen that of the Crown.

Indeed, the first legislation aimed against blasphemy on the stage was the famous statute of 1605, enacted some five years

---

[1] Quoted in F. Fowell and F. Palmer, *Censorship in England* (London, 1913), p. 13. See also V. C. Gildersleeve, *Government Regulation of the Elizabethan Drama* (New York, 1908).

[2] Fowell and Palmer, pp. 14 and 26.

after scriptural drama had ended.[1] In this statute, King James forbade players to pronounce the names of God, Christ, the Holy Ghost, or the Trinity on the stage, and by 1623 the censor was busily removing even such harmless phrases as the italicized words in Justice Shallow's comment, 'Death, *as the Psalmist says*, is certain to all.'[2] Censorship of the drama on grounds of sacrilege came, therefore, too late to have contributed to the cessation of biblical drama.

(iv) The Rungs of Sanctity

Since neither the Puritan opposition to the stage nor the restrictive legislation aimed against its exploitation for religious polemic can be held responsible for the discontinuance of scriptural drama, the remaining possibility is that it resulted from internal rather than external causes. We have seen that once the puppet-like theatre of the mystery cycles became humanized, and the haloes disappeared from the scriptural figures, God could no longer appear on the stage. This required no legislation but was felt instinctively by the dramatists themselves. The next development was to exclude Christ from the list of characters, and the lengthy discussions of the early Reformers on this point revealed again that no external pressure was required. New Testament drama now practically disappeared except for plays devoted to John the Baptist and the prodigal son, who were merely peripheral figures in the Gospel narrative. The Old Testament, as the less sacred part of the Scriptures, was the ideal subject-matter for religious drama, since it was, in a sense, peripheral as long as it was regarded merely as a prefiguration.

[1] This is not true of the Scottish Church which banned all biblical plays as early as 1575 on grounds of sacrilege. The Act of the General Assembly of the Kirk reads:
'Forasmuche as it is considered that the playing of clerk-playes, comedies or tragedies, upon the canonicall parts of the Scriptures, induceth & bringeth with it a contempt and profanation of the same, it is thought meete and concluded, that no clerk-plays, comedies or tragedies, be made upon canonicall Scriptures, other New or Old, in time coming.'
[2] *II Henry IV*, iii, ii, 41.

The growing sanctity of the Old Testament was, as we have noted, brought about by the Reformation demand for an open Bible and by the sense of identification with biblical heroes implicit in the doctrine of election. But it was a slow process, going hand-in-hand with the onerous and dangerous task of sixteenth-century biblical translation. The Geneva Version of 1560, beloved by the Calvinists, was, despite its Protestant origin, heavily encrusted with prefigurative interpretation, each chapter being prefaced by a lengthy 'key' to the typological cypher. The Authorized Version of 1611 provided the first English edition which printed the Old and the New Testaments as of equal sanctity, with the marginal comments restricted to purely linguistic aids, and with brief headings to chapters merely indicating the nature of the contents. Of course, this version contained traces of Christological interpretation, particularly in the messianic sections of *Isaiah*, but these were negligible in comparison with the heavy commentary of previous editions. The Old and the New Testaments lay side by side in the same volume, open to all readers in their naked form. Christ no longer pervaded the entire Bible from *Genesis* to *Revelation*, and the first part had become the self-explanatory history of the Jewish people and of the progressive revelation of God's covenant with them and with their seed. The sanctity of the Old Testament had been significantly heightened.

The idea of an Authorized Version was first mooted in 1604 when, on January 16, John Rainoldes suggested the project to James at the Hampton Court Conference. The King, at once struck with the idea, gave orders for work to begin, adding the caveat 'that no marginall notes should be added, having found in them which are annexed to the Geneva translation (whiche he saw in a Bible given him by an English lady) some notes very partiall, untrue, seditious, and savouring too much of dangerous and trayterous conceits.'[1] At the turn of the century, therefore, the climate was in favour of a Bible free from prejudiced commentary, which allowed the Old Testament to speak for itself.

[1] See J. Isaacs, 'The Authorized Version and After', in *Ancient and English Versions of the Bible*, ed. H. Wheeler Robinson (Oxford, 1940), p. 197, D. Daiches, *The King James Version of the English Bible* (Chicago, 1941), and A. W. Pollard, *Records of the English Bible* (London, 1911).

The Rungs of Sanctity

This new sanctity of the Old Testament is the real reason, it seems to me, for the dramatist's disinclination to write biblical drama on Old Testament themes. In the sixteenth century as opposed to the present day, the Bible was not regarded as mythology to be exploited for literary symbols; nor was it merely an alternative to Holinshed. It was still a sacred book to be treated with reverence, and any dramatist who turned to it for the theme of his drama necessarily respected the sanctity of his material. Shakespeare unhesitatingly altered, moulded, and transformed the secular histories and dramatic sources which he used, but whatever slight alteration the biblical dramatist might make was weighed carefully lest it damage the original story. True, Ovid and Seneca dominated much of the later biblical drama of the period, but only as a tinting to the biblical narrative; the essentials of the story had to be preserved.

The dramatist, therefore, who chose the Old Testament as the source of his subject-matter was a man with some religious sense, innately sensitive to the suggestion that the Bible was too sacred for the stage. We have seen that Greene, Lodge, and Nashe answered the Puritan attack on the stage not (as did many other dramatists) by jibes at the hypocrisy and narrow-mindedness of their opponents, but with real concern. They acknowledged that the stage was becoming a source of immorality, and they attempted to improve the moral tone of the theatre by presenting noble and edifying plays based upon biblical themes. But it was too late to stem the tide of immorality. The theatre was unquestionably the resort of vagrants, prostitutes, homosexuals, and gamblers and, as in every age, it attracted to its ranks a group of professionals whose moral standards were often conspicuously low. The dramatists themselves, now that the sanctity of the Old Testament had risen almost to the level of the New, began to experience qualms over the use of such holy matter for profane purposes.

If this theory that the growing sanctity of the Old Testament discouraged dramatists from exploiting it has any validity, we would expect those playwrights interested in religious themes to move one step downwards in sanctity of theme in the same way as they had previously shifted from New Testament to Old. And that is precisely what we do find. Immediately subsequent to the cessation of biblical drama came a spate of plays based

117

either upon the less sacred Apocrypha or upon the histories of Josephus, which provided a biblical setting without the problems of a sacred text. Apart from a few drolls, interludes and masques, Peele's drama is the last biblical play whose text has survived, although we know of other plays performed if not written until 1602 – just two years before work was begun on the Authorized Version.[1]

It is significant that the alternative of the Apocrypha and of Josephus to the sacred Bible itself had been exploited earlier when the mystery plays were under attack for their 'perversion' of the Scriptures. In 1564, Lincoln chose the more innocuous *Tobias* to replace the traditional cycle, and in 1584, Coventry commissioned a Mr. Smythe of Oxford to write a play on *The Destruction of Jerusalem*. Now the process was repeated with Legge's *Destruction of Jerusalem* (1591).

The clearest testimony to the prevailing shift from sacred themes to the less sacred apocryphal stories appeared in the introduction to the English edition of the *Christian Terence* published in 1592. This edition, omitting the truly biblical plays by Schonaeus, restricted itself merely to *Tobaeus*, *Iuditha* and *Pseudostratiotes*, the editor explaining:

'There is an old familiar proverb, *It is not good to play with*

---

[1] We know of the following performances of biblical plays whose texts have not survived: R. Greene, *Jobe* (1587); ?*Abrame and Lot* (1593/4); ?*Hester and Ahasuerus* (1594); ?*nabucadonizer* (Nebuchadnezzar), (1596); Wm. Houghton, *Judas* (Maccabeus?), (1601); Dekker and Munday, *Jephthah* (1602); Henry Chettle, *Tobias* (1602); S. Rowley, *Joshuah* (1602); Rowley and Jewby, *Sam(p)son* (1602); Rowley and Jewby, *Absalom* (1602). Most of these appear as entries in Henslowe's *Diary*. The play, *Hester and Ahasuerus*, may be the original of an extant German translation of an English play on that theme. This translation contains a subplot, probably a German addition, but the main plot remains close to the biblical story, emphasizing the theme of divine justice. W. W. Greg denies that this was based on *Godly Queene Hester* in his edition of the latter, p. 159. Creizenach, *English Drama*, p. 162, suggests that the *Samson* by Rowley and Jewby (or Jubye") may be the source of the allusion in Middleton's comedy, *The Family of Love*, in which the gallants speak admiringly of the biblical hero's strength:

'Why I tell thee we saw Sampson bear the town gates on his neck from the lower to the upper stage, with that life and admirable accord that it shall never be equalled, unless the whole new livery of porters set [to] their shoulders.'

sacred things. And what is holier and more sacred than the divinely inspired canonical scriptures? Therefore, to add, subtract, to omit anything from them, to insert speeches and characters, as poetic license permits, becomes a scruple in the eyes of some whom we do not want to offend needlessly.'[1]

The change was clearly reflected in the English biblical drama of the period. A few years later, Lady Elizabeth Carew (or Cary), to whom Nashe had dedicated his *Christ's Tears Over Jerusalem* and who was therefore aware of the recent trends in biblical drama, applied Peele's 'romantic' treatment of the Scriptures to the works of Josephus in her *Tragedy of Mariam, the Faire Queene of Iewry* (1613). This new Herod, no longer merely the cruel, ranting tyrant of the mystery cycles, but now the passionate lover as well, dogged by an overpowering jealousy, appeared again as the hero of the play by Gervase Markham and William Sampson entitled *The True Tragedy of Herod and Antipater . . . According to Josephus, the learned and famous Iew* (1622),[2] and in the following year, Massinger's *Duke of Milan* borrowed the same Herod-Mariamne theme from Josephus. These dramas marked the beginning of a spate of pseudo-biblical plays which exploited the oriental exoticism of the biblical setting and the popular interest in scriptural themes while yet avoiding the charge of sacrilege. The seventeenth century continued the genre with a work by William Heminge (the son of Shakespeare's actor friend who helped edit the First Folio) entitled *The Jewes Tragedy or their Fatal and Final Overthrow by Vespasian and Titus His Son, Agreeable to the Authentick and Famous History of Josephus.*[3]

[1] The tragedy is merely initialled *E.C.* but is generally attributed to Lady Carew, the mother of the Lord Falkland of Civil War fame. Nashe had written that 'Logique, Rethorique, History, Philosophy, Musique, Poetry, all are the hand-maides of Divinity'. He felt a need for the arts to fulfil some 'divine' purpose, and Lady Carew's play attempted to carry out the advice.

[2] For the history of dramas based on the Herod theme, see M. J. Valency, *The Tragedies of Herod and Mariamne* (New York, 1940); W. W. Greg, 'Herod on the English Stage', *Spectator lxxxv* (1905); A. C. Dunstan's examination of the dramas by Lady Carew and by Markham and Sampson (Königsberg, 1908); and J. B. Fletcher, 'Herod in Drama', *SP xix* (1922), 292.

[3] It was published in 1662, but must have been written much earlier as the author died some time before 1653.

It is clear, therefore, that to attribute the cessation of biblical drama to the Puritan opposition is to ignore that gradual move down the ladder of sanctity necessitated on the one hand by the growing reverence for the Old Testament and on the other by the humanization of character inherent in the development of dramatic technique. The mystery cycles, with their stylized figures and austerely simple scenes, could depict God himself and the central figures of the Gospels without irreverence, although even there such livelier dramatization as was possible was confined to the Old Testament and the pre-Nativity world. In the sixteenth century, the staging of God and Christ became an irreverence, and biblical drama was restricted almost entirely to Old Testament themes. By the end of the century, however, the Old Testament was no longer a prefigurative subsidiary of the New, but had become, particularly for the Protestant, a holy text relating those earlier stages of divine history in which the Chosen People had first been elected to that Covenant with God which the Protestant believed he had inherited. The dramatist attracted to its themes grew increasingly conscious that he was verging on sacrilege, and the *Noli me tangere* of the New Testament was extended to the Old. Yet the urge to dramatize the scriptures was still strong, and the playwright moved a rung down in sanctity first to the Apocrypha and, when that too became sacrosanct, to the histories of Josephus which provided scriptural settings and associations without the awkwardness of divine authority.

The revival of biblical drama for stage performance was delayed some three centuries until the nineteenth-century attacks upon the Bible had so weakened its authority that dramatization was less an irreverence than an attempt at its defence; and in those intervening centuries, the obstacle to its stage presentation was not legal prohibition but the universal assumption in Protestant England that such dramatization would constitute sacrilege. It was the same fear of sacrilege as had brought an end to biblical drama at the close of the sixteenth century.

(v) SHAKESPEARE AND THE BIBLICAL DRAMA[1]

Eliot has recorded that, 'No author exercised a wider or deeper influence upon the Elizabethan mind or upon the Elizabethan form of tragedy than did Seneca,' and the work of J. W. Cunliffe and others makes it unnecessary to labour the point here.[2] The publication of *Seneca His Tenne Tragedies* in 1581, mainly the work of Jasper Heywood, raised him to the status of the leading model for the contemporary stage, and both Hoole's *New Discovery of the Old Art of Teaching Schoole* (1660) and the curriculum of Rotherham school in Shakespeare's day testify to the large part he played in the education of the Elizabethan dramatists. The blood-tragedy of revenge, the love of epigrammatic dialogue, the moral posing, the ghosts, and the sententious rhetoric which he bequeathed to the English stage do not concern us directly here, but rather the vein of Stoicism, of resignation to a blind fate, which the Elizabethan dramatists inherited together with his dramatic techniques.

It has been suggested that among Seneca's main attractions for the Elizabethan dramatist was his cosmopolitanism.[3] He wrote not from a narrow, national viewpoint, not from within a purely local religious system as did the Greek, but from the centre of the Roman Empire whose territory embraced the major portion of the known world. His cultural background consequently reflected a mixture of varied races and creeds which, in effect, cancelled each other out, leaving in their void a cynicism which recognized no tribal deities and could perceive no claim to superiority in any one of the innumerable gods with whom Rome had come into contact. In Stoicism, fate is blind, callous, and impervious to man's suffering; and man, in his turn, if he is to retain sufficient self-respect to avoid becoming a snivelling wretch, must learn to raise himself above the vicissitudes

[1] Some of the ideas in this section appeared in an article of mine under the same title in the *Iowa English Yearbook* (1964), and I am grateful to the editors for permission to make use of that material.
[2] In the introduction to the reprint of the 1581 translation of Seneca (London, 1927). See also J. W. Cunliffe, *The Influence of Seneca*, and T. S. Eliot, *Shakespeare and the Stoicism of Seneca* (London, 1927).
[3] Cunliffe, p. 15.

of his environment, to treat with equal scorn the triumphs of success and the bitterness of failure. The ideal of Senecan Stoicism is the man who is no longer vulnerable to his own emotions:

> *A Kyng he is that feare hath layde aside*
> *And all effects that in the breast are bred.*[1]

For the Renaissance humanist, dazzled by those very splendours of the temporal world which the Middle Ages had despised, and by the sudden change from medieval humility to a sense of personal dignity in a challenging world, this Stoic superiority to fate had a peculiar fascination. The idea of subduing emotion to a calm, objective weighing of fact had a novelty about it strangely in tune with the embryonic empiricism of the age. Brutus possesses that calm detachment in the face of all danger:

> *Set honour in one eye and death i' th' other,*
> *And I will look on both indifferently.*

because his priorities have been rationally defined and no emotions will sway his judgement.

> *. . . I love*
> *The name of honour more than I fear death.*

Honour, the Stoic justification for living, outweighs the medieval fear of death, and at this early stage of the play his credo appears a noble and admirable ideal. But in the interests of that honour, Brutus, we discover, is misguidedly prepared to throw into the scales not only his own death but that of his friend Caesar, too. The heart must be offered upon the altar of cold Reason. Hence the play's recurring imagery of cold, impassive statues gushing with blood. The climactic speech of the play scorns the 'honourable' Brutus by means of this very contrast with the warm blood of pity and love:

> *Through this the well-beloved Brutus stabb'd*
> *And as he pluck'd his cursed steel away,*
> *Mark how the blood of Caesar followed it,*

---

[1] Seneca, *Thyestes*, in the reprint of *Seneca His Tenne Tragedies* (1581), published London/New York, 1927, i, 66.

As rushing out of doors to be resolv'd
If Brutus so unkindly knock'd or no;
For Brutus, as you know, was Caesar's angel.
Judge, O you gods, how dearly Caesar lov'd him!
This was the most unkindest cut of all;
For when the noble Caesar saw him stab,
Ingratitude more strong than traitor's arms,
Quite vanquish'd him: then burst his mighty heart;
And in his mantle muffling up his face,
Even at the base of Pompey's statue,
Which all the while ran blood, great Caesar fell.

Within his apparent Renaissance admiration of Stoicism, then, Shakespeare harboured some serious doubts about its ultimate validity.

His reservations are, perhaps, most clearly focused in Hamlet, the later and fuller treatment of the Brutus figure. There Horatio, as the embodiment of Stoicism *par excellence*, represents all that Hamlet longs for in himself–that calm superiority to Fate's buffetings, that control of blood by cool judgement:

> *. . . for thou hast been*
> *As one in suff'ring all that suffers nothing,*
> *A man that Fortune's buffets and rewards*
> *Hast ta'en with equal thanks; and blest are those*
> *Whose blood and judgment are so well commingled*
> *That they are not a pipe for Fortune's fingers*
> *To sound what stop she please.*

The opening of this speech–'Nay do not think I flatter'–leaves no doubt of Hamlet's sincerity; and here is the crux of the play. For if Hamlet is drawn so powerfully towards the Stoic philosophy, what prevents him from becoming a Stoic himself, from translating his admiration into belief? The obstacle to this belief lies at the heart of his tragic dilemma.

The starting-point for Stoicism was, after all, the conviction that this universe is devoid of order and justice. Gods there may be, but they have lost all interest in human affairs, and distribute their blows and caresses with a blind disregard for right and wrong. As Seneca put it:

The Later Renaissance

Res humanas ordine nullo
fortuna regit, spargitque manu
munera caeca, peiora fouens.[1]

The Stoic, obsessed by this sense of cruel, arbitrary Fate, scorns death as no more than a sleep, a painless reabsorption into the *anima mundi*, and hence as a happy release from the suffering of this world. Dispassionately he measures the point at which life ceases to be worthwhile and, having reached it, calmly commits suicide. Cato, Paetus Thrasea, and Seneca himself led the way for the hundreds of Roman Stoics who chose for themselves this path into honourable oblivion; and it was a path which sorely tempted the Elizabethan too in moments of world-weariness and disillusionment. Abused by an 'outrageous' fortune, Hamlet yearns above all

> *to die, to sleep —*
> No more; *and by a sleep to say we end*
> *The heartache and the thousand natural shocks*
> *That flesh is heir to. 'Tis a consummation*
> *Devoutly to be wished.*

If the sleep is a consummation, an ending to all, then it is wholly good. But deeply rooted in the consciousness of the Elizabethan, beneath his apparent sang-froid was an ineradicable awareness of an impending Day of Judgement, a settling after death of all scores accumulated in this mortal world. And what is *To be or not to be* but the monologue of a man torn between the temptation of a Stoic suicide ('When he himself might his quietus make/With a bare bodkin') and the biblical doctrine that the Eternal has inexorably set his canon against self-slaughter? For all the attractions of oblivion, Hamlet can find no assurance that death will, in fact, provide that longed-for consummation:

> *to die — to sleep —*
> *To sleep, perchance to dream, ay there's the rub*

and the conscience that makes a 'coward' of Hamlet (but not of Horatio) is

[1] *Hippolytus*, 980 f.: 'Fortune rules human affairs with no order and scatters her gifts blindly, cherishing the worse gifts.'

Shakespeare and the Biblical Drama

. . . that the dread of something after death
The undiscovered country, from whose bourn
No traveller returns, puzzles the will
And makes us rather bear those ills we have
Than fly to others that we know not of.[1]

Within this speech Hamlet, rigorously unfair to himself, oversimplifies his own problem. Were he merely afraid of punishment in the world to come, he might indeed appear a coward. But it soon becomes apparent that his baroque struggle, his dissatisfaction with the irreconcilability of philosophies goes far deeper; for his hesitancy over becoming an adherent of Stoicism arises, paradoxically, from a dread lest the Stoic assumptions be true. If death is oblivion, then, ostensibly at least, it is attractive. But if death *is* oblivion, then life itself loses all meaning to a man of Hamlet's sensitivity. Horatio is unmoved by the implications of Yorick's skull—' 'Twere to consider too curiously to consider so'; but for Hamlet the thought that the infinite jest of man should end in a rotting skull crawling with maggots makes his gorge rise in more than a physical sense. Until he can be convinced that there is some ultimate order and purpose in the world, there seems little point in contributing to the restoration of that order by avenging his father's murder.

We, the audience, have already been predisposed to reject the Stoic view by the Ghost's chilling, if veiled account of purgatorial torture:

> *Doomed for a certain term to walk the night,*
> *And for the day confined to fast in fires,*
> *Till the foul crimes done in my days of nature*
> *Are burnt and purged away.*

In the setting of the play, we have no doubt that Purgatory and Hell are real; and this theme of salvation and damnation dominates the play. Claudius's sin is biblical rather than hierarchical. His crime is less the usurpation of the throne than the fratricidal sin of Cain, bearing 'the primal eldest curse'. He is unable to

[1] See Hiram Haydn's *Counter-Renaissance* (New York, 1950), pp. 651 f. and Virgil K. Whitaker, *Shakespeare's Use of Learning* (San Marino, 1953), pp. 251 f.

enjoy the fruits of his crime, for he knows that the account with heaven cannot be settled with a bribe as here below:

> *In the corrupted currents of this world,*
> *Offence's gilded hand may shove by justice,*
> *... But 'tis not so above.*

and his stifled prayer deliberately echoes the biblical source:

> *... What if this cursed hand*
> *Were thicker than itself with brother's blood,*
> *Is there not rain enough in the sweet heavens*
> *To wash it white as snow?*

It recalls Isaiah's famous insistence on spiritual purity as a prerequisite for prayer: 'Though you offer many prayers, I shall not hear; your hands are full of blood. Wash, clean yourselves. ... Though your sins be as scarlet, they shall grow white as snow' (Is. i. 15). Hamlet, seeing his prayerful mood, determines to catch Claudius about some act that 'hath no relish of salvation in't.' Ultimately, it is Hamlet's sense of a divinely ordered universe and his concern with the 'audit' in this world for the retributive after-life – the 'things in heaven and earth' that are not dreamt of in Horatio's philosophy – which lead him to reject the Stoic concept of death as mere dissolution of the human frame.

Similarly, Macbeth's readiness to 'jump the life to come', to risk the consequences of his deed in the next world is, for the audience, his self-damnation; we recognize at once the blasphemous futility of the attempt. If the play's imagery reiterates Macbeth's hierarchical unsuitability for the regal robes, it broods no less on the Isaiah image of blood which cannot be washed off, on the summoning to Heaven or Hell, and on the *Amen* which sticks in the throat of the unrepentant sinner. There is ample evidence, then, that the biblical ethos served as a counterpoise to Senecan Stoicism on the Elizabethan stage, providing a moral framework within which the characters might rise or stumble in their search for inner salvation and regeneration.

This biblical sense of retributive justice of course formed part of the general Christian climate of the age; but it is too deeply embedded in the Elizabethan theatre, in the structure and themes of the plays performed there, to be merely a 'climatic' importation, and its origins need to be traced back at least partially within the stage tradition which Shakespeare and his contemporaries inherited. In recent years there has been increasing recognition of Shakespeare's debt to the medieval Moralities. Tillyard noted that the 'hierarchical order' of the history plays was largely derived from them through the *Mirror for Magistrates* and the *Chronicles* of Edward Hall; Bernard Spivack sees in Richard III and Iago extensions of the Allegory of Evil; and Miss Madeleine Doran has argued that the Moralities helped mould the universality of the Elizabethan dramatic form.[1] But surprisingly enough, the large body of scriptural plays performed so frequently in the Tudor era and occupying so prominent a place in the repertory of the theatre in which Shakespeare learned his craft, has been almost ignored as a source. From Henslowe's diary we know of at least a dozen biblical plays which he was personally responsible for staging at a time when (for reasons we have discussed) they were already disappearing. And in the earlier part of the century, many such plays had been performed in the schools and universities where the University Wits had been studying. To ignore their influence, therefore, would seem a serious omission.

The quintessence of the Morality play is, after all, the prostration of all men before the Judgement Seat, the contempt for petty differences in temporal rank and power, and the depiction of this mortal world as valuable solely for the acquisition of good deeds in preparation for the world to come. The Shakespearean hero's astonishment that this splendid creature man should serve one day to stop a bung-hole is the very antithesis of the Morality viewpoint, *Media vita in morte sumus*. Macbeth's crime horrifies us, but we never doubt that the royal throne for which he committed it was a prize that might tempt any man. If this interest in worldly prizes is set against the sombre backcloth of a moral order, it is rather the practical moral order of the

[1] E. M. W. Tillyard, *Shakespeare's History Plays* (New York, 1947); Bernard Spivack, *Shakespeare and the Allegory of Evil* (New York, 1958); and Madeleine Doran, *Endeavours of Art: a study of form in the Elizabethan drama* (Madison, 1954). Irving Ribner's *Patterns in Shakespearian Tragedy* (London, 1962) offers the best discussion yet of retribution and the biblical ethos in Shakespearean drama but, apart from occasional allusions to the Moralities, makes no attempt to connect it with earlier stage traditions.

Old Testament than the symbolic, eschatological order of the Moralities. In the latter, Good Deeds are a vague, unspecified commodity to be placed upon the scales on the Day of Judgement; whereas the Tudor Old Testament plays, like the Shakespearean drama itself, examined the actions of individual men, underscoring the implications of those actions in the scheme of retributive justice. The Shakespearean heroes possess a universality as valid as Everyman's; but it is a universality rooted in the vigorous realism of the Renaissance world, in the foibles and potentialities of creatures of flesh and blood. And this ability to perceive in the lives of individual men, particularly in their struggles against temptation and evil, an archetypal significance for all mankind is a quality specifically cultivated in the postfigurative Tudor dramatizations of the Bible.

The story of Susannah and the Elders, for example, had long been a favourite among Renaissance dramatists for its neat illustration of God's vindication of the righteous. Garter's *Godlye Susanna* published in London in 1578 had, like all these plays, aimed at depicting the triumph of justice in this world and the theme was familiar to all theatregoers of the age. Shakespeare's *Merchant of Venice* consists of a laminated pattern of Ser Giovanni's tale, the residue of the Morality plays in Shylock's Vice, Launcelot Gobbo, and a somewhat distorted Crucifixion play in which Antonio, the 'tainted wether of the flock', awaits the spilling of his blood by the red-haired Judas. But when, at the climax of the play, Portia enters disguised as a lawyer, Shylock's exclamation 'A Daniel come to judgement' suddenly highlights a new indebtedness which adds considerable dramatic irony to the play. On the basis of the Susannah story, Portia is seen to represent the divinely appointed judge about to rectify a miscarriage of justice within the law, her pseudonym Balthazar echoing Daniel's pseudonym in the Bible. The irony is one which a modern audience can easily miss but which a Shakespearean audience would grasp unhesitatingly. Shylock's exclamation shows that he has 'postfiguratively' identified himself as the reincarnation of Susannah, the wronged innocent awaiting divine redemption. But by the audience he is at once seen to be (with Tubal) the Elder of the Synagogue perverting justice to suit his own illicit ends. Hence Gratiano's gleeful reiteration of the phrase at the moment of triumph:

Shakespeare and the Biblical Drama

A Daniel, still say I, a second Daniel!
I thank thee, Jew, for teaching me that word.

The recent outcrop of books arguing for the Christian elements in Shakespeare makes any detailed examination superfluous here.[1] Sylvan Barnet and Roland M. Frye have pointed to the dangers of overstating the case, of trying to turn Shakespeare into a Christian preacher. But with all scholarly caution it is, I think, justifiable to perceive within the great tragedies an ultimate sense of retributive justice which suggests that there is, after all, some order in the universe even if we cannot perceive it in its entirety; it is enough if at the end of the play we catch a glimpse of that supernal power. For those, like J. W. Cunliffe, who have argued that a cruel, Senecan fatalism 'runs through Elizabethan tragedy from the very beginning' there seems to be ample evidence in Gloucester's bitter cry:

> *As flies to wanton boys are we to the gods,*
> *They kill us for their sport.*

and even Wilson Knight, who (with great circumspection) leads the 'Christian' school, points out that the heavens do not take Lear's part, his curses on Regan and Goneril have no effect, and the winds continue to roar.[2] But this is merely the tardiness of justice; for by the end of the play the curses on Regan and Goneril have taken their effect, the winds are stilled, and

[1] G. Wilson Knight, *The Christian Renaissance* (Toronto, 1933), has been followed by Virgil K. Whitaker, *Shakespeare's Use of Learning* (San Marino, 1953), Paul N. Siegel, *Shakespearean Tragedy and the Elizabethan Compromise* (New York, 1957), R. W. Battenhouse, 'Shakespearean Tragedy: a Christian Interpretation', in N. A. Scott ed., *The Tragic Vision and the Christian Faith* (New York, 1957), John Vyvyan, *The Shakespearean Ethic* (London, 1959), J. A. Bryant, *Hippolyta's View* (Lexington, 1961), Ribner's, *Patterns*, and the studies of individual plays by Roy Walker and G. R. Elliott. There have been parallel studies of the Jacobean drama by Ribner and Robert Ornstein. See also the consecutive articles by Battenhouse and Ribner in *CRAS viii* (1964), 77. The counter movement is led by Sylvan Barnet, 'Some Limitations of a Christian Approach to Shakespeare', *ELH xxii*, 81 and Roland M. Frye, *Shakespeare and Christian Doctrine* (Princeton, 1963). R. Noble, *Shakespeare's Biblical Knowledge* (London, 1935), provides a useful checklist of scriptural quotations and allusions.

[2] *The Wheel of Fire* (New York, 1957), p. 193; also W. R. Elton, *King Lear and the Gods* (San Marino, 1966).

Gloucester's mood has changed to one of patience and contrition:

> *You ever-gentle gods, take my breath from me;*
> *Let not my worser spirit tempt me again*
> *To die before you please.*

This framework of divine justice does not, of course, express itself with the neat simplicity of a moral tract for children. Tragedy must present the disturbance of equilibrium, the dreadful picture of a world chaotic in its disorder and purposelessness; and only gradually is the supernal order felt as an unseen Presence. The trial scene in *Lear*, with the naked Tom cast as the 'robed man of justice', symbolizes Lear's growing awareness of the corruption and miscarriage of formal human law and his as yet tentative belief that only in nature itself can the workings of Providence be perceived. Cordelia's death cannot be revoked – the pain of her innocent suffering accompanies us as we leave the theatre; but in the larger view, Lear has atoned for that initial perversion of justice which led to it, the evil instruments of punishment have met their violent deaths, and even Lear himself finds his purgation in death, his release from 'the rack of this tough world'. This torment of human passion ends with Albany's assurance that those who have survived will try in their limited way to restore the order that has been so grievously disrupted.

> *All friends shall taste*
> *The wages of their virtue, and all foes*
> *The cup of their deservings.*

We have gazed into the abyss, and the horror is yet with us, but the assurance that all may yet be well acts as a balm. With its echo of 'The wages of sin is death', it is not unlike the didactic close to religious drama, when Noah, for example, comforts his wife:

> *Dame all ar drowned, late by thy dyne,*
> *And sone þei boughte þer synnes sore.*
> *Gud lewyn latte vs be-gynne*
> *So þat we greue our god nomore.*[1]

[1] *York Plays*, ed. cit., p. 63:
> Dame, all are drowned; hush thy din!
> And some have paid their sins' full score.
> Good living let us now begin,
> So that we grieve our God no more.

Shakespeare and the Biblical Drama

We who have been bred on post-medieval drama tend to accept the final retributive scenes as a natural ingredient of tragedy. But the Attic stage depicted an unjust world in which the righteous suffer in a manner totally unrelated to their merits. The cycle of the blood-feud involved each generation in the fatal ancestral curse irrespective of their individual virtues. As Butcher has shown, the *hamartia* which Aristotle demanded of great tragedy was 'a single error, whether morally culpable or not'[1] and *Oedipus Rex*, Aristotle's ideal play, presents us with a hero foredoomed to commit patricide and incest in ignorance of his parents' identity, and hence as morally guiltless. Antigone goes to her doom for saving her brother's soul, and Hippolytus, guilty only of chastity, is sent plunging to his death for having rejected his step-mother's incestuous advances. In a sense, the Hippolytus story is the tale of Joseph's rejection of Potiphar's wife translated into Greek terms, and the contrast in ending is significant: Hippolytus is slain by the gods, and Joseph rewarded by being elevated to the highest post in the land. In Greek tragedy, the injustice is offset by the subtle technique of *hybris* and *nemesis*, whereby the sin itself does not cause the hero's downfall so much as the manner in which he commits it. Agamemnon is fated to die long before he returns home, and every detail of his murder has been prepared; but he must first step on the purple carpet in order technically to have offended the gods. In this way, the appearance of ultimate order so necessary to tragedy is brilliantly preserved. But in the Senecan plays which served as the Elizabethans' classical model there is no such subtlety. A grim obsession with an inexorable ancestral curse presents the innocent victim chained at the opening of the drama to his irrevocable fate and ends the play with ominous hints of the death in store for the successful 'avenger'. Had Shakespeare's indebtedness to Senecan tragedy not been offset by the biblical sense of a moral, orderly universe, his plays might well have lacked their firm dramatic structure and harmonious endings.

Tom F. Driver's perceptive study of the sense of history in

---

[1] S. H. Butcher, *Aristotle's Theory of Poetry and Fine Art* (London, 1902), p. 321.

Shakespeare serves to strengthen this view.[1] He argues that the Greek search for a fundamental stability within the cyclical movements of nature resulted in an essentially static concept of history, while the ancient Hebrew, seeing through nature the purposive sovereignty of a Creator, regarded history as linear, moving inevitably towards the end for which the world had initially been created. Both Orestes and Hamlet must avenge a father's murder. But Orestes is fated to act as part of the unbroken cycle of the blood-feud (broken in Aeschylus by the extraneous intervention of a *dea ex machina*); while Hamlet is, in a sense, 'chosen' for his task, and must work out his own salvation, bearing the moral responsibility for his acts.

For all the eagerness with which the Elizabethan exploited the Senecan mode, in the new drama Roman Stoicism never overcame that sense of divine providence which biblical drama had established on the stage, and by the later dramas such as *Lear* the two had blended in the Christian Stoicism of Kent. The rebirth of drama within the Church had, from its very beginnings, the avowed aim of impressing audiences with the Doomsday which should decide how well they had hearkened to the message of the Crucifixion; and the religious drama of the Tudor era had transferred the emphasis to man's actions in this world and their place in the pattern of an orderly, just universe. Audiences and playwrights had come to expect the fall of villains, and the reward of the upright. As Cornwall plucks out Gloucester's eyes, the servant voices our own sentiments:

> *I'll never care what wickedness I do*
> *If this man come to good.*

and by the next scene Cornwall is dead. It was a feeling which had its roots in the drama of Shakespeare's predecessors.

Nor was this feeling confined to tragedy; for the parallels may be perceived even in so unlikely a play as Jonson's *Volpone*. In Italy, Machiavelli's *La Mandragola* had dealt with an almost identical theme – the young man eager to seduce a married woman and devising a trick to win the husband's approval. The

---

[1] *The Sense of History in Greek and Shakespearean Drama* (New York, 1960).

husband, led to believe that a fertility potion will kill the first man to sleep with her, gladly welcomes the suitor into his house and ushers him into his wife's bed. Our sympathies are with the suitor throughout, and the play ends with the amusing success of the ruse. In *Volpone* our sympathies are with the suitor and his Mosca no less, as they deceive with their gay resourcefulness the revolting carrion crows waiting for the pickings of Volpone's corpse. They too trick Corvino into ushering his pretty wife towards the bed of an apparently senile Volpone; but at that moment the two plays part ways. Instinctively, Jonson knows that he has gone as far as the English (predominantly Protestant) stage will allow him. That is not to suggest that he felt constrained. It may well be and, indeed, is more likely, that with his training on the English stage his own sentiments coincided with that desire for the visible punishment of immorality. At all events, at the risk of ruining the comic potentialities of his play, he brusquely transforms Volpone and Mosca into the villains of the piece, and concludes by condemning them both to cruel penalties far beyond the normal limits of the comic world. Only with the sharp break in stage tradition created by Restoration drama, partly imported from the Continent and partly reflecting the irreligion of a Hobbesian age, could comedy allow Mirabell to remain the hero after getting Mrs. Fainall with child and unconcernedly marrying her off to someone else. And even then, the temporarily submerged moral tradition was at work, soon to overthrow the Restoration drama through the attacks of Jeremy Collier, Richard Steele, and others. This Protestant sense of visible retribution had been too firmly established on the English stage to be suppressed for long.

(vi) The Dramatic Unities

A further divergence from the Senecan form lay in the Elizabethan rejection of the Three Unities. These had, of course, been wrongly attributed to Aristotle in Castelvetro's 1570 edition of the *Poetics*. Aristotle had merely demanded Unity of Action, suggesting Unity of Time in the general comment that 'tragedy endeavours, as far as possible, to confine itself to a single revolution of the sun, or but slightly to exceed this limit.' Greek drama frequently transgressed this latter rule, as in the *Eumenides*, the *Trachiniae* and the *Supplices*, while the Unity of Place, although generally observed on the Attic stage, was not even hinted at by Aristotle. But through Sidney and others, these Three Unities were vigorously defended as having been sanctioned by Aristotle, causing endless trouble and unnecessary concern to later dramatists, so that Corneille's kings had to receive ambassadors in their private rooms.[1]

Despite the bastard growth of the theory and the frequent transgressions within Greek drama, in fact Seneca followed the Unities closely, and the Elizabethan dramatist, modelling himself upon the Latin playwright, might well have been seriously inhibited by a set of Unities easier to observe in declamatory recitals (as Seneca's plays are assumed to be) than in actual presentation upon the stage. Yet *The Winter's Tale* spans intervals of many years, the Chorus of *Henry V* wafts his audience across the seas to Harfleur, and only the unity of action essential to all drama is consistently observed.

It would be foolish to suggest that Shakespeare consciously looked to biblical drama for guidance in the matter of the Unities; but tradition exerts a powerful force on men's minds, and it was through medieval scriptural drama that the traditions of the revived stage had been established. The focus upon eternity, as we have seen, telescoped the events of this world so that an interval of many years was but a passing moment. The concept 'A thousand years in thy sight are but as yesterday when it is past, and a watch in the night' made nonsense of the unity of time in a drama relating God's covenant with man; and a God 'who maketh the clouds his chariot and walketh upon the wings of the wind' made a journey from Palestine to Egypt seem merely a few steps across the stage. The Latin liturgical drama had moved round the 'stations' within the narrow confines of the Church, and the presentation of the play as a series of what I have termed 'stained-glass windows' established the technique of rudimentary signposting of locale adopted by the Elizabethan stage. Moreover, even in the more developed scriptural drama of the sixteenth century, the strict adherence to the biblical

[1] Sir Philip Sidney, *Apologie for Poetrie* (written 1580, published 1595).

story left little opportunity for compression into one or more of the Unities. If the Bible recorded that David had spied Bathsheba in Jerusalem, but conducted the operations against Absalom from Mahanaim, the dramatist could not make those convenient changes in locale common in the secular dramatist's treatment of Holinshed. Nor could he compress time, pretending that the incident with Bathsheba occurred on the same day as Absalom's revolt when the audience knew full well that the first child of their illicit union must be born and die before the revolt takes place. Not only did Shakespeare's transgression of the Senecan unities require no violent break with tradition, but in fact he merely followed an established precedent in ignoring them.[1]

Further, when Polonius informs Hamlet that the approaching players are the best actors in the world: 'either for tragedy, comedy, history, pastoral, pastoral-comical, historical-pastoral, tragical-historical, tragical-comical-historical-pastoral, scene individable or poem unlimited', he is (whether consciously or not)commenting not only on the rejection of the Unities implicit in 'scene individable or poem unlimited' but also on the break-up of the rigid classical genres separating, primarily, tragedy from comedy. The separation of the two is, indeed, natural, and their coalescence requires explanation rather more than their divorce. To this day, critics are divided over the validity of the theory of 'comic relief'. Whether the comedy be merely a minor element in a dominantly tragic play (in Shakespeare, usually reflecting the tragic theme, as in the graveyard scene from *Hamlet* or the Fool in *Lear*) or alternatively the major theme containing tragic elements (as in *The Merchant of Venice*) dramatic problems inevitably arise. Shakespeare's mastery of the stage turned a potential hindrance into a valuable device which has continued to be exploited fruitfully in our own day.

In the most recent full-length study of tragicomedy as a genre, Marvin T. Herrick passes in one enormous leap from classical times to the Christian Terence movement as if the medieval cycles had played no part in introducing this hybrid genre to the

---

[1] Willard Farnham's *Medieval Heritage of Elizabethan Tragedy* (Berkeley, 1936) is concerned with the debt to the moralities rather than the mysteries.

English stage.[1] But no historian can afford to ignore their contribution. Where, as in Greece and Rome, the stage had room both for comedy and tragedy, the two existed side by side in watertight compartments. At the Dionysiac festival, the dramatist was expected to offer a tragedy, a comedy or a satyr play, and mythologically each was the domain of a separate Muse. The satyr play seems to have contained some mingling of the two in its own separate genre but, since only one play of this type has survived, tragicomedy could not trace its source to the Greek stage. The arguments centring on Guarini at the end of the sixteenth century which tried to establish a classical source for tragicomedy were merely an unsuccessful attempt to find classical authority for a genre that had long been accepted on the contemporary stage, and did not, as Herrick suggests, reintroduce the fashion. For example, the Plautine use of the term *tragicomoedia* was eagerly seized upon as proof of classical sanction when in fact Plautus had merely used it jestingly in the prologue to his *Amphitruo* to excuse his introducing divine characters into the comedy itself. The Roman stage maintained a clear distinction between the two genres, and there is no trace of comedy in the sombre works of Seneca, nor of tragedy in the plays of Plautus and Terence.

The resurgence of drama within the medieval Church, however, left no room for comedy as a distinct genre. Religious plays had to justify themselves either as contributions to the liturgy or, later, by their dissemination of Christian doctrine and their strengthening of religious faith. But man's natural desire for comedy and burlesque, particularly among the unsophisticated audiences of the mystery plays, could not be long thwarted by such restrictions; and the humour which found no expression outside religious drama, was forced to find it within. Minor characters became comic without detracting from the overall seriousness of the drama, and the medieval audience saw no contradiction between the ribaldry of Noah's domestic strife and the divine covenant of the rainbow.

It was this which led to a confusion of terminology – a confusion never visible in classical literature. Dante applied the term *Commedia* to a work profoundly serious in tone but justify-

[1] *Tragicomedy: its origin and development in Italy, France, and England* (Urbana, 1955).

ing its title by the happy ending, and although the conclusion of a play became the generally accepted criterion for calling it a tragedy or comedy, the decision seems frequently to have been purely arbitrary. Bale entitled his *Temptacyon of Our Lorde* a comedy and *God's Promises* a tragedy, even though they probably form part of the same work. Bèze, despite the lack of any humour in his *Abraham Sacrifiant*, declared 'It is partly tragical and partly comicall . . . And because it holdeth more of the one than of the other; I thought best to name it a tragedie.' This confusion of terminology served at the same time as a convenient method of introducing humour to an otherwise tragic play, and by the time of Garter's *Susanna*, it was normal practice for a play to contain 'matter grave and sad' yet 'mixed with myrth'. Indeed, audiences had become accustomed to the mingling of the two and expected that the gravity of theme (which is, of course, present in all biblical drama) should be relieved by lighter touches. Although this mixture was paralleled on the continent too, the English love of compromise coupled with its dislike of excessive gravity (witness the 'babwyneries') had developed it much further. Elizabethan audiences did not feel it incongruous when Duncan's murder was followed by the coarse clowning of the Porter.

The Renaissance rejection of medievalism and, particularly, the English rejection of Catholic medievalism had removed from the Elizabethan stage many theatrical traditions established during the flowering of ecclesiastical drama. For this reason it was more indebted to the revenge motifs and rhetorical devices of Senecan tragedy. The Puritan attack upon drama had driven the playwright further into the secular world of classical history and mythology, and the growing fear of sacrilege had ensured that even the few dramatists who might otherwise have exploited biblical themes kept clear of holy ground. Shakespeare, of course, wrote no biblical plays and the religious themes in some of his plays escape identification until they are ferreted out.[1]

But no literary revolution, however radical, could tear out completely the traditions established on the stage during the previous four hundred years. The medieval disregard for unities of time and place gave to *Antony and Cleopatra* a grandeür and

---

[1] Cf. Barbara K. Lewalski, 'Biblical Allusion and Allegory in *The Merchant of Venice*', *SQ xiii* (1962), 327.

universality that swept the action back and forth over half the world. And that mingling of tragedy and comedy typical of all scriptural drama bequeathed to the Elizabethan stage a technical device which, in the hands of Shakespeare, invested his major tragedies with greater depth and subtlety. Shakespeare's debt to biblical drama is by no means as apparent as his debt to Seneca, but it helped in no small way to raise his own writings above the level of the somewhat frigid Latin plays.

CHAPTER IV

DRAMA WITHOUT A STAGE

(i) Pageants, Masques, and Drolls

More than three centuries were to pass before biblical drama reappeared on the professional stage in England. Included in the general ban on drama under Cromwell, it found no place in the Restoration theatre, which catered to a predominantly anti-Puritan audience antagonistic to anything resembling religious sermonizing. Moreover, the abrupt closure of the theatre by the Puritans consequent upon the vitriolic attacks of Prynne and others, had left the almost ineradicable impression on the English people that there was something inherently blasphemous in the dramatic presentation of biblical themes. Even the Englishman who continued to attend the theatre often did so with the conviction that he was risking eternal damnation. Pepys frequented the theatre '. . . against my judgement and conscience (which God forgive, for my heart knows that I offend God in breaking my vows herein).'[1] This assumption that biblical drama was unsuited to the professional stage was not paralleled on the continent where in France, for example, Racine's scriptural plays, written for the schoolgirls of Saint Cyr at Madame de Maintenon's request, were after Racine's death denied performance on the professional stage merely out of respect for the author's extreme religious views. On the death of Louis XIV who had imposed the ban, the plays were at once presented on the legitimate stage, *Athalie* appearing in 1716 and *Esther* in

---

[1] On attending a performance of Sir William D'Avenant's tragi-comedy, *Love and Honour*, on October 21st, 1661; *Diary*, ed. H. B. Wheatley (Boston/New York, 1893).

1721. In England, however, the prohibition of biblical drama was, until the nineteenth century, largely self-imposed as a restriction justified by the veneration due to Holy Writ. Nevertheless, the composition of biblical dramas did not cease, although they were no longer written with the intention of professional performance. Drolls[1] and puppet shows on biblical themes continued to draw crowds in the seventeenth century, and the following century saw an outcrop of generally pious compositions aimed not at the spectator but the reader.

The period of transition from Elizabeth to Cromwell produced only two works worthy of note, though not of more detailed examination. The first of these, the *Stonyhurst Pageants*, survived as an undated manuscript gathering dust in the library of Stonyhurst College, North Lancashire until unearthed by Carleton Brown and published by the Johns Hopkins Press in 1920 under his editorial supervision. On linguistic grounds, Professor Brown was able to establish 1625 as the *terminus ad quem* for its composition, while the indebtedness of the pageants to the Douai version of the Bible (1609–10) set the earlier limit to its dating. The use of the Douai version further indicates Catholic authorship (a fact not otherwise apparent in the text itself) and the stage directions of the plays make it clear that they were written for stage presentation. From this evidence it is not difficult to deduce that the pageants were written in England, probably by a Jesuit priest or novice, for performance by the pupils of the English college in France, or in the hope of the reopening of Jesuit schools in England. The presence of women among the *dramatis personae* is explained by the ruling issued from Rome in 1602 that women may be portrayed in school plays provided they be soberly and decorously presented.

Even in its present fragmentary form, its length (8,740 lines) exceeds the longest of the previous mystery cycles, and the ambitious project must be viewed as an attempt to provide a more modern version of those cycles which had only just ceased to be performed in England. But one change is significant – the pageants are devoted entirely to the Old Testament. Even if the missing continuation of the pageants had contained New Testament scenes, the total length of the cycle would have needed to reach inordinate proportions to maintain any balance between

[1] Comic sketches, often excerpted from longer plays.

the two sections. It would seem that the move from New Testament themes to those of the Old which dominated sixteenth-century biblical drama had made even this new Catholic mystery cycle omit the New Testament stories as ineligible for dramatic portrayal.

Moreover, the cycle, unlike its predecessors, is devoid of comic scenes. Even Balaam and his ass, who had rejoiced the hearts of previous audiences, disappeared as drama and their tale was recounted by the chorus. Thus the greater dramatic opportunity afforded by Old Testament themes was nullified by that augmented sanctity which precluded the possibility of ribaldry and humour. The result is a tedious and almost unrelieved work, rarely rising above the level of schoolboy drama.

Lest it be thought that biblical themes in this period always had so deadening an effect, it may be worth mentioning here that a contemporaneous masque entitled *Solomon and the Queen of Sheba*, performed before King James and the King of Denmark in 1607, ended in bacchanalian revelry. The revelry appears to have been induced less by the nature of the masque than by the condition of the performers and audience; for according to Sir John Harrington the pageant drew to a riotous close when the Danish King attempted to dance with the tipsy Queen of Sheba but was unable to keep his footing and fell sprawling to the floor.[1]

Nebuchadnezzars Fierie Furnace, a fragmentary manuscript of a political parody based upon the story of Shadrach, Meshach and Abednego, remains something of an enigma. Margarete Rösler has perceived in the versification and imagery such marked indebtedness to the style of Josuah Sylvester as to make ascription to him almost definite.[2] The play, with its tiresomely repetitive theme of the divine right of kings, reads today like an excerpt from a Gilbert and Sullivan opera, although its original intention was not, of course, comic. The most banal utterance of the king is acclaimed by the fawning courtiers, who

[1] M. S. Steele, *Plays and Masques at Court* (New Haven, 1926), p. 151.

[2] The play, edited by Margarete Rösler, was published in 1936 as volume xii of *Materials for the Study of the Old English Drama* (Louvain).

in turn sing praises to his wisdom and affirm their undying loyalty to the crown. Even the three dissenters who refuse to bow to the idol fervently declare their allegiance to the throne, an allegiance only exceeded by their obedience to the King of Kings.

It is unlikely that the theme of divine kingship was intended to refer directly to James I since it would have been, to say the least, an awkward compliment—the biblical story portrays Nebuchadnezzar as an idolatrous tyrant forced by a miracle to acknowledge his transgression. Since James had favoured Sylvester by appointing him groom of his son's chamber, we may assume that the author had no reason for attacking him even in so clumsy a fashion. In all probability, the author was merely recounting the biblical story in accordance with the current royalist views, and no specific allusion was intended.

Apart from these two manuscripts, no further plays on scriptural themes were published until after the Restoration. As was indicated earlier, drolls and puppet shows probably continued to employ such themes, although there is no definite evidence of the presentation of scriptural subject-matter during the Cromwellian period even in this stylized form. A droll on the subject of *Susannah* we know to have been popular at Bartholomew Fair during the seventeenth century (a reference to it appearing in an old song about the Fair) and one on the subject of Noah, entitled somewhat inaccurately, *The Creation of the World*.[1] John Locke records in a letter dated 1664 the performance of a droll at the same fair entitled *Judith and Holofernes*, which may be identical with the puppet play recorded by Pepys in the same year. At the end of the century, in 1698, a visiting Frenchman named Sorbière related how at Bartholomew Fair he found himself surrounded by 'a hundred People' crying 'Monsieur, See *Jephtha's Rash Vow*.'[2] The popularity of these simple playlets makes it likely that the tradition went back without interruption to the 'Motions' on scriptural themes which marked the end of the morality plays, particularly since the Puritans had no objection to watching puppet drama.

[1] E. D. Coleman, *The Bible in English Drama: an annotated list of plays* (New York, 1931), p. 92.
[2] H. Morley, *Memoirs of Bartholomew Fair* (London, 1880), p. 337.

(ii) Milton and the Stage

The religious dramatist of the early seventeenth century who might otherwise have been prompted to compose a drama upon a biblical theme had, as we have seen, found the most serious impediment within his own religious scruples. The Puritan himself had, with righteous zeal, torn down the playhouses as dens of iniquity. Yet, paradoxically enough, the most important biblical drama of this period and one of the most important in all such drama came from the pen of a dramatist who was both deeply religious and a leading Puritan. It is a paradox which can only be explained by that profound sense of spiritual isolation and individual responsibility which permeated Milton's life and writings.[1]

He was that strange mongrel, the Puritan humanist, and both as Puritan and humanist he insisted upon substituting for the theological authoritarianism of the church his own personal examination of scriptural and hermeneutical sources. For Milton, the risk of eternal damnation as a heretic was preferable to a timorous subservience to ecclesiastical dogma. Only by first-hand examination of sources could he determine his own religious doctrines, and the inevitable result was radical divergence not only in the question of divorce but also in fundamental points of faith. He abandoned the Calvinist doctrine of predestination, he denied the equality of Father and Son, he opposed the theory of *creatio ex nihilo*, and accepted 'mortalism'. These doctrinal divergences from accepted theological dogma he justified from his own reading of the Bible and of the numerous commentaries to which he had access in Buxtorf's edition of the Bomberg Bible and elsewhere.[2] But he chafed even under

[1] The numerous instances of such independence in Milton's life include his refusal to take holy orders in his youth because of his objection to episcopal authority and to the necessity of accepting the Thirty Nine Articles. The same individualism and sense of isolation is to be found in *Comus*, where the Lady stands utterly alone, and in *Samson Agonistes*, which presents a hero who finds neither comfort nor faith in the solicitations of his visitors, but must blaze his own path to spiritual regeneration.

[2] For Milton's use of Hebraic sources see below, particularly, the works by Fletcher and Saurat referred to. For his use of patristic

the authority of the biblical text, and before long found, in the 'variable guardianship' to which God had committed the text of the Bible, grounds for suspicion of its accuracy, which indicated that 'the Spirit which is given to us is a more certain guide than Scripture'.[1] Such intrepid independence of spirit lay behind his conviction, in the teeth of Puritan dogmatism, that music should be returned to the Church, poetry cultivated once more, and (what concerns us more closely) that drama, cleansed of its immorality, could be a valuable instrument for good.

In his early years, when the Puritan pamphleteers were fulminating against the contemporary stage and citing innumerable ecclesiastical authorities as proof that the theatre was intrinsically evil, Milton imperturbably attended the theatre both at Cambridge and, during his vacations, at London. In his *Elegia Prima* addressed to Charles Diodati he relates with enthusiasm how, when wearied of his books, '. . . the magnificence of the arched theater diverts me and the chattering actors invite me to applaud them. Sometimes the speaker is a shrewd old man, sometimes he is the wastrel heir, and sometimes the wooer. Or the soldier lays aside his helmet and appears, or the barrister who has fattened on a ten-year suit volleys his barbarous verbiage at an illiterate court-room.'[2] Although the plots and characterizations he describes suggest that he restricted his attendance to the academic exercises of the University students rather than to the stage proper, his sympathy for drama is apparent. No doubt the purely extraneous factors of the professional stage—such as its use as a place for assignations—discouraged him from attending; but in any case his warm approval of Shakespeare makes it likely that he had witnessed performances at first hand. He followed his epitaph to Shakespeare with a further tribute in *L'Allegro*:

writings and those of later Christian commentators see J. P. Pritchard, 'The Fathers of the Church in the Works of John Milton', *Classical Journal xxxiii* (1937/8), 79. The list of biblical commentators either cited or referred to in Milton's works is impressive.

[1] *De Doctrina Christiana*, in *Works*, Columbia ed., 20 vols. (New York, 1931–40), xvi, 279.

[2] Translation from Merritt Y. Hughes, *John Milton: Complete Poems and Major Prose* (New York, 1957), p. 8. The turgid translation of the Columbia edition is unquotable.

Milton and the Stage

Then to the well-trod stage anon,
If Jonsons *learned Sock be on,*
Or sweetest Shakespear *fancies childe,*
Warble his native Wood-notes wilde.

and a little earlier in the poem wrote with similar enthusiasm of the court masques:

There let Hymen oft appear
In Saffron robe, with Taper clear,
And pomp, and feast, and revelry,
With mask, and antique Pageantry,
Such sights as youthful Poets dream
On summer eeves by haunted stream.

He did more than dream of these masques, and both his *Arcades* and *Comus* were actually performed at Harefield and Ludlow Castle, the latter certainly and the former probably after the publication of William Prynne's vicious attack on the stage, the *Histriomastix*. His journey to Italy in 1638 brought him into contact with the thriving Italian stage, and, although the evidence is not conclusive, Voltaire maintained that, while there, Milton had watched a performance of Giovanni Battista Andreini's *Adamo* which helped to determine his choice of the theme for his own epic.

At all events, he was closely in touch with the theatrical world during these early years. By the time of his return, however, Milton's enthusiasm for the drama had been blunted, though by no means crushed; for the fury of the Puritan attack had not left him entirely untouched. He castigated the divinity students acting in University plays, who were 'seen so often upon the stage, writhing and unboning their clergy limbs to all the antic and dishonest gestures of Trinculoes, buffoons and bawds; prostituting the shame of that ministry which either they had or were nigh having, to the eyes of courtiers and court-ladies, with their grooms and mademoiselles.'[1] The attack is on the prostitution

---

[1] *An Apology for Smectymnuus* (1642). In this work, Milton answers the charge of having frequented playhouses by neatly sidestepping the issue. He claims that attendance at college exercises was sufficient to give him the knowledge of the stage which had provoked the charge, but he does not deny explicitly his attendance at the professional theatre. At this time it would have been impolitic to admit it.

of their holy calling rather than on drama itself, but at the same time the tone implies a general disapproval of buffoonery on the stage. The further, perhaps milder, implication that participation by divinity students in more seemly theatricals would not have profaned the holiness of their calling is borne out by his more explicit statement on the function of drama, published in the same year. Like the school of Elizabethan biblical dramatists discussed above, Milton saw nothing essentially immoral in the stage, and hence opposed its abolition; but he did demand 'eloquent and gracefull inticements to the love and practice of justice, temperance and fortitude . . . not only in Pulpits, but . . . at set and solemn Paneguries, in Theaters, porches, or what other place or way may win most upon the people to receiv at once both recreation & instruction'. Provided it performed a moral and didactic function, the theatre was in his eyes a noble vehicle for the artist, divinely sanctioned, as he pointed out on Origen's authority, by the presence in the scriptural canon of a pastoral drama, the *Song of Solomon*.

In a famous passage Milton debated whether to adopt the epic, lyric, or tragic form for his own projected work:

'Time serves not now and perhaps it might seem too profuse to give any certain account of what the mind at home in the spacious circuits of her musing hath liberty to propose to her self though of highest hope, and hardest attempting, whether that Epick form whereof the two poems of *Homer*, and those other two of *Virgil* and *Tasso* are a diffuse, and the book of *Job* a brief model. . . . Or whether those *Dramatik* constitutions, wherein *Sophocles* and *Euripides* raigne shall be found more doctrinal and exemplary to a Nation . . . Or if occasions shall lead to imitat those magnifick Odes and Hymns wherein *Pindarus* and *Callimachus* are in most things worthy.'[1]

Sir Arthur Quiller Couch, on the basis of Milton's interest in the stage, assumed that *Paradise Lost* was originally planned as a drama, and he explained the reasons for the change with the bold rhetorical flourish: 'I give you the answer to that in a dozen words. *In 1642 Parliament closed the Theatres; which remained*

---

[1] *Reason of Church Government*, Col. ed., iii, 240 and 237–8. Milton's definition of Job as an epic followed a lengthy tradition. For details, see Barbara K. Lewalski, *Milton's Brief Epic* (Providence/ London, 1966), pp. 10 f.

shut until the Restoration.' He added later that Milton planned to
reform the theatre with his own drama 'and behold! of a sudden
there was no theatre to reform'.[1] This, I believe, is an over-
simplification, the evidence being by no means as conclusive as
Quiller Couch suggests. There can be no doubt that in the early
plans Milton did consider very seriously the possibility of
composing *Paradise Lost* as a drama. But his final reasons for
the rejection of that form in favour of the epic included, besides
the physical closure of the theatres, his own growing suspicion
that the contemporary Puritan attack on the immorality of the
stage was not entirely unjustified.

The Trinity College manuscript, assigned by most scholars to
the years 1639–41, lists nearly a hundred possible subjects for
the projected tragedy, of which fifty-three were on Old Testament themes, eight on New Testament themes, and thirty-eight
on themes drawn from British history.[2] Of these only a few
consist of more than titles, and the fullest by far of the more
developed outlines is that devoted to the fall of man, of which
four drafts are included. Of some significance in this history of
scriptural drama is the greater emphasis upon the human
characters in these drafts as contrasted with their subordination
to Satan in the final epic form of the work. According to the most
elaborate of the four drafts:

'Adam then & Eve returne accuse one another but especially
Adam layes the blame to his wife, is stubborn in his offence
Justice appeares reason with him convinces him the chorus
admonisheth Adam, and bids him beware by Lucifers example
of impenitence . . . at last appeares Mercy comforts him promises
the Messiah, then calls in faith, hope & charity, instructs him
he repents gives god the glory, submitts to his penalty the
chorus briefly concludes.'[3]

[1] *Studies in Literature: Second Series* (Cambridge, 1923), pp. 140
and 146. Masson had suggested this with greater reservation in his
Life of Milton (London, 1880), vi, 663.
[2] The list is reprinted in Col. ed. xviii, 228 f. W. R. Parker, 'The
Trinity Manuscript and Milton's Plans for a Tragedy', *JEGP xxxiv*
(1935), 225, maintains that Milton could not have been considering
a tragedy rigidly adhering to the Greek form since the number of
characters in the more expanded topics transgressed the limits imposed
by Greek tragedy.
[3] Col. ed., xviii, 231–2.

The necessity in tragedy for fallible characters with whom the audience can feel some identity leads Milton instinctively to make Adam and Eve the central figures. Allegorically Adam is depicted as checking the injustice of his outburst against Eve, repenting, and resigning himself to his just punishment. The epic, on the other hand, demanded heroic characters (in the original 'demi-god' sense of the word), into which category Satan fitted far more easily.

A. H. Gilbert makes the point that the fortuitous survival of this manuscript detracts from the importance which should be attached to it, since Milton may well have made similar lists for projected epics or lyrics that have not survived.[1] While it is true that the list provides no proof that he was at this time thinking exclusively in terms of drama, his nephew Edward Phillips makes specific mention of Milton's work on a tragedy of the fall of man, which can be dated almost exactly to the time of the Trinity Manuscript. According to Phillips, Milton showed him 'several years before the Poem was begun' some verses describing the glories of the sun which were designed for the very beginning of the tragedy but were later incorporated into *Paradise Lost* (iv, 32–41). In Aubrey's memoir of Milton which preceded that of Phillips, the chronology is more exact, and the author quotes Phillips as placing the incident some fifteen or sixteen years before the poem was begun. This Masson shows to be about 1642, the year of the closure of the theatre and probably a year or two after the compilation of the list of projected tragedies.[2] Thus there can be no doubt that at this early stage Milton had actually begun composing a biblical drama on the theme of *Adam Unparadiz'd*.

Moreover, many of the models which are thought to have influenced Milton in his treatment of the subject-matter were themselves dramas. Andreini's *Adamo*, Vondel's *Lucifer* and, particularly, the *Adamus Exul* of Grotius (whom Milton met in Paris) may well have tempted him to turn to the tragic muse,[3]

---

[1] A. H. Gilbert, 'The Cambridge Manuscript and Milton's Plans for an Epic', *SP xvi* (1919), 172.

[2] Masson's edition of Milton's poems (London, 1882), ii, 20.

[3] The autobiographical nature of Grotius's drama, *Sophompaneas* (1635), provides an interesting continental parallel to that post-figurative sense of personal identification with biblical characters

while Du Bartas's pseudo-epic on the theme of the creation, translated by Sylvester in 1605 and enormously popular with the Protestants, may have helped to swing his final choice towards the epic.[1] Among other reasons suggested for the eventual selection of the epic, Saurat argues that Milton, as a man 'that could look evil in the face, see its force, its grandeur, its fascination even, and then judge, condemn and reject it', could find no way of introducing himself into a drama restricted to these few characters.[2] But it is a weak argument. *Samson Agonistes*, apart from the opportunity it offers for such identification, exploits the chorus for this purpose too, and to suggest, as Saurat does, that Milton had not yet discovered the trick of speaking through the chorus is unconvincing in the light of his excellent knowledge of Greek drama and the techniques it employed.

But whatever the reasons for Milton's final choice of the epic form, not least among them was the contemporary disrepute of the theatre. Repeatedly Milton refers to the tragedy of the Greeks as to something pure and untainted, and his close adherence to the Aristotelian rules in *Samson* testifies to the respect in which he held Greek drama.[3] In the period of Athens' greatest power, the theatre formed part of a religious ritual in which leading citizens participated and which brought honour and respect to its playwrights. Aeschylus, Sophocles, and Euripides were of noble family and in no way degraded by their theatrical associations, whereas in England contact with the professional stage in any capacity other than patron or spectator constituted a social stigma. When Shakespeare chose to become a respected citizen, he left the stage for his native

which found its English climax in *Samson Agonistes*. Grotius saw himself, a Dutchman entering the service of the Swedish throne, as Joseph about to aid his own people by working for a foreign power. The play, translated by Francis Goldsmith, was published in London in 1652.

[1] See G. C. Taylor, *Milton's Use of Du Bartas* (Cambridge, Mass., 1934), for a detailed examination of Milton's indebtedness to Sylvester's translation of the work.

[2] D. Saurat, *Milton, Man and Thinker* (London, 1944), p. 185.

[3] For articles discussing the Greek elements in the play see W. Brewer, 'Two Athenian Models for *Samson Agonistes*', *PMLA xlii* (1927), 910, and W. R. Parker, *Milton's Debt to Greek Tragedy in 'Samson Agonistes'* (Baltimore, 1937).

Stratford, breaking his association with the prostitutes, wastrels and tavern life of the contemporary stage. There was thus a distinction in Milton's mind between the noble tragedy of Athens and the less noble theatre of his own day:

> *Som time let Gorgeous Tragedy*
> *In Scepter'd Pall come sweeping by,*
> *Presenting* Thebs, *or* Pelops *line*
> *Or the tale of* Troy *divine*
> *Or what (though rare) of later age,*
> *Ennobled hath the Buskind stage.*[1]

The parenthesis suggests regret rather than condemnation, and his later return to the tragic form in *Samson* – though the purified Greek tragic form – probably at a time when the theatres had been reopened leaves little doubt that his choice was affected in some way by the state of the contemporary stage.

In a certain restricted sense, therefore, *Paradise Lost* may be regarded as a biblical drama radically transformed into an epic. This is not to suggest that the epic was, in the final analysis, a less appropriate choice for the subject-matter; but since it was originally conceived as a drama, some traces of dramatic technique are visible in the work. Merritt Hughes calls it 'an epic built out of dramas' and he notes further the way in which these dramas provide repeated contrasts with each other.[2] The council of hell in Book iii parodies the council of heaven in Book ii; Satan's assumption of power for his proposed seduction of man parallels Christ's assumption of power for his proposed redemption of man and, as Rajan notes, Satan, Sin and Death form an infernal counterpart to the Holy Trinity.[3] While not actually prefigurative, this double focus is an extension of the medieval technique of seeing in one story a mirror of another – a technique which had become indigenous to biblical exegesis and thereafter to biblical drama. Moreover, no clearer instance could be cited of the concept of divine justice in scriptural themes than this epic's simple acknowledgement of its lofty purpose – to 'justify the ways of God to men'. The entire work revolves

---

[1] *Il Penseroso*, Col. ed., i, 43.

[2] *ed. cit.*, p. 173.

[3] See B. Rajan, *'Paradise Lost', and the Seventeenth Century Reader* (London, 1947), p. 50.

around this weighty, didactic theme, the ultimate justice of God and his intimate concern with man's welfare. Even when expelled from the Garden of Eden, man and woman remain within his jurisdiction:

> *The World was all before them, where to choose*
> *Thir place of rest, and Providence thir guide.*

They must choose, but under the watchful eye of a benevolent heaven.

Similarly, the 'postfigurative' aspect of biblical drama, while not so apparent as in the true drama *Samson*, is nevertheless actively present in *Paradise Lost*. The transference of Milton's own rebelliousness to Satan and the consequent ennobling of the latter to heroic proportions in the early books, although, as Werblowsky argues, an almost inevitable result of the Christian conception of God as Love,[1] is also part of that emotional identification with biblical narrative fundamental to the Protestant tradition; and the topical allusions in the Council of Hell develop that postfiguration further.

But the most impressive identification of all is more general. It is Milton's adoption of the mantle of the biblical prophet who, unwaveringly certain of his election for a holy mission, speaks with the full authority of God in his condemnation of man's backslidings and his triumphant vindication of God's righteousness. Milton's choice of subject was one that would have intimidated a lesser man; yet his conviction that he and God stood together against Satan (for all his sympathy with that rebellious spirit) gave him the confidence to transgress the limits of orthodoxy. His invocation at the opening of the work is more than the conventional epic appeal to the muses. Conscious that he is embarking on things unattempted yet in Prose or Rhyme, he is yet confident that, with the aid of the divine Muse, he will succeed in 'asserting' Eternal Providence. Unlike the potential biblical dramatist of his day who had deserted biblical themes as

---

[1] R. J. Z. Werblowsky has pointed out that the Old Testament concept of Satan as part of the divine family, obtaining (as in *Job*) permission for his acts of temptation, changes when the New Testament identifies God as a Christ figure representing love and mercy, and stripped of martial power. The Promethean qualities of energy, progress, and stoical self-possession are thus transferred to Satan. See his *Lucifer and Prometheus* (London, 1952), p. 74.

too sacred for dramatization, Milton felt himself to be divinely chosen as the bearer of God's message to men. Like Isaiah who, in a vision of the heavenly court, had been the sole volunteer to win back the recalcitrant Israelites to God, so Milton, at a time when none dared to dramatize the Scriptures, chose the most challenging theme of all, the justification of divine dispensation through the theme of the Fall. What was originally conceived as drama eventually appeared as epic; but in *Samson* he recounted the same intimidating theme of divine justice dramatically, and this time in more personal terms. Both in the epics and in the drama Milton's greatest triumph is that he never falls below the soaring heights of his theme. No reader could seriously accuse him of profanity in the treatment of his scriptural figures; and what raises him to the level of his subject-matter is that burning conviction of personal election, that unshakable certainty of a divine call in the tradition of the biblical prophet.

(iii) 'Samson Agonistes'

Milton's choice of Attic tragedy as the model for *Samson Agonistes* made it abundantly clear that he had not intended it for stage performance in the public theatre of his day. Its publication together with *Paradise Regained* in 1671 has, with the lack of any further evidence, made it impossible to determine the date of composition, and scholars offer a range of possible dates from 1640 to 1670;[1] but whether or not the theatres had been reopened (or even yet closed) at the time it was composed, the rarefied atmosphere of Greek tragedy was not intended for the common people. Indeed, the space devoted in the preface to justification of its dramatic form on the autho-

---

[1] A. H. Gilbert, in *PQ xxviii* (1949), 98, suggests the 1640's, W. R. Parker in the same volume of the periodical (p. 164) puts it between 1647 and 1653, A. S. P. Woodhouse, in 'Samson Agonistes and Milton's Experience', *TRSC* 3rd series xliii (1949), 157, places it between 1660 and 1661, while Masson's earlier view had proposed 1666 to 1670. None of the evidence is more than circumstantial, but my own feeling is for a later date. See also Ernest Sirluck, 'Some Recent Changes in the Chronology of Milton's Poems', *JEGP lx* (1961), 749.

rity of St. Paul, Gregory Nazianzen, and others confirms the suspicion that Milton at this period felt qualms about writing a biblical drama even in so venerable a tradition as that of the Athenian stage; and he left no doubt of his opposition to its actual performance by his note: 'Division into Act and Scene referring chiefly to the Stage (to which this work was never intended) is here omitted.'

The choice of theme had been under consideration for many years. The Trinity College Manuscript had contained the brief entry:

(19.) Samson pursophorus or Hybristes, or Samson marriing or in Ramath Lechi Jud. 15.

(20.) Dagonalia. Jud. 16.[1]

But although five possible approaches had been suggested, all were left undeveloped, from which we may assume that the theme had not yet been considered very seriously. As Milton did not become blind until 1652, the close parallel which it was later to provide with his own life was not yet apparent. Nevertheless, the magnificent symbol offered by the story of Samson appealed to him even at this early date. In the *Reason of Church Government*, he described Charles I as a Nazarite Samson, educated in the precepts and practice of temperance, but laying his illustrious locks among the strumpet flatteries of prelates who wickedly shaved them off.[2] In the *Areopagitica* Samson appears again, this time representing the English people 'rousing herself like a strong man after sleep, and shaking her invincible locks',[3] and there were further references in *Iconoclastes* (1649), the *First Defence* (1651), and *Paradise Lost* (ix, 1059).

The attraction of the theme for Milton from the first was the duality of its symbolism, both aspects reflecting elements in his own religious philosophy which were enormously deepened by his later experiences. The overt theme of hirsute virility lost by the treachery of woman appealed, even in this primitive form, to that conviction of male superiority and feminine guile which Adam expressed so forcefully in *Paradise Lost*. It also provided divine support for his own views of chastity (hinted at in *Comus*) that even in marriage there was to be continence, reason, and suppression of lust. But the symbolic value of the

[1] Col. ed., xviii, 236. [2] Col. ed., iii, 276.
[3] Col. ed., iv, 344.

theme was greatly enhanced by its association with the Nazarite vows. The oath imposed on Samson's parents never to allow the razor to touch his hair was a visible affirmation of his election to the divine task of leading Israel. The hair, in accordance with biblical injunction,[1] itself became sanctified, to be dedicated in the flames of the altar on completion of the vow; and thus the loss of Samson's locks symbolized his own pollution, by surrender to physical lust, of his divinely appointed task.

Milton's Samson is, of course, a very different figure from the coarse braggart of the biblical narrative, but the transformation was achieved without straining or, indeed, even altering the original story in any significant detail. Even in assuming that Dalila was Samson's wife and not his mistress he merely adopted an ancient interpretation of a point unspecified in the Bible. But by emphasizing Samson's physical beauty, enlarging his intellect, and endowing him with a profound moral consciousness, Milton succeeded in elevating him to the dignity of a tragic hero.[2]

Krouse has argued with much learning that this transformation was not Milton's but that of the historical tradition which he inherited. Paul's *Epistle to the Hebrews* had numbered Samson among the Old Testament saints; Augustine's *Sermo de Samsone* had established allegorical parallels between Samson and Christ; medieval tradition had equated him with the classical Hercules; and the hermeneutical literature of the Church had followed Augustine's lead in pursuing Christological interpretations of the story. Moreover, the traditions established in English secular literature previous to Milton had done much to bestow heroic qualities upon the Old Testament champion. The *Cursor Mundi*, *The Monk's Tale*, the *Confessio Amantis* had all depicted him as a mighty figure brought low by female treachery, and this reading (which is, after all, the literal reading of the biblical text) was echoed in Burton's *Anatomy of Melancholy* and Spenser's *Faerie Queene*.[3] Krouse might have added the

[1] *Numbers* vi, 18.

[2] Cf. E. M. Clark, *Milton's Conception of Samson*, Texas University Studies in English viii (1928), 88–99.

[3] For details and further references see F. M. Krouse, *Milton's Samson and the Christian Tradition* (Princeton, 1949), particularly chapters iii and iv.

medieval proverb which forms part of the same tradition: 'Who was strenger than Sampson, wyser than Salomon, holyer than David? And ȝit they were al overcomen by the queryntise and whiles of women.'[1] But the very profusion of variant sources which Krouse adduces, both religious and secular, vitiates his own argument. In these manifold traditions, Samson was a Christ figure, a Herculean champion, a luster after women, a holy saint, a suicide, a martyr, an iconoclast, and much more. With such a plethora of interpretations to choose from, the credit of creating a figure so distinctly Miltonic as the hero of *Samson Agonistes* must finally belong to Milton himself.

To give but one example from the more contemporary versions of this complex tradition, Thomas Hayne's *General View of the Holy Scriptures* (1640) provided a diagrammatic tabulation of the parallels between Samson and Christ. These consist (I paraphrase) of Annunciation, Redemption, Triumph over Evil, Victory over the Enemies, Solitude, Betrayal, Binding, Entombment (in Gaza), and Martyrdom. The central parallel is, of course, the equation between Judas and Dalila, for in the biblical narrative this betrayal forms the climax of the story. Yet Milton rejects the parallel out of hand; for such an equation suggests that Samson is, like Christ, the innocent victim of treachery. In *Samson Agonistes*, the full burden of responsibility rests solely upon Samson himself, guilty of allowing physical desires to over-ride his spiritual dedication. To suggest, therefore, that Milton borrowed from these traditions more than the general elevation of the biblical figure to heroic proportions is to ignore the specifically original features of Milton's Samson.

Attempts are still being made by critics to identify Milton's Samson as a Christ figure. Scott-Craig feels that the true title of the drama is *Christus Agonistes* and he perceives in Manoa's pathetically futile attempt to ransom his son an 'ironic counter-theme' to the Christian redemption.[2] Samson, he maintains in another article, must be a Christ figure 'as practically everyone

---

[1] Quoted in G. R. Owst, *Literature and Pulpit in Medieval England* (Cambridge, 1933), p. 385.

[2] T. S. K. Scott-Craig, 'Miltonic Tragedy and Christian Vision', in N. A. Scott (ed.), *The Tragic Vision and the Christian Faith* (New York, 1957), p. 108.

from Jerome to John Donne and John Diodati agree'.[1] It is not difficult to cite medieval and Renaissance scholars who followed St. Ambrose in the view that *'Samson nascens, vivens et moriens Christum in plurimis exprimebat'*[2] but then almost every Old Testament character bearing the faintest resemblance to Christ —Noah, Isaac, Jacob, Jephthah—had been similarly equated. As long as both religious and secular literature preserved contrary traditions, there is not even a *prima facie* case for suspecting that Milton was relying on the Christological reading. True, Donne maintained that Samson died 'with the same zeal as Christ', but, on the other hand, John Lightfoot, in a sermon preached on *Judges* xi, 39, regarded his death as a clear case of suicide.[3] Even Krouse, who argues in favour of a Christological reading, admits that there is 'almost no vestige' of a Christ parallel in the play except as implicitly suggested by reliance on the tradition. The dangers of reading traditions into the play where there is no evidence to support such interpretation has been amply illustrated by a recent article which purports to see in the ransom scene of the play a figure of Socrates refusing to be ransomed by Crito.[4] If such interpretation has any validity—and I would admit some echo of a Christological identification—it is a matter of purely academic interest. Although the sacrificial and redemptive nature of Samson's death is vaguely evocative of the Crucifixion,[5] there is an enormous gulf between the altruistic purpose of the Crucifixion and the distinctly personal motive of Samson's vengeance. Christ's last words are to pity and beg forgiveness for his enemies, while Samson rejoices in their slaughter.

The subtle changes which Milton effected in Samson's character, while yet preserving fidelity to the original story, produced, then, a tragic figure specifically Miltonic not only in

[1] T. S. K. Scott-Craig, 'Concerning Milton's Samson', *RN* v (1952), 46–7.

[2] Quoted without source in W. Kirkconnell, 'Six Sixteenth-Century Forerunners of Milton's *Samson Agonistes*', *TRSC* 3rd series, xliii (1949), 73. He has an interesting collection and catalogue of analogues in his *That Invincible Samson* (Toronto, 1964).

[3] Krouse, p. 75.

[4] A. Gossman, 'Ransom in *Samson Agonistes*', *RN* xiii (1960), 11.

[5] Cf. D. Saurat, *Milton, Man and Thinker*, p. 238 and M. M. Ross, *Poetry and Dogma* (New Brunswick, 1954), p. 12.

its grandeur and inner struggle but also in its remarkable resemblance to Milton himself. The work can be read as a drama entirely dissociated from Milton's personal life; yet the points of contact are unmistakable. The tendency of modern scholarship has rightly been to view with suspicion Visiak's autobiographical interpretation of the play as *Milton Agonistes*. Yet with all due scholarly circumspection, the similarity in fundamentals, if not in detail, is too marked to be ignored. Milton shared with his Samson a bitter disillusionment arising from the triumph of his enemies, the treachery of a wife, and the dreadful affliction of blindness; above all both were obsessed by the need to reconcile their suffering with the doctrine of divine justice. And behind this sense of personal identification, more potent than any in the history of biblical drama before or since, lies a shift in the Protestant attitude to the ancient Hebrews peculiar to the political and religious state of contemporary England.

That sense of identity with Old Testament characters so typical of the Protestant Reformation had now been significantly deepened, producing distinctly philosemitic tendencies. The most striking of these concerned the ritual law. The mistrust of medieval Christian exegesis central to Puritanism and the re-examination of the biblical text which it demanded had led to the realization that nowhere in the New Testament was there any official abrogation of the ritual laws of the Old. Consequently doubts arose whether they ought ever to have been abrogated by the Church, and, indeed, whether the Church had the right to annul laws specified as divine in Holy Writ. Some Puritans began to practise circumcision (particularly since this constituted the mark of the covenant with the elect) and to observe the seventh day of the week as the Sabbath in accordance with the requirements of the Decalogue. In 1600, the Bishop of Exeter complained of the prevalence of 'Jewism' in his diocese,[1] and in 1624 James Whitewall of Christ Church, Oxford was one of many prosecuted for 'Judaistic' opinions, he himself being accused of teaching them as well.[2] The followers of the Puritan extremist, John Traske, were imprisoned between 1618 and 1620 for pursuing literalism to the extent of 'judaizing', and

[1] Cecil Roth, *A History of the Jews in England* (Oxford, 1949), p. 149.
[2] *State Papers, Domestic*, 1624, p. 435.

the validity of the accusation was confirmed when some of them, who later settled in Amsterdam, formally joined the local Synagogue.[1] In 1635, Mary Chester was ordered to be released from Bridewell on the condition that she acknowledge the error of her ways in adopting such Jewish practices as the dietary separation of meat from milk, and the observance of the Jewish Sabbath.[2]

The majority of Puritans did not, of course, go so far as to adopt these practices; but the very presence of the problem presented the 'Pharisaical' ritual of the Jews in a more favourable light, and their obstinacy in refusing to surrender it became regarded as a virtue rather than a vice. Moreover, this new sympathy for the contemporary Jews led to the hope that Christianity, purified of the 'superstitious' medievalism of the Catholic Church, might succeed in converting them where previous attempts had failed so lamentably. The multiplication of Christian sects in England promoted a demand for religious liberty of conscience, and the logical extension of such a claim was bound to include Jews too. The Baptists who pressed the demand most vehemently had their case presented in Leonard Busher's *Religions Peace, or, a Plea for Liberty of Conscience* (1614) which suggested that the exclusion of the Jews from England acted as an impediment to their conversion; and this was followed in the next year by a fellow Baptist's demand that Jews should be converted only by argument and never by force.[3] Such publications expressed a growing sympathy for the contemporary Jew, and the tide of pamphlets continued to rise. One particularly noteworthy example was Sir Henry Finch's treatise, *The World's Great Restauration* (London, 1621) for which he was thrown into jail, since it attempted to persuade the Jews to return to Palestine where they could receive the homage of the Christian world. Without requiring conversion as a prerequisite, he visualized the Jewish people who shall 'sit as a Lady in the mount of comelinesse, that hill of beautie, the true *Tsion* and heavenly *Ierusalem* to the worldes admiration'.[4]

---

[1] Roth, p. 149.

[2] *State Papers*, *Domestic*, 1635, pp. 111, 122, and 132.

[3] John Murton, *Objections answered by way of dialogue* . . . (1615).

[4] In the *Epistle Dedicatory* of the work. Cf. Rembrandt's sympathetic portraits both of Old Testament figures and of contemporary Jews.

It was a vastly different picture from that of the medieval usurer identified with Satan, and it parallels the shift from Marlowe's Barabas to Milton's Samson.

Furthermore, even those less eager to identify themselves with the Jews and their Old Testament traditions had a motive for extending a hand of friendship. The waves of false messianism which swept over Europe in the seventeenth century had touched off an enormous interest in the conditions to be fulfilled before the millennium, among which was the total dispersion of the Jews to the four corners of the Earth. Since the name 'Angleterre' suggested that England formed one of those corners, it was felt that the exclusion of the Jews was serving to delay the messianic era, and this fear formed the main platform for Menasseh ben Israel's *Spes Israelis* (1650). His subsequent visit to England aroused wide interest and the English version of his work contained a preface by its Christian translator which, after praising the breadth of the author's learning, added the significant comment that 'he may wel be set for a pattern to us Christians, who profess much better than he, but live much worse'.[1] By the 1660's Jews were being allowed to settle in the country, if not officially, then by silent consent.[2]

Milton, in the heart of the Puritan activity as Cromwell's Latin Secretary, was in close contact with this rising sympathy and, what was more important, with its source in the growing suspicion that the Old Testament, so far from being a Pharisaical document superseded by the New and sanctified only by its prefigurative elements, was a prelude to it whose validity may never have been annulled. And its effect upon Milton was intensified by his contact with the parallel movement, the recent revival of semitic and, more specifically, of rabbinic studies.

The mistrust with which medieval Catholic exegesis had come to be regarded by Protestants led not only to a re-examination at first hand of the biblical text itself, but also to a search for an alternative body of biblical commentary, to be found, of course,

---

[1] According to p. 61 of the work, the translator was Moses Wall.
[2] Cromwell had an additional motive for encouraging Jewish settlement since he made wide use of Jewish spies whose ease of access to Jewish communities abroad kept him fully informed of Charles' whereabouts. See Lucien Wolf, *Cromwell's Jewish Intelligencers* (London, 1891).

only among the rabbis. Kimchi and Ibn Ezra had, it is true, been occasionally referred to even by Catholic commentators of earlier centuries, but the main impetus for the close examination of Hebrew commentaries was the spate of biblical translation in the sixteenth century coupled with the need of the Protestant to substantiate his divergences from Catholic dogma. Erasmus, the Scaligers, and Isaac Casaubon began this revival of semitic studies, and they were soon followed by such brilliant Hebraists as the Buxtorfs, Cartwright, Drusius, Selden, Pococke, Whitgift and, indeed, Milton himself.[1] For these scholars the commentaries of the rabbis were not, as they had been regarded in the Middle Ages, deliberately corrupt,[2] but were now a more reliable link with the true traditions of biblical exegesis than the suspect commentaries of the Catholics. The elder Buxtorf, although always insistent in his desire to convert the Jews and not always sympathetic towards their customs, was on the warmest personal terms with the rabbis and other Jewish scholars of his community, whom he repeatedly consulted on matters of interpretation. On one occasion, he was even fined a hundred gulden for attending a circumcision in the home of a Jewish friend.

Milton's acquaintance with rabbinic writings, by allowing him to see the Old Testament figures through Jewish eyes, deepened the sense of identity he felt with them. Whatever Christological significance he might attach to them later, during the actual reading of the commentaries he saw these figures bare of typological connotations, as men of flesh and blood, triumphing in success or downcast by despair. Of all biblical drama composed during the preceding century, none overcomes completely that barrier of sanctity which prevents total identification between author and character. Bèze may feel deeply the similarity between his own exile and that of Abraham, but the analogy is confined to one restricted aspect of the patriarch's life. Similarly

[1] H. F. Fletcher, *Milton's Semitic Studies* (Chicago, 1926), and *Milton's Rabbinic Readings* (Urbana, 1930).

[2] As late as 1597 Hugh Broughton, one of the finest of Puritan biblical scholars and one excluded from appointment as a translator of the Authorized Version merely for personal reasons, stated in his *Epistle to the Learned Nobilitie of England* that 'bad Iewes invented all this disturbance of very malice'. See D. Daiches, *The King James Version*, p. 156.

Udall's identification of Henry VIII with Hezekiah is intended as little more than a graceful compliment to the king. But in *Samson Agonistes* Milton has so immersed himself in the biblical character that the drama is, in a sense, a catharsis for Milton even more than for the audience.[1] Poetry, Milton had maintained, has the power 'to allay the perturbations of the mind and set the affections in right tune'.[2] He may have intended this to apply to the reader, but it is even truer, particularly in this instance, of the poet.

We have noted that Milton altered little of the original story in adapting it to the dramatic form but, while preserving factual accuracy, transformed Samson from the vindictive and lustful braggart of the Scriptures into a tragic hero struggling to find the path to his own spiritual regeneration – a figure bearing a remarkable likeness to Milton himself. This is postfiguration carried to its fullest lengths. The biblical figure of Samson is translated into personal, contemporary terms to lend a vicarious sanctity to Milton's own sense of spiritual dedication. And such passionate identification could only be achieved when that mild disdain for the Old Testament Jews which predominated in medieval drama had been replaced in the Reformation by a new and deep respect for them as men closer to the purity of divine revelation than the saints and martyrs of the Catholic church.

Masson asks, perhaps a trifle naïvely, why Milton finally picked Samson as the theme for this play, when in 1640 it had merely been mentioned briefly in a lengthy list of possible themes.[3] But in 1640 Milton had not yet become blind, his first marriage had not been solemnized, and that bitter disillusionment with the political state of his country had not yet revealed the extent to which he could find in Samson a mirror of his own life. When it did, the 'idolatry' of the Philistines became for him a symbol of formal Christianity, both Catholic and Anglican, and the triumph of the God of Israel over Dagon was the longed-for victory of purified religion over the superstitious rites of the

---

[1] J. H. Hanford, *'Samson Agonistes* and Milton in Old Age', in *Studies in Shakespeare, Milton and Donne* (New York, 1925), p. 188, makes this point, developed in Woodhouse's article quoted above.

[2] *Reason of Church Government*, Col. ed., iii, 238.

[3] Introduction to *Samson Agonistes* in his edition of *Milton's Poetical Works* (London, 1882).

churches. That identification with the tradition of the biblical prophet apparent in his invocational opening to *Paradise Lost* takes on a more personal note when he visualizes himself in *Samson* as the divinely appointed champion, dedicated from birth to the fulfilment of his holy task. Visiak's identification of Harapha with Salmasius takes the autobiographical reading to extremes[1]; but there does emerge from the work Milton's own vision of Samson as typifying the validity of willed action and the rejection of Stoic passivity which is central to the drama itself.

Paradise Lost, although technically based upon Old Testament narrative, was, in fact, a reading through New Testament spectacles of the account of man's disobedience as related in *Genesis*. The Fall of Lucifer, Satan's determination to revenge himself, and the specifically Christian doctrine of original sin with its consequent need for redemption in the form of the Christian Messiah robbed Adam and Eve of their freedom of choice to a degree which left Milton, with his own insistence upon that freedom, in an anomalous position. On the one hand Adam and Eve fall entirely through their own weakness; yet on the other hand these puny, innocent creatures are pitted against the Arch Fiend, and act as pawns in a game between God and the Devil in the vast setting of heaven, hell, and eternity. Moreover, their fall had long been preordained, and Milton was conscious of the contradictions inherent in this position. God reassures his angels after the Fall with the reminder:

> *. . . When first this Tempter cross'd the Gulf from Hell.*
> *I told ye then he should prevail and speed*
> *On his bad Errand, Man should be seduc't*
> *And flatter'd out of all, believing lies*
> *Against his Maker; no Decree of mine*
> *Concurring to necessitate his Fall,*
> *Or touch with lightest moment of impulse*
> *His free Will, to her own inclining left*
> *In even scale.*[2]

But the scale is heavily weighted against Adam nonetheless. Moreover, obedient passivity is eulogized throughout. The only

---

[1] E. H. Visiak, *Milton Agonistes* (London, 1922), p. 99.
[2] *Paradise Lost*, Col. ed., ii, 306.

active participant is Satan himself, to whose flattery and specious logic Eve succumbs in a moment of weakness. *Paradise Regained* preaches a similar doctrine of passivity, Christ's refusal to be tempted by the devil paralleling man's fall.[1] Yet the implied contrast between Adam's weakness and Christ's triumph is essentially false, since both are in a sense preordained and hence non-volitional. Adam's fall is the corruption of the guileless mortal by the superhuman and almost invincible powers of evil, while Christ's triumph over temptation is the victory of the infallible Messiah and representative of heavenly goodness over the corrupt and damned Tempter of hell.[2] The opening of the poem, neatly adapting Paul's phraseology,[3] equates Adam and Christ by means of that misleading term *man*:

> *I who e're while the happy Garden sung,*
> *By one mans disobedience lost, now sing*
> *Recover'd Paradise to all mankind,*
> *By one mans firm obedience.*

But the one is man reduced to insignificance in the battle of heaven and hell, while the other is a heavenly creature merely clothed temporarily in mortal flesh.

In *Samson*, however, we enter the world of the Old Testament itself. Samson is a mortal, bearing upon his own shoulders the full responsibility for his actions. He has fallen entirely through his own weakness and his path to spiritual regeneration lies equally within his own power. 'Whom', he asks, 'have I to complain of but myself?' and however bitterly he may bemoan his lot, never does he conceal from himself his total responsibility for whatever has befallen him. Action has brought his downfall, but action too offers the means of personal redemption. Where Adam's redemption can be attained only vicariously through

---

[1] Cf. E. M. W. Tillyard, *Milton* (London, 1956), p. 328.

[2] Barbara K. Lewalski argues in 'Theme and Structure in *Paradise Regained*', *SP* lvii (1960), 186, that the three temptations mark Christ's progress from human uncertainty to a condition of perfect human freedom from enslavement to worldly desires. But even in the first stage Jesus is described as 'This perfect Man, by merit call'd my Son' (166), which suggests that his victory is never in doubt. On divine perfection, see Aquinas, *Summa Theol.*, i, iv.

[3] 'For as by one man's disobedience many were made sinners, so by the obedience of one shall many be made righteous.' Rom. v. 19.

Christ, Samson's is achieved by his own deliberate self-immolation.

(iv) SAMSON AND JOB

The apparently calm resignation of the opening lines

> *A little onward lend thy guiding hand*
> *To these dark steps, a little further on;*
> *For yonder bank hath choice of Sun or shade . . .*

has made it a commonplace of Miltonic criticism to assume that Stoicism forms a main, motivating force in the play, particularly since Tillyard's remarkable statement that by the very opening of the drama Samson 'has yet achieved his personal integrity. He has purged his pretensions by an utter humility and is content with his hard lot, however servile.' Tillyard summarized: 'That is Samson in his Protestant-Stoic citadel.'[1] But in fact that superficial calm of the play, its quiet opening reminiscent of Oedipus at Colonus, is shattered almost at once by Samson's bitter outburst against his own folly. A turmoil of crushed pride, self-condemnation, and longing for revenge is churning below the deceptively calm exterior and, as the play progresses, the surface too grows stormier, till he violently upbraids the treacherous Dalila, warning her not to approach

> *. . . lest fierce remembrance wake*
> *My sudden rage to tear thee joint by joint.*

That passion which underlies all Old Testament history – the denunciations by the prophets, the ecstatic paeans of the Psalmist, the desperate prayers for help in time of trouble – underlies this Old Testament drama too, despite its sophisticated Attic form. Calm of mind, as the closing line suggests, is to be achieved only when passion has been spent, and consequently the Stoic superiority to misfortune has little part in the play. As Milton himself put it elsewhere, Stoicism is the opposite to true patience 'as may be seen in Job and the other saints, when under the pressure of affliction'.[2] Man must bear full responsibility for his deeds, and the true patience of the Old Testament

---

[1] E. M. W. Tillyard, *The Miltonic Setting* (London, 1938), pp. 85–86.
[2] *De Doctrina Christiana*, Col. ed., xvii, 253.

is that which is realized not by blind submission to fate, but by wrestling with one's own soul until some reconciliation has been achieved between the grievous injustice apparent in the real world, and the believer's abiding sense of an overall equity not always visible to man. This contrast between the passivity of Christian Stoicism and the willed action of Old Testament narrative echoes the distinction noted earlier between the Senecan and Hebraic aspects of Shakespearean drama. In the same way as the fatalism inherent in Senecan Stoicism was there checked by the Hebraic sense of personal responsibility in a divinely organized world, so Milton's transition from the macrocosm of *Paradise Lost* to his study of Samson the man entailed a deeper sense of personal identity both with Samson and with the Old Testament setting of individual responsibility for sin.

Despite the acknowledgement by critics of Milton's debt to *Job* in this play in such minor matters as the visitation by the comforters, the profundity of that debt has, I believe, never been fully recognized.[1] Whether or not *Job* is a tragedy in any formal sense (and definition of genres is at best somewhat nebulous)[2] the materials of *Job* are essentially tragic. Tragedy demands above all a conflict between two irreconcilable sets of values, a protest against the apparent blindness of fate and a gradual if incomplete reconciliation with it, usually culminating in the purgative death of the hero. Job does not die and is, of course, fully reconciled with heaven in the final scene; but the first thirty-seven chapters suit the tragic situation ideally. The Bible, with its absolute set of values, might appear to offer no

---

[1] Ann Gossman, 'Samson, Job, and "The Exercise of Saints" ', *ES xlv* (1964), 212, goes furthest in acknowledging the relationship. But she argues for an additional identification – 'implied rather than stated' – of Samson as a Christ and saint figure; and there, of course, our paths part. See also H. Fisch, *Jerusalem and Albion* (London, 1964), p. 145.

[2] Although generally termed an epic in patristic literature, it was also often regarded as a drama or tragedy. In 1918, Horace M. Kallen's *The Book of Job as Greek Tragedy* presented it as Attic drama. His theory, together with a similar theory by R. G. Moulton, was effectively dismissed by Morris Jastrow, *The Book of Job: its origin, growth and interpretation* (Philadelphia, 1920), which denied that the book as it stands is dramatic in form but suggested that the situation and development of plot may be.

possibility of inner conflict, and George Steiner, maintaining that 'tragedy is alien to the Judaic sense of the world', places *Job* on 'the outer edge' of Judaism.[1] It is an attractive theory because the lines of demarcation seem so clean. The Bible insists on the unfailing justice of heaven; *ergo* any tragic sense of heavenly injustice is excluded. But tragedy concerns itself not with philosophical systems but with the agony of an individual at the moment of his dilemma. There are no perfect Jews in the Old Testament, no saints to epitomize the ideal religious standpoint. Stunned by catastrophe, a man's instinctive response is to protest and challenge no matter how deep his faith. If it be deep and strong he will, after that initial protest, painfully come to terms with his fate, and only a haloed figure seen retrospectively smiles beatifically at the moment of spiritual torture. If the Jobian predicament lies outside the Judaic and, more specifically the Old Testament tradition, how are we to read Abraham's incredulous plea for Sodom: 'Wilt thou also destroy the righteous with the wicked?' or the bitter cry so often heard in *Psalms*: 'O God, why hast thou cast us off for ever? why doth thine anger smoke against the sheep of thy pasture?'

There is, I believe, no tragedy in the Bible which conforms to the Greek or Shakespearean pattern—nor, indeed, is there any drama in the technical sense of the word, since Job is narrative and the *Song of Songs* is a series of lyrical monologues. But we should beware of denying to the scriptural figures the possibility of tragic dilemma and protest on the grounds of the theological framework of the Bible as a whole. On the same principle, the climactic tragedy of Christian history, the Crucifixion, might be denied its tragic quality on the grounds that Jesus was a divine figure merely shedding his mortal clothing in the interests of mankind. Theologically that may be so; but what are we to make of his agonized cry quoting the words of the Psalmist: 'My God, my God, why hast thou forsaken me?' It was the very duality of the mortal and immortal within him which impressed the Christian world with a sense of his human suffering.[2] And one strand of this present study traces how those periods more

[1] George Steiner, *The Death of Tragedy* (New York, 1966), p. 4.

[2] For a valuable discussion of the specifically Christian view of tragedy, see Nathan A. Scott, Jr., *The Broken Center* (New Haven, 1966), pp. 135 f.

concerned with Jesus as a mortal than as a god substituted for the earlier stylization of Christ a more tragic concept of the *man born to be king*.

Job, then, momentarily shattered by his unexpected suffering, hears his own inner voice speak through his wife's lips: 'Curse God, and die!'; but he longs for a solution which will reconfirm his faith in the ultimate justice of the world. The so-called 'comfort' offered by his visitors is shallow and unsatisfying, for however involved and casuistic it becomes, its starting-point is the conviction that all suffering in this world is meted out with scrupulous attention to desert. The more he argues, the more deeply he sinks into that very disbelief which his soul abhors. One part of him proclaims: 'Behold I cry out of wrong, but I am not heard: I cry aloud, but there is no judgment,' while the other maintains with triumphant conviction: 'I know that my Redeemer liveth, and that he shall stand at the latter day upon the earth.' At this point, when he has reached the zenith of religious faith and the nadir of religious doubt, when his soul is being torn in two, God speaks from the whirlwind to remind Job that man is not God, able to bind the sweet influence of Pleiades or loose the bands of Orion; that the inequalities of this world are an indication not of a purposeless creation but of the limits to man's understanding. The bitter conflict is not resolved by denying reality but by assuring man of an ultimate justice not apparent to his limited comprehension, of a justice which weighs with care the deeds of mortals created in the image of God. Job, having in all sincerity risen to challenge God as an equal, is gently reminded of his presumptuousness, calmed like a fretful child, and rewarded for the faith which prompted him to justify the ways of God to men at the risk of his own soul.

That same inner conflict between belief in God's justice and the conviction that his own suffering outweighed his deserts permeates *Samson Agonistes* and constitutes the essence of the tragedy, the very title connoting inner agony as well as championship.[1] Milton's other writings had prepared the way. Refusing to accept the ancient view that Teiresias had been deprived of his sight as a punishment for divulging Jove's

---

[1] Krouse traces this connotation to medieval sources, such as Irenaeus's description of St. Paul as *bonus agonista* (pp. 108 f.). See also Paul R. Sellin, 'Milton's Epithet *Agonistes*', *SEL iv* (1964), 137.

secrets, he asserted with empathic relevance to his own position that the loss of sight which '. . . this inspired sage, who was so eager in promoting knowledge among men, sustained, cannot be considered as a judicial punishment'.[1] In the sonnet he composed on his own blindness, one detects beneath the apparently calm exterior a desperate longing to reconcile himself to an undeserved fate; but in *Samson* the bitterness of his complaint erupts through that determination to accept with pious resignation the decision of a totally just God.

As he gropes his way towards the cool, shady bank, we learn that the shade will only provide

> *Ease to the body some, none to the mind*
> *From restless thoughts, that like a deadly swarm*
> *Of Hornets arm'd, no sooner found alone,*
> *But rush upon me thronging.*

In *Job,* question after question, each cutting close to the roots of religious faith, expresses the book's passionate search for truth at all costs. 'Why died I not from the womb? Why did I not give up the ghost when I came out of the belly? . . . Wherefore is light given to him that is in misery, and life unto the bitter in soul? . . . Why is light given to man whose way is hid, and whom God hath hedged in?' Yet however radical the questions, they never cross the bounds of blasphemy; for the deep faith which both prompts the questioning and hopes for eventual satisfaction keeps them in check. His first utterance tersely suggests that tension between protest and faith. We have watched the advent of disaster after disaster, his wife has urged him to curse God and die, he has sat brooding and grieving in ominous silence and at last he opens his mouth to speak.

> *After this opened Job his mouth, and cursed . . .*

For a moment it seems that he will curse God after all. But the verse concludes by harmlessly deflecting the curse against himself:

> *. . . and cursed his day.*

Samson begins with the same series of passionate questions:

---

[1] *Second Defence*, Col. ed., viii, 63–65.

> *O wherefore was my birth from Heaven foretold . . .?*
> *Why was my breeding order'd and prescrib'd . . .?*
> *Why am I thus bereav'd thy prime decree . . .?*
> *. . . why was the sight*
> *To such a tender ball as th' eye confin'd?*

and at each stage the questions are checked or deflected against himself as Samson realizes their implications:

> *Yet stay, let me not rashly call in doubt*
> *Divine Prediction.*

and:

> *But peace, I must not quarrel with the will*
> *Of highest dispensation, which herein*
> *Happ'ly had ends above my reach to know.*

His more sober judgement tells him that his passionate outbursts are rash; and the clash here between reason and emotion is, in fact, the Jobian clash between a longing for theodical affirmation and the dreadful suspicion that theodicy is merely a figment of the imagination. On the one hand he affirms:

> *Whom have I to complain of but myself?*

yet a moment later, in a passage vibrant with emotion, he complains of that loss of sight which has made him inferior to the vilest, and he looses a veritable fusillade of bitter questionings. If A. S. P. Woodhouse has rightly pointed to the play's Christian rather than Hellenic insistence on willed action, his argument that: 'From the conviction of his own responsibility Samson never wavers' is surely untenable once this agonizing spiritual dichotomy has been perceived.[1]

The partially autobiographical reading of *Samson Agonistes* which gives increased force to this Jobian interpretation of the play has been rejected by C. B. Tinker and others because of the absence in Milton's own life of any crime paralleling Samson's betrayal of his sacred trust.[2] To the best of our knowledge he never consciously violated the ideals to which he had dedicated

[1] A. S. P. Woodhouse, 'Tragic Effect in *Samson Agonistes*', *UTQ* xxviii (1958/9), 205.

[2] In *Tragic Themes in Western Literature*, ed. Cleanth Brooks (New Haven, 1955).

his life. But the answer lies within this Jobian interpretation. If we recall that deep-rooted Protestant need to discover in the world around, including the world of material wealth, tangible evidence of blessing at the hand of God, we are at once faced by a Milton at one level convinced that his suffering is undeserved, but at another searching into his own conscience for some faint hint of that sin which would alone justify his grievous punishment. At the latter level, he is forced to consider, if only momentarily, that 'weakness' which we know formed a central paradox within his own life – the eternal contradiction between his idealistic ennobling of wedded bliss and his disgust at the physical 'lust' it inevitably involved. Nowhere does he betray this more clearly than in Book ix of *Paradise Lost*, where before the act of love woman is beautiful, innocent, and pure:

> *But come, so well refresh't, now let us play,*
> *As meet is, after such delicious Fare:*
> *For never did thy Beauty since the day*
> *I saw thee first and wedded thee, adorn'd*
> *With all perfections, so inflame my sense*
> *With ardor to enjoy thee, fairer now*
> *Than ever.*

But satiated, Adam is filled with the 'guilty shame' of Samson:

> *So rose the* Danite *strong*
> Herculean Sampson, *from the Harlot-lap*
> *Of* Philistean Dalilah, *and wak'd*
> *Shorn of his strength.*

In a moment the beautiful Eve has become a harlot, and it is her fault that Adam was roused by her beauty. In that context, is it so strange that the ascetic Milton, committed from his youth to scorning delights and living laborious days, should unconsciously endow his dramatic hero with that very sin of which he did not feel entirely guiltless – particularly when such sublimation allowed him in Samson's guise momentarily to transfer the ultimate responsibility to the blandishments of treacherous woman:

> *. . . into the snare I fell*
> *Of fair fallacious looks, venereal trains,*
> *Softn'd with pleasure and voluptuous life.*

The parallels should not be pressed too far – an artist need not be autobiographical in order to express the problems and suffering of his own being; but that intense yearning for truth and spiritual regeneration which motivates the play has too personal a ring to be divorced from Milton's own life. And seen as a partial projection of his own agony, the play's true impetus can be related more closely to that urgent postfigurative identification with Old Testament characters which formed so central a part of the new Protestant typology.

In the twentieth century we have, perhaps, a predisposition to dismiss as slightly absurd the guilt felt by a man whose wife attracts him physically. But two historical factors should not be forgotten. First, that for all the iconoclastic vigour of the Reformation, there was still a strong vein of medievalism within the Calvinist conscience, and the stern maxim *omnis ardentior amator propriae uxoris adulter est* ('any man too passionately in love with his own wife is an adulterer') had not been entirely eradicated. Secondly, it would be fallacious to ignore the biblical insistence that authority, notably when divinely delegated, carried with it enormous responsibility. Samson's surrender to feminine charms might today be regarded as a venial sin; but so would Moses' striking of the rock for which he was denied entry into the Promised Land, or Saul's compassion towards Agag for which he was deprived of the hereditary monarchy. Milton's concern was less with Samson's 'lot unfortunate in nuptial choice' than with the profanation of 'the mystery of God giv'n ... under pledge/Of vow' which such unfortunate choice involved. For that, as Samson repeatedly insists, there can be no excuse. He reminds Dalila:

> *All wickedness is weakness: that plea therefore*
> *With God or Man will gain thee no remission.*

but he was honest enough to apply the same principle to his own weakness too.

This theme of profaned vocation is brilliantly suggested in the play by Milton's distinction between *service, servitude,* and *servility.* This is not mere word-play, but a Mannerist sense of meaningful ambivalence stemming from the Hebrew sources with which he was familiar. In the Hebrew Bible, *'avodah* ('service') in isolation denotes the purity of Temple worship, but in conjunction with *zarah* ('foreign') is transformed to mean idolatry and hence whoring after strange gods and strange women; the word *'eved* ('slave') is a derivative. For Milton, then, to serve truly was to submit to no yoke other than that of the King of Kings; and servitude to woman constituted idolatry, leading appropriately enough to physical enslavement at Gaza:

> *. . . foul effeminacy held me yok't*
> *Her* Bond-slave; *O indignity, O blot*
> *To Honour and Religion!* servil mind
> Rewarded well with servil punishment!
> *The base degree to which I now am fall'n*
> *These rags, this grinding, is not yet so base*
> *As was my former* servitude, *ignoble*
> *Unmanly, ignominious, infamous*
> True slavery, *and that blindness worse than this*
> *That saw not how degeneratly I* serv'd.

Throughout the play this ignoble service to idolatrous powers is contrasted with the noble service to which he was originally dedicated:

> *Now blind, disheartn'd, sham'd, dishonour'd, quell'd,*
> *To what can I be useful, wherein* serve
> *My Nation and the work from Heav'n impos'd*
> *Here rather let me drudge and earn my bread,*
> *Till vermin or the draff of* servil *food*
> *Consume me . . .*

But Manoa reminds him that only by spurning such servility will he achieve the regeneration of a return to the true service of God.[1] With this encouragement, Samson moves through his remorse towards those 'rousing motions' which inform him that he has yet 'some great service' to perform whereby he will atone for his violated vow. The ignominy which he brought upon himself has been cancelled by his last great mustering of strength whereby he razes the temple of the idolaters, symbolically purging away the idolatrous taint of Dalila. His death, as in all great tragedy, marks a reconciliation with the powers that be, with the heavens which have generously granted him the opportunity for one final act of atonement:

[1] Col. ed., i, 351 and 357. The emphasis is mine.

. . . but death who sets all free
Hath paid his ransom now and full discharge.

The passion has been spent, the calm of mind achieved; and like
Job he has struggled through protest and bitter complaint to
perception of that order within the universe which is so often
obscured:

> *All is best, though we oft doubt,*
> *What the unsearchable dispose*
> *Of highest wisdom brings about,*
> *And ever best found in the close.*
> *Oft he seems to hide his face,*
> *But unexpectedly returns*
> *And to his faithful Champion hath in place*
> *Bore witness gloriously.*

There is an echo here of the didactic close traditional in biblical
drama; but it is more subtle. The term 'faithful Champion' is
not intended ironically. Unlike Abraham, Samson has sinned
grievously and betrayed his trust: but through the agony of his
spiritual odyssey he has achieved at last re-acceptance into the
covenant of the faithful. In its concern with that covenant, in its
intense postfigurative identification with the Old Testament
setting, with the fallibility but undimmed moral vision of its
characters, *Samson Agonistes* marks the finest flowering of the
Protestant biblical drama.

(v) THE JOSEPHUS PLAYS

The reopening of the theatre at the Restoration saw a revival
of that pseudo-biblical drama of which the plays by Lady Carew,
by Markham and Sampson, and by Massinger had set an
example. The importation from French romances of impossibly
noble heroes and exceedingly virtuous heroines caught in the
toils of lecherous villains had, together with the audience's
desire for lavish settings of oriental splendour, made it convenient to choose plots from the stirring historical adventures
of foreign tyrants and princesses. For this, the themes of
Mariamne and of the destruction of Jerusalem were ideal, since,

in addition to fulfilling these requirements, their slight biblical association served automatically to increase the grandeur of the heroes and to prepare the audience for events of spectacular magnitude.

The first to be performed was Samuel Pordage's *Herod and Mariamne*, produced in 1673, probably at Dorset Garden. By furnishing Mariamne with a noble lover (for whom there was no historical foundation), the author provided that four-cornered overlapping of triangles so beloved by the French. Herod, enamoured of Mariamne, is jealous of Tyridates; while Salome, enamoured of Tyridates, is jealous of Mariamne. The two noble, if illicit, lovers meet their gory deaths together with the villains, the male rivals swearing with their final breath to continue the duel in ghostly form. Perhaps the wisest critical comment was the earliest. According to literary gossip, Pordage, having left the manuscript with the Earl of Rochester in the hope of obtaining his patronage, returned a week later to find scrawled across its cover:

> *Poet who e'er thou art, God damn Thee.*
> *Go hang thy self, and burn Thy Mariamne.*[1]

Roger Boyle, the Earl of Orrery, who first popularized the rhymed heroic tragedies copied from France, was, as the comparatively recent discovery of an unsigned letter has shown, prevented by a series of misfortunes from either producing or publishing his own *Herod the Great*, although it was printed posthumously in 1694. The Theatre Royal was gutted by fire just before his play was due to appear, and the subsequent staging of Pordage's play made Boyle's superfluous.[2] The loss to the English stage was not great, nor, indeed, did any of these Josephus plays rise above the mediocre, probably because they were pandering to popular taste. Both parts of John Crowne's *Destruction of Jerusalem* (1677) achieved a phenomenal contemporary success, which can only be attributed to the lavish décor and the sensational scenic devices that it employed. The text

---

[1] Quoted in W. S. Clark, 'Pordage's *Herod and Mariamne*', *RES v* (1929), 61, which defends Dorset Garden as the place of first performance against Allardyce Nicoll's claim for Lincoln's Inn Fields.

[2] W. S. Clark, 'The Published but Unacted Plays of Roger Boyle', *RES ii* (1926).

itself, leaning heavily on Dryden's *Conquest of Granada* and Racine's *Berenice*, has little to recommend it to the modern reader. Otway's *Titus and Berenice*, acted at the Duke Theatre in 1677 and, like Crowne's play which it rivalled, derived largely from Racine, was (understandably) never revived after its initial performance. In fact, this sudden interest in Josephus plays seems to have created some theatrical congestion. In the same way as Boyle's drama had been forced off the stage by Pordage's, so Crowne was compelled to transfer his play from the Duke's Theatre to the Theatre Royal since the former had already accepted Otway's *Titus and Berenice*.[1] The sole member of this group to deserve some of its success was the somewhat later *Mariamne* (1723) by Elijah Fenton which, although only mildly superior, treated the theme with more sympathy and gentleness than its predecessors. The author, more widely known today for his collaboration with Pope over the translation of Homer, is said to have netted a profit of over one thousand pounds from the performance of this play.[2] Apart from Francis Peck's dramatic poem of 1740 and one negligible tragedy published in 1839,[3] this marked the end of the Mariamne plays until Stephen Phillips' drama of 1900. Josephus's account of the destruction of Jerusalem continued to be dramatized, notably by Mary Latter in 1763, by Mary Eleanor Bowes, Countess of Strathmore, in 1774, and by Henry Hart Milman in 1820.

(vi) DRYDEN'S 'STATE OF INNOCENCE'

The sidelight which Dryden's poem *Absalom and Achitophel* sheds upon seventeenth-century veneration for biblical and

---

[1] A. F. White, *John Crowne: His Life and Dramatic Works* (Cleveland, 1922), p. 35.

[2] E. Harlan, *Elijah Fenton* (Philadelphia, 1937), pp. 115–16. Both Allardyce Nicoll, *History of English Drama* (Cambridge, 1952), ii, 436, and M. J. Valency, *Tragedies of Herod and Mariamne* (New York, 1940), mention the indebtedness of Fenton's play to Voltaire's *Mariamne*; but the latter was first published in 1724 and Fenton's produced in 1723 and neither author suggests that Fenton had sight of Voltaire's manuscript before publication.

[3] William Waller's *Mariamne*. Henry Solly's *Herod the Great* (1896) is not a Mariamne play but an attempt to defend Herod against Josephus's unflattering picture of him.

pseudo-biblical characters justifies a momentary digression, even though it is non-dramatic. The poetic exploration of scriptural parallels for the purpose of political polemic had reached a high level of ingenuity long before Dryden's day, and even the equation of the English King with David and of his false counsellors with Achitophel had a long history among the Puritan pamphleteers before Dryden borrowed it.[1] But Dryden's treatment of the theme is more remarkable for its innovations than for its similarities.

The fourth book of Cowley's *Davideis*, for example, is patently a defence of the Commonwealth against the growing desire for restoration of the monarchy. Samuel rejects the people's plea for a king with the scornful reminder:

> *Cheat not your selves with* words: *for though a* King
> *Be the mild Name, a Tyrant is the Thing.*

The sincerity of Cowley's republicanism retrospectively became suspect when he subsequently supported Charles II; but the reiterated emphasis in this poem on the sacredness of the theme leaves little doubt that, at least while he was composing it, he was fully committed to the republican cause. His note on this couplet displays a bitter antipathy to the Royalists:

'It is a vile opinion of those men, and might be punished without Tyranny, if they teach it, who hold, that the *right* of Kings is set down by *Samuel* in this place.'

Samuel's outburst is followed, as in the biblical text, by the voice of God himself castigating the people for their implied dissatisfaction with the King of Kings, and warning them of the abuses attendant upon a monarchy. Throughout, Cowley is at pains to stress the divine sanction for his poetic message. The subtitle reads *A Sacred Poem of the Troubles of David*, and the lengthy invocation, addressed not to the Muse but to Christ himself, proclaims the holy task to which the poet has been called:

> *But* Thou, *Eternal Word, has call'd forth* Me
> *Th' Apostle, to convert that* World *to* Thee.

---

[1] A. H. Nethercot, *Abraham Cowley: the Muse's Hannibal* (Oxford, 1931), p. 154, traces some of the earlier examples. See also R. F. Jones, 'The Originality of *Absalom and Achitophel*', *MLN xlvi* (1931), 211.

Dryden's State of Innocence

Like his predecessors in this form of polemic, Cowley finds in his use of the biblical theme a vicarious sanctity, suggesting in the postfigurative tradition that the archetypal story of the Israelite kings will be cyclically repeated in his own era.

Dryden's poem has no such fervour. It is detached, sardonic, and devoid of religious veneration, deliberately verging at times upon the blasphemous. Absalom's birth, recounted in the lines:

> *Whether, inspir'd by some diviner Lust,*
> *His Father got him with a greater Gust.*

presents an incongruous picture of divine participation in human affairs, and there is a note of cynicism in the wry comment:

> *But Life can never be sincerely blest:*
> *Heaven punishes the bad and proves the best.*

In effect, Dryden was merely using the biblical text as a novel alternative to classical mythology. It was novel in that his use of it was as free from religious connotations as his use of the pagan works of Greece and Rome. The neo-classical flair for translating contemporary events into mythological terms was now being applied to scriptural 'mythology', and it is significant that this application could not have been successfully attempted any earlier in English history; for the wit involved in such identification demands from the reader a ready familiarity with the details of the original story. In the Middle Ages even the more educated layman interested in religious matters had only the sketchiest knowledge of the Scriptures, and that culled mainly at second hand from paintings, sermons, and plays. Only after the publication of the English Bibles and the intense seventeenth-century interest in biblical study could an author assume on the part of his readers a detailed knowledge of Holy Writ. But piety forbade its exploitation for purposes other than religious until the neo-classical cultivation of a religion free from enthusiasm made permissible the use of biblical parallels for entirely secular purposes.

Although Dryden's poem is, in a sense, an extension of 'postfiguration', it marks a radical departure from earlier traditions. Even Milton's *Samson*, published only a decade before *Absalom and Achitophel*, had preserved the main motivation behind both prefigurative and postfigurative readings. Past, present, and future were envisaged as parts of the enormous sweep of history, moving inevitably towards the fulfilment of divine destiny and repeating within each generation the eternal stories of man's struggles embodied in the biblical 'figures' or 'types'. Adam and Noah were at the same time historical figures, 'types' of Christ, and symbols of the whole of mankind. The ability to see within one's own life the pattern of a biblical figure gave a sense of individual destiny, an increased importance in the scheme of universal history. By visualizing himself even subconsciously as Job, Milton could suffer his misfortunes with greater forbearance, and apply himself with a more profound sense of divine election to the task of justifying God's ways to men.

Dryden sees no such cyclical repetition. The story of David is little more than a convenient peg on which to hang his satire, and, unlike Milton, he identifies himself with none of the biblical characters. He is, in conformity with the ideals of the age he was inaugurating, merely the spectator, watching with an amused and somewhat disdainful smile the antics of his fellow man. No hint of sanctity elevates those he identifies with biblical figures, except insofar as the equation of Charles II with David is intended as a graceful compliment to the King. The interpretation of contemporary events in the light of biblical history has become in Dryden's poem a literary tool, and perhaps even constituted a parody of the biblical equations employed by the Puritan pamphleteers.

In his 'operatic' dramatization of *Paradise Lost*, entitled *The State of Innocence and Fall of Man* (1677), Dryden's cool detachment made him incapable of recapturing that emotional force and conviction of holy purpose which had inspired Milton's work. It remains, therefore, little more than a literary husk, presenting the same story and even preserving many of the same details, but lacking the kernel of prophetic insight and dedication. The regularity of its rhymed couplets reflects Dydren's restrained treatment of the material, but, above all, his conscious desire to win applause for his wit and learning distracts attention from the subject-matter which is rarely more than a vehicle for that wit. At times the effect is almost ludicrous, as when Adam's opening speech anachronistically offers a digest of Cartesian philosophy:

> *What am I? or from whence? For that I am*
> *I know because I think.*

With such frigidity and intellectual word-play there can be no serious grasp of character, no attempt to revitalize the significance of scriptural events; and although as neo-classical poetry the work has some merit, as biblical drama it fails abysmally. Indeed, Milton's epic is far more dramatic than Dryden's dramatization, and the latter never reached the stage.

Johnson is reported to have explained that *The State of Innocence* could not be 'decently represented on the stage' because it was 'an attempt to mingle earth and heaven by praising human excellence in the language of religion'.[1] Since he finds it necessary to explain its failure to reach the stage, his comment raises once more the problem of the legal basis for prohibiting stage presentations of biblical themes in the Restoration and early eighteenth century. Apart from one vague reference to the granting in 1662 of a licence 'to George Bayley, of London, musitioner, to make show of a play called Noah's Flood' (which appears to have been some sort of musical presentation and hence not a biblical dramatization in the fullest sense), there is no record of any stage performance of biblical drama until a further dubious reference in 1793.[2] And yet the numerous allusions to the possibility of such stage performances suggests that the prohibition of biblical dramas was regarded as by no means automatic. The return of Sir Henry Herbert to the post of Licenser at the Restoration was brief, and his replacement by D'Avenant and Killigrew was to ensure that plays did not contain 'Prophenation, scurrility or obscenity'.[3] This left the question of biblical drama open. Presumably the Licenser could himself determine whether it came under the category of 'prophenation' and since Killigrew was the author of one of the coarsest of dramas, he might be expected to be broad-minded.[4]

[1] D. E. Baker, *Biographia Dramatica* (London, 1812), iii, 299.
[2] Bayley's play is recorded in W. C. Hazlitt, *A Manual . . . of Old English Plays* (London, 1892), p. 167.
[3] F. Fowell and F. Palmer, *Censorship in England* (London, 1913).
[4] *The Parson's Wedding*, played between 1637 and 1642 and published in 1664.

179

Drama Without a Stage

Jeremy Collier's *Short View of the Immorality and Profaneness of the English Stage* (1698) (which, of course, was not aimed at biblical drama, since none existed on the stage) prompted William II to ban scenes 'contrary to Religion and good manners' and encouraged the cloyingly moral drama of sentiment. But theatrical censorship throughout the eighteenth century (particularly after Fielding's *Tom Thumb* had roused Walpole's ire) was aimed primarily at political attacks on the government and was only casually concerned with religious indiscretions. We must assume, therefore, once again that the absence of biblical drama from the stage during this period was due less to legal prohibition than to a tacit assumption that the dramatization of scriptural themes was in some sense profane.[1]

Roger Boyle's *Tragedy of King Saul*, published both posthumously and anonymously in 1703, seems to have been written with the distinct aim of stage performance in mind; for, according to the publisher's preface, the 'Persons that have the Government of the Stage have Rejected this Heroick Poem, as being freighted with too much Vertue, and Morality to gain 'em a full Audience'.[2] The reason given in this preface is perhaps no more than a disgruntled response to the play's rejection on literary grounds. It attempts to portray the heroic qualities of Saul and David, but in fact does no more than translate the biblical account into dull verse. Nevertheless, since his *Herod the Great*, which is only slightly better, would have been staged but for the burning of the theatre, and his seven other complete plays were all performed, is it more likely that the reason for the refusal of *Saul* was its biblical theme. The preface adds the interesting note that, in despair of its being performed on the professional stage, the publisher had set the poetical interludes to music 'which may Recommend it to be Acted in Schools, and Universities, as a proper Entertainment for those that have Ingenious and Liberal Education, on Solemn Occasions'.

Then again, a few years later a suggestion came from the

---

[1] For the situation at the end of the century, see the discussion of Hannah More's plays below.

[2] *Dramatic Works*, ed. W. S. Clark, ii, 705. This play was attributed by the *Biographia Dramatica* to Joseph Trapp, but Clark makes out a convincing case for Horace Walpole's attribution of the play to Boyle. See Clark's edition, i, 57.

higher echelons of the Church that Milton's *Samson Agonistes* be altered for the purpose of a stage performance. Bishop Atterbury about 1722 urged his friend Pope to divide the dramatic poem into acts and scenes in order that it might be performed by the students of Westminster. Admittedly, the performance was to be staged by schoolboys and not by professionals, but he must have known that a version by so eminent an author as Pope would be likely to interest the professional stage. His reminder to Pope in a subsequent letter suggests that he was aware of this difficulty when he adds 'always allowing for its being a story out of the Bible, which is an objection that, at this time of day, I know is not to be gotten over'.[1] Apparently he regarded the suppression of biblical drama as a merely temporary phenomenon. At all events, Pope did nothing about it and the problem of its performance never materialized.

(vii) THE HANDELIAN COMPROMISE

But biblical drama could not be kept off the stage for long, and a method was discovered for reviving performances of scriptural themes without causing offence to the religious scruples of either licenser or audience. It will be recalled that the main reason for the cessation of biblical drama in the early seventeenth century was that the greater humanization of biblical figures detracted from their sanctity. As long as the figures remained 'haloed' and somewhat wooden, this respectful distance could be preserved, the barrier of their stylization preventing any excessive familiarity. The increased realism of the stage could not be artificially retarded merely to accommodate biblical themes, and until some alternative technique could be devised, scriptural drama had to be excluded from the stage.

The technique which was discovered eventually was to combine the dramatization of a sacred theme with the solemnity of church music, and thus to create a semi-religious performance easily distinguishable from the 'profanities' of the professional

---

[1] *Memoirs and Correspondence of Francis Atterbury*, ed. F. Williams (London, 1869), i, 379.

theatre. Despite the Puritan disapproval of ecclesiastical music,[1] its power of evoking an atmosphere of prayerfulness and of elevating the audience from mundane thoughts to a mood of awe and humility had never waned. The device of setting scriptural drama to solemn music provided that very barrier to complete realism which was needed in this period in order to permit the dramatization of sacred figures. And it achieved a twofold purpose. On the one hand biblical drama could now be staged without fear of sacrilege, and on the other hand the more puritanically minded, who denied themselves attendance at the theatre because of its immorality, could salve their consciences when attending a Handel oratorio on the grounds that they were improving their souls. As Lady Warrington put it some years later in Thackeray's *Virginians*:

'Far be it from me to object to any innocent amusement, much less to the music of Mr. Handel ... Music refines the soul, elevates the understanding, is heard in our churches, and 'tis well known was practised by King David. Your operas I shun as deleterious; your ballets I would forbid to my children as most immoral, – but music, my dears! May we enjoy it, like everything else in reason.'

The invention of the oratorio as a means for reviving scriptural drama was a gradual process, beginning at the Restoration. In 1656 D'Avenant had applied the term 'opera' to his *Siege of Rhodes* in a successful attempt to deflect Puritan disapproval at a time when all plays were banned. Over twenty years later, Dryden employed the same inoffensive term to his *State of Innocence* (even though it was really a dramatic piece interspersed with songs) but this time probably as a guard against those who should object to his dramatization of a biblical theme. The ruse was ineffective, and if Johnson's explanation is correct, it was ineffective because the mingling of religious and profane could not be concealed merely by nomenclature. Two years after its publication Edward Ecclestone followed his lead by publishing an opera, also based upon Milton but transposing the theme of *Paradise Lost* to *Noah's Flood or the Destruction of the World*. In this piece Lucifer and his associates determine to

[1] Calvin had not denied the place of music in the church (*Institutes III*, xx, 32), but the later distrust of art forms had been extended to include music too.

destroy Noah, first by sending Belial into the ark in the guise of a beast, and later by open assault. Noah resists all attacks until finally he succumbs to wine, and mankind is punished accordingly.[1] The indebtedness of the opera both to Milton and Dryden is obvious and (to the honour of the author) acknowledged, but that did not save it from a deserved neglect.[2] After some twelve years had elapsed, its title was changed twice in the hope of attracting renewed interest, but it then was allowed to die a quiet death.[3] The addition of musical passages to Boyle's *King Saul* after its rejection by the theatre was a move in the same direction as these operas and equally unsuccessful. But however fruitless these early experiments may have been, they showed that an attempt was being made to edge biblical drama onto the stage under the cover of its musical accompaniment.[4]

Where the so-called 'opera' failed, the scriptural oratorio became almost at once a cherished part of the English heritage, to be performed enthusiastically in every village and city hall by professional and amateur alike. Nor was its success fortuitous. Handel, so far from being inspired by a happy stroke of genius, found himself forced with great reluctance away from his beloved opera to these biblical works, and his unwilling surrender to popular taste is sufficient indication that his oratorios were supplying a deeply felt need. His two theatrical masques *Acis and Galatea* and *Esther*, composed for the Duke of Chandos between 1718 and 1720, did not see public performance for more than a decade, and even their immediate

---

[1] The fullest discussion of the piece appears in J. R. Baird, 'Milton and Edward Ecclestone's *Noah's Flood*', *MLN* lv (1940), 183.

[2] '*Mr. Dreydon's* State of Innocency and Fall of Man, is of the same Nature with this, from whose Incomparable Piece I drew this rugged draught; and Milton's Paradise Lost is full of the same Adornments.' Whether 'the same' refers here to Dryden or Ecclestone must be left open to conjecture!

[3] 'This play not going off, a new Title and Cuts were affix'd to it in Hillary Term, 1684, it then going under the Title of The Cataclism, or General Deluge of the World', G. Langbaine, *An Account of the English Dramatic Poets* (Oxford, 1691), p. 186. It was reissued in 1690 as *The Deluge, or The Destruction of the World*, still without achieving performance.

[4] The earlier attempt of George Bayley in 1662 did, apparently, win a licence for the performance of *Noah's Flood* because of its musical form.

popularity prompted only two further such works during the next seven years. It was solely the failure of his attempts at opera in 1738 and the financial crisis involved which persuaded him to try his hand once more at this musico-dramatic genre and to produce fourteen oratorios in as many years.[1] The public was prepared to throng to the oratorio but not to the opera. The story of the attacks upon the Italian opera in the eighteenth century lies outside the province of this study, but *Spectator No. 18* gives some indication of the Englishman's attitude to the ludicrous mixture of Italian and English, the awkwardness of the translation, and the distrust of a foreign importation.

To enquire into the reasons for the oratorio's immediate success is not to assume that it was artistically undeserved. Not every work of genius is appreciated in its own day. Moreover, modern music critics have frequently argued that Handel's operas equal and at times even excel the oratorios artistically.[2] Their failure is to be attributed primarily to the unfavourable climate of contemporary taste; and, conversely, the success of the oratorio must be traced at least partly to that same climate.

Handel was among the first to recognize that despite the eighteenth-century veneration for the classics, the English people as a whole were more familiar with their Bible than with Ovid's *Metamorphoses*. Moreover, like the authors of the pseudo-biblical Herod dramas of the Restoration, he realized that scriptural themes had an appeal sufficient to put the audience into a sympathetic and receptive frame of mind even before the performance began. After his initial use of Ovid in *Acis and Galatea*, he devoted the remainder of his oratorios, apart from three on classical themes, to *Esther, Deborah, Athalia, Saul, Israel in Egypt, Messiah, Samson, Joseph, Belshazzar, Judas Maccabaeus,*

[1] For much of the technical information on Handel's works I am indebted to Winton Dean's excellent study, *Handel's Dramatic Oratorios and Masques* (Oxford, 1959). R. M. Myers, *Handel's Messiah: A Touchstone of Taste* (New York, 1948), provides an interesting examination of the reception accorded to the most famous of the oratorios.

[2] W. C. Smith, for example, in his article on Handel contributed to the 1954 edition of *Grove's Dictionary of Music and Musicians*, describes the operas as 'artistically excellent', and there has recently been a marked revival of interest in these operas.

The Handelian Compromise

Alexander Balus (based on the book of Maccabees), *Joshua*, *Solomon*, *Susanna*, *Theodora* and *Jephtha*. All, with the exception of *Theodora* and the *Messiah*, were drawn exclusively from the Old Testament and even the latter consisted largely of quotations from it.

Handel's choice of the Old Testament stories in preference to those of the New was a *tour de force* not to be explained by that need for fallible human characters which had motivated previous biblical dramatists. On the contrary, a fundamental reason for the success of these oratorios was, as has been noted, the blunting of vivid dramatization necessary in a musical performance. The Latin oratorios of Carissimi in the seventeenth century, prompted by the Jesuit desire to strengthen the religious element in opera and to divert audiences from secular performances, had adopted the tradition of these secular operas by paying more attention to the isolated expression of each emotion as it arose than to vivid characterization. The extent to which Handel followed this lead is indicated by his readiness to split a part between two singers, and although he himself only rarely indulged this licence, a libretto of *Saul* printed in 1786 allocates each part to two or more singers, regardless of the pitch of the voices and with frequent interchanges among the cast of ten.[1] Realism, therefore, was not a primary consideration in oratorio and cannot be regarded as substantiating in this era the preference for Old Testament themes.

The true reason lay in that Protestant identification with Old Testament heroes which had animated such works as Milton's *Samson*. By broadening its narrower sectarian bounds so that the God of Israel became the universal God of the World, and the people of Israel became reincarnated in eighteenth-century England, Handel succeeded in glorifying in biblical terms the confident patriotism of the English people as they rose on the wave of imperial expansion, convinced that they were carrying the true word of God to the pagan corners of the world. The heroic, martial splendour of *Deborah*, of *Judas Maccabaeus*, and of *Joshua* was adopted enthusiastically as symbolic of English integrity and courage. The words and music were English, the marches reminiscent of English tunes, and the rousing rhythms, by their appeal to the simplest musical taste, were evocative of

[1] W. Dean, p. 139.

democratic pride in the equality of free people. As a British audience heard the words:

> *While lawless tyrants, with ambition blind*
> *Mock solemn faith, waste worlds, and thin mankind;*
> *Israel can boast a leader just and brave,*
> *A friend to freedom and ordained to save.*
> *Thus bless'd to heav'n your voices raise*
> *In songs of thanks and hymns of praise.*[1]

they were thinking less of Joshua and his army than of their own intrepid spirit of adventure, their love of justice, and their sincere, if somewhat vague, religious aspirations.[2]

The appeal to the rising middle class was inevitably greater than to the aristocracy. The middle class was less inclined to cynicism, more chauvinistic, and more deeply impressed by Britain's expansion of trade than the conservative upper class; and the oratorios became increasingly directed towards this new audience. In a calculated attempt to win them, single tickets were issued in addition to seasonal subscriptions, and Handel's remark to Gluck in 1746 that the English liked something to which they could beat time probably explains the addition of more rousing marches to such subsequent works as *Judas Maccabaeus*. In fact, the frequent equation of Handel with Orpheus in this era was intended as a sly dig at his ability to charm those dumb beasts, the British *plebs*. The bourgeoisie was lulled into the soothing conviction that attendance at a Handelian oratorio was, if not a substitute, then at least a valuable supplement to attendance at church. It began to be regarded as an infallible cure for profligacy, an irresistible source of spiritual elevation, so that occasional examples of its inefficacy aroused the concern and amazement of pious ladies. 'Alas!' one cried, 'It is too true, that one of the most profligate poor wretches I know, and the most lost and insensible to all serious considerations, is the most constant frequenter of all oratorios.'[3]

---

[1] The final recitative of *Joshua*.

[2] Paul Henry Lang's *George Frideric Handel* (New York, 1966) offers some valuable observations on Handel's choice of Old Testament themes, and would seem to support the theory argued here (briefly outlined in my *Prophet and Poet*) that the oratorio filled a need created by the prohibition of staged biblical drama.

[3] Dean, p. 137. The association of the oratorios with haritable

The Handelian Compromise

This emphasis upon the edification to be obtained from oratorios was an attempt to justify, even to oneself, attendance at a combination of a biblical drama and a musical performance. The end of the Commonwealth had left a residue of Puritanism which was assimilated largely by that very middle class to whom the oratorio had made a particular appeal. By falling into the no-man's-land between the church and the theatre, on the one hand it suffered attack from both institutions, but on the other hand it afforded those willing to exploit it the possibility of indulging a frustrated craving for music and drama without impairing their moral integrity. The High Church Tory might sanctimoniously write to his newspaper:

'An *Oratorio* either is an *Act* of *Religion,* or it is not; if it is, I ask if the *Playhouse* is a fit *Temple* to perform it in, or a Company of *Players* fit *Ministers* of *God's Word* . . . If it is not perform'd as an *Act* of *Religion,* but for *Diversion* and *Amusement* only (and indeed I believe few or none go to an *Oratorio* out of *Devotion*) what a *Prophanation* of *God's* Name and Word this is, to make so light Use of them?'[1]

But such a view failed to perceive that it was intended neither as a diversion nor as an act of religion, but as something falling neatly between the two categories. The intervention of the Bishop of London in 1732 to forbid the use of costume or action in the stage performance of *Esther* had the salutary effect of reducing the theatrical element in oratorios to a minimum; and the prohibition of a performance of the *Messiah* in church some thirty years later shows that it had never been regarded as liturgical.[2]

Although the artistic value of the oratorios lies today almost exclusively in the musical score, the importance of the libretto for contemporary audiences should not be underestimated. The subtitle *An Oratorio, or Sacred Drama* was intended to remind

causes was a deliberate attempt to increase the impression of its nobility of purpose, and consequently to attract the middle class even further. The eleven performances of the *Messiah* at the Foundling Hospital are reputed to have brought in nearly £7,000 for its funds. See C. Burney, *Sketch of the Life of Handel* (London, 1785), p. 28.

[1] From a letter published in the *Universal Spectator,* 19th March, 1743.

[2] In 1763 the Rev. William Hanbury was denied this permission, even though there was an isolated precedent in the performance at Bristol Cathedral in 1758. See Myers, p. 119 and Dean, p. 140.

the audience that the work consisted of a biblical dramatization set to music. Unlike the imported Italian opera, its English text was intelligible to all. Indeed, Handel's ability to compose a score whose solemnity and majesty did not fall short of his sacred text was soon recognized as his greatest asset, and the audience watched carefully for the harmonious synthesis of the two. Thus the poet Shenstone, after lavishing praise on the *Messiah*, added: 'Yet I fancied I could observe *some parts* in it, wherein Handel's judgment failed him; when the music was not equal, or was even *opposite*, to what the words required.'[1] In fact, although the audience did not realize it at the time, the reverse was true of those oratorios which did not employ quotations from the Holy Writ, for it was the music which elevated a dull libretto.[2] To give but one example, that exquisite air from *Jephtha*:

> *Waft her, angels, through the skies,*
> *Far above yon azure plain;*
> *Glorious there, like you, to rise,*
> *There, like you, for ever reign.*

is flat and uninspired when divorced from its musical setting. It is the delicate rise and fall of the first line, the translation into musical terms of the word *waft*, which lends dignity and grace to the text. When, as in the *Messiah*, the music was matched by words that were truly great, the combination produced a triumphant work of art.

The contemporary concern with the texts of the various oratorios confirms the theory argued here that they formed a disguised revival of biblical drama, satisfying in musical form the people's craving for scriptural pageantry. In medieval times the biblical characters had been revitalized by the gleaming vision of the *praesepe* or the haloed figures of the triptych. The

[1] In a letter to Richard Graves, 25th November, 1758.

[2] The librettists included Charles Jennens, Thomas Morell, Newburgh Hamilton, James Miller, and Samuel Humphreys, none of them distinguished in the realm of literature. Dean defends Jennens' reputation by attributing to him much of the credit for the structural unity of *Saul*, but even he can only credit him with 'something approaching eloquence'. Jennens and his colleagues may have had some flair for selecting incidents in order to create a unified presentation of the story, but they were not poets.

earliest dramatizations had provided magnificent décor to add dignity to the scriptural heroes, and the more developed drama used the magic of words to conjure up scenes of grandeur and heroism. Since both art and drama had fallen under the ban of the Puritan, the English middle class, which had preserved much of this puritanical outlook, turned instead to the music of the oratorio as a means of recapturing the dignity and solemnity of sacred narrative. It was a magnificent substitute, but it was not drama in the true sense of the word, as a glance at *Samson* will show. This adaptation of Milton's drama by Hamilton retains much of the beauty of the original text and restricts alteration of Milton's words to the minimum; yet an element which evaporates at the first touch is that desperate inner struggle which forms the core of *Samson Agonistes*. Where Milton's hero is torn between vituperation of Dalila and the admission 'but true/I to myself was false ere thou to me', Hamilton's dismisses her with the disdainful:

> *Traitress to love, I'll hear no more*
> *The charmer's voice, your arts give o'er.*

The succession of comparatively brief airs essential to an oratorio offers no opportunity for the elaboration of emotional conflict, and although the latter may be replaced in a modified form by the musical score, the music can never achieve that distinct articulation of emotional experience which forms an integral part of drama.

Yet in its own day the oratorio came to be regarded as a new literary form, as an alternative to the dramatic poem and one which had the added advantage of being eligible for public performance. During the years following the first public performance of Handel's oratorios, over twenty dramatic poems on Old Testament themes were published or performed as 'oratorios'. This number excludes anonymous works on themes identical with Handel's which were possibly reissues of his own librettos,[1] and they number among them works by Oliver

---

[1] I have been able to trace the following works: W. Huggins, *Judith* (1733), J. Lockman, *David's Lamentation* (1736), J. Hoadly, *Jephtha* (1737), E. Tollet, *Susanna* (1755), J. Free, *Jephtha* (1757), B. Stillingfleet, *Paradise Lost* (1760), J. Hawkesworth, *Zimri* (1760), I. Bickerstaff, *Judith* (1761), ?*Ruth* (1763), J. Brown, *Cure of Sau*

Drama Without a Stage

Goldsmith and Christopher Smart.[1] For the author interested in biblical themes, the oratorio provided a new opportunity for dramatization.

Goldsmith chose as the theme for his oratorio *The Captivity* (1764) the fall of Babylon to Cyrus of Persia and the consequent salvation of the Hebrew captives there. He portrayed the ancient Hebrews as pious and dignified patriarchal figures, despising the ribald merriment of their captors and preferring the simple honesty of their own faith to the corruption and debauchery around them. And behind this lay a subtle change in the English attitude to the Bible. The Protestant of the preceding centuries and, indeed, the librettists of the Handelian oratorio, had found in the scriptural narrative heroic figures engaged in stirring actions, and they seized upon them as symbolic of their own militant qualities. But the movements of primitivism and orientalism, in their reaction against the urbanization of eighteenth-century England, had begun to lay greater emphasis upon the picture of Eastern ease and luxury evoked by the imagery of the Bible. The colourful accounts of the orient which the seventeenth-century traveller had brought back with him conjured up in the mind of the Englishman a life of immeasurable wealth, luxuriant vegetation, and languorous ease. The voluptuous and exotic imagery of the *Song of Songs*, the pastoral simplicity of Ruth, and the equality of king and commoner in ancient Palestine captured the imagination of the pre-romantic

(1763), C. Smart, *Hannah* (1764), O. Goldsmith, *Jews in Babylon* (1764), B. Stillingfleet, *Joseph, Moses and Zipporah*, and *David and Bathsheba* (1765), C. Smart, *Abimelech* (1768), J. Hawkesworth, *Fall of Egypt* (1774), H. Brooke, *Ruth* (1778), R. Jago, *Adam* (1784), C. Davy, *Balaam* and *Ruth* (1787), T. S. Dupuis, *Elijah* (1789). Most are recorded with fuller details in vols. ii and iii of Allardyce Nicholl's *History of English Drama* (Cambridge, 1952), and in E. D. Coleman's bibliography. I have only recorded here the eighteenth-century versions. They continued to be written during the following century too.

[1] Smart's oratorios consisted of undistinguished hack-work. Both were publicly performed, *Hannah* at the King's Theatre, Haymarket, and *Abimelech* at the Theatre Royal in Covent Garden. See E. G. Ainsworth and C. E. Noyes, *Christopher Smart: a biographical and critical study*, University of Missouri Studies xviii (1943), pp. 132 and 138, and R. Brittain, *The Poems of Christopher Smart* (Princeton, 1950), p. 45.

writer. Robert Lowth's recognition of the dignity of the biblical Hebrews, 'There were no empty titles, no ensigns of false glory. . . they were contented with those arts which were necessary to a simple and uncultivated (or rather uncorrupted) state of life',[1] led a few years later to Sir William Jones's depiction of the ancient orientals, quietly watching their flocks and camels, and singing their native songs '. . . which they pour out almost ex tempore, professing a contempt for the stately pillars and solemn buildings of cities, compared with the natural charms of the country and the coolness of their tents'.[2]

As a result, the active, martial element of Holy Writ began to be supplanted by a more passive quality. The prophet was no longer, as in Milton, the dedicated man of action, providing vigorous leadership in politics and warfare, but became identified with the ancient bard, whose divine inspiration expressed itself (or sometimes dissipated itself) in songs of praise.

> *But, hush! see, foremost of the captive choir,*
> *The master-prophet grasps his full-ton'd lyre,*
> *Mark where he sits, with executing art,*
> *Feels for each tone, and speeds it to the heart.*
> *See inspiration fills his rising form,*
> *Awful as clouds, that nurse the growing storm;*
> *And now his voice, accordant to the string,*
> *Prepares our monarch's victories to sing.*

The people and their leaders remain passive throughout. Commanded to sing songs of Zion, they decline in words reminiscent of *Pslam* cxxxvii, and as they lament their lot with calm resignation and noble restraint, their deliverance comes in the form of an invading army. At the conclusion of the oratorio the mercy of God is eulogized and his powers of salvation acknowledged, but it is a very different form of salvation from Milton's. Where Samson had wrestled desperately for atonement and self-regeneration, Goldsmith's prophets quietly await the

---

[1] *Lectures on the Sacred Poetry of the Hebrews*, tr. G. Gregory (Oxford, 1787), but originally delivered in Latin, 1741–51.

[2] *Essay on the Poetry of the Eastern Nations*. For an account of the stories of the East brought back by English travellers, see S. C. Chew, *The Crescent and the Rose* (New York, 1937), which recounts the relationship between Islam and England during the Renaissance.

moment of their redemption, singing gentle airs in praise of heavenly goodness.

Furthermore, the choice of theme reflects the growing contemporary concern with national freedom and the consequent hatred of tyranny. Rousseau's *Du Contrat social* (1762) and the continental preoccupation with the rights of man were producing echoes in England, and in scriptural drama the enslavement of the Hebrew people as a whole began to excite more sympathy than the fall of a single biblical hero. Loss of political independence had become more 'tragic' than loss of spiritual integrity, and had a greater appeal to the eighteenth-century reader since it verged less on problems of religious enthusiasm.[1]

The pre-romantic interest in the Bible as oriental literature was focused primarily on the *Song of Songs*, rich in unbridled passion and uninhibited love. Numerous 'dramatic' paraphrases and translations appeared throughout the century, some genuinely attempting to recapture the spirit of the original, while others merely revealed the author's penchant for the voluptuous and the erotic.[2] Samuel Croxall's *The Fair Circassian*, published anonymously in 1720 and running through numerous editions during the century, explained in the preface that the author visualized Anna Maria Mordaunt, to whom it was dedicated, as the Shulamite of the drama and himself as Solomon. He seemed unaware of the consequent indelicacy of placing in the lady's mouth the lines:

> *Tell me, my lovely Spoiler, thy Retreat;*
> *I now forgive: for Oh! the Theft was sweet.*

or

> *Behold, my Life, our dear expecting Bed*
> *With coverlets of lively Verdure spread.*[3]

Despite (or perhaps aided by) a sharp attack on its indecency published in 1751,[4] the work remained popular, partly because

---

[1] Byron's *Hebrew Melodies*, which depicted the conquered Hebrews lamenting their exile and sadly raising their 'fast-Fetter'd hands that made vengeance in vain', marked the culmination of this trend.

[2] See B. Simmons, *Some Aspects of the Treatment of the Psalms and the Song of Solomon in English Eighteenth Century Literature* (1937), an unpublished thesis at London University.

[3] Quotations from the 1743 edition published posthumously in London.   [4] James Craig, *Spiritual Life: Poems* (Edinburgh, 1751).

of the erotic, oriental flavour emphasized in the title. It is, however, drama in only a restricted sense. The speeches are assigned to the male and female of the duet, but there is no other attempt at dramatization. Even those translators like Ann Francis who attempted to provide the book with some dramatic structure by means of the addition of a chorus of virgins succeeded merely in creating an empty shell.[1] The book itself is essentially undramatic, so that any successful dramatization must be at the expense of fidelity to the original.

The eighteenth century is, at best, a lean period for serious drama, both through the stultifying effects of the Licensing Act and through the concern with wit and urbanity which tended to turn tragedy into epigrammatic rhetoric. In consequence, the biblical drama of the period, apart from the oratorios, has little to offer. Aaron Hill, whose preface to *Creation* (1720) had revealed a serious interest in the literary quality of the Bible and who, as a theatrical manager, had launched Handel on his English career, tried his hand at a tragedy entitled *Saul* but deserted the project after the first act.[2] The language is stilted and the dramatization wooden, but it shows signs of a freer treatment of the material – the type of freedom, in fact, which was to become common during the twentieth century. Without alteration of the original story, the embellishments of incidents and of plot shifted interest to an imaginary sequence of events which might conceivably have occurred within the framework of the biblical text. Jessida, the supposed sister of David, warns Jonathan that her brother, hiding at Endor, is in danger of discovery during Saul's visit there. Although these events are without scriptural foundation, they do not directly contradict the text and hence came to be regarded as

---

[1] *A Poetic Translation of the Song of Solomon* (London, 1781), reprinted in G. A. Kohut, *Hebrew Anthology* (Cincinnati, 1913), ii, 965. Other eighteenth-century dramatizations of the song include versions by John Bland (London, 1750), Thomas Percy (London, 1764) and Elizabeth S. Bowdler (Edinburgh, 1775). Percy's marked a turning point in the movement towards those translations which achieved literary excellence by means of fidelity to the text, but it was not a drama.

[2] See Dorothy Brewster, *Aaron Hill: Poet, Dramatist, Projector* (New York, 1913), p. 86. *Saul* is published in his *Dramatic Works* (London, 1760), vol. ii.

justifiable by dramatic licence. In all previous biblical drama, embellishments had been restricted almost entirely to the introduction or elaboration of minor characters, and never intentionally at the expense of the major figures. This new treatment of the biblical material meant that the major figures were themselves elaborated and, on the assumption that the audience was well acquainted with the main features of the hero's life, the old stories were given new twists. The resultant tendency was that biblical drama became less a dramatization of existent narrative than the construction of new incidents and plot on the foundations of the text. Apparently the Bible was becoming too familiar to be dramatized without the introduction of novel dramatic situations.[1]

Hannah More, however, took scrupulous care to ensure that fidelity to the text take precedence over realism, and informed her readers in the preface to her *Sacred Dramas* (1782) that she did not imagine herself at liberty 'to invent circumstances'. The detrimental effect which this restriction was liable to have upon her dramas she recognized in admitting that she 'rather aspired after Moral Instruction than the purity of Dramatic Composition'.

Since, according to the sub-title, her playlets were intended solely for the edification of young children, it might be thought unfair to judge them as dramatic works, were it not that a mingling of coy humility with unwarranted pride suggests that she had thoughts of a wider audience. She modestly confesses in her introduction:

> *Nor prophet's burning zeal,*
> *Nor muse of fire, nor yet to sweep the strings*
> *With sacred energy, to me belongs;*
> *Nor with Miltonic hand to touch the chords*
> *That wake to ecstasy.*[2]

[1] Thomas Holcroft, in his translation of Madame Genlis mentioned below, stated that in his experience French audiences were abysmally ignorant of the Bible when compared with the English. His explanation that this arose from the Catholic practice of restricting the reading of biblical passages smacks of religious prejudice, but his experiences, related in some detail, do suggest that the English acquaintance with their Bible made the introduction of new plots necessary in order to sustain interest.   [2] *Works* (New York, 1835), vol. vi.

yet she pretentiously affixes as the epigraph to her first play the Miltonic lines:

> *Let me assert eternal Providence,*
> *And justify the ways of God to man.*

Two other plays take their epigraphs from Racine's works, and to confirm the impression that she was hopeful of having her plays meet with a success similar to Racine's biblical dramas, she adds a note to her introduction:

'It would not be easy, nor perhaps proper, to introduce Sacred Tragedies on the English Stage. The pious would think it profane, while the profane would think it dull. Yet the excellent Racine, in a profligate country and a voluptuous court, ventured to adapt the story of *Athalia* to the French Theatre.'[1]

In fact, of course, Racine had restricted the performance of his scriptural plays to the school stage, while Hannah More's plays, despite the hesitancy of the above paragraph, saw public performance during her lifetime. And the incident throws some light on the current attitude to the staging of scriptural plays.

Tate Wilkinson informs us (somewhat ungrammatically) in his *Wandering Patentee* that a gentleman 'of distinguished fortune, character and tastes' altered two of her plays so expertly 'as to please the most devout ear, and indeed impossible to offend the most rigid, as improper for the stage'. In 1793, the dramas were received in Doncaster with applause, but when the adapter planned to stage the plays in Hull during the following month, the religious people of the town objected so strenuously to the proposal of presenting biblical characters on the stage

---

[1] A few years later, a parallel to Hannah More's plays, also intended for children and inspired by Racine, was published in London, when Thomas Holcroft's translation from the French of the plays by Mme la Comtesse de Genlis appeared in 1785 and again in 1786. Perhaps the best comment on their literary value would be to offer a quotation from *The Death of Adam*:

Seth: Curse! – My father! – I! – Oh, with what transport would I now resign my life to prolong his! – Providence of God! – his head declines, his features stiffen. – Adam! – My father! – My father! – breathest thou? Livest thou?

that he was forced to abandon the attempt.[1] A further note on
the prevailing attitude to scriptural drama was provided a few
years later when in 1832 Genest commented on Hannah More's
hesitancy to allow their performance:

'There could be no reasonable objection to the performance
of Sacred Dramas, provided they were acted in a proper place
and by proper persons – but without being very profane, one
might venture to say that Sacred Dramas would, generally
speaking, be dull.'[2]

His insistence on 'proper persons' suggests that he would not
have approved of a performance by professional actors.

Despite the success of her *Percy*, due more to Garrick's
reputation and direction than to its intrinsic merits,[3] Hannah
More was no great dramatist. Where Racine applied his talents
and experience to transform the biblical account into drama,
Hannah More, perhaps excessively conscious of what she
described as 'the holy ground' on which she stood, hoped that
the sacred material would shape itself, and consequently confined herself to a versification of the existent story. The result
is a curious mixture of simplicity and elaboration. Aware of
the innocent children to whom the plays were addressed, she
larded her characters with noble piety and moral edification;
yet at the same time her desire to 'dramatize' the material
resulted in involved rhetorical speeches, sprinkled with Greek
idioms and often unintelligible to a younger audience. One
wonders what a child (or, indeed, an adult) would have made of:

> *Thou Great Unseen! who causest gentle deeds,*
> *And smil'st on what thou causest, thus I bless thee,*
> *That thou didst deign consult the tender make*
> *Of yielding human hearts, when thou ordain'dst*
> *Humanity a virtue!*

[1] M. A. Hopkins, *Hannah More and her Circle* (New York, 1947),
p. 102. Although Miss Hopkins relates the story in connection only
with *Daniel*, E. D. Coleman records a performance of her *Moses* in
Doncaster during the same year, from which I assume that both
plays were presented by the same 'gentleman'.

[2] *Some Account of the English Stage* (Bath, 1832), vi, 250–1.

[3] See M. G. Jones, *Hannah More* (Cambridge, 1952), for an account
of its reception. The failure immediately after Garrick's death of her
second play, *The Fatal Falsehood* (which is not inferior to *Percy*), shows
how far *Percy*'s success was due to him.

The Handelian Compromise

Yet, despite these occasional flights of 'rhetoric', the plays did succeed in presenting the biblical stories simply and effectively for children, and if they failed as drama, they served to convince many readers that biblical plays could prove a useful educational device. England had never benefited from the Jesuit school drama which had achieved so much on the continent, and after the early Christian Terence, religious school drama had been practically ignored until Racine's plays drew attention to its possibilities as a means of conveying precepts to the young. In poetry as well as drama, the increased interest in the 'innocence' of children now led to a spate of poetry intended specifically for them. Ambrose Phillips's attempts at the beginning of the century had been laughed to scorn, earning him the name of 'Namby Pamby'; but by now Smart's *Hymns for the Amusement of Children* and Blake's *Songs of Innocence* revealed a growing concern with the moral welfare of the child.

The popularity of Hannah More's plays and the new readiness to provide religious and moral instruction for the young resulted in a spate of pious dramatizations of biblical themes, pared down to remove any hint of immorality. The combination of eighteenth-century 'sensibility' with this fresh concept of the moral delicacy of children resulted in an intense prudery which robbed biblical stories of their vigour and fire. The prophet was no longer the fierce condemner of social abuse, nor the sacred bard, but an unfailing source of moral platitudes. Throughout the nineteenth century, biblical dramas were composed by elderly ladies, educationally-minded clergymen, and laymen filled with a righteous zeal to improve the minds of young and old alike. But the result was neither drama nor the Bible; for drama could not survive on a diet of sanctimonious piety, while the Bible, rich in vivid stories of passion, lust, and hate, became merely a diluted discourse on virtue when reduced to the tastes of the Victorian moralists.

CHAPTER V

THE BIBLE ROMANTICIZED

(i) Byron's 'Cain' and 'Heaven and Earth'

An examination of the biblical dramas of the nineteenth century
reveals a disproportionate resurgence of interest in the story of
Cain and Abel.[1] Admittedly, Byron's provocative play prompted
imitations and refutations, but as the growth of this interest in a
theme ignored since the mystery cycles can be traced back to the
mid-eighteenth century, the revival cannot be attributed entirely
to him. Nor, indeed, would it explain why Byron himself was
intrigued by this scriptural story. The thesis I propose to
advance here is that the Cain plays together with such dramas
as Robert Jameson's *Nimrod* (1848) and Alfred Austin's *Tower
of Babel* (1874) form a disguised reinterpretation of the theme
of the Fall, and hence a re-examination of the justification of evil
offered by Christian exegesis.

The neo-classicist's conceptualization of God as the Supreme

---

[1] I have traced fourteen such plays between 1822 and 1877. Apart
from the three recorded above, there were Cain plays by David
Lyndsay (two) in *Dramas of the Ancient World* (1822), William
Battine, *Another Cain* (1822), an anonymous female's, *Another Cain*
(1822), H. Wilkinson, *Cain* (1824), J. E. Reade, *Cain the Wanderer*
(1829), Owen Howell, *Abel* (1843), Elizabeth B. Browning, *Drama
of Exile* (1844), William Harper, *Cain and Abel* (1844), and Lady
F. C. Dixie, *Abel Avenged* (1877). Arthur Hugh Clough published
a *Mystery of the Fall* on the theme of Adam in 1869.

Byron's Cain *and* Heaven and Earth

Being in a static and plenitudinous Chain[1] had resulted in such facilely 'optimistic' treatises as Soame Jenyns' *Free Enquiry into the Nature and Origin of Evil* (1757). The more sensitively religious Christian such as Dr. Johnson could not but reject with scorn the superficial solution it offered; yet he himself suggested no more effective answer. In an age inimical to religious passion, to the kind of spiritual quest typified by Job and Milton, he sadly resigned himself to the almost unmitigated sufferings of this world in the hope, rather than the conviction, that some recompense would be offered in the after-life. But for others, an open scepticism replaced the gnawing doubts of the thinking Christian, and Hume, Gibbon, and Paine marked the new freedom of religious thought by boldly questioning the validity of the Bible and hence of the Christian religion *in toto*. By the end of the century, what Professor Lovejoy called the new 'diversitarianism' had encouraged, even among the less recalcitrant, a radical reappraisal of traditional Christian cosmogony.

In the realm of biblical drama, this questioning of the concept of an 'ordered' world meant that where Milton had seized upon the theme of the Fall as a means of impressing upon man a sense of responsibility for his lot, the romantic poet approached the story with a predisposition to sympathize with the errant human and to view with distrust the scriptural portrayal of God as the merciful and benevolent father.

Milton, however, had made the story so much his own, he had so inspired the potential dramatist with the fear of imputations of plagiarism for anything remotely resembling *Paradise Lost*, that this reinterpretation of original sin was side-tracked into the subsequent story of Cain's fratricide. If the tasting of the forbidden fruit signified man's first disobedience of divine commandment, the murder of Abel marked the first transgression of the moral law; and the expulsion from Eden into the toilsome world of thorns and painful childbirth was closely paralleled by the primal elder's curse of exile and incessant wandering away from the happier security of his native surroundings.

[1] See A. O. Lovejoy, *The Great Chain of Being* (Cambridge, Mass., 1950), particularly chapter vii. The so-called 'optimism' of the Leibniz school contained, as he has shown so brilliantly, paradoxical elements which suggested a deeper dissatisfaction, and the gulf between Jenyns and Johnson was not so wide as it then appeared.

Moreover, the Cain incident provided the dramatist with a story more readily suited than that of Adam to the new romantic sensibility. The seduction of man by his vain helpmate had served ideally the medieval glorification of celibacy and its contempt for the world of the flesh; and even the later Puritan who rejected celibacy–for all his hymns to wedded love– tended for much of the time to regard the female as little more than a procreative chattel. But the nineteenth-century idealization of womanhood–an idealization which made a virtue of her weakness and her need for male comfort and protection– made the theme of the Fall appear both unchivalrous and distasteful. In the disguised versions of the Fall produced by the romantics, the wives of Cain, Nimrod, and Aran are neither the instigators of their misfortune, nor even their accomplices. The hero surrenders to the devil's blandishments entirely on his own responsibility. The tender, righteous pleas of a loving and virtuous wife prove powerless against his masculine vigour and fearless curiosity. Where Adam falls through weakness, the romantic Cain is raised to heroic proportions both by the strength which leads to his downfall and by the love which he has inspired in a noble woman.[1]

In 1760, the publication of Salamon Gessner's *Der Tod Abels* touched off this new interest in the theme of Cain.[2] Its enormous popularity, beginning in England with Mary Collyer's translation published in the following year, won the comment in 1814 that 'no book of foreign growth has ever become so popular in England as the *Death of Abel*' and it provided the impetus for the versions by Coleridge and Byron.[3] Although both the

---

[1] This tendency is closely paralleled by the relationship in Goethe's *Faust* between Gretchen, the symbol of pious faith, and the hero, representing the courageous male searching for truth. For a discussion of the Faustian elements in Byron's *Cain*, see S. C. Chew, *The Dramas of Lord Byron* (Göttingen, 1915), pp. 126 f.

[2] Alfieri's play, *Abele*, was not translated into English until 1815, and Byron records in the preface to *Cain* that he had never read it.

[3] *Quarterly Review xi* (1814), p. 78. Byron vigorously denied the influence, maintaining in the preface to *Cain* that he had not read it since the age of eight. But he protests too much, and his denial suggests that he was aware of some indebtedness even though he wished to assure his reader that it was only general. He records elsewhere that whilst his German master 'was crying his eyes out over its pages,

original and Mrs. Collyer's translation employed what the latter described as 'a kind of loose poetry' set out as prose, the work was at once compared with Milton's epic – which indicates how difficult it was to tackle the theme of the Fall, even in disguised fashion, without inviting invidious comparison with Milton's work. An anonymous critic in 1766 commented in an access of enthusiasm that 'it traces and often gains upon Milton in his very brightest tracts',[1] and at the turn of the century W. C. Oulton was moved to offer a translation into hexameters as being most suited to 'an evident imitation of Milton's celebrated *Paradise Lost*'.[2]

In fact Gessner's so-called epic followed Milton neither in style nor in treatment of theme, but in conformity with the new sentimental tendencies of the age, depicted the characters as successively bursting into floods of tender tears. Cain is portrayed from the first as a callous brute or, as Gessner put it somewhat whimsically in the preface, as a 'rough Cossack'. But the conclusion marked an entirely novel approach which appealed at once to the susceptibilities of his contemporary readers. After the perpetration of the murder, Cain's bitter remorse, although completely out of character, transforms him from a villain into an object of sympathy. As he returns to his wife and children with the burden of his crime on his conscience, Cain 'could give no answer to the little innocents. He embrac'd them. He hugg'd them in his arms, while his tears ran on their faces. Then unable to support his anguish, he fell on the earth, at the feet of his wife.'[3] His wife, unhesitatingly loyal and with her devotion deepened by his new need of her, steadfastly insists on accompanying him into exile, and the story ends as they advance together 'by the light of the nocturnal star' into the desert regions never violated by human foot.

In 1798, immediately prior to the composition of the *Ancient Mariner* with its underlying theme of the Wandering Jew,

I thought that any other than Cain had hardly committed a crime in ridding the world of so dull a fellow as Gessner made brother Abel'. Thomas Medwin, *Journal of the Conversations of Lord Byron* (Baudry, 1824), p. 125. See also Bertha Reed, *The Influence of Solomon Gessner upon English Literature* (Philadelphia, 1905).

[1] Quoted in Reed, p. 16.

[2] W. C. Oulton, *The Death of Abel* (London, 1811), p. vi.

[3] I have used the Boston edition of 1768.

Coleridge became interested in the essentially similar wanderings of Cain and began a prose poem with that title. In a prefatory note written some thirty years later, he recalled the friendly rivalry between himself and Wordsworth to determine which of them could compose a canto on the subject more quickly. Wordsworth came a poor second because, as Coleridge modestly explained, it was impossible 'for a taste so austerely pure and simple to imitate the Death of Abel'. Since Coleridge's own attempt was written in a rhythmical prose, there can be little doubt that he was alluding to Gessner's version as the model.[1]

The fragment which Coleridge then composed but never completed is a 'Gothic' episode with a shrieking ghost and desolate crags reminiscent of ancient battlements. But most significant of all was his portrayal of the Wandering Cain, stricken with remorse and unwittingly polluting all that he touched:

'And the innocent little child clasped a finger of the hand which had murdered the righteous Abel.'

Cain pathetically stifles the groans which rise from his soul and as though to underscore the new sympathy which the romantic felt for the suffering sinner, Coleridge puts into his mouth a lament unmistakably echoing that of Job, the accepted symbol of undeserved suffering:

'O that a man might live without the breath of his nostrils. So I might abide in darkness, and blackness, and an empty space! Yea, I would lie down, I would not rise, neither would I stir my limbs till I became as the rock in the den of the lion, on which the young lion resteth his head while he sleepeth.'

Despite the presence of his child, Cain is spiritually isolated, conscious of his own moral failings, and yearning eternally and vainly for relief from his pain. He has been transformed from a callous villain into a member of the romantic brotherhood.

Implicit in this reinterpretation of the first murder is a condemnation of divine dispensation. For a whitewashing of Cain could only be achieved by transferring the guilt in some way to the world at large, and hence to the powers which direct it. And

[1] J. L. Lowes, *The Road to Xanadu* (Boston/New York, 1927), pp. 257 f., discusses more fully the evidence for his indebtedness to Gessner.

this implicit condemnation becomes explicit towards the end of the brief canto. The 'Shape' of Abel which appears moaning and shrieking in the wilderness prompts from Cain the legitimate query: 'Didst thou not find favour in the sight of the Lord thy God?' Abel's answer subverts the fundamentals of Christianity with the words: 'The Lord is God of the living only, the dead have another God,' and Cain understandably rejoices secretly in his heart. The heresy is further elaborated into a rejection of the after-life as recompense or punishment for earthly acts:

' "Wretched shall they be all the days of their mortal life," exclaimed the Shape, "who sacrifice worthy and acceptable sacrifices to the God of the dead; but after death their toil ceaseth. Woe is me for I was well beloved by the God of the living, and cruel wert thou, O my brother, who didst snatch me away from his power and domination." '

The canto concludes with Cain's determination to seek the God of the dead and to conciliate him in preparation for his own ghostly life.

The effect of the heresy is to cut from Cain's neck the albatross of his guilt. The dichotomy between the worlds of the living and the dead, and, even more, between the ruling powers of this world and the next denoted a dual scale of morality and hence absolved him automatically from the responsibility for his crime. The absence of a third canto (since Coleridge's was intended to be the second of three) leaves the continuation to conjecture, but a Faustian theme is suggested, perhaps free from moral strictures.

Neither Gessner's version nor Coleridge's had been dramatizations, but they show beyond doubt that Byron's *Cain* was part of a new trend to transform Cain from villain to hero, to romanticize him into a pathetic creature overwhelmed by remorse and yet retaining the grandeur and dignity of the seeker after truth. Gessner's figure moving towards the untrodden wastes of his exile contains more than a hint of the explorer about to plot uncharted regions, while Coleridge's Cain is, at the conclusion, eager to set out upon a quest for the new God of whom he has just learned. The interpretation of Cain as the symbol of intellectual curiosity had begun.

In the preface to his drama, Byron stressed that although he calls it a *mystery* play, it will observe a greater fidelity to the original text than did the ancient cycles. In fact, despite the startling divergence of his Cain from conventional characterizations, only in the smallest details is there any discrepancy between the scriptural account and the Byronic. In order to preserve Cain's manly dignity, for example, it is his wife Adah who begs for mitigation of sentence. And Byron succeeds in combining fidelity to the text with his novel presentation by triumphantly quoting Bishop Watson's answer to all such objections: 'Behold the Book!'[1] Removing the exegetical encrustations of time, the prejudiced interpretations of previous generations, he saw the story in its naked form, and perceived that the brief biblical account, by restricting itself as usual to the actions and words of the participants, gave almost no indication of their motives or religious inclinations. If Byron's *Cain* shocked readers by its rejection of the traditional reading, it left them with little that could be specifically attacked on the grounds of divergence from the text. After the long and bloody battle for an open Bible, it was difficult for a Protestant country to prohibit even the devil from quoting Scriptures for his own ends.

The new cosmogony of numerous inhabited worlds, whose ordered plenitude had formed the basis for Leibnizian optimism, was a two-edged weapon. By the end of the century it had filled the romantic with a depressing sense of his own insignificance in the vast universe of whirling planets and immense stars. Thus the central act of *Cain*, the tour of the heavens conducted by Lucifer, deliberately contrasts the new scientific cosmos and the traditional biblical world-picture of the opening act.[2] The result, as Byron anticipated, was that his drama was welcomed in some quarters as deliciously wicked, and in others as a piece of calculated blasphemy.[3] In fact, it was neither.

[1] Preface to *Cain*.

[2] Cf. Edward E. Bostetter, 'Byron and the Politics of Paradise', *PMLA lxxv* (1960), 571.

[3] R. Heber's discussion of certain theological heresies in the work gives some indication of its reception. See *Quarterly Review liv* (1822), 476 and, for a more general account of its reception, S. C. Chew, *Byron in England* (London, 1924), chapter vi. Stopford Brooke's 'Byron's Cain', published posthumously in *HJ xviii* (1919), 74, provides a more subjective interpretation of the theological problems it poses.

Byron's Cain *and* Heaven and Earth

On the one hand there can be no doubt of a partially iconoclastic intent. Both during its composition and after, he repeatedly linked it with *Manfred,* the study of an unjust and capricious God.[1] His portrayal of Cain as the rationalist defending the serpent betrayed an unwillingness to accept the story on its face value:

> *The snake spoke truth; it was the tree of knowledge;*
> *It was the tree of life: knowledge is good,*
> *And life is good; and how can both be evil?*

and by justifying the snake he transferred to God the guilt for man's disobedience. But to interpret the entire play as a condemnation of the traditional story or of the traditional cosmogony is to ignore the positive assertions of the drama. On the guided tour, for example, Cain is indeed overwhelmed by the 'scientific' world; but his breathless 'O altitudo!' is no rationalist acceptance of a mechanistic universe but an ecstatic marvelling at the splendour of creation:

> *Oh God! Oh Gods! or whatsoe'er ye are!*
> *How beautiful ye are! how beautiful*
> *Your works, or accidents, or whatsoe'er*
> *They may be.*

In its mingling of faith and scepticism, it echoes the agnostic's prayer: 'O Lord, if there is one, save my soul if I have one!'

Even more remarkable are the implications of the conclusion in which Cain, by following the attractively reasoned arguments of Lucifer, murders an innocent brother and is cast out from society as a polluted thing. The intellectual rebel of the earlier scenes, heroically crusading for truth and for freedom from hypocrisy, ends as a guilt-ridden exile, crushed by the horror of his gratuitous crime. By slaying Abel he has destroyed not only a brother but the hope of future redemption for mankind and for himself:

> *And he who lieth there was childless! I*
> *Have dried the fountain of a gentle race*
> *Which might have graced his recent marriage couch,*
> *And might have tempered this stern blood of mine,*
> *Uniting with our children Abel's offspring!*

[1] Ernest J. Lovell, *Byron: the Record of a Quest* (Austin, 1949), p. 208.

Where is that fascinating Lucifer now? Cain's rebellion against heaven has led not, as he half-believed, to a thunderbolt from the jealous tyrant of heaven but to his own self-imposed, self-created torture. Adah's gentle prayer for Abel: 'Peace be with him' elicits from Cain the pathetic cry: 'But with *me!* –' and the play ends in a chastened mood of remorse – the very reverse of that confident iconoclasm with which it began.

The paradox of a play which both idealizes and crushes the heretic can be traced to that deliberate cultivation of inconsistency typical of Byron's personality. He remarked of the diary on which he was engaged: 'God knows what contradictions it may contain. If I am sincere with myself . . . every page should confute, refute, and utterly abjure its predecessor';[1] and this was no mere posturizing. The stern Calvinist upbringing to which he had been subjected as a child produced a violent antipathy to the doctrines of original sin and predestination, while yet leaving an ineradicable mark on his soul. In the resulting polarity, he vacillated between the gay, amoral diabolism of Don Juan and the guilt-ridden self-pity of Childe Harold; and in neither character was he fully himself.[2] His predisposition for rationalism was offset by the dread conviction that his physical deformity was a symbol of divine wrath, and the dualism of this belief was reflected vividly in the drama itself.

The dualism, which has so frequently been given the inappropriate name of Manicheism,[3] is not an opposition of good and evil; for Lucifer is certainly not depicted as evil nor God as good. Indeed, for the first time in the history of biblical drama the benevolence of God is boldly refuted,[4] Lucifer and Cain describing themselves as:

[1] *Letters and Journals of Lord Byron*, ed. R. E. Prothero (London, 1898–1901), ii, 366.

[2] E. W. Marjarum, *Byron as Skeptic and Believer* (Princeton, 1938) is the best presentation of the view that *Cain* reflects Byron's religious confusion, although, as I have indicated, I do not always agree with the author's more detailed arguments.

[3] In the original draft of the Preface, Byron wrote that he 'was prepared to be accused of Manicheism' and would readily defend himself against the charge. But, since Heber's article, the term has been generally applied by critics.

[4] Milton's Satan, although rebelling against God, never, of course, denies the latter's benevolence. He merely challenges his authority and power.

Byron's Cain *and* Heaven and Earth

> *Souls who dare look the Omnipotent tyrant in*
> *His everlasting face, and tell him that*
> *His evil is not good.*

And lest it be thought that this is a reversal of Manicheism with
Lucifer representing the good and God the evil, the noble Adah,
symbolic of love and goodness, upbraids Lucifer:

> *Fiend! tempt me not with beauty: thou art fairer*
> *Than was the serpent, and as false.*

Similarly, Marjarum's description of the dualism as a contrast
'between authority and rebellion, between enforced ignorance
and knowledge' is only partially true. For these are merely the
surface expression of a deeper spiritual dichotomy remarkably
similar in many ways to that experienced by Job and Milton,
with the significant difference that the latter triumphantly
resolved the problem (at least to their own satisfaction), while
Byron retired from the spiritual fray only vaguely aware of the
direction in which the solution lay.

The apparent injustice of the world and, more particularly, the
disproportionate enormity of the punishment for man's first sin
obsessed Byron as it had Milton. Both saw in the Fall of man an
allegory of the origins of evil and one which demanded rational
justification.[1] It was the need for that justification which
prompted Milton to compose his epic defence and it was, to some
extent, his own awareness of the deficiencies of that defence
which led to the more personal dramatization in *Samson
Agonistes* of the spiritual conflict involved in unravelling the
mystery. Byron's *Cain* is no less concerned with the Fall,
although ostensibly dramatizing the story of a later generation,
and the opening of the play reiterates Cain's overwhelming
sense of injustice that he, the innocent child, should bear his
parents' guilt—particularly since he questions repeatedly
whether that original guilt was itself deserved:

> Cain: . . . *Toil! and wherefore should I toil?—because*
>   *My father could not keep his place in Eden.*

---

[1] Schaffner's neat comment that Byron seeks 'to justify the ways of
man to God' is misleading, since, as I argue below, it is true only of the
opening scenes. See A. Schaffner, *Lord Byron's Cain und seine Quellen*
(Strassburg, 1880), p. 32.

What had I done in this?—I was unborn:
I sought not to be born; nor love the state
To which that birth has brought me. Why did he
Yield to the serpent and the woman? or,
Yielding, why suffer? What was there in this?
The tree was planted, and why not for him?
If not, why place it near him, where it grew,
The fairest in the centre? They have but
One answer to all questions, ''Twas his will,
And he is good.' How know I that? Because
He is all-powerful, must all-good, too, follow?
I judge by the fruits—and they are bitter—
Which I must feed on for a fault not mine.

Again like Milton he insists upon personal responsibility and the freedom to enquire and demand explanations even from the Creator of the universe. But where Milton began his quest for truth with the Jobian longing for reconfirmation of his faith, Byron's spiritual foundations rested on the slippery soil of religious superstition, scepticism, and youthful rebelliousness.

Indeed, Cain is as patently a projection of Byron's inner struggles as Samson is of Milton's. His club foot and that 'wild blood' he inherited from his father were gifts of birth with which he believed a cruel destiny had unjustly plagued him, and Cain's protest against the doctrine of hereditary guilt implicit in the Christian interpretation of the Fall had an intensely personal significance for Byron. So far from rebelling against Protestantism, he was in his resolute individualism, his desire to return to the literal text of the Bible, his rejection of ritualism, and his ability to identify himself passionately with biblical narrative, entirely typical of the basic Protestant tradition. Even his rationalism and rebelliousness were inherited from the Puritan revolt against the shibboleths of medieval Christianity, and while his ostentatious cultivation of immorality would make it ludicrous to label him a Puritan, it is important to recognize that his Cain and, indeed, much of his own scepticism resulted not so much from a conflict with the Protestant tradition as from an excess of it.

The resultant dualism of the play is, therefore, more complex than the mere opposition of a cruel, despotic God and a rationalist, freethinking Lucifer. It is rather a dualism between this rebelliousness on the one hand and the vindication of God on the other. For the obviously sincere depiction of God's callousness and Lucifer's nobility is an allegorical representation of Job's initial and dangerous blasphemy – his demand for the human right to question the apparently unjust ways of God. But the Faust theme, whose shadowy presence is felt throughout as Cain succumbs to reasoned persuasion, predisposes the reader to mistrust the Mephistophelian Lucifer. Adah, as we have seen, recognizes Lucifer's falsity and the speciousness of his arguments and, despite Byron's dislike of the principle of Christian redemption (he maintained that the Crucifixion 'no more does away *man's* guilt than a schoolboy's volunteering to be flogged would exculpate the dunce'[1]), the play moves towards a glorification of the Crucifixion and hence towards an implicit justification of God. When Cain, under the influence of Lucifer, heartlessly demands that his parents should die for their own sin and thus absolve him from responsibility, Adah reproaches him with overt allusion to the Christian doctrine of vicarious atonement:

> *Would* I *could die for them, so* they *might live!*

Moreover, critics have generally ignored the significance of Byron's identification of Abel as a Christ figure, dying with the prayer:

> *Oh God! Receive thy servant, and*
> *Forgive his slayer, for he knew not what*
> *He did.*

At this point, any attempt to glorify Cain and whitewash him of his guilt is shattered by his prefiguration as Christ's murderer.

Part of the confusion of this dualism lies in that dramatic preference for fallible characters so apparent in the medieval cycles. With the exception of Cain, Lucifer, and Adah, all the *dramatis personae* are flat and lifeless, and of these exceptions, Cain alone is truly human. Adah's gentleness and devotion make her a haloed symbol of love, while Lucifer, as a being half celestial and half diabolic, represents allegorically (and with certain Mephistophelian characteristics) reason and the pursuit

---

[1] *Letters*, ii, 34.

of knowledge. Cain alone is a man, striving upwards towards truth and intellectual comprehension, yet dragged down by his cynicism and iconoclasm. Inevitably he gains the reader's sympathy by his dignity, intellect and courage—a sympathy enhanced by the love which he has inspired in Adah. And the most serious dramatic flaw in the play is that, in consequence of this, his sudden anger at Abel and the wild attack upon a defenceless brother is totally out of keeping with the thoughtful, idealistic, and grandiose presentation of character which had preceded it.

Byron laboriously explained in a letter that, as a result of his lengthy colloquy with Lucifer, Cain kills Abel in a fit of dissatisfaction 'partly with the politics of Paradise, which had driven them all out of it, and partly because (as it is written in Genesis) Abel's sacrifice was the more acceptable to the Deity'. Yet a short time later he categorically denied the latter motivation, stating that the catastrophe resulted 'from mere *internal* irritation, *not* premeditation, or envy of Abel (which would have made him contemptible)'.[1] The reason which he offers in this revised explanation as the true cause of the murder is 'rage and fury against the inadequacy of his state to his conceptions'. This motivation Lovell and others have accepted as elevating the murder to lofty heights by displaying Cain's depression at man's insignificance after his tour of the heavens.[2] But where, we are entitled to ask, does this appear in the play? The dialogue at the point of the murder has no hint of inadequacies but rather a childish and frenzied spite against Abel. In anger against the bloody sacrifices of his brother as contrasted with his own purely vegetarian offering, he indulges in the illogical outburst.

> *Give way! —thy God loves blood! —then look to it:*
> *Give way, ere he hath* more!

and expresses his disgust at the murder of innocent animals by murdering an innocent brother. The illogicality is, of course, camouflaged in the play by the swiftness of the dialogue and the sudden rush of anger which prompts Cain's cry, but it is a dramatic incongruity nonetheless, suited perhaps to the brutal Cain of

[1] *Letters*, v, 368 and 470.
[2] Chew, for example, maintains that this phrase of Byron's 'has comprehended the central idea of the poem' (*Dramas*, p. 128).

the mysteries but not to the sophisticated intellectual of Byron's drama. The author's involved explanation must, therefore, be regarded either as an attempt at a retroactive justification or as a plan which he failed to realize effectively in the drama itself. It certainly does not explain away the dramatic inconsistency, and Byron's contradictory justifications of the murder suggest that he himself had not resolved the problem.

Both Milton and Byron insisted upon a vigorous individualism, a salvation which must be achieved by personal action. But where Milton's Samson attains through this individualism that self-fulfilment which he believed he had forfeited for ever, the intellectual independence of Byron's hero leads him only to the perpetration of a ghastly and morally indefensible crime which robs him of even the faintest hope of spiritual regeneration. The contradiction involved deepens the confusion inherent in the play's dualism. Byron has questioned, like Job, the justice of the world and done so extraordinarily effectively. But his meek submission at the conclusion is, unlike Job's, an unexplained *volte face* which leaves the reader merely perplexed. Byron's lack of a consistent religious (or even anti-religious) philosophy is patent at the end of the play.

However, this does not mean, as many critics (Chew among them) have maintained, that the play fails through lack of a dramatic conflict. According to this view Adah represents the attractions of comfortable acquiescence to traditional theology, while Lucifer, as the exponent of reason and intrepid speculation, is 'but a glorified Cain',[1] so that Cain's rejection of Adah for Lucifer is a foregone conclusion. If this is partially true, it ignores Adah's additional function as the representative of goodness, loyalty and love; and Lucifer, as too many critics forget, is the direct cause of his downfall. Nor should it be forgotten that the scriptural source of the play provided the reader in the opening scene with the foreknowledge that Cain would end as the branded outcast from society, banished for a crime deserving even more rigorous penalties than had been meted out by a merciful heaven. Whatever the attractions of Lucifer, therefore, both author and reader recognized that the essentially virtuous Cain was being torn between good and evil, and it is soon apparent that this conflict is, as has been argued

---

[1] Cf. G. Rebec, 'Byron and Morals', *IJE xiv*, 39 f. and Chew, p. 130.

here, an allegory for Byron's own inner conflict—a curious mixture of indictment and vindication of the Fall.

If the blasphemies of *Cain* formed, at least ostensibly, an indictment of Christianity, *Heaven and Earth* was, despite Murray's rejection of it as 'another *Cain*',[1] an almost innocuous defence. Byron himself described it as 'less spectacular than *Cain* and very pious' and perhaps as a result of his experiences with its predecessor, he expressed a readiness to soften any hints of impiety to which readers might object.[2] Erected on an even flimsier biblical foundation than *Cain* (which, though not contradicting the text, was largely an elaboration)[3], it took as its hero Japhet, the righteous son of Noah, suffering the pangs of unrequited love for a maiden consorting against divine commandment with a celestial creature. The allegorical representation of divine justice is here not the expulsion from Eden but the Flood which, as Wilson Knight has pointed out,[4] had a special significance for Byron, fascinated by the enormous power of the ocean. But it goes further than that; for the ocean symbolized to him the immanence of God in nature and man's insignificance before such might. He described it in *Childe Harold* as:

> *Thou glorious mirror, where the Almighty's form*
> *Glasses itself in tempests . . .*
> *. . . boundless, endless and sublime,*
> *The image of eternity, the throne*
> *Of the Invisible.*

and there is in this Hebraic sense of wonder before the divine presence in the natural world, a recognition of the hand of the Creator holding its might in check and directing its course.[5]

[1] Medwin, *Journal*, p. 231.

[2] *Letters*, vi, 31 and 47.

[3] Apart from the verses from *Genesis* prefixed to the work, Byron was indebted also to the apocryphal book of *Enoch*, but even this debt is very general. See M. Eimer, 'Das apokryphe buch Henoch und Byrons mysterien', *Eng. Stud. xliv* (1912), 18.

[4] *Lord Byron: Christian Virtues* (London, 1952), pp. 111–12.

[5] *Childe Harold iv*, clxxxiii. Cf. *Psalm civ*, 6: 'The waters stood above the mountains. At thy rebuke they fled: at the voice of thy thunder they hasted away . . . Thou has set a bound that they may not pass over; that they turn not again to cover the earth.'

Byron's Cain and Heaven and Earth

In *Heaven and Earth* man is not seduced by Lucifer but dismisses his arguments as specious. The rebellious Spirit, cynically asking Japhet whether man will be good after the Flood, is answered with calm conviction:

> The eternal will
> Shall deign to expound this dream
> Of good and evil; and redeem
>   Unto himself all times, all things;
>   And gather'd under his almighty wings,
>   Abolish Hell!
> And to expiated Earth
> Restore the beauty of her birth,
>   Her Eden in an endless paradise.

Similarly, the fallen angels, although portrayed as creatures of dignity and grandeur, are outshone by the radiance of Raphael, the loyal servant of God. True, Japhet is a questioner like Cain, unable to comprehend the need for divine wrath in the world, but where Cain's intelligent thrusts are left unparried, Japhet's are gently but firmly dismissed by a merciful Raphael:

> Patriarch, be still a father! smooth thy brow:
> Thy son, despite his folly, shall not sink:
> He knows not what he says.

Again the allusion to the forgiveness of Christ on the cross. Moreover, Noah, the representative of that unthinking, doctrinaire spirit so distasteful to Byron, is reproved for the abruptness of his reply to Japhet's outburst, with the effect that the rigidity of Calvinism is condemned and true Christianity portrayed as kindly, understanding, and just.

Yet Byron had not turned pious overnight, and the defiance which marked the figure of Cain finds its counterpart in Aholibamah—scornful of authority, vigorously independent, and penetrating in her religious cynicism. Her pride in her descent from Cain leaves no doubt of her function in the drama. Yet here again the sharpness of her attack is blunted by the presence of Anah, who, as the object of Japhet's love, timorously attempts to restrain her sister's impiety but proves the weaker of the two. That polarity of religious belief which distinguished Byron's character was reflected in the close of this fragmentary play. The rebellious angels, instead of drowning in the Flood, are permitted to fly with their loves to another star, and, whatever the author may have planned for them in the unwritten sequel, those 'sons of God' and 'daughters of men' who, according to *Genesis*, had been the prime cause of the retributive Flood, were spared, at least temporarily, the watery death of mankind. Similarly, a mother's pathetic plea that Japhet should take her innocent babe aboard again challenges heavenly justice:

> *Why was he born?*
> *What hath he done—*
> *My unwean'd son—*
> *To move Jehovah's wrath or scorn?*

But these challenges are offset by the calm faith of an anonymous drowning mortal speaking with Jobian echoes for all mankind:

> *And though the waters be o'er earth outspread,*
> *Yet, as his word,*
> *Be the decree adored!*
> *He gave me life—he taketh but*
> *The breath which is his own.*

Heaven and Earth is by no means a theodicy but, like *Cain*, it constitutes an examination of divine justice, counterbalancing the scepticism of the earlier work by its more generous appraisal of divine benevolence. And, like *Cain* it too is unmistakably concerned with the Fall of Man, although the Fall is presented in an even more camouflaged form. The image of the serpent seducing mankind is prominent in the opening scene, the colloquy between Raphael and the rebellious angels is patently reminiscent of Satan's speeches in *Paradise Lost*, the sin of Anah and Aholibamah is their transgression of divine prohibition, and the Flood itself parallels the expulsion from Eden. The criticism that greeted Byron's plays, particularly his *Cain*, showed that the parallels they afforded to Milton's work had not been overlooked, despite Byron's hesitant disclaimer in the preface: 'Since I was twenty I have never read Milton; but I had read him so frequently before, that this may make little difference.'[1] But the parallels were less in the literary techniques

---

[1] For details of the pamphlet warfare arising out of the publication of *Cain* see S. C. Chew, *Byron in England*, pp. 80 f., which also contains an interesting account of non-dramatic poems imitating or rebutting Byron's play.

employed than in the two poets' projection of their own religious searchings into the theme of the Fall.

(ii) OTHER VERSIONS OF THE FALL

The dramatizations of the story of Cain that followed hard upon Byron's plays cannot be regarded as part of this nineteenth-century interest in the Fall since they were mere appendages to his work. William Battine's *Another Cain*, A Mystery (1822), sought to rewrite Byron's plays from a religious standpoint, the author modestly admitting that he was not disputing the laurels with Lord Byron. 'His Cain', he explained in the Preface, 'has the merit of poetical talent; my Cain the merit of Truth', and the truth, as he saw it, was the more conventional depiction of Cain as the villain, rebelling against a righteous God. But Byron had imaginatively coloured the biblical story so effectively that no one who had read his play could see the biblical account in quite the same light as before. Even Battine's rewriting presents a Cain nearer to Byron's than to that of the mysteries. He symbolizes Reason, is seduced by the clever arguments of Satan and ignores the wise counsel of a devoted wife. The portrayal of Cain as a sensitive, intelligent seeker after truth had replaced the rowdy ruffian of the cycles even in the pious rebuttals of Byron's drama.[1]

Cain the Wanderer (1829) by J. E. Reade was even more indebted to Byron, being the work of an enthusiastic admirer who maintained in a lengthy dialogue prefacing the work that the latter had 'unmasked all hypocrisy, moral and political . . . laid bare the darkest and most secret workings of the human soul, and showed, in their grandeur and abasement, all that sinks and elevates man'. The title of Reade's work recalls Coleridge's prose poem and, like him, Reade depicted the sequel to Abel's murder. But Cain had changed since Coleridge's day, and Reade's drama is a reworking of Byron's play so slavishly imitative in characterization, plot, and poetic style as to

---

[1] Owen Howell's *Abel: written, but with great humility, in reply to Lord Byron's Cain* (London, 1843), was a similar attempt to defend the more traditional view, but with Abel as the central character, successfully resisting the temptations of the devil.

constitute little more than a carbon copy. It required real skill to produce lines so deceptively similar to Byron's as the apostrophe to Death:

> *Thou senseless degrader of all lovely things!*
> *. . . Feels't thou delight*
> *In seeing forms once beautiful become*
> *Like thyself, gaunt and hideous? Abhorred mockery!*
> Thou *art the dupe, not they—they did but yield*
> *To the fate it were vain to oppose, but thy blind fury*
> *Is ever baffled thus in their renewal.*

and had it preceded *Cain* it would have merited serious attention. But the originality of presentation and the sharpness of the scepticism which had intrigued readers of Byron was secondhand in Reade's work and, despite the popularity which it achieved in its day, it remains no more than a literary oddity.

A truly original work on the theme of the Fall and one of considerable merit was Elizabeth Barrett Browning's *Drama of Exile* (1844), which she described as 'the longest and most important work (to *me*!) which I ever trusted into the current of publication'. Her preface substantiates the theory offered here that these plays were disguised dramas of the Fall, for she alone of these dramatists admits that fear of the charge of plagiarism had driven her from the subject of her choice to the period subsequent to the Fall. She determined, as she put it, 'to shut close the gates of Eden between Milton and myself, so that none might say I dared walk in his footsteps'.[1]

In fact, the gulf between the masculine vigour, grandeur and strength of Milton's epic and the gentle, loving trust which pervades the poetess's version would have protected her from any charge of plagiarism, and it was, indeed, her recognition of the specifically feminine approach to her subject-matter which encouraged her to proceed. She noted in her Preface that 'the self-sacrifice belonged to [Eve's] womanhood, and the consciousness of originating the Fall to her offence', so that it appeared '. . . more expressible by a woman than a man.' Where as has been noted, these disguised dramas of the Fall depicted woman as innocent, loyal and virtuous, in this drama alone Eve bears the full responsibility for her guilt as the sinful

[1] Preface to *Poems* of 1844.

corrupter of mankind. As a woman, the authoress did not offend against the code of chivalry by attributing the sin to Eve, and by her natural sympathy with Eve she portrayed with far greater vividness the poignancy of her suffering. In consequence the dominant theme of the play is Love. Where Milton's Adam, determining to perish with Eve, reviles her nonetheless for her sin, Adam here offers a prayer of thanksgiving.

> *That rather thou hast cast me out with* her
> *Than left me lorn of her in Paradise,*
> *With angel looks and angel songs around*
> *To show the absence of her eyes and voice.*

Eve in her turn begs him to desert her that he may eventually receive heavenly grace, but is refused with declarations of undying devotion.

Since this mortal love is merely a reflection of divine love there is, inevitably, no serious questioning of divine dispensation. Insofar as there is a conflict, it is between despair and hope. The justice of her punishment Eve recognizes fully, and the enormity of her crime is so clearly visualized as to make her despair of spiritual regeneration; her passionate prayers for heavenly pardon provide full acknowledgement of her guilt. But the eventual appearance of Christ[1] assures them of their future redemption, admonishing them to:

> *Fasten your souls so high, that constantly*
> *The smile of your heroic cheer may float*
> *Above all floods of earthly agonies,*
> *Purification being the joy of pain.*

A danger inherent in this unquestioning acceptance of suffering is that untroubled piety usually robs drama of that spiritual struggle essential to its success. The trite theology of the opening scene between Gabriel and Lucifer is, indeed, discouraging, but the intensity of Eve's remorse, the delicacy of her characterization, and, not least, the quality of the verse

---

[1] She is at pains to explain in the Preface that the introduction of Christ into the drama is justified by her conviction that all life 'is a continual sacrament to man', and that there should, therefore, be no profanity in depicting holy figures participating in human affairs.

itself lend realism to Eve's almost desperate yearning for forgiveness:

> *. . . leave us not*
> *In agony beyond what we can bear*
> *Fallen in debasement below thunder-mark,*
> *A mark for scorning – taunted and perplext*
> *By all these creatures we ruled yesterday,*
> *Whom thou, Lord, rulest alway!*

The title of the play indicates once again the contemporary interest in spiritual isolation typified by the Wandering Jew. The parents of mankind, exiled from Eden, set out into the wilderness weighed down by their guilt like the Cains of Gessner, Coleridge, and Reade.

Of the other disguised Fall plays it is only necessary to give two examples, both sad instances of diffuse nineteenth-century closet drama at its worst. But they serve our purpose here by exemplifying even further camouflaging of the story of the Fall than those dramas already examined. Robert W. Jameson's *Nimrod*, published anonymously in 1848, is an extraordinary mixture of melodrama, spectacle, fantasy, and religious didacticism. If we ignore the lengthy theological discussions among the angels, the plot concerns the hunter Nimrod (a descendant of Cain) who despite his squeamishness kills animals solely to protect mankind. His beloved Nahmah (who worships him as a god) is horrified to see him gradually corrupted by Satan. Intellectual freedom and religious faith lie somewhat obscurely behind the temptation, but we are assured by the ever-flitting angels that this is so. Nimrod achieves the power to which he aspires by learning to slay mortals with indiscriminate callousness, and the play concludes with the saintly Nahmah offering herself as a sacrifice in order to redeem him. All the 'noble' characters cast themselves into the flames (including the dog), and Nimrod lives to regret the error of his ways. Through the thick covering of extraneous material it is still possible to discern the underlying pattern common to these Fall plays. Nimrod is the upright, intelligent, and sensitive man seduced by Satan despite the wise counsel of a loyal woman. The scene is set in the early chapters of *Genesis* a few generations after Adam, and the 'conflict' of the play lies in the choice between intellectual freedom and submissive faith—the same choice as had faced Adam and Eve before they ate from the forbidden Tree of Knowledge.

Alfred Austin's *Tower of Babel* (1874) exploited a further theme as a drama of the Fall—the Fall this time symbolized by the tower whereby man presumes to challenge heavenly authority. Again the hero goes to his doom ignoring the gentle protests of his pious wife. Angels, of course, continue to debate the possibilities of rebellion, and in this play one of the more saintly angels who, despite his saintliness, had been making amorous advances to Aran's wife, obtains special dispensation to be transformed into a mortal in order to make a (dramatically) honest woman of her. From this absurd situation the author —later a Poet Laureate—deduces the moral:

> *Though the Earth*
> *May not ascend to Heaven, by Tower or aught*
> *Of man's devising, Heaven descends to Earth*
> *For those who will receive it.*

By now, the disguised drama of the Fall was mere melodrama; yet even in the sanctimonious 'moral' quoted above there can be faintly discerned in vastly oversimplified terms the problem which had vexed Job, Milton, and Byron—the problem of the limitation of man's intellect in his attempt to comprehend the workings of heaven.

(iii) The Pitfalls of Orthodoxy

The nineteenth century offered a selection of biblical drama quantitatively rich yet qualitatively poor and in this it reflected the general state of the theatre. Of more than sixty scriptural plays published during this period, almost all have sunk into a deserved obscurity—an obscurity disturbed only by the patient researcher vainly hoping to uncover a forgotten gem. Fortunately, in a study such as this, concerned less with detailed documentation than with the overall pattern of scriptural drama, our investigation may be confined to the reasons for their collective failure, to the peculiar circumstances which foredoomed the majority even before they were composed, and the reader may be spared a tiresome account of their various plots and literary defects.[1]

Central to this failure was the confidence of the author that the sacredness of his plot would suffice to elevate the play above the works of secular dramatists. This fallacious belief in the transcendent value of biblical themes had a lengthy history but had not produced serious practical effects until the nineteenth century. The mystery cycles and, indeed, biblical drama as late as the sixteenth century had been performed before a predominantly illiterate audience delighting in a simple substitute for a reading of the original text. Moreover, the liturgical origins of ecclesiastical drama had enhanced the audience's readiness to witness even a mere repetition of the previous year's play; for liturgy is the translation of spontaneous prayer into a formal pattern for reiterative public worship. But the popular evangelical movements of the eighteenth century coupled with the increased nineteenth-century concern over the spiritual welfare of the young had so effectively completed the work begun by the Reformation that Bible reading occupied a prominent place in the educational curriculum and family routine, particularly among the members of the middle class. No self-respecting reader could (as in our own day) plead ignorance of any but the most obscure scriptural stories, and consequently mere versification of a familiar, and perhaps even a hackneyed biblical tale robbed the play of that vitality, suspense, and originality which form the primary ingredients of good drama. The biblical plot, so far from lending force to the dramatization, threw its full weight upon the versification which except in the rarest of instances, needed all the support it could get. That florid rhetoric shared by the nineteenth-century poetasters has little lasting appeal, and the combination of insipid verse with an excessively familiar plot lies at the root of their failure. Finally, the impossibility of staging these dramas meant

---

[1] Again the reader is referred to Coleman's bibliography for titles of these works. Not all of them are extant, but I was able to read more than thirty. Typical examples are G. F. Savage-Armstrong, *Tragedy of Israel* (London, 1872), a 3-vol. work on Saul, David and Solomon; P. Bayne, *The Days of Jezebel* (London, 1872); E. Carpenter, *Moses* (London, 1875); A. W. Buchan, *Esther* (Glasgow, 1873); and *Joseph and his Brethren* (London, 1887) – the latter a rare omission from Coleman's list.

that no limit was imposed on length, and they frequently run to more than two hundred pages of execrable verse.

The Greeks, faced with the similar problem of revitalizing traditional mythology, had been aided by their audience's preoccupation with artistic form; yet even they found it necessary within the short interval between Aeschylus and Euripides to refashion the plots by introducing such novel devices as a duplicate Helen;[1] for their mythology, despite its overt religious significance, was by no means sacrosanct. Yet Milton and Byron had provided excellent proof that the sacred biblical stories could be revitalized without alteration of the original account. Each, from somewhat different motives, had solved the problem by projecting himself into the biblical character, by transferring himself imaginatively not so much into the physical situation as into the spiritual perturbation and religious conflicts of the scriptural protagonist. Milton, obsessed by his own Hebraic sense of personal election, had seen in the Samson of the Old Testament a prefiguration not so much of Christ as of himself, and by his emotional identification had infused new vigour and fresh poignancy into the somewhat brutish figure of the Scriptures. Byron, on the other hand, determined to expose the irritating complacency involved in the traditional reading of Cain's character, and prompted by his iconoclastic impulse to dispel the aura of sanctity surrounding the story, had endowed his hero with his own spirit of bold intellectual curiosity.

Each, despite the profound religious convictions of the one and the almost superstitious Calvinism of the other, was essentially an unorthodox rebel, and the success of their dramas derives primarily from this very unorthodoxy. Substitute for their Samson and Cain the noble warrior and black-hearted villain of the Sunday School and the drama evaporates; yet that was precisely what these pusillanimous biblical plays of the nineteenth century insisted upon doing. It is the old story of the fallible versus the infallible character. Those very haloes which had, as we have seen, inhibited the dramatic portrayal of New Testament characters throughout the history of biblical drama had now been solemnly reaffixed by the Victorian pietists to all

[1] It will be recalled that in his *Helena*, Euripides portrayed her as having been innocently held captive on a remote island while a spirit in her guise consorted with Paris.

but the most reprobate of the Old Testament figures, and these latter wore horns and a spiked tail. Even those few dramatists who felt the need for some condiments in these otherwise tasteless dishes either inserted extraneous sub-plots or sprinkled the dull story with 'purple' passages. A brief examination of the two most outstanding of these dramatists, Henry Hart Milman and Charles Jeremiah Wells, will illustrate these techniques employed at their best and the failure resulting from their intrinsic defects. The reader may imagine *a fortiori* the disastrous results in the work of less gifted writers.

Milman, whose popular drama *Fazio* had been instrumental in obtaining for him the Chair of Poetry at Oxford, was a man of primarily ecclesiastical bent, known best today for his researches into the history of early Christianity. His *History of the Jews* offended many by its philosemitic tolerance and it was perhaps natural that he combined his literary and historical interests in two plays set in ancient Palestine. The first and more successful of these, *The Fall of Jerusalem* (1820), portrayed sympathetically the dilemma of a beautiful Jewish heroine torn between loyalty to her family and love for a young Christian, the dilemma symbolizing, of course, the conflict between Jewish conservatism and the New Truth. The second of the two was pseudo-biblical in a different sense, for although set earlier in the biblical period and taking as its ostensible plot the theme of *Belshazzar*, in fact it was biblical in no more than its setting.

Milman, apparently recognizing that a versified account of Belshazzar's feast would hold little interest for his potential readers, inserted into the sketchy framework of the incident a melodramatic plot recounting the adventures of the 'spotless virgin' Benina forced to become the 'bride' of the Babylonian god or, as the reader guesses only too soon, in fact of his lecherous high priest. With echoes of *The Castle of Otranto*, a disembodied voice prevents the rape at the final moment and as the walls of Babylon crumble before Cyrus's troops, Benina is reunited with her love. The biblical setting serves the sole function of providing the play with a supposedly more 'noble' plot and of larding it with a heavy orientalism:

> . . . *they shall feast*
> *Around me, all reclined on ivory couches,*

The Pitfalls of Orthodoxy

Strew'd with Sidonian purple, and soft webs
Of Egypt; fanned by bright and glittering plumes
Held in the snowy hands of virgin slaves;
And o'er their turban'd heads shall lightly wave
The silken canopies, that softly tremble
To gales of liquid odour.[1]

The lush epithets may not be suited to modern taste, but compared with the best of contemporary closet drama, the verse was by no means negligible, and Milman was frequently compared to Byron by his contemporaries.[2] Nevertheless, this play met with a poor reception in its day, largely, we may suspect, because its attempt to enliven the biblical account by the interpolation of foreign material produced mere pastiche.

Wells's *Joseph and his Brethren*, published in 1824 under the pseudonym of H. J. Howard, fell still-born from the press, greeted by scant and unflattering criticism before it disappeared from view. Its author, known otherwise only by the sonnet addressed to him by his schoolfriend Keats (and a remarkable ability to call up spirits of the dead[3]) immediately lost interest in the play and in later years was reluctant to make the slightest effort to resuscitate it. Yet within half a century it had become what Gosse described as 'a kind of Shibboleth – a rite of initiation into the true poetic culture' of Rossetti's circle. Its grandiose verse, fired with vivid passion, appealed to them by its obviously Shakespearean affinities, and at Rossetti's instigation Swinburne contributed an enthusiastic article to the *Fortnightly Review* commending the 'wonderful ease and stateliness of manner which recall the more equable cadences of Shakespeare in his earliest period'.[4] Nor was the praise unjustified and, although the play's excessive length makes it tiresome reading, the quality of the verse is sustained throughout. The characterization is at times excellent, Potiphar's wife particularly possessing an imperiousness, a seductive power, and a venomous wrath

---

[1] *Poetical Works* (London, 1839), i, 276–7.
[2] Shelley objected strenuously to this comparison in the Preface to *Adonais*.
[3] Watts-Dunton recalls this strange quality in his introduction to the 1908 edition of the play.
[4] *Fortnightly Review xxiii*, New Series xvii (1875), 217 f.

not unworthy of Shakespeare's Cleopatra on whom she is modelled. Enamoured of Joseph she describes his

> *. . . marble front a veined tablet fair,*
> *Whereon my lips shall trace my history;*
> *His hair of that rare tint, nor black nor brown,*
> *Of olive amber'd in the sun's bright rays,*
> *That love to linger in its massy folds;*
> *Which o'er his shoulders, like a vexed wave,*
> *Rolls in disorder'd order, gracefully*
> *Meandering and curling on itself.*

Yet once the stir created by its republication in 1876 had died down, the play disappeared from the public eye almost as completely as it had some fifty years before. This time Swinburne himself unconsciously provides the clue to its failure in his admiring appraisal that:

'The pure dramatic quality is perhaps best shown in the characters of Reuben and Issachar, where the poet has found least material for his workmanship in the original story.'

The fidelity of the plot to the original is so slavish as to deprive it of any originality outside the characterization of the minor figures. Joseph is no more than a prig and, since he bears the entire drama upon his shoulders, it falls with him. Phraxanor's sensuous advances he repels with frigidity and, what is worse, with a sanctimonious piety which robs him of all human sympathy:

> Joseph: *It is enough.*
> *'Tis time this hopeless contest had an end.*
> *I have borne this besieging patiently,*
> *Still hoping to arouse your modesty.*

This is not the stuff of which great drama is made – even closet drama never intended for the stage – and the quality of the verse failed to rescue from oblivion a drama which relied upon a well-known biblical story, unenlivened by any flashes of originality and made even more ineffective by the elevation of its central character to the cold immobility of a sacred figure.

The faults of Milman and Wells are magnified in the even less distinguished biblical dramas of the period. Their moral lessons may have been clothed in the garb of poetic drama but their verse rarely constituted poetry and their use of dialogue made them dramatic in no more than a technical sense. Without a revitalization of character, a realization that the biblical heroes were men struggling with agonizing religious doubts and almost invincible temptations to immorality, the so-called dramatizations were doomed to a deserved neglect.

(iv) BIBLICAL MELODRAMA

The last years of the century witnessed a new birth–that prodigy biblical melodrama, of which Jameson's *Nimrod* and Austin's *Tower of Babel* had been harbingers. Handel's oratorio had used religious sentiment as a means of drawing the middle-class to the concert hall, if not to the theatre itself; but the religious sentiments had been genuine and no one could charge the authors of the libretto or the score with compositions un-suited to the sanctity of the subject-matter. Biblical melodrama, however, was patently mercenary in its intent, and if the authors occasionally wrote from sincere religious impulse, a crude sensationalism almost invariably obscured any nobler motives.

In 1896, Wilson Barrett brought his *Sign of the Cross* to the Lyric after its American tour, and it proved an instant and highly lucrative success. The story, set in the time of the early Christians, relates how a Prefect of Rome, Marcus Superbus, attempts to seduce a Christian maiden. She remains steadfast to her principles and the Prefect, now deeply in love, becomes a Christian and dies with her in the arena. If *Arms and the Man* parodied the secular melodrama, Shaw's *Androcles and the Lion* clearly had Barrett's production in mind–a production which he castigated in his own review. Similarly the London *Times* justifiably attacked this spectacle of Christian conversions 'brought about under the influence of sexual passion' and the theatrical hodge-podge which such meretriciousness produced;[1] but the public appetite had been whetted and the long series of such melodramas had begun. In the following year, Barrett produced *The Daughters of Babylon*, and three years later

[1] 7th May, 1900, quoted in G. Weales, *Religion in Modern English Drama* (Philadelphia, 1961), p. 26.

adapted *Quo Vadis* for the stage. The greatest success of all, also an adaptation of a novel, was, of course, General Lew Wallace's *Ben Hur*, produced at Drury Lane in 1902. In all these productions, the sadism of the gladiatorial arena vied for first place with the passionate love theme, and these melodramas have retained their popularity into our own day. In the same way as the non-biblical melodrama, with its heroine rescued from the villain's clutches by the last-minute arrival of the hero, moved naturally from the stage into the cowboy films of the new cinema screen, so the semi-biblical melodrama became the ideal theme for the Technicolor film epic. It would be unfair to ignore the sincerity of some later versions—notably Cecil B. de Mille's *Ten Commandments* which did try to convey the religious impact of the Sinaitic revelation; and more recently Christopher Fry has written of the heart-searching which went into the screenplay he wrote for the Twentieth Century Fox film, *The Bible* (1966). But the public has been trained to expect sensationalism from the biblical epic, and any artistic version will have to overcome this expectation at the risk of commercial failure. However, if the cinema took over the financial advantages of the biblical melodrama together with its artistic defects, it did at least perform the service of freeing the theatre of those epic associations with the Bible which inhibit the film producer. We must, in a sense, be grateful to the cinema for clearing the stage for those biblical plays discussed in the following chapter.

(v) Nineteenth-Century Censorship

The censorship of biblical drama underwent an almost unnoticed change during this period, and one which was to have serious consequences in later years. The prohibition of biblical drama, previously enforced (as we saw in the public outcry at Hull) by public respect for the sanctity of the Scriptures, was gradually given legal status, so that when public opinion veered towards a more lenient view, the more puritanical elements in the country were able to insist upon the enforcement of the law. The means whereby custom could be transformed into law without public knowledge lay in the anomalous position of the Censor, who had legal authority to enforce his decisions but no precise instructions for the criteria on which they should be based. Generally he looked to precedent, and if no previous censor had permitted biblical plays, then, the Censor assumed, they were to be prohibited by his legal power. The history of this legalization deserves some attention.

In 1778, John Larpent had been appointed Examiner of Plays and from the collection of manuscripts which he left behind him it appears likely that no plays on scriptural subjects were even submitted.[1] The treatment such a play would have received may be gauged from his insistence in 1809 that the line 'Bring my grey hairs in sorrow to the grave' be expunged from a farce by Thomas Hook on the grounds that biblical quotations were profaned by usage on the stage. His successor Colman (a profligate author of indecent plays) went even further than Larpent by prohibiting the stage lover from calling his mistress *angel* on the grounds that this constituted a slight on a scriptural figure. Such absurdities began to irritate and at times even to infuriate the dramatist whose purposes were entirely innocuous, and during Colman's tenure of office Thomas Wade complained that on the submission of his manuscript 'the revered name of the Deity, wherever it occurs, was erased by the great religious and moral pen of the licenser and altogether abjured in stage utterance'.[2] The author obtained his revenge by printing the play in its original form and capitalizing the censored portions in order, as he explained in the Preface, that 'the liberal reader will smile in perusing them; and deign, perhaps, to anticipate with some pleasure the speedy abolition of a childish tribunal'.

A later Censor, William Donne, who supervised licensing from 1849 to 1874, stated categorically, 'I never allow any association with Scripture or theology to be introduced into a play', and a successor, Redford, answered a letter requesting a

---

[1] *Catalogue of the Larpent Plays in the Huntington Library* compiled by Dougald MacMillan (San Marino, Calif., 1939). Since, until the twentieth century, almost every biblical play contained a reference in its title to the scriptural nature of its contents, the absence of any such title from the list makes the above assumption almost certain.

[2] Thomas Wade, *The Jew of Arragon* (London, 1830), which was based upon the book of Esther but set instead in the thirteenth century, probably in order to make its stage performance possible. Wade was one of a small Christian band who, led by Macaulay, were fighting for Jewish emancipation in England. The play, superior to much contemporary drama, was booed from the stage because of its pro-Jewish bias.

licence for a biblical drama by hiding behind the rule of precedent which he now regarded as binding:

'I have no power as Examiner of Plays to make any exception to the rule that Scriptural plays, or plays founded on or adapted from the Scriptures, are ineligible for licence in Great Britain. It would appear from your letter that your play would come under this rule and I may say for myself that I am glad to be relieved of the difficult and delicate duty of deciding on the fitness of treatment in each particular case.'[1]

In 1902, the same Examiner refused to license Laurence Housman's *Bethlehem* for similar reasons, although the opera *Samson and Delilah* was, during the same period, suddenly licensed after a lengthy prohibition, presumably on the assumption that the musical form prevented too realistic a portrayal (the same assumption as had aided the popularity of the Handelian oratorio). But, as the number of biblical plays submitted to the Examiner indicates, the dramatists themselves were now convinced that the legal prohibition was totally unjustified,[2] and searched diligently for loopholes through which to slip biblical plays despite the rigorous censorship. Stephen Phillips, who had achieved a phenomenal success with his pseudo-biblical *Herod*, composed a drama on the theme of *David and Bathsheba*, and on its expected refusal by the Examiner he transferred the same plot to the setting of the English Civil War, provocatively naming it *The Sin of David* (1904). Through the thin disguise of Puritan garb the biblical characters of David, Uriah, and Bathsheba are clearly visible.[3] Three years later a play entitled

[1] Quoted F. Fowell and F. Palmer, *Censorship in England*, p. 212.

[2] An interesting symposium entitled 'The Bible and the Stage' appeared in the *New Review viii* (1893), 183 f. There were three participants. Alexandre Dumas *fils* expressed his amazement that the English, unlike the French, should have greeted Wilde's *Salome* with horror and have denied it stage presentation; Dean Farrar voiced the traditional ecclesiastical opposition to biblical drama; and the playwright H. A. Jones insisted vigorously that there was no justification for such banning and 'no reason why the great human stories of the Bible should not be utilized on the stage'. Jones had published similar views some years earlier in his article entitled 'Religion and the Stage', *Nineteenth Century Review*, January, 1885.

[3] There is a detailed account of the play and its sources in R. E. Glaymen, *Recent Judith Drama and its Analogues* (Philadelphia, 1930), p. 106.

Kings in Babylon by Miss A. M. Buckton was performed at the Haymarket Theatre as a result of a similar subterfuge. The plot was identical with that of Shadrach, Meshag, and Abednego set in Babylon itself, but merely by altering the names of the characters the authoress succeeded in circumventing the censorship. The first scriptural play to be licensed was Gwen Lally's *Jezebel* in 1912.

It is abundantly clear that, from the time of the closure of the theatres in the early seventeeth century until the beginning of the twentieth, the banning of scriptural drama from the professional stage was either tacitly assumed or legally enforced. The rare instance of the performance in Doncaster of one of Hannah More's plays made, if possible, even more innocuous before presentation, merely indicates that the provinces were less conscious of the impropriety involved than was London, the centre of dramatic activity (although the neighbouring town of Hull contained, apparently, a more militant puritanical element). There were, we may be sure, occasional performances of biblical themes in country areas lacking a professional stage, and one account of such a bucolic performance has been preserved in the *Cornhill Magazine*.[1] It records with some amusement the performance in Gornal, South Staffordshire of Richard Jukes' *Joseph and his Brethren* by the 'young men and other friends' of the local Wesleyan Chapel. The placard advertising it described it as 'The Grand Sacred Cantata', which suggests that music was again being used as a camouflage; the spectator records only an opening hymn and musical interludes by the local choir of girls, the play itself being free of musical accompaniment. The performance, apparently reminiscent histrionically of Bottom and his crew, was in costume but without any form of scenery, and this lack of décor in an age which had come to identify drama with spectacle, coupled with the 'redeeming' feature that the proceeds were to be devoted to the renovation of the Chapel, suggests that such performances formed no exception to the ban on biblical plays proper. Similarly, the puppet dramas at Bartholomew Fair noted above constituted no real infringement of the prohibition.

One exception to this rule has, however, escaped the notice of critics and remains a puzzling instance of the fish that slipped

[1] *Cornhill Magazine*, New series xvi (1891), p. 282.

through an apparently impenetrable net.[1] A play by Elizabeth Polack entitled *Esther, the Royal Jewess; or the Death of Haman* was given public performance at the Pavilion Theatre, London, on March 7th, 1835, and a later (undated) edition of the play gives details of the lavish oriental costumes used in this performance. A stage direction reads 'Splendid banners, &c. A magnificent Banquet in the Eastern style; the Vases, Cups &c. of the most costly appearance. The Stage as full as possible', and the account of the costumes worn at the stage performance suggests that these directions were followed closely. The play itself is a prose dramatization of the biblical story in no way remarkable for originality either of presentation or of plot, apart from the depiction of Haman in typically melodramatic terms as the secret admirer of Vashti, suggesting her banishment in order to bring her into his clutches. How such a drama obtained a licence for stage performance at a time when, as we have seen, the Examiner of Plays was prohibiting the use of the endearment *angel* remains a mystery, but there can be no doubt that it was afforded fully professional treatment and hence constitutes the sole recorded exception to the ban on biblical drama during a period of some three centuries.

The plays of Oscar Wilde provide a classic instance of the moral tone demanded by the English stage. Although he was an ostentatious adherent of the Decadent group with its flaunting of traditional morality, his secular plays are remarkably conventional in form. No heroine will commit herself to an official engagement before obtaining the formal consent of her parent or guardian and the worst crime is a little 'Bunburying'. If there is any subversion of Victorian convention, it is introduced humorously and unobtrusively. But one play, his *Salome* (1893), gives full rein to his Decadent licentiousness, for the simple reason that he knew it would never be performed on the English stage because of its biblical theme. He wrote it, therefore, in French. It was translated into English the same year not by himself but by Lord Alfred Douglas, and was of course refused a licence in England; but it saw performance in Paris in 1896. In this dreadful yet strangely beautiful work, Salome epitomizes the ideal of Art for Art's sake by her readiness to bespatter

[1] A note of its performance appears without comment in the bibliographies both of E. D. Coleman and of Allardyce Nicoll.

herself with a lover's gore, to slay an innocent prophet, and to throw away her own life solely to enjoy the exquisite depravity of biting the dead lips of a man who had fascinated but refused her. In Salome we have a figure of lustful pride, scornful of the world's opinion, and imperiously demanding the gratification of her evil whims. She stands exulting in her nauseating triumph:

'Ah! I have kissed thy mouth, Iokanaan, I have kissed thy mouth. There was a bitter taste on thy lips. Was it the taste of blood? . . . Nay; but perchance it was the taste of love . . . They say that love hath a bitter taste . . . But what matter? what matter. I have kissed thy mouth, Iokanaan, I have kissed thy mouth.'[1]

We feel a sense of relief at Herod's terse command 'Kill that woman!' She is devoid of all that gentleness which allows man to idolize woman, and her perverse use of her beauty horrifies even the bloodthirsty Tetrarch. This was certainly too rich a diet for the as yet abstemious English stage.

Unacted drama, or rather drama not intended for stage performance, is a contradiction in terms. Impersonation forms an essential part of drama proper and only the fruitful co-operation between playwright and actor can transform dialogue into drama. The divorce of scriptural drama from the stage, both amateur and professional, for so lengthy a period deprived it of the opportunity to flourish, and despite Milton's magnificent exploitation of the Attic form and Byron's theatrically unactable but vividly dramatized closet plays, the history of scriptural drama during these three centuries is notable more for the insight which it affords into the prevailing attitudes to the Bible and its heroes than for the intrinsic merits of the plays. Certainly by the end of the period the plays had reached the nadir both of unactability and of stock characterization. Yet the very profusion of biblical plays in Victorian England, whatever their literary inadequacies, suggests that the frustrated desire for biblical dramatization which had produced the eighteenth-century passion for oratorio was seeking a new outlet in closet drama.

The extraordinary resurgence of biblical drama which forced its way past the twentieth-century censor and provided the modern stage with some of its most distinguished drama–both

[1] *Complete Works* (New York, 1927), ix, 182–3.

religious and anti-religious – confirms the thesis argued throughout this study that a people concerned with the sacred text of the Bible experiences an urgent impulse to visualize its characters in human terms. The fallacious impression in England, inherited from the less enlightened Puritans, that drama was an essentially unholy vessel had resulted in the excessive artificialization of biblical characters to counterbalance any possible charge of sacrilege; but the eventual victory in the twentieth century of the more liberal view that drama was as valid an artistic device as painting or versification led to a spate of vividly naturalistic portrayals of biblical themes by some of the leading dramatists of the day.

The fear that such a legalization of scriptural drama might lead to flagrant heresy proved amply justified; but even the most pious would be forced to admit that, whatever the heresies involved, the imaginative interpretations of the Bible on the twentieth-century stage demanded from both playwright and audience a far greater identification with scriptural narrative than the dull, pretentious, and stereotyped versions of the Victorian age. The move from closet to theatre provided, at the very least, a breath of badly-needed fresh air, and at best it meant that the sacred figures of the Scriptures could be brought down from their pedestals and transformed into creatures of flesh and blood – sinful, arrogant, and at times despicable, but wonderfully alive.

CHAPTER VI

THE MODERN ERA

(i) THE FALL OF THE BASTION

The nineteenth-century battle between the biblical fundamentalists and the protagonists of scientific empiricism ended in a rout, with the Bibliolaters (to use Coleridge's term) retiring from the field both bloody and bowed. To ease their flight, they had flung aside such basic tenets as belief in miracle, and by now the account of Creation was no longer an allegory over and above its historical truth but at the expense of it. Yet it was not through oversight that the previous chapter omitted mention of this contemporary religious ferment; for while the effect of these changes on the dramatization of the Scriptures was inevitably profound, it was delayed until the present century, partly through England's insularity from the intellectual movements on the continent, and partly through the innate conservatism of all but the most sophisticated of English intellectual circles.

The clash between science and religion was, of course, by no means an exclusively nineteenth-century phenomenon. At least as early as Epicurus, the theory that matter had originated in the chance displacement of an atom had challenged the belief in a purposeful universe directed by mysterious yet ultimately beneficent powers. But the patent orderliness of the physical world and the complexity of organic nature militated against this theory of chance creation, and more modern atheists began to speak in terms of an immutable law, which so closely resembled a deity as to cause the Christian little intellectual discomfort. Newton's gravitational theory could be interpreted as confirmation either of the contemporary form of deism or of revealed religion. It was the transfer of the empirical system from the inorganic to the organic sphere that cut at the roots of Christian belief; for to recreate man in the image of the ape was to rob him of that hope of spiritual redemption out of which Christianity had sprung. Moreover, Darwinism posited an empirically supportable theory of chance creation which yet succeeded in explaining the orderliness and complexity of the natural world without postulating the existence of supernal powers.

The publication of the *Origin of Species* in 1859 offered the opposition a new and powerful weapon, but disquietude over the religious implications of empiricism had been felt much earlier. Coleridge, accepting the concept of religious evolution, had maintained that the literal interpretation of the Bible 'petrifies at once the whole body of Holy Writ', and he learned to rely instead upon the principle that 'whatever *finds* me' is thereby shown to derive from the Holy Spirit.[1] The subjectivity of this principle placed it safely beyond the realm of scientific evaluation. Charles Lyell's *Principles of Geology* (1830–33) raised doubts about the biblical account of Creation and prompted Tennyson's fearsome description of Nature 'red in tooth and claw', careless not only of the individual but even of the species. Yet comparatively few were aware of the impending threat to conventional religious beliefs.

George Eliot, for example, despite her wide reading and alert sensitivity to ecclesiastical sectarianism, had quietly been pursuing her aim of modelling herself upon St. Paul, Wilberforce and Hannah More when Hennell's *Inquiry Concerning the Origin of Christianity* (1838) exploded her calm assumptions.[2] Nor was Hennell himself aware of the attacks upon the infallibility of the Scriptures which were being made with increasing vehemence on the continent, and Strauss, whose famous *Leben Jesu* had been published some three years earlier, commented in a preface to the German translation of the *Inquiry* that despite the similarity of Hennell's work to that of the German critics, 'He is un-

---

[1] *Confessions of an Inquiring Spirit,* Letter i.
[2] Basil Willey's *Nineteenth Century Studies* (New York, 1949), particularly chapter viii, provides an interesting account of the Hennell circle. The best study of the demythologizing of Jesus is, of course, Albert Schweitzer's *The Quest of the Historical Jesus,* tr. F. C. Burkitt (New York, 1957).

acquainted with what the Germans have effected in the Criticism of the Gospels since Schleiermacher's work on Luke.'[1] As late as 1851, George Eliot remarked that the demythologizing of the Scriptures, although known long to German critics, was 'still startling to the English theological mind',[2] from which it is clear that the circle of Bray, Hennell, and Eliot formed little more than a provincial oasis of advanced thinkers.

For the wider public, the *Essays and Reviews* published in 1860 by six clergymen and one layman was the first indication that the attack had begun both from within and from without the fortress of orthodox Christianity. In his article *On the Study of the Evidence of Christianity* Baden-Powell argued that a change in the 'external accessories' of Christianity did not necessarily affect the ultimate validity of its essentials, and he proceeded to throw to the Cerberus of empiricism the sop of those miraculous occurrences in Scripture which he felt were no longer indispensable to modern Christianity. In an age which demanded such miraculous evidence these legends had, he suggested, served a useful function, but to the enlightened nineteenth-century thinker they formed a mere encumbrance and should be discarded forthwith. Where a century earlier Hume's similar essay on miracles had been dismissed by believing Christians with the scorn due to the scoffer, Baden-Powell's article found numerous sympathizers within the body of the Church – a group which continued to grow during the century until even the traditionalists became chary of claiming the veracity of such biblical accounts without adding some naturalistic explanation of the supposed miracle. The effect of this apparently minor change was a tacit rejection of the principle of direct revelation in favour of inner urges, visionary dreams, and imaginary 'voices' – a change which suggested divine intervention without assuming any suspension of the immutable laws of nature.

Matthew Arnold expressed most vividly the perturbation of the religious intellectuals of his day, forestalling them in some of his conclusions and providing an early summary of the future tendencies of English Protestantism. Following Coleridge and hence Spinoza, Arnold adopted the intuitive method of biblical

[1] Willey, p. 219.
[2] In her review of R. W. Mackay's *Progress of the Intellect* in the *Westminster Review liv* (1851).

interpretation in preference to the rationalistic, philological, and historical. Although condemned repeatedly as anti-Christian and anti-religious, he persisted in his attack on the Bibliolaters on the one hand and the iconoclasts on the other, centring his own interpretation of the Scriptures on the problem of miracle. In *God and the Bible* (1875) he suggested that a miracle was a credulous elaboration through the ages of an initial supernatural pheno- menon which itself did not 'interrupt the settled order of nature'.[1] The story that Jesus walked upon the waves he interpreted as having its source in the weird, bright light which appeared at the moment of baptism (recorded in the apocryphal *Gospel of the Hebrews*). The light itself was miraculous in its timing but contra- dicted no fundamental law of nature as did the supposition that water could support the weight of a vertical human body.

Arnold ridiculed his adversaries' interpretation of miracle by applying their methods to the fairy-tale of Cinderella. The fundamentalist, feeling that some concession to rationalism was necessary, would maintain that the fairy godmother transformed the pumpkin not into a coach-and-six but into a one-horse cab; while the rationalist, perceiving the 'true' story concealed be- neath the legendary account, would insist that she really sold the pumpkin in order to hire a cab with the proceeds. Arnold wisely stopped short of offering his own version of the story, but we may wonder whether his would be much better. Accord- ing to his interpretive method, the godmother substituted a coach-and-six for the pumpkin so quickly that Cinderella imagined a miraculous transformation had occurred, although (he would add circumspectly) it was miraculous that a coach- and-six just happened to be standing by at the time.

The ridicule, therefore, could be applied to all three parties, for it was equally 'reasonable' to interpret miracle as worthless folklore, or as a temporary interruption of natural law by an omnipotent God, or as an elaboration of an instance of divine intervention occurring within the framework of natural law. However, of the two religious interpretations, the latter was, once the innate conservatism of religious belief had been over- come, infinitely more attractive to the enlightened nineteenth- century Christian, since it implied no contradiction of those

---

[1] Matthew Arnold, *God and the Bible* (London, 1906), p. 30.

empirically proven laws which the scientists had declared to be inviolable. Among the more advanced thinkers, therefore, the choice lay between total rejection of the validity of the Bible (assisted by the Higher Critical theory of multiple authorship) and the attempt to recover the 'pure' message of a divinely inspired literature which had been garbled in transmission to disciples and subsequent generations.

The biblical dramatist of this period, busily engaged in his attempt to confirm the faith of the believer, was almost oblivious of the religious battle raging around him. Byron's *Cain* had, it is true, provided an early model of the intellectual inquirer demanding rational explanations of Christian belief; but his Cain never questioned the veracity of the biblical account and eventually even withdrew his suspicions of its implications. However, once the religious intellectuals surrendered their faith in the literalcy of the biblical text, it was inevitable that biblical drama should undergo a fundamental change, particularly in its portrayal of scriptural heroes.

The assumption that the original message of the Scriptures had been perverted by the credulity and superstition of its trans-mitters (an assumption into which the thinking Christian was forced by the rationalist view of miracles rather than by his own convictions) automatically placed the biblical figures in an entirely new light. The world of the Scriptures, so far from being elevated above the contemporary by its aura of holiness and divine inspiration, was suddenly viewed with some condescen-sion as peopled by an ignorant mob unable to distinguish be-tween fact and fiction, and demanding miraculous accounts in order to confirm its wavering faith. Even the leading biblical figures, respected still for their dedication to spiritual concepts and for the loftiness of their ideals, were, once robbed of their miraculous powers, brought closer to the level of ordinary men. Their haloes were explained away both literally and meta-phorically, and in consequence the sanctity which had since the late sixteenth century prevented their dramatic portrayal was reduced, even amongst the religious, to a degree which made such prohibition absurd. The resistance met by biblical drama-tists in the early twentieth century merely reflected the tardiness with which people were prepared to surrender their traditional standpoint.

Moreover, the new view of the Bible was confirmed by subsequent scholarship, until the evidence appeared overwhelming. Frazer's *Golden Bough* and his subsequent *Folklore of the Old Testament*, by perceiving parallels between the cultures of ancient peoples both primitive and civilized, argued that the Hebrews were as prone to 'savagery and superstition' as the most unenlightened African tribes. And the new science of Freudian psychology explained away the spiritual strivings of man in terms of libidinal perversions. As William James complained in 1902:

'Medical materialism finishes up St. Paul by calling his vision on the road to Damascus a discharging lesion of the occipital cortex, he being an epileptic. It snuffs out St. Teresa as an hysteric, St. Francis of Assisi as an hereditary degenerate. George Fox's discontent with the shams of his age and his pining for spiritual veracity, it treats as a symptom of a disordered colon. . . . And medical materialism then thinks that the spiritual authority of all such personages is successfully undermined.'[1]

What is more important, for many laymen the authority of such personages *had* been undermined, and one of the characters in Aldous Huxley's *Point Counter Point* describes the same St. Francis as 'a smelly little pervert who can only get a thrill out of licking lepers' ulcers'. This Christian symbol of spiritual self-sacrifice, humility, and altruism had been summarily dismissed as a masochistic pervert.

But whatever the cavilling of the extreme rationalists, the Bible still possessed a powerful fascination for reader and writer alike, and the centuries of veneration could not be swept aside in a moment, however intense the adverse criticism. The surge of interest in biblical themes during the twentieth century by religious and anti-religious alike testifies to the persistence of its appeal, although the treatment of these themes differed radically from that of preceding generations. Behind this new interest lay a desire to reassess the biblical narrative by discounting the miracles and visualizing the biblical figures in entirely human terms. In the new determination to expose the historical persons faintly visible through the 'distorting' biblical account, the traditional exegetical whitewashing of the more noble characters was

[1] William James, *Varieties of Religious Experience* (New York, 1958), p. 29.

pointedly ignored, and their actions judged impartially (or often antagonistically) by modern ethical criteria. The fear of blasphemy that had inhibited and restrained earlier writers had been interestingly inverted; for now worse than blasphemy against orthodox Christian doctrine was blasphemy against the new 'religion' of scientific materialism. To portray Jacob as a hypocrite was merely to rectify the myopia of the orthodox; but to introduce angels or miracles into a biblical play except for the purpose of comic effect or deliberate fantasy was to invite the derision of the rationalists and the scorn of the enlightened Christian.

The sudden lowering of biblical sanctity, therefore, encouraged the dramatization and stage presentation of its themes in much the same way as its rise prior to the publication of the Authorized Version had prohibited them. But it will be recalled that, even in the fifteenth and sixteenth centuries when biblical drama had flourished, a distinction had been preserved between the Old and the New Testaments. Quite apart from the difficulty of dramatizing New Testament narrative because of the infallibility of its main characters, the dramatist hesitated to cross the threshold of the Christian Holy of Holies by dramatizing the Gospels themselves. Once the wooden figures of the mystery cycles had been humanized, God could no longer appear on the stage, and since the majority of Gospel narrative revolves around Christ himself, stage dramatization of the Gospels was ruled out.

In the twentieth century too the distinction continued to operate, although for slightly different reasons. Essentially it still arose from the greater sanctity of the Gospels, but the nineteenth-century discussion of miracle now underscored the point. The historicity of the Old Testament miracles was surrendered almost at once, since it had little if any bearing on the validity of Christianity itself. It merely confirmed the impression that the deniers of Christ were no more than a superstitious rabble. The Protestant identification with the Old Testament characters was now a thing of the past, and the remnants of the sentimental attachment visible, for example, in the continued popularity of the Handelian oratorios was insufficient to withstand the onslaught of the empiricists. The conflict raged instead over the so-called 'evidences of Christianity' as related in the Gospels themselves. Arnold and others were prepared to discard such 'external accessories' as Christ's walking over the waves in order to defend on more rational grounds the essential truths which lay behind scriptural account. Yet if, as the enlightened Christian now maintained, miracles occurred only within the framework of the immutable laws of nature, then by logical extension the central mystery of Christianity, the Immaculate Conception, ought to be discarded too. Some Christians, it is true, felt impelled to take this final step and to regard Jesus as no more than a mortal of remarkable spiritual nobility, but it is questionable whether such belief belongs any longer within the framework of Christianity itself. To surrender faith in the divinity of Jesus was to deny the basis of Christianity, and as a result all but the most blatant atheists were chary of pressing the attack home too close to this central mystery. On the continent, writers were more outspoken and Ludwig Noack, for example, argued with some ingenuity that Jesus's illegitimate birth had led him to embrace God as a father substitute.[1] In England, though, if the portrayal of Jacob as a hypocrite was now acceptable, the presentation of Jesus himself in terms of modern psychological diagnosis was felt instinctively to be taking matters further than was permissible in an officially Christian country. As late as 1931, D. H. Lawrence's *The Man Who Died* (originally *The Escaped Cock*), despite the deep reverence with which it treated the Christ of flesh and blood, was greeted with a storm of protest for its suggestion that Christ could indulge in carnal love. The dramatist was free to interpret the Old Testament as liberally as he wished, but public opinion was too strong to allow similar liberties to be taken with the Gospels themselves. Once again, therefore, the resurgence of biblical drama was restricted almost exclusively (Sunday School drama apart) to the stories of the Old Testament.

(ii) Biblical Suffragettes

Although this demythologizing of Scripture and the pursuit of the authentic history it concealed were faintly reflected in biblical drama during the early decades of this century, no fundamental change occurred until as late as the twenties, when Shaw's *Back to Methuselah* replaced God in the story of Eden by the Berg-

---

[1] *Die Geschichte Jesu* (1876), quoted in Schweitzer, p. 177.

sonian Life Force. The earlier plays, despite their scriptural subject-matter, seemed more concerned with the sociological than the religious revolution of the contemporary scene – although the very application of contemporary problems to the biblical world did in itself presuppose an attempt, perhaps even subconscious, to visualize the sacred figures in human and hence contemporary terms. As in the nineteenth century, it is possible to perceive in the apparently heterogeneous conglomeration of dramas an underlying theme which unifies them despite their diversity.

If, as was suggested in the last chapter, the nineteenth-century preference for the Cain theme over that of Eve was prompted at least partially by the new idealization of woman, then the early twentieth-century group may be interpreted as reflecting the reaction – her demand for political and legal independence and the right to be treated as man's intellectual equal. Ibsen's Nora had firmly closed the door on matrimonial subservience and stepped out bravely into the world of the new feminism; and Shaw's *Candida* (1898) had transmitted the message to the English stage. The predominance, therefore, of female pro-tagonists in the biblical drama of the period may be viewed as part of the same movement. During the first quarter of the century some dozen plays appeared on the themes of Judith, Jezebel, Esther, Vashti, Salome, and Mariamne, in each of which the female character dominated the drama by her independent spirit and bold determination. Throughout the history of biblical exegesis, Judith and Jezebel had symbolized respectively the virtues and dangers of female participation in political affairs, and in this period they served admirably to highlight the hopes and fears inspired by the suffragettists. But the new militancy led both sides to invert the traditional reading when it suited their propagandist purposes. Jezebel was at times transformed into a virtuous and noble woman misunderstood by the ignorant Pharisees and hence vilified in their histories; and Judith, despite the praise of her piety in the apocryphal account, emerged in one dramatization as an erotic sensualist, slaying Holofernes merely in order to preserve unspoiled the perfect moment of love.

The first example of this feminist interpretation of scripture was scarcely encouraging. P. M. Barnard's *Jezebel* (1904), the work of a clergyman, continued the tradition of his predecessors in biblical drama by providing a 'poetized', literal recounting of the story in archaic diction; and despite the contemporary clash of views on miracle, he related unselfconsciously the wonders of Elijah on Carmel as though totally unaware of the dispute. Yet his Jezebel and Athaliah do possess a harshness, cruelty, and masculine intrepidity which contrast vividly with the gentle creatures of the disguised Fall plays, and King Ahab is but a poor creature, jeered at by his wife for his 'timorous fears'. Indeed, Jezebel's dominance over Ahab in the biblical story was the original attraction of the theme for the anti-feminists, and the transformation of Jezebel in some versions into a noble figure supporting a weak king by taking upon herself the blame for his transgressions was the feminists' answer to the charge.

Thomas Sturge Moore's *Mariamne* (1911) was probably inspired by the extraordinary success of Stephen Phillips' Herod play in the Beerbohm Tree production of 1900, but the lapse of just over a decade marked the transition from the nineteenth to the twentieth century in interest as well as date. For Phillips the theme was the romantic love of a king and his queen in the orientally luxuriant setting of the ancient biblical world. For Moore it was the story of two powerful female figures – Mariamne and Salome – whose conflict so dominates the play that Herod is simply dropped from the title as of merely minor interest. Salome is another Jezebel, seeking by her cunning insinuations and bribery of servants to rid her brother of his 'Delilah'. But Mariamne's affinity to the feminist movement is even more marked. Instead of turning against Herod because of her brother's murder (as in the Josephus account) her prime motive now is the conviction that Herod loves her not for herself but merely for her wit, beauty, and nobility. While most women might rejoice to be admired for such qualities, with echoes of Ibsen and Shaw she insists:

> *Is wit and beauty, beauty, wit and crown,*
> *My sum and total hold?*

Her love has prompted her to serve a man inferior in station and lineage. But unlike her nineteenth-century forebears with their noble loyalty and humble devotion, she resents impositions on her freedom:

Biblical Suffragettes

. . . 'tis no service, slavery it is
That will content thee!

She is the new woman, insisting that her fulfilment of matrimonial obligations be conditional on her husband's respect for
her individuality–for her somewhat ill-defined 'self' as opposed
to the sum of her attributes. In her death-cell at the conclusion of
the play she debates the possibility of demeaning herself by
begging his forgiveness but, although when it is too late she
eventually weakens for her child's sake, her determination to die
for her feminist principles is strong:

> *My husband loved me–not indeed as I*
> *Hoped, being foolish,–still he gave me much.*
> *And even now I am in reach of love,*
> *If I could only force these lips to cry;*
> *But pride has sealed them fast.*

Ultimately, it is her concern with her dignity as a woman and
her refusal to surrender her independence that prevents her from
returning his love.

In 1912, Gwen Lally's *Jezebel* finally broke the ban on stage
performances as the first licensed biblical drama of the twentieth
century, and was performed at the Comedy Theatre in March
of that year. It is unfortunate that the honour should have been
bestowed on so poor a work–dull, conventional, and written in
execrable verse. But perhaps those very defects allowed it
through the net, since it contained nothing to arouse the ire of
the Lord Chamberlain nor of those staider members of the public
whom he represented. At least, it had cleared the way for more
impressive plays. Beerbohm Tree's 1913 production of *Joseph
and his Brethren* by Louis N. Parker was not one of these more
impressive plays, but it gave greater publicity to the Lord
Chamberlain's new policy, which was now officially welcomed
by *The Times*. The showing during Christmas 1912 of an American film on the life of Christ–Reinhardt's *From the Manger to
the Cross*–demonstrated the relaxing of strict censorship.[1]

The outbreak of the Great War had thrown the doors of

---

[1] Gerald Weales, *Religion in Modern English Drama* (Philadelphia,
1961), p. 32. It incorrectly names Parker's as the first staged biblical
play of the century.

factories, hospitals, and business offices wide open to the suffragettes, and by its conclusion the satisfaction of their electoral demands had left them the less radical task of quietly extending the social bounds of their victory. The dramatizations of biblical heroines, while they continued to reflect the current concern with female independence, began to veer away from this central theme towards a greater concern with realism and consequently towards that reassessment of biblical morality which was soon to become typical of biblical drama in general. Moore's *Judith*, although published three years before the outbreak of the War, and performed at the Queen's Theatre in 1916, provided some hint of the new interests. The heroine is still a symbol of feminine courage, her courage being heightened by the moments of terror and weakness which precede the murder. But the most interesting innovation of the play was the patent suggestion (never made explicit) that in order to slay Holofernes she first submitted to his amorous advances. The Apocryphal account, by stressing Holofernes' drunkenness, suggests that she murdered him before he could seduce her, and the conclusion of the account insists that (in the biblical sense) 'none knew her all the days of her life after that Manasses her husband was dead'. For the modern dramatist, attempting to visualize the scene realistically and no longer inhibited by the *Noli me tangere* of biblical sacrosanctity, the scriptural story appeared to be deliberately concealing the less ennobling aspect of the incident in the cause of moral didacticism. Accordingly, Moore's Judith sheds tears of shame as she overhears the soldiers' jocular description of Holofernes as 'deliciously engaged'. The innuendoes, repeated by the Eunuch, are echoed in the maid's dream that Judith bathed naked in a stream and 'rose up black', and her prayer to God: 'Change not the heart because the hand is soiled' has, therefore, deeper implications than the defilement of murder. Such a presentation, of course, effectively removes Judith from her spotless pedestal, but at this early stage of biblical reassessment her dignity is still retained. The author acknowledges with admiration the patriotism of a heroine in performing a deed even more courageous than that recorded in the Bible – and his very respect suggests the application of new moral criteria to the ancient story.

In the following year, Lascelles Abercrombie's *Emblems of*

Love took this suggestion a degree further. As the title indicates, the underlying theme connecting these brief playlets is the varied aspects of love, and in consequence the two biblical plays included are distinctly un-Hebraic in tone. *Judith* opens the section devoted to 'Virginity and Perfection', and her virginity is the mainspring of the drama. The author was faced with the obvious problem that, as a widow, Judith's virginity had long ago been sacrificed on the altar of matrimony. Abercrombie carefully disposed of this by his interpretation of her refusal to wed after Manasses' death. In a woman who has once been clasped by the man she loves there is, he suggests, 'a fiercer and more virgin wrath' against subsequent suitors, and Judith has transformed her widowhood into an allegorical virginity. Her stern reproaches as the citizens consider surrender inspire the people's trust, and she decides after due deliberation that her virginity must be sacrificed once more, but this time for patriotism and not for love. What had been guardedly implicit in Moore's version is explicit in Abercrombie's, and before the curtains are modestly drawn on the scene in the bedchamber, Judith prays:

> *Show me the way to loathe this vile man's rage . . .*
> *So that not fainting, but refresht and astonisht*
> *And strangely spirited and divinely angry*
> *My body may arise out of its passion,*
> *Out of being enjoyed by this fiend's flesh.*

After the murder, she is filled with loathing at her defilement, at her having allowed a 'filthy verminous beast' to make his lair in her soul's chamber, and she is only restrained from suicide by the sympathetic persuasion of Ozias. By a final neat twist of the story, Abercrombie explains the omission of this defilement from the Apocryphal account: Ozias bids the people, for Judith's sake, to suppress the more sordid elements of the brave deed in relating the story outside the city walls.

Again Judith is transformed from myth to flesh, and female courage is eulogized. But in an earlier section of this book Abercrombie provided further evidence of the theory offered here that these plays were motivated by the feminist movement. *Vashti* opens the section named 'Discovery and Prophecy', by which we may assume from what follows that he meant the

discovery of the true meaning of love from the woman's viewpoint and her prophecy that it would be acknowledged in later
years. For the play is concerned with Vashti's refusal in the book
of *Esther* to answer the King's summons and to display her
beauty to the assembled guests. Earlier in the play, Ahasuerus's
assertion that woman was made for man's delight is scornfully rejected by Vashti with the familiar suffragettist question:

> *Now therefore tell me, Man, my king, my master:*
> *Lovest thou me, or dost thou rather love*
> *The pleasure thou hast in me? This is not nice,*
> *Believe me. They're more sundered, these two loves,*
> *Than if all the braving seas marcht between them.*

(The poverty of the verse explains why these minor plays are
of merely historical interest.) Ahasuerus, so far from being
resentful, is delighted by her intellectual prowess, and determined to let no man gaze upon this rare combination of wit and
beauty. In the following scene, however, the Poet's lengthy
praise of feminine charms prompts Ahasuerus to break his vow
and order her to appear. But the summons is inopportune. At
that moment Vashti is engaged in persuading her maidens how
unfair is the principle 'Man, please thyself, and woman, please
thou man'. In no mood to respond to the summons, she chooses,
like Nora, to surrender the comforts of her royal home and her
marriage in favour of her feminist ideals, and departs for exile
rather than submit to male arrogance. At this point we should
recall the contrast with the biblical account, which endorses the
counsel that 'every man should bear rule in his own house'.
Biblical history was, once again, being adapted to suit contemporary standards.

The year following the conclusion of the War saw the staging
of a biblical play which marked a notable break with the conventional depiction of scriptural heroes and heroines. Although
the subject-matter was still vaguely suffragettist, the audience's
interest was directed to the more erotic aspects of the biblical
story, in line with the hints apparent in the work of Moore and
Abercrombie. In fact, the play arose in a sense out of the staging
of Moore's *Judith*. For at the end of 1918, the actress Lillah
McCarthy, who had created the part of Moore's heroine, re-

quested Arnold Bennett to write her a play on the same theme.[1]
Bennett at once complied, and within just over three weeks it
was ready with the main part tailored to fit. The text itself was
less startling in its originality than the production, although it
lent itself to this more erotic interpretation and had, moreover,
the full blessing of the author. For in the performance Judith
more closely resembled Salome in her dance of the seven veils
than the dignified and decorous heroine of the Bible. Her
costume, the author informs us in his *Journal*, frightened one of
the lessees of the Eastbourne theatre at which it was first
produced.

'Above a line drawn about ½ inch or 1 inch above the *mont de
Venus* she wore nothing except a 4-inch band of black velvet
round the body hiding the breasts and a similar perpendicular
band of velvet starting from between the breasts and going
down to the skirt and so hiding the navel . . . The skirt was slit
everywhere and showed the legs up to the top of the thigh when
she laid [*sic*] down there at Holofernes' feet. She looked a
magnificent picture thus, but a police prosecution would not
have surprised me at all.'[2]

It appears that more than haloes were being stripped from
the biblical figures. Moreover, the apparently slight alteration
of the Apocryphal account to conclude with Judith's marriage
to Achior (where the original stresses her fidelity to Mannasseh's
memory) took on a deeper meaning in the light of the stage
presentation. She was transformed literally into a creature of
the flesh, and at the London performance a month later the
scantiness of her costume together with the erotic characterization evoked the wrath of the critics. *The Times* complained that,
although her lascivious advances to Holofernes must be accepted
as justified by the original text, her immodest behaviour to
others was indefensible:

'She ogles the Governor. She ogles a young captive, whom
she ultimately marries. She even ogles the Chief Eunuch.

---

[1] Yeats spoke contemptuously of her performance as having ruined
Moore's play, but Moore himself defended her. See *W. B. Yeats and
T. Sturge Moore: Their Correspondence*, ed. Ursula Bridge (London,
1953), pp. 24–25.
[2] *Journal of Arnold Bennett* (New York, 1933), p. 684. Bennett
later wrote the libretto for Eugene Goossens' opera *Judith*.

And all the time she is talking fervently of the God of Israel.'[1]

The public, apparently, was not yet ready for such lively dramatization, and after a short run the play closed as a box-office failure.

Yet the most significant originality of the play was ignored by the critics, although it may well have contributed to their righteous indignation. For the first time in centuries, biblical drama was being enlivened by broad humour, and the supernumeraries, like their forebears in the mystery cycles, were treated as comic figures. Ozias and Chabris squabble over a bottle, insist with obvious topical allusion that theirs will be the war to end all wars, parody biblical genealogy, make wry comments about women, and scoff at each other's ages. Later in the play the other minor characters continue the light-hearted banter. The brutish Ingur, smitten by the 'charms' of Judith's ugly maid, the eunuch Bagoas vainly attempting to keep order among his master's numerous mistresses, serve to remove from the play that aura of sanctity which had for so long paralysed biblical drama. It pointed forward to the more successful humour of Bridie's scriptural plays.

John Masefield's *Esther* (1922) was no more than an insipid adaptation of Racine for a small amateur group, but his play *A King's Daughter*, published in the following year and performed twice at the Oxford Playhouse, marks a significant change in the twentieth-century presentation of the Jezebel story. Applying to the theme the new conception of the Old Testament as a series of Pharisaically biased accounts, he transposed the virtuous and the guilty to reveal the supposed truth concealed by the historian's prejudice. Jezebel herself emerges as a loyal wife, a believer in the purity of her inherited religion, and a devoted queen, struggling to establish justice and peace among her fanatically hostile and crafty subjects. Naboth, a coarse, stubborn braggart, answers her gentle reasoning with a stream of insults, and since in this play the central theme of Ahab's desire for the vineyard is transformed from mere personal cupidity into a matter of national strategic necessity, the righteous cause passes from Naboth to the queen. What had begun as an attempt to reassess the moral integrity of the

[1] *The Times* (London), May 1, 1919.

biblical heroes in the light of modern ethical criteria was becoming an arbitrary rewriting of the story with the express purpose of whitewashing the villains and blackening the heroes. It was a form of deliberate iconoclasm rather than a pursuit of the truth.

Of particular interest is Masefield's denigration of the prophet as a political schemer, hypocritically justifying his self-interest by his claim of divine inspiration. In league with the plotter Jehu from the first, he comments cynically:

> *Truly our work is godly, since it prospers.*

and his oath 'Gods!' echoed repeatedly by Jehu leaves no doubt of the superficiality of their religious faith. Jezebel muses:

> *How blest to be a prophet, who forever*
> *Does but condemn another man's endeavour.*
> *How blest, not to decide, nor be, nor do,*
> *But help the many to condemn the few.*

Apparently chary of naming him Elijah directly, the author chose instead to call him simply 'The Prophet', but under this innocuous title he unobtrusively fused Elijah and the false prophet Zedekiah in order to discredit the former.[1]

The parallel between Masefield's approach and that of the Higher Critical school is interestingly demonstrated by a lengthy review of his play which appeared a few months later in the *Sewanee Review*.[2] The reviewer endorsed the attempt of 'this nobly imagined and finely written tragedy' to reconstruct the original scene whatever departures from the records the needs of the task might require, and he provided a learned dissertation in Wellhausen terms of the historical background to the biblical account. When Jezebel introduced the worship of Astarte and Melkart into the predominantly Yahwe tradition of Palestine, no one, he informs the reader, was sufficiently enlightened to perceive that there can be no such thing as a false religion 'given due earnestness', and he describes Elijah as a fanatical patriot opposed to the introduction of the Tyrian Baal Melkart primarily

---

[1] Masefield's quotation of Ahab's famous cry to Elijah, 'Hast thou found me, O my enemy?' and of Zedekiah's, 'horns of iron' symbol leaves no doubt that he was aware of the distinction.

[2] G. H. Clarke, 'John Masefield and Jezebel', *SR xxxii* (1924), 225.

through fear of the commercial infiltration involved. He admits that the obscene rites of the Baal worship may have acted as an additional motive, but Elijah emerges from his summary as a political economist rather than a prophet and is consequently dismissed as a mere chauvinist in much the same way as St. Francis had been dismissed as a masochist.

Naboth's Vineyard (1925) by Clemence Dane (a pen-name for Winifred Ashton) is a more sensitive attempt to reinterpret the biblical story since it reassesses the moral integrity of the protagonists without sacrificing the essentials of the original account. The incident of the vineyard, for example, is left intact in so far as Ahab's motive is personal greed and Naboth's refusal to sell arises from respect for an ancestral inheritance. Yet the guilt is shifted nonetheless by the expedient of converting the simple tale of greed versus filial piety into a complex politico-religious intrigue in which Naboth and Ahab are pawns in a larger game. From the opening scene the petty bickering between the priests of Ashtoreth and those of the Jewish God prepare the audience for the central scene in which Jezebel and Naboth confront each other. Jezebel, eager for power and for the command of an expanding empire, is nevertheless a creature of gentleness and kindness when not compelled to act harshly. In the court scene where she has acted as a second Solomon, protecting the marital rights of the woman by a clever legal move, she complies readily with Naboth's insistence on renting rather than selling the plot. All is amicably agreed between them, when the prophet Zedekiah whispers to Naboth that he should insist upon her swearing to the contract by the Jewish God instead of Ashtoreth. Jezebel, understandably, refuses and her reasonable offer that each should swear by his own god is scornfully rejected by the roused mob. Thus, while the guilt of cupidity and murder is technically retained, the audience's sympathies are transferred to the murderess.

The depiction of the Hebrew priests as self-seekers inciting an ignorant and fickle rabble in order to further their own ends becomes a stereotype for almost all twentieth-century biblical drama, in contrast to the noble orientals of the preceding era. It was a healthy realism encouraging the portrayal of truly human characters, but it indicated also the extent to which the relationship between the Old and New Testaments had changed as a result of the empiricists' attacks. For this fickle, jeering rabble now represented the Pharisees of the New Testament, the deniers of Christ, rather than such heroic figures as the Maccabees, and even the hitherto venerable prophets were portrayed unsympathetically. In a sense the wheel had come full circle. The stern rebukes meted out to Isaiah and others in the ancient *Ordo Prophetarum* for their reluctance to testify on Christ's behalf were being paralleled by the twentieth-century conviction that the supposed virtues of the rejecters of Jesus should be regarded with the gravest suspicion. The subordination of the Old Testament to the New was being repeated.

The most extreme European instance of this demythologizing of Scripture is, perhaps, Giraudoux's *Judith* (1931) which treated the Apocryphal story in much the same way as Anouilh's *Antigone* treated Greek mythology. For both dramatists the ancient myth was little more than a convenient framework for a fundamentally new tragedy, with the advantage that the contrast between the ancient and modern treatments of the subject-matter lent an added spice of interest. For Giraudoux the biblical subject-matter had no greater sanctity than any other ancient myth, and he simply adapted the original framework to fit his own needs. Judith is here a virgin, and Giraudoux, unlike Abercrombie, is writing in an era which requires no explanation of the discrepancy. Divine inspiration is no longer in vogue: 'Don't talk prophecy to me. Let's call it by its name: mass hysteria'; and God is treated for the most part as somewhat less than human. 'Tonight', Judith is told by an admirer, 'even Jehovah is flattered because His name starts with the same letter as yours.' Moreover, the theme of female heroism triumphing in the cause of divine righteousness is replaced by that of a pleasure-loving, vain, and self-centred woman slaying an intelligent and kindly Holofernes merely to preserve the moment of love. Her motives are, however, faintly patriotic and her arrogance makes her squirm at the thought that she may have to share some of the praise with a jealous God.

'God writhes with jealousy. That divine hypocrite, I can feel him all around me, grasping, trying to take all the credit for himself.'[1]

[1] Translation by J. K. Savacol in *The Modern Theatre*, ed. Eric Bentley (New York, 1955), p. 185.

The play returns to the biblical setting only in the concluding scene in which a sentry, seized by a divine spirit, explains that there was a miracle despite Judith's conviction to the contrary since angels had accompanied her throughout – for 'God reserves the right to project saintliness on sacrilege, and purity on self-indulgence. It's all a question of knowing how to light the stage.' The play is thus concerned, like *Murder in the Cathedral* (also written in the thirties), with the idea that the greatest treason may be 'To do the right deed for the wrong reason.' It was, perhaps, the twentieth-century version of faith versus works.

These dramatizations of biblical heroines had by now lost their original 'suffragettist' impetus and had grown more intimately concerned with the attempt to disclose the truth concealed beneath the superstitious reverence or deliberate forgery of the biblical historian. Yet however radical such rewriting had become, the themes of Judith and Jezebel were not the best clinical specimens for the demythologizers. They were, in a sense, peripheral. As Judith was derived from the Apocrypha, and Jezebel was a non-Jewish villainess, their respective denigration and whitewashing involved little that could be called blasphemy by the orthodox. If Elijah was transformed from prophet to schemer, the transformation took place anonymously, under the guise of the Beggar or Prophet. To perceive fully the change in the treatment of biblical figures, we must examine those plays devoted to the traditional heroes themselves, the dramatizations of Moses, Samuel, and David, whose faith and nobility of purpose had been virtually unquestioned in preceding generations.

(iii) The Nietzschean Moses

The earliest plays of this group formed little more than the backwash of the previous century. Thomas Ewing's *Jonathan* (1902) merely versified the story in terms of sacred heroes and blackguardly villains, and C. W. Cayzer's *David and Bathshua* (1903), published under the pseudonym of C. W. Wynne, did much the same, although in more respectable verse than its predecessor. The only important change in Wynne's version was an attempt to exculpate David from the guilt of Uriah's murder, and this attempt to whitewash a biblical hero is itself sufficient indication of the author's awareness of twentieth-century trends.[1] Stephen Phillips' *Sin of David* (1904) avoided the problem of censorship by placing the story in a seventeenth-century setting, as was noted above, and A. R. Thorndike's *Saul* (1906) swung back to medieval typology in order to depict the triumph of David over Saul as symbolic of the victory of the New Testament over the Old. The only worthwhile scriptural drama was Thomas Sturge Moore's *Absalom* (1903) which preceded his Judith and Mariamne plays by almost a decade. While not a great play, it has a dignity and delicacy of characterization which elevates it above the uninspired biblical drama of its period, and the verse itself is one of the earliest attempts to discard the bombastic rhetoric and archaic diction thought appropriate for scriptural plays. Moore's concern with the future of poetic drama—a concern which he shared with Yeats and Bottomley—marked the first serious if not fully successful attempt to break with this unfortunate tradition.

One quality common to almost all these early biblical dramas is their concern with the life and times of King David. Indeed, apart from the feminist plays, the overwhelming majority of scriptural dramas published during the first forty years of the century were devoted to this one era. Nor was the predominance fortuitous, for the stories connected with David's life form, in one respect, the least suspect section of biblical history. Old Testament miracle had by now lost favour even with the so-called fundamentalists, and the dramatist instinctively retreated to those less vulnerable areas of scriptural narrative which contained no instances of the temporary suspension of natural law. Such previously popular figures as Adam, Cain, Noah, Abraham, Joseph, and Moses were all concerned with divine participation in human affairs and heavenly visions of the future, but the richly dramatic vicissitudes of David's life were recorded in realistically human terms. Despite the divine election which had preceded his victory over Goliath—an election which, incidentally,

---

[1] Charles M. Doughty, the author of *Travels in Arabia Deserta*, wrote a play entitled *Adam Cast Forth* (London, 1908) which both in subject-matter and treatment clearly belongs to the nineteenth-century disguised Fall plays. Its inversions of word-order and grotesque ellipses were attacked in the *Athenaeum cxxxii* (1908. George Moore's *The Passing of the Essenes*, staged in 1930, was, like his earlier *The Apostle* (1923), merely a dramatization of his novel *The Brook Kerith*.

took the form not of the usual vision but of a simple anointing at the hand of a fellow human-being – the victory itself was achieved by the mundane device of a pebble and sling. And for all their spirituality, his magnificent *Psalms* consist not of ethereal visions of the celestial throne but of humble prayers in time of mortal danger and of thanksgiving to the Creator of the sheep, the mountains, and the natural beauties of this visible world. Although Moses, Abraham and, indeed, all the Old Testament characters were fallible, none fell so low as David and was yet redeemed; and the nature of his fall was one to capture the imagination and excite the interest of the dramatist. Moreover, of all biblical characters none is delineated so fully in the text itself as David, from his innocent boyhood, through his idyllic friendship with Jonathan and his military prowess, and on to his feeble dotage, when the beautiful Abishag fails to warm the blood of the dying old man. The stories of David's life were, by their freedom from the supernatural and by their striking realism, ideally suited to the needs of the twentieth-century dramatist and they were exploited accordingly.

However, there were those among the dramatists, as the feminist plays have indicated, who were specifically interested in depicting the miraculous episodes themselves, either in order to expose the miracle-workers as charlatans or, less belligerently, in order to re-examine these episodes stripped of their supernatural elaboration. The most popular figure for the demythologizers proved to be Moses. But the treatment of this theme reveals that the motivation was more complex than mere opposition to miracle. For in the twentieth-century dramatizations of Moses he is depicted as a Nietzschean superman dragging by the sheer force of his own personality and vigour a reluctant and illiterate rabble on to victory and upward in the scale of human dignity and achievement. Frequently ruthless, and unshakable in his certainty of success, he emerges less as a servant of destiny than as its creator, and where the miracles are admitted into the play in a significantly attenuated form, they arise out of the sheer force of his will rather than as a sign of divine approval.

Surprisingly little has been written on the literary effects of the Nietzschean superman, although a study of the biblical drama alone reveals how profound was the influence. Carlyle's admiration for the national hero and Nietzsche's idealization of

The Nietzschean Moses

the *Übermensch* had received powerful support both from the Darwinian theory of the survival of the fittest and from the twentieth-century intellectual's instinctive antipathy towards the bourgeois results of mass education.[1] Shaw's *Man and Superman* (1903), in preface, play, and Revolutionist's Handbook, popularized the concept in England and in an age dominated by anxiety neuroses and lack of direction the ancient heroes became further idealized for their steadfastness and conviction of purpose. In the same way as Eliot's Prufrock gazed with longing and envy at such unswervingly defiant figures as John the Baptist and Michelangelo, so Moses began to typify in scriptural drama the vigorous leadership of a powerful national hero, imposing law and justice on a barbaric and aimless mob.

The first such Moses drama was Isaac Rosenberg's brilliant but brief play published in 1916. It had the merit of a threefold originality. It was the first play to present a scriptural theme stripped bare of its miracles; it was the first of what I have called the Nietzschean dramatizations; and, perhaps most important of all, it was the first play to substitute for the pompous archaic diction of most scriptural dramas the refreshing touch of true poetry, with colourful images and exciting verbal combinations. One might have suspected from its brevity that the play's two scenes were merely drafts for a full-length play, but since it was published during Rosenberg's brief lifetime, it seems likely that he had no intention of expanding it. Yet within its narrow compass much was achieved.

The two scenes are restricted to the incident of the Egyptian's murder, but they suffice to depict Moses himself as a Colossus in the midst of petty men, driven on by his intense personal ambition, and eager to trample on men's lives in order to satisfy his egotistical lust for power:

> . . . *my hands ache to grip*
> *The hammer – the lone hammer*
> *That breaks lives into a road*
> *Through which my genius drives.*[2]

[1] Eric Bentley, *A Century of Hero-Worship* (Boston, 1957), published in Great Britain as *The Cult of the Superman* (1947), deals primarily with the political implications.

[2] *Collected Poems*, ed. Gordon Bottomley and Denys Harding (London, 1949), p. 48.

Commanded by Pharaoh to extract the teeth of the Jews (an idea derived from a famous instance in medieval England), Moses refuses not through squeamish pity for his fellow creatures but as a means of testing Pharaoh's trust and of obtaining the Israelites' adulation. So far from experiencing a divine call, he speaks contemptuously of 'This miasma of a rotting god' and it is his own Life Force which provides the momentum for the exodus. One admiring young Israelite records that as he lay almost dying, the touch of Moses' vitality was sufficient to restore him to life:

> *O what a furnace roaring in his blood*
> *Thawed my congealed sinews and tingled my own*
> *Raging through me like a strong cordial.*

Finally, Moses slays the Egyptian not as in the original story in the cause of justice but to prevent the premature disclosure of his Hebrew origin. Yet at the moment of this calmly callous murder, there is a hint of the noble achievements which will result from his selfish lusts – the beneficial consequences of the superman's power:

> *I'd shape one impulse through the contraries*
> *Of vain ambitious men . . .*
> *. . . All that's low I'll charm;*
> *Barbaric love sweeten to tenderness.*
> *Cunning run into wisdom, craft turn to skill.*
> *Their meanness threaded right and sensibly*
> *Change to a prudence, envied and not sneered.*
> *Their hugeness be a driving wedge to a thing,*
> *Ineffable and useable, as near*
> *Solidity as human life can be.*
> *So grandly fashion these rude elements*
> *Into some newer nature, a consciousness*
> *Like naked light seizing the all-eyed soul,*
> *Oppressing with its gorgeous tyranny*
> *Until they take it thus – or die.*

And in the concluding words we return to the cold brutality that lies behind the lofty aim.

The poetry has an excitement and power that matches its

theme and in many ways, both poetically and in treatment of subject-matter, it forestalls by some thirty years the most recent version of the same theme, Christopher Fry's *The Firstborn*. It was an impressive departure from the dull nineteenth-century tradition, and served as a bright harbinger of the new school of biblical drama.

(iv) SHAVIAN WIT

In 1921, Shaw announced in his lengthy preface to *Back to Methuselah* that he had written it 'as a contribution to the modern Bible', and provocatively subtitled it *A Metabiological Penta-teuch*. As the first portion of the play, he rewrote the opening chapters of *Genesis* in a scintillating rebuttal of neo-Darwinism, and if the Bible suffered in the process, so much the worse for the Bible. Assuming with typical *sang-froid* that no intelligent man now 'outraged' his intellectual conscience by accepting the veracity of biblical legend, he urged his readers with mock earnestness not to neglect the Bible completely, particularly 'the chronicles of King David, which may very well be true, and are certainly more candid than the official biographies of our contemporary monarchs'. But miracle he rejected out of hand, insisting that it was this adulteration of religion that made it reel at the impact of every advance in science. Yet for all his iconoclasm and reformatory zeal, he was theologically rooted in the nineteenth-century tradition, embodying and extending the religious assumptions of the Arnold school.[1] The more closely one examines the contradictions inherent in his use of the Bible, the more apparent it is that beneath the caustic wit and ostensible empiricism lay an awareness of some mysterious power over and above that Life Force for which he argues so learnedly and so pungently.

His rejection of neo-Darwinism in favour of the Bergsonian Life Force was based, as he explicitly states, on his antipathy to

[1] Julian B. Kaye, *Bernard Shaw and the Nineteenth Century Tradition* (Oklahoma University Press, 1958), and Anthony S. Abbott, *Shaw and Christianity* (New York, 1965), examine in very general terms the religious vein in Shaw's writings. See also Dean Inge, 'Shaw as a Theologian', in *G.B.S.* 90, ed. S. Winten (New York, 1946).

the principle of circumstantial selection. The theory he had advocated in *Man and Superman* that Will, the inner urging to create and survive, was the motivating and preservative force in the history of mankind, he now applied to the biblical world. However, his dramatic innovation of a disembodied Voice to represent this inner Force – a device, incidentally, which was to be adopted in almost all subsequent scriptural drama to represent divine intervention – revealed an instinctive dissatisfaction with the Bergsonian theory itself. For while the Voice was originally intended to suggest an inner prompting of will or conscience, it could serve also as a symbol of external prompting, of a force directing puny man from without towards the fulfilment of an ultimate universal purpose. And this is precisely the change that occurs almost imperceptibly in the course of his biblical scenes.

The first mention of the Voice clearly restricts it to an inner prompting. Adam insists that he can distinguish it from all other sounds because 'it is so near that it is like a whisper from within myself'. Yet he speaks later of 'the sentinel set by the Voice', in which the voice has taken on a new meaning as an independent being. The Serpent assures Adam that the Voice he hears is merely his own voice, but Adam now insists that 'it is something greater than me: I am only a part of it'. By the Cain scenes at the conclusion of the section, it has become a symbol of divine Authority making all men but Cain 'listen and tremble in silence'. Adam accuses his son of 'blasphemy' for attempting to tame the Voice and they proceed to argue how far this Voice proves the existence of 'divine justice'.

What the terms 'blasphemy' and 'divine justice' are intended to mean in the supposedly amoral setting of Darwinism and the Life Force it is difficult to conceive, unless they suggest an unconscious return to the traditional setting of a universe directed by a supernal, anthropomorphic power. And we should recall here that both the conventional Adam and the rationalist Cain argue in favour of this divine justice. The Voice has suddenly become strangely reminiscent of Arnold's 'Power not ourselves that makes for righteousness'.

The problem of miracle, so far from being suppressed, forms the main theme of the 'biblical' opening act, and, particularly, the miracle of childbirth in which the will to reproduce is interpreted as the miraculous force. The Serpent's suggestion of the word *conceive* to denote this process of imaginatively willed procreation is a *tour de force*, but even at Shaw's most convincingly earnest moments there is always a suspicion of sly mockery, and we almost forget to ask who had willed Lilith (Adam and Eve's mother) into existence. With the skill of the consummate debater, he has neatly deflected his audience's attention from the main point by means of a fascinating side issue.

Similarly the original story of *Genesis* is unobtrusively twisted to fit the needs of this metabiological Pentateuch, and by suppressing awkward details Shaw gives the impression of having proved his point from the scriptural account itself. He adroitly ignores Cain's expulsion from Eden and the punishment of eternal wandering, and seizes triumphantly on the merciful addendum of a protective mark as proof of divine approval and justification. The effect is, of course, to exonerate Cain entirely and to provide that inversion of moral guilt beloved by the twentieth-century dramatists. The murder of Abel is conveniently relegated to the distant past and the remorseless Cain triumphs in this victory. 'Anybody', he boasts to Adam, 'could be the first man: it is as easy as to be the first cabbage. To be the first murderer one must be a man of spirit,' and it soon becomes clear that Cain is another Nietzschean figure of ruthless will, exulting in bloodshed and warfare as tests of manly prowess. 'There is', he says twirling his moustache, 'something, higher than man. There is hero and superman.' In Byron's *Cain*, it will be recalled, the vegetarian hero slays Abel in a moment of anger. Here we have the vegetarian Shaw condoning murder in a moment of calm. But of course there was nothing he would not condone for the pleasure of shocking his audiences out of their complacent assumptions, and it is perhaps unfair to examine too seriously the delightful parries and thrusts of Shavian dialogue.

Rosenberg's play apart (which in all likelihood the prosaic Shaw had never troubled to read), this self-contained act was a startling innovation in biblical drama and may be regarded as the turning-point dividing the old school of reverent bibliolaters from the fearless and often iconoclastic reinterpreters of scriptural themes in the light of modern criteria. Once Shaw's wit had pecked away on the public stage at these hitherto sacred stories, they were fair game for his fellow dramatists, and if this reinterpretation involved an inversion of the moral lessons they taught, it did, at least, infuse a new vitality into the stock characters.

The effect was at once noticeable, and in the same year there appeared an amusing playlet by the humorist A. P. Herbert entitled *The Book of Jonah.* (*As almost any modern Irishman would have written it.*)[1] Although only a minor piece not intended for stage presentation, it had the distinction of being the first frankly comic dramatization of a leading biblical character. The supernumeraries had frequently been treated humorously in the mystery cycles and the practice was revived in Bennett's *Judith*; here not only the central figure but even the central story was treated with gentle mockery. It is difficult to convey briefly the delightful flavour of the original, but as the scene opens Mrs. Joner is discovered seated in front of her house next to an enormous statue of her 'late' husband. In a broad Irish brogue she relates to her amorous suitor Timothy James O'Leary the events which led up to his sad demise:

Mrs. J.: It was the sailors of the ship that did be saying they would sail the ship no longer when they found that himself was in the Post Office, and him travelling for the Government. And there was a great storm and the ship tossing the way you wouldn't know she was a ship at all, or a cork that a boy throws in the water out of a bottle; and the sailors said it was the English Government – and why would it not be? – and they cried out against himself, and he rose up out of his bed and 'Is it sinking the ship I would be?' he said, and he threw himself over the side into the water – and that was the way of it.

T.J.: (*reflectively*) And him with the rheumatics – God rest his soul! And have you any pension taken from the Government?

Mrs. J.: I have so. And it's worth more to me he is now he's dead than ever he was when he was alive, with all his praying and preaching and prophesying.

As she accepts her suitor, Mr. Joner returns in person to relate

[1] In the *London Mercury iii* (1921), 601.

his miraculous survival in the whale. His two hearers are incredulous, but suggest, with Joner's acquiescence, that it might be profitable to exploit his supposed experiences financially in order to compensate for the loss of the pension. Joner wisely agrees to alter the whale to 'a big fish' when it is pointed out to him that a whale's throat is too small to admit a man.[1]

Behind the comedy lies a delicate ridiculing of miracle and hence of the authenticity of the scriptural story; but more important was Herbert's ability to translate the ancient characters into vividly modern terms, largely by means of the incredulity with which such a story would be greeted today. It is not so far removed from the mystery cycles' depiction of Noah's wife nagging mercilessly at her workmanlike husband and scoffing at his warning of an imminent deluge.

The Shavian influence was even more marked in a work by the British-born Lawrence Langner who settled in America where he founded the famous Washington Square Players and later the Theatre Guild which supplanted them. His play *Moses* (1924) was, like those of Shaw, preceded by a preface almost as long as the play itself which, after discussing the theme of the play, exploited the opportunity for castigating the evils of shoddy manufacture, poor work-rates, advertising, American soft-living, and mass education.[2] Although Langner lacked that wit which served to sugar the bitterest of Shavian pills, he had a similar ability to twist almost anything into convincing proof of his own viewpoint, and the play is an impressive piece of reassessment, perhaps too long ignored.

The story of Moses he treats as mere legend, as 'part of the folklore of all the western nations'. In a stimulatingly original, if somewhat suspect, examination of the Hebraic tradition, he applies contemporary scientific discoveries to the ancient account. From Freud he deduces that both Moses and the conception of God which he created are father images in their threat of punishment for disobedience of stringent rules. On Marxist

[1] In fact, the whale tradition is post-biblical; the Bible itself refers only to 'a great fish'.
[2] Published in New York, it was never performed. Langner's *Susannah and the Elders* (1940) is, despite its title, not a biblical play, but a comedy devoted to the religious 'communist' settlements of nineteenth-century America.

lines, he sees Joseph's insistence on the need for granaries as an attempt to exploit the liquid assets of the country and become the first capitalist-monopolist. He even suggests that the invention of monotheism marked the beginning of modern scientific inquiry since the sun was no longer a god but merely a giant heating and lighting machine. But like many of his theories it is too glib; it ignores the theories of divine immanence, the animistic element of Hebraism in which all creation joins in praise of God, and (the very antithesis of his suggestion) the mystery of divine creation as opposed to a purely mechanistic interpretation of the universe.

The main story is changed radically into a conflict between law and beauty, with Moses and Miriam as their representatives. Moses, as a man who often exposed his vices 'under the mistaken impression that they were virtues' (a remark which typifies the inversion of biblical morality) forbids all graven images, and Miriam, who is Langner's mouthpiece as well as Beauty's, insists:

'It is given our people to dream; to feel the infinite beauty of the universe which God has created, and to desire to create in the image of his handiwork; and by creating, they partake of the spirit of God Himself, for thus they come closest to knowing Him and loving Him.'

The crucial scene is, of course, that of the Golden Calf which Miriam claims is a cleaner form of sacrifice than the blood-offerings instituted by Moses and a form of art essential to this imaginative people. It would seem that Langner's ideal is the cultivation of art and beauty in a people sufficiently civilized to abstain from idolatry, but he has no constructive suggestions for educating the erstwhile slaves of the Exodus.

The passage quoted above indicates how far the diction of scriptural drama had moved from the archaisms of nineteenth-century rhetorical drama towards a robust modern prose. In fact, the diction of twentieth-century plays on scriptural themes fluctuated between biblical *thees* and *thous* on the one hand and modern prose or verse on the other; but at least the vernacular was no longer regarded as inappropriate and if the playwright chose the artificiality of biblical jargon, his choice was no longer dictated by convention. There was still the risk of offending the die-hards who insisted that the language 'becomes too ordinary and colloquial for the dignity of the Bible situation' or who felt that colloquialisms were 'rather undignified speech for a prophet'[1], but usually the dramatist was sufficiently intelligent to ignore such advice. The aim at this period (unlike that of more recent years) was to achieve realism, and not to allegorize by deliberate artificiality.

In accordance with this need for realism in an age of reason, the miracles of the biblical story were dropped entirely. The manna was dismissed with the remark that they were 'supping on dates and sleeping on thistles,' while the ten plagues preceding the Exodus are reduced to one, and that rationally explicable. The danger in demythologizing the Scriptures was that the baby was only too frequently thrown out with the bathwater. The story of the Exodus stripped of its miracles, its sense of divine purpose, its ethical lessons, and its national significance, leaves little for the dramatist but the figure of Moses as a primitive lawgiver, narrow-mindedly excluding, like Plato, all art and non-didactic literature from the state; and that is precisely the figure Langner's Moses becomes. Yet because of the associations which readers bring to the play, Moses' dignity and power seem to have roots extending more deeply into the soil of human experience than the dialogue itself warrants and this vicarious quality is the prime advantage gained by the dramatizer of scriptural themes.

The contemporary attempt to visualize scriptural scenes realistically in terms of the modern world is nowhere more refreshingly suggested than in the American folk-play *Green Pastures* (1930) by Marc Connelly.[2] Based on Roark Bradford's *Ol' Man Adam an' His Chillun*, it presents with guileless simplicity the Negro's view of heaven in which God, who remarkably resembles the local Negro preacher, participates with his Negro angels in a celestial fish-fry. The reason for the play's success is partly, as the author suggests in the preface, that the illiterate Negro is unburdened by theology or fidelity to the details of the biblical text and hence can allow his imagination full rein; but it might be truer to note that the uneducated

[1] Rose E. Glaymen's comment on Masefield's *Judith* in her *Recent Judith Drama and its Analogues* (Philadelphia, 1930), p. 98.

[2] Eugene O'Neill's *Lazarus Laughed* (1925) stands at the other extreme. A sophisticated experimental play of masks and symbols, it is only biblical in starting-point. It relates the story of Lazarus after the Crucifixion, his laughter symbolizing the discovery of eternal life.

Negro of the twentieth century is also not burdened by the need to rationalize. What is more important, the non-Negro audiences could suspend their rationalist criticisms with a feeling of pleasant indulgence rather than of disloyalty to the New Age. The charming *naïveté* of the Negro characters protected it, moreover, from any charge of blasphemy in much the same way as a child could not be castigated for visualizing God as his grandfather, and the Negro preacher's rejoinder to all awkward questions: 'De answer is dat de Book ain't got time to go into all de details', succeeded by its very ingenuousness in prompting a willing suspension of disbelief. For the sophisticated audiences it constituted the same type of escape from intellectualism as primitivism has offered in every era of excessive refinement.

(v) W. B. Yeats and D. H. Lawrence

If Locke in an earlier era had welcomed Reason as 'the candle of the Lord' placed in the minds of men to confirm and direct their religious as well as their secular thoughts, for the Shavian school it had become an incandescent lamp dispelling once and for all the shadowy mystery of Christian belief. There were still lessons to be learnt from the Nietzschean supermen directing class-warfare among the ancient tribesmen of Palestine; there were even charming tales that could be cleverly inverted to teach the new Bergsonian theories; but the magic of the Scriptures had vanished. The death and rebirth of Jesus and the prohibition of work on the Sabbath no longer constituted part of a divine plan but had become mere fertility totems and taboos masquerading as religious truths. But for Yeats and Lawrence that very primitivist reading which had apparently invalidated the Bible formed its most potent attraction. Chilled as they were by the analytical materialism of their age, they perceived within the anthropological search for folkloristic parallels a new validation of the Scriptures as having emanated from man's intuitive responses to the archetypal cycles of nature in contrast to the artificial scientism of the contemporary world. Paradoxically, the Bible's appeal now lay in its 'paganism'.

While Lawrence saw the natural urge for procreation, the

'naked hunger and inevitability of . . . loving' as a primary
symbol of man's creativity, Yeats was more of a dreamer, view-
ing such natural primitivism as only one aspect of man's incessant
struggle with the supernatural, with the cyclical forces which
mysteriously create the ebb and flow of human civilization. Man
the individual craves for identification with the cosmic Oneness,
but the cosmos is indifferent to him and he is left with his immortal passions vainly beating their wings against the constrict-
ing walls of his own mortality. The vein of despair in Yeats'
writings—a despair often concealed beneath the heroic anti-mask
—probably has its source in the engaging scepticism of his father.
Like his own heroes, Yeats was born out of phase with the cultural cycle of his day. At a time of filial insurrection, when such
contemporary writers as Samuel Butler were vigorously over-
throwing the weighty authority of the Victorian father-image,
Yeats found within his own home that the revolt was long over
and the battlements stormed. His father had already performed
the religious and social *volte-face* by rejecting Christianity in
favour of scepticism and abandoning a promisingly secure career
as a barrister in favour of the precarious and bohemian life of an
artist. Richard Ellman, who first perceived this frustrated rebellion in Yeats' early years, has suggested that in self-defence the
adolescent Yeats retreated into the world of religion;[1] but perhaps it is unnecessary to cast about for a specific cause. He was
by nature a child of fantasy, withdrawing with distaste from the
reality into which he was continually being jolted, and for such
a nature the world of the spirit offered by religion was infinitely
more attractive than a scepticism insisting on provable facts. But
the boisterous atheism of a father whom he greatly admired had
closed the door of religion in his face, and he was compelled to
turn to an adjacent door—mythology and the occult—as a means
of establishing contact with the timeless world beyond reality.
As he himself put it:

'I was unlike others of my generation in one thing only. I am
very religious, and deprived by Huxley and Tyndall, whom I
detested, of the simple-minded religion of my childhood, I had
made a new religion, almost an infallible church of poetic tradition, of a fardel of stories and of personages, and of emotions,

[1] Richard Ellman, *Yeats—the Man and the Masks* (New York,
1958), p. 25.

inseparable from their first expression, passed on from generation to generation by poets and painters with some help from
philosophers and theologians.'[1]

The world of Blake, whose work he edited, and of the Kabbalah which he had come to know through Macgregor Mathers'
The Kabbalah Unveiled, convinced him that '. . . images well up
before the mind's eye from a deeper source than conscious or
subconscious memory' and throughout his life he stumbled with
a strange mixture of perceptiveness and gullibility from one
occult society to another in search of a spiritual panacea, combining an image from here, a myth from there to create the richly
complex structure of his own eclectic symbolism.

In his early period, Yeats toyed with the idea of collaborating
with Katharine Tynan on a miracle play based on the Adoration
of the Magi, and he inserted in his *Countess Cathleen* (1892)
a theme echoing the medieval morality plays, the selling
of her soul to the devil. But it was in his *Calvary* (1920) and
Resurrection (1931) that he applied to the central Christian
themes his own mythological and symbolist reading.[2] In the
tradition of the No play, which had offered to Yeats a stylized
dramatic timelessness rooted in the ancient past, *Calvary* introduces Jesus as a ghost about to retrace the final scene of his
earthly life:

> *Good Friday's come,*
> *The day whereon Christ dreams His passion through.*
> *He climbs up hither but as a dreamer climbs.*
> *The cross that but exists because He dreams it*
> *Shortens His breath and wears away His strength.*
> *And now He stands amid a mocking crowd,*
> *Heavily breathing.*

Peter Ure, in the best analysis of these plays yet to appear, has
remarked that this 'dreaming-back' serves to make the suffering
more remote, to place Christ at the centre of the scene not as a
tortured victim but as '. . . the pantokrator, Byzantine and un-

---

[1] *The Trembling of the Veil,* i, 2.
[2] His *King of the Great Clock Tower* (1935) contains elements
of the Salome theme but not sufficient to constitute it a biblical
drama.

realistic, rigid like the figure in an icon'.[1] Ure was doubtless employing the term 'Byzantine' here in a Yeatsian sense, but it is misleading. The stylization of Christ in Byzantine art—a stylization preserved in the mystery cycles—derives from a religious awe which instinctively elevates Christ above mere human suffering. Hence the contrast noted in an earlier chapter between the physical realism of the hammering in of the nails and the almost detached spirituality of Christ himself in the York Passion play. For Yeats, however, Byzantium epitomized an aesthetic rather than a religious sanctity, the artifice of eternity where he visualizes himself transformed out of nature into the form of a bird wrought from hammered gold and set upon a golden bough. In *Calvary*, Christ's passive immobility serves less to elevate him to superhuman sanctity than to abstract him into a universalized symbol of rejected Christianity—an artifact of the mind.

Within this dehumanization of Christ lies the clue to the play's ultimate failure; for the symbolism functions at two contradictory levels, and to hold both antithetical readings in mind at the same moment is dramatically unfeasible. At one level the play constitutes a symbolic re-enactment of the original Crucifixion in terms of Yeats' theory of the cycles of civilization. Here Christ represents the initiation of the objective Christian age. The heron, self-sufficient in its subjective loneliness, prepares us for the appearance of Lazarus and Judas who resent the intrusion of Christianity into the privacy and self-sufficiency of their lives.

> *Motionless under the moon-beam,*
> *Up to his feathers in the stream;*
> *Although fish leap, the white heron*
> *Shivers in a dumbfounded dream.*

> *God has not died for the white heron . . .*

> *But that the full is shortly gone*
> *And after that is crescent moon,*
> *It's certain that the moon-crazed heron*
> *Would be but fishes' diet soon.*

[1] Peter Ure, *Yeats the Playwright* (New York, 1963), p. 117. See also Leonard E. Nathan, *The Tragic Drama of William Butler Yeats* (New York/London, 1965), pp. 202 f.

The Modern Era

In the lunar cycle of Yeats' system, the heron is almost consumed by the fish (an ancient symbol of Christianity – the Greek ἰχθύς containing the initials of Christ's title); but the phase will pass, the full moon move into the crescent, and Christianity itself wane in the course of time. Lazarus protests that he has been robbed by Jesus of the comfortable seclusion of death:

> *Alive I never could escape your love,*
> *And when I sickened towards my death I thought,*
> *'I'll to the desert, or chuckle in a corner,*
> *Mere ghost, a solitary thing.' I died*
> *And saw no more until I saw you stand*
> *In the opening of the tomb; 'Come out!' you called;*
> *You dragged me to the light as boys drag out*
> *A rabbit when they have dug its hole away . . .*

and Judas insisting upon his right to make his own decisions, has betrayed Christ not because he no longer believes but in order to be free:

> *I could not bear to think you had but to whistle*
> *And I must do; but after that I thought,*
> *'Whatever man betrays Him will be free';*
> *And life grew bearable again.*[1]

The indifference of the Roman soldiers who 'lay beyond His help' is more discouraging to Christ than the active antagonism of Lazarus and Judas, and with the cry of 'My Father, why hast Thou forsaken Me?' Jesus withdraws into his own spiritual loneliness. It is a loneliness not identical with that of the birds, since theirs is self-imposed and his results from mankind's rejection; but there is some bond with the solitude of the sea-bird, the ger-eagle, and the cygnets who have flown from the empty lake.

Even at this first level of meaning, we are left with an enigma. If Christ represents the New Revelation at the beginning of the

---

[1] I can see no reason for the suggestion in Helen H. Vendler, *Yeats's 'Vision' and the Later Plays* (Cambridge, Mass., 1963), p. 175, that we are meant to think of Judas's suicide although it is not explicitly present in the play. In a play which inverts the normal interpretation of Judas's motives, the omission of any mention of the hanging is, I think, proof enough that Yeats did not wish us to recall it, especially as it would invalidate Judas's protest.

Christian 'lunar' cycle, the play should close with his acceptance by mankind as he ousts the Roman world from its place of eminence. The reason is supplied by the second level of meaning, the contemporary implications of which interested Yeats more than a merely historical re-enactment, however symbolic the presentation. In that contemporary reading, Christ represents an exhausted Christianity about to be replaced by the new cycle, by what Yeats called elsewhere the 'rough beast' with gaze blank and pitiless as the sun. Here Lazarus and Judas represent the twentieth-century dialecticians intellectually demolishing the outmoded selflessness and asceticism of Christianity; and the Roman soldiers are the common people, heedless as usual of all but their own games of chance. Hence the rejection of Christ at the close of the play, a rejection tinged with the author's own sympathy for the lonely figure representing that spiritual world which Yeats sometimes felt he was championing in vain. Not that Yeats consciously regretted the end of Christianity; theoretically he insisted that no preference should be given to the antithetical forms of the cycle, which must simply be allowed to take their course. But he did admit nonetheless that he regarded himself as the voice of 'a greater renaissance – the revolt of the soul against the intellect – now beginning in the world'[1] and in that sense he betrays a latent sympathy with the rejected Christ.

This dual symbolism which serves to represent both the historical and the contemporary change of the cycles, ultimately collapses. Christ as the image of the nascent Christianity of the first century vigorously replacing the old dispensation with a New Revelation cannot function at the same time as a symbol of a debilitated twentieth-century Christianity withdrawing before the onset of more powerful forces. The two readings are mutually exclusive.

If *Calvary* proved dramatically unsuccessful, for Yeats it served as a valuable experiment in Christian symbolism, preparing the way for his more impressive *Resurrection*, which ranks among his most notable dramatic achievements. The latter play concentrates attention almost exclusively on the historical event, the revelation of Christianity at the beginning of its cycle, with

[1] *The Letters of W. B. Yeats*, ed. Allan Wade (New York, 1955), p. 221.

only occasional and very generalized allusions to the twentieth-century scene. After an opening chorus, we are introduced to a Hebrew and a Greek who are guarding the disciples; the latter never appear in the play and the economy in cast sharpens the focus upon these two central figures. Christ has already been crucified and they together with the absent Syrian guard are waiting, each in his own way, for the confirmation of their responses to the Revelation. The Hebrew, with his Old Testament affinity to the temporal world of flesh and blood, sees Jesus sympathetically as a noble man misled into messianic pretensions:

'He was nothing more than a man, the best man who ever lived. Nobody before him had so pitied human misery. He preached the coming of the Messiah because he thought the Messiah would take it all upon himself. Then some day when he was very tired, after a long journey perhaps, he thought that he himself was the Messiah. He thought it because of all destinies it seemed the most terrible.'

Like Judas in *Calvary*, the Hebrew had shuddered at the thought that he might have to surrender all knowledge, all ambition, allowing God to take complete possession, and the Crucifixion came as a relief, proving that Jesus was only a man after all. The Greek, combining within himself the best elements of the later Greek world, a fusion of sophisticated polytheism and Platonic idealism, is convinced that Jesus was no more than a phantom in human form:

'We Greeks understand these things. No god has ever been buried; no god has ever suffered. Christ only seemed to be born, only seemed to eat, seemed to sleep, seemed to die.'

The proof he is expecting is that Christ, having risen from the tomb, will reappear as a disembodied wraith, and for this purpose he has sent the Syrian to inquire at the tomb. The Syrian returns, joyfully announcing that Christ has risen: something has occurred beyond the bounds of rationality and a new cycle has begun. At that moment the figure of Christ enters, wearing a 'recognizable but stylistic mask'. The Greek calmly announcing that it is the phantom he has been awaiting as proof of his theory, runs his hand along the figure to demonstrate that it is disembodied, and screams in horror: 'The heart of the phantom is beating!' Acknowledging the revelation, he proclaims:

Yeats and Lawrence

'O Athens, Alexandria, Rome, something has come to destroy
you. The heart of a phantom is beating. Man has begun to die.
Your words are clear at last, O Heraclitus. God and man die in
each other's life, live each other's death.'

Such is the plot in brief outline; but it assumes far greater
subtlety and complexity than such an outline can suggest, both
by its poetic choruses and by the introduction of the Dionysian
ritual which occurs offstage and is only reported by the guards
as they gaze out at the rabble. The pagan substratum of Christianity, which had invalidated it for the Higher Critics but provided the 'natural' primitivism so attractive to Yeats, is here
represented by that Dionysian ritual. Yeats, as Ellman has
shown, was fascinated by the parallels between the two god-
figures suggested by the *Golden Bough*. Apart from their death
and resurrection, both Christ and Dionysus had died and been
reborn in March when the sun was between the Ram and the
Fish, and when the moon was beside the constellation Virgo who
carries the star Spica in her hand.[1] The latter image he saw, of
course, in terms of the Virgin and the Star of Bethlehem. Hence
the significance of the opening chorus, seeing in the rise of
Christianity the beginning of a cycle replacing the exhausted
Dionysian era and foreshadowing the scene of the pulsating
heart later in the play:

I

I saw a staring virgin stand
Where holy Dionysus died,
And tear the heart out of his side,
And lay the heart upon her hand
And bear that beating heart away;
And then did all the Muses sing
Of Magnus Annus in the spring,
As though God's death were but a play.

II

Another Troy must rise and set,
Another lineage feed the crow,
Another Argo's painted prow
Drive to a flashier bauble yet.

[1] R. Ellman, *The Identity of Yeats* (London, 1954), p. 260.

The Modern Era

The Roman Empire stood appalled:
It dropped the reins of peace and war
When that fierce virgin and her Star
Out of the fabulous darkness called.

This poem, together with the concluding chorus, was published separately in *The Tower* and seems to have been a later addition to the original plan of the play. Ure, for example, refuses to include them in his discussion as being extraneous to the play itself. But it seems to me that within that very heterogeneity, the dichotomy between chorus and play, can be perceived a clue to the ambivalence of the play as a whole. On 24th May, 1926, Lady Gregory recorded in her journal: 'And I hear Yeats "purring" next door, and he has just come in and said, "I meant this to be a poem of Christianity and it has come out like this:"' and she appends an early form of the above poem. If the discrete opening chorus betrayed an attempt to write a poem of Christianity and was subconsciously transformed into a poem to Dionysus, the play itself reveals the opposite pole of Yeats' ambivalence. Theoretically, as we have seen, Yeats insisted that no preference should be given to one cycle over its antithesis; yet in the play itself the Dionysian ritualism has reached the nadir of its orbit and is reduced to mere animalistic orgy as compared with the refined intellectualism and spirituality of the rising Christian faith. By choosing this moment in history, he implies, perhaps unintentionally, that Christianity marked an elevation of religion above bestiality and public copulation to the ascetic idealism of the Christian life. Even the rarefied intellectuality of the Greek world must submit to the mystery of the Passion and the Resurrection with all that they imply. Each of the guards, after an initial resistance to the change, accepts unconditionally, both as individual and as representative of a distinct cultural phase in the human cycles, the evidence of the new Revelation. The evidence which they accept is, we may note, that very miracle that had troubled the Higher Critics and the twentieth-century rationalists, but which constituted for Yeats the mystery of the faith by its transcendence of an inhibiting scientism. That the supernatural was more than a mere literary device for him is evidenced quite apart from his general interest in the occult by comments he made on these two Christian plays.

On *Calvary* he notes in all seriousness: '. . . once at Gogarty's when I was reading out my *Calvary* and came to the description of the entrance of Lazarus, the door burst open as if by the blast of the wind where there could be no wind, and the family ghost had a night of great activity.'[1] And in *Wheels and Butterflies* he gave as the source of his climactic *Resurrection* scene Sir William Crookes' *Studies in Psychical Research* which '. . . after excluding every possibility of fraud' related how he touched the beating heart of a materialized form. Yeats records that on reading the passage he had felt the 'terror of the supernatural described by Job'.

At a conscious level, then, Yeats seems to have intended the play to record in much the same way as *Calvary* the shock offered to thinkers by the advent of a new cycle and their reluctance to desert the old in favour of the new. But by placing his drama at the historical moment which marked the rise of Christianity in contrast to the degenerate Dionysian ritual, the overall effect of the play is of identity with the accepters of Christ and the new faith. Perhaps it was a stirring deep within him of that religious sensibility suppressed during his adolescent years, but the final cry of the Greek as he proclaims the new belief is a cry that we, the audience, are intended to accept as valid. It is followed by the second chorus, again an addition suggesting the contrary view that even Christ's kingdom will pass in its turn from the earth:

> *Everything that man esteems*
> *Endures a moment or a day:*
> *Love's pleasure drives his love away,*
> *The painter's brush consumes his dreams;*
> *The herald's cry, the soldier's tread*
> *Exhaust his glory and his might:*
> *Whatever flames upon the night*
> *Man's own resinous heart has fed.*

But the play itself, with its dramatic tension mounting towards the climactic revelation scene, affirms a more positive response. The enveloping choruses thus suggest the need to submit to change but the play betrays in Yeats a certain hankering after the old dispensation, the glory and might which must pass at the advent of the new era. This contrast between Yeats' intellectual

---

[1] *Letters*, ed. cit., p. 729.

and emotional commitments lends the play its dramatic vitality, providing that spiritual struggle between dream and reality which marked for him the ideal of drama:

'Now the art I long for is also a battle, but it takes place in the depths of the soul and one of the antagonists does not wear a shape known to the world or speak a mortal tongue. It is the struggle of the dream with the world – it is only possible when we transcend circumstances and ourselves, and the greater the contest, the greater the art . . .'[1]

Yeats' early contact with scepticism soon diverted his religious penchant from Christianity to the occult. In contrast, D. H. Lawrence, born in the conservative Midlands of England with their staunch chapel-going and evangelical preaching, had been imbued from childhood with the 'odd sense of wild mystery or power about, as if the chapel men had some dispensation of rude power from above'. His mother, as a Congregationalist, scorned the Primitive Methodists with their 'cheeky' inspirationalism, but Lawrence came to love the religious hymns which he heard during those 'strange marvellous black nights of the north Midlands, with the gas-light hissing in the chapel, and the roaring of the strong-voiced colliers'. There was a marked vein of this evangelical inspirationalism in his own crusade against hypocrisy, in his intense moral concern, and in his sensitivity to the immanence of God in the life-forces of nature. If to churchgoers he sometimes seemed the embodiment of anti-Christ, he wrote of himself in 1914: '. . . primarily I am a passionately religious man, and my novels must be written from the depth of my religious experience.'[2] His religion was not, of course, a traditional Christianity; he rejected out of hand the parochialism and myopia of organized religion which he termed the religion of Christ Crucified, fighting instead for a revitalized Christianity, reunited with that creative and procreative impulse in nature which he identified as God:

'Jehovah is the Jews' idea of God, not ours. Christ was infinitely good, but mortal as we. There still remains a God, but not

---

[1] *The Poet and the Actress* (1915).

[2] *The Letters of D. H. Lawrence*, ed. Aldous Huxley (New York, 1932), p. 192. The earlier quotations are from the opening pages of his *Apocalypse*. For the best study of Lawrence's religious quest, see George A. Panichas, *Adventure in Consciousness* (The Hague, 1964).

a personal God: a vast, shimmering impulse which waves on-
wards towards some end, I don't know what – taking no regard
of the little individual, but taking regard of humanity.'[1]

He denied, then, the basic tenet of Christ's divinity, but he
did so not from atheistic motives but from a genuine desire to re-
implant religion within the physical world, to identify the divine
as the dynamic force of a nature vibrant with life. Despite his
unorthodoxy, he found the Christian story an ideal framework
for his task, and in *The Man Who Died* his reverent retelling of
the Resurrection with his careful avoidance of Christ's name,
belies any suggestion of blasphemy. There is a hush of sanctity
about the work as he returns Jesus to earth not as a disembodied
wraith but as a man whose torn flesh is still aching from its
wounds and whose soul must discover through that flesh the spiritual wholeness of physical communion. It is the communion of Osiris
with Isis, the blending of the Christian with the pagan cycle; but
it is above all a revalidation of physical love, aimed at restoring
to that sordid bodily act the flame of purifying passion which the
twentieth century had dampened and almost extinguished.

His play *David* (1926) reflects this dual response to the Bible,
this mingling of reverence and annoyance. Lawrence recorded
in his *Apocalypse* that, like any other nonconformist child, he had
the Bible '. . . poured every day into my helpless consciousness,
till there came almost a saturation point. . . . So that today,
although I have "forgotten" my Bible, I need only begin to read
a chapter to realise that I "know" it with an almost nauseating
fixity. And I must confess, my first reaction is one of dislike,
repulsion, and even resentment. My very instincts *resent* the
Bible.' The Bible has been temporarily 'killed' for him because
its meanings had become petrified, not least by means of the
'. . . pie-mouthing, solemn, portentous, loud way in which every-
body read the Bible, whether it was parsons or teachers or
ordinary persons'. His response is, of course, typically Protestant in its desire to return to the original meaning of the text
unspoilt by the formal church. If his 'first reaction' was dislike
and repulsion, Lawrence's deeper conviction was that the Bible
did possess an inherent vitality, and *David* exemplified the re-
reading he demanded.

[1] Ada Lawrence and G. S. Gelder, *Young Lorenzo* (London, 1932),
p. 72.

The play was written at a crucial period in Lawrence's life, as he lay recuperating in New Mexico from an almost fatal bout of the illness that was to kill him. Frieda Lawrence felt as she watched him that 'in that play he worked off his struggle for life'. His purpose within the play was, I think, to perform for religion what he had fought to achieve for love – to restore to it the flame of passion; in this instance that burning sense of divine vocation which the Higher Critical school on the one hand and the church parsons on the other had almost snuffed out. In a magnificent prose which echoed biblical parallelism yet skilfully avoided pastiche, he rejected the twentieth-century stereotype of the prophet as political intriguer in favour of a Samuel dignified by his vocation, demanding retribution for sin, yet compassionately grieving for the suffering sinner:

'Speak to me out of the whirlwind, come to me from behind the sun, listen to me where the winds are hastening. When the power of the whirlwind moves away from me, I am a worthless old man. Out of the deep of deeps comes a breath upon me, and my old flesh freshens like a flower. I know no age. Oh, upon the wings of distance turn to me, send the fanning strength into my hips. I am sore for Saul, and my old bones are weary for the King. My heart is like a fledgling in a nest, abandoned by its mother. My heart opens its mouth with vain cries, weak and meaningless, and the Mover of the deeps will not stoop to me. My bowels are twisted in a knot of grief, in a knot of anguish for my son, for him whom I anointed beneath the firmament of might.'[1]

It was this 'primitive religious passion' that he hoped above all to transmit to his London audience, and the transcendent mystery of this passion was for him infinitely more valuable than any scholarly pursuit of historical accuracy. Eliab the atheist offers the usual objection to the 'howlings of priests in linen ephods' and is answered by his father Jesse with calm confidence:

'There is a path that the gazelle cannot follow, and the lion knows not, nor can the eagle fly it. Rare is the soul of the prophet that can find the hidden path of the Lord. There is no open vision, and we, who can see the lion in the thicket, cannot see the Lord in the darkness, nor hear Him out of the cloud. But the word of One is precious and we perish without it.'

[1] Quotations from the 1930 London edition.

The manuscript itself has the title *David* crossed through and the name *Saul* substituted; for the theme of the play concerns them equally. In a manner reminiscent of Yeats' theory of the changing cycles of civilization and of the themes he himself explored in *The Plumed Serpent* (published that same year), he saw the anointing of David during Saul's lifetime as symbolizing the rise of a new religious sensibility in place of the outmoded. He had experimented with the idea in an earlier biblical play, *Noah*, in which religious transition formed the motive force, but he had abandoned the play in favour of *David*. Here Lawrence injects into his attempt to recapture the spiritual dedication of its protagonists the idea of a progressive revelation which Saul in the bitterness of his own rejection expresses in pagan terms:

'The gods do not die. They go down a deep pit, and live on at the bottom of oblivion. And when a man staggers, he stumbles and falls backwards down the pit—down the pit, down through oblivion after oblivion, where the gods of the past live on. And they laugh and eat his soul. And the time will come when even the God of David will fall down the endless pit, till He passes the place where the serpent lies, living under oblivion . . .'

The reason for Saul's rejection is, as in the original story, his disobedience of divine command. But for Lawrence the act constituting that disobedience had special significance. Saul's failure to slaughter the sheep captured from the Amalekites is interpreted here as the kind of selfishness which cuts man off from the divine, bountiful surge of nature. Man must surrender himself unreservedly to the thrust of the grasses and the call of the peewits, and hoarding one's own little store is to be unworthy of God. Hence the sun image in Samuel's denunciation, the suggestion that Saul has denied the God of life-giving nature:

'Thou hast turned away from the Hidden Sun, and the gleam is dying from out thy face. Thou hast disowned the Power that made thee.'

And Saul acknowledges that his inner flame has been extinguished:

'Lo, I have sinned, and lost myself, I have been mine own undoing. But I turn again to the Innermost, where the flame is, and the wings are throbbing. Hear me, take me back! Brush me again with the wings of life, breathe on me, and be with me, and dwell in me. For without the presence of the awful Lord, I am an empty shell.'

In contrast the youthful David is a symbol of guileless altruism, submitting himself to the will of God and thereby representing the ideal of passionate reabsorption into the divine forces of nature:

'. . . when I feel the Glory is with me, my heart leaps like a young kid, and bounds in my bosom, and my limbs swell like boughs that put forth buds.'

Even in these brief extracts one can perceive Lawrence's tendency to use un-biblical circumlocutions in order to avoid the church-associations of *Lord* and *God.* The latter do occur from time to time to make it clear that he is speaking of the biblical God, but he calls him the Innermost, the Glory, the hidden Sun, the Power, to lend freshness to the vision. But that God makes heavy demands and by the end of the play, even David is waning and has lost the 'blitheness' and altruistic 'nakedness' of his youth, and the play closes with Jonathan's withdrawal from his beloved friend:

'I would not see thy new day, David. For thy wisdom is the wisdom of the subtle, and behind thy passion lies prudence. And naked thou wilt not go into the fire.'

Yet with all its virtues, the play is unsuccessful as drama. The characters come alive, the prose is at times wonderfully lyrical, and this vignette of mankind striving towards reintegration with divine will does indeed convey that inner fire of divine vocation. But the play suffers from two serious blemishes. First, although the language of the main speeches revitalizes biblical idiom, the dialogue often lapses into that very jargon they so studiously avoid:

'*Adriel:* Yea and blithely. And tomorrow even in the early day will I set her on an ass and we will get us to my father's house.'

Secondly, drama requires a plot; it needs some tension mounting to a climax, and there is none. In the lengthy Goliath episode the audience's foreknowledge of the outcome robs the scene of its interest. This problem of the audience's familiarity with the plot is, of course, shared by all biblical drama; but we have seen that Milton and Byron infused new vitality into the scriptural story by projecting into the protagonists their own inner anguish. If Lawrence's David symbolizes one aspect of Lawrence's philosophy, he reflects the author himself in little but name. And what a missed opportunity! For within the David story lay a theme ideally suited to his own experiences, to that passion for Frieda which cut across class barriers to blend the atavism of the aristocrat with the noble savagery of the artistic plebeian—a theme worked out in part in *Lady Chatterley*. David the plebeian poet and psalmist rising from the sheepfolds to win the heart of Michal, the daughter of King Saul, lay ready to hand; but he by-passed it in favour of a more traditional focus on the Saul-David relationship. The interpretation he offered was new, the language for the most part vivid and poetic; but the plot trailed off into what the *Spectator*'s reviewer rightly called a 'series of chromolithographic "views"'; and we can but regret the failure.

(vi) HUMOUR AND WRATH

The twentieth-century dramatist soon discovered an alternative to that projection of personality which had distinguished successful drama of the past—an alternative hinted at by A. P. Herbert's version of *Jonah*, and successfully developed by James Bridie. Not only was the scriptural narrative translated into warmly human and contemporary terms by means of humorous anachronism, topical allusion, and light-hearted banter, but Bridie introduced a new device that succeeded in preserving, or at times reinterpreting, the ethical lessons of stories more effectively than the more serious dramatizations could hope to do. Instead of ignoring miracle or attempting to rationalize it, he simply made it part of a world of fantasy in which archangels, demons and whales chatted amicably with amusingly unheroic heroes. The humorous acceptance of these supernatural manifestations relieved the author of the need for rationalist explanations and, by winning the audience's indulgence in this way, it succeeded also in evoking their sympathy for the human characters in the drama. Where in more serious plays the miracle-working prophet had to be denigrated and vilified as a charlatan in an attempt to gain the credence of the more sophisticated audience, Bridie's Jonah is such an absurd, rotund little man that we feel paternally concerned when a jackal's howls terrify him into reluctantly fulfilling his prophetic task.

For the first of these plays Bridie chose a section of the Apocrypha, perhaps in order to test the reactions of the pietists by beginning with the less sacred portion of the Scriptures, but perhaps also because no one could challenge the fairy-tale atmosphere of his play. *Tobias and the Angel* (1931) was, apart from a few negligible dramatic poems,[1] the first dramatization of the book of *Tobit* since the sixteenth century. Nor is this surprising; for it solemnly recounts the story of the archangel Raphael sent to instruct the righteous young Tobias in the magical properties of a mysterious fish. By its aid he not only cures his father's blindness but also rescues the beautiful Sara from the clutches of the demon Asmodeus, a malevolent spirit who had strangled each of her previous husbands on the wedding night. Sara, who had, it seems, a natural antipathy to spinsterhood, had already lost seven bridegrooms in this fashion but was not to be discouraged. Tobias, as the eighth successful suitor, was successful also in surviving the marriage night with the aid of the magical fish, and everyone lived happily ever after. The Apocryphal account is, of course, entirely devoid of humour in its preoccupation with the moral lesson that heaven preserves the righteous.

In Bridie's version, the noble Tobias who wins the hand of the fair Sara is introduced as 'a little fat young man with reddish fair hair becoming prematurely bald'. In *Prufrock*, T. S. Eliot's more serious concern with the gulf between suburban mediocrity and the heroism of such biblical figures as John the Baptist had prompted him mockingly to visualize Prufrock's head:

> . . . (*grown slightly bald*)
> *brought in upon a platter.*

The baldness is used there to widen the gulf between the biblical and the contemporary world by debasing the contemporary. Bridie reverses the process by depicting the baldness of the biblical hero in order to lessen the gulf, and hence to revitalize the biblical story.

---

[1] Cf. James Jacobson, *Tobias, a dramatic poem* (London, 1818).

Humour and Wrath

Accordingly the language makes almost a fetish of such colloquialisms as 'I am a proper old nuisance' and 'I bumped myself all over' – a fetish which might become tiresome were it not that the humour arises out of the very ordinariness of this workaday world. Raphael, in the guise of a human, explains glibly that he always bathes alone because of 'a slight abnormality in the region of my shoulder blades', and describes his capture of the demon in the topically aeronautical terms:

'. . . He nearly gave me the slip in the Caucasus first, but we had a straight burst across Anatolia and I got him just over the Nile delta.'[1]

This is a welcome fresh breeze for the somewhat stuffy atmosphere of biblical drama, but it is more than mere comedy. For as the audience well knows, this realistic portrayal is undoubtedly more authentic than the traditional deification of biblical heroes. If the Apocryphal story has any historical foundation, it is more likely that Tobias greeted the appearance of the fish with the Hebrew equivalent of 'By gum!' than with those flights of edifying rhetoric common in nineteenth-century dramatizations of the Bible.

In *Jonah and the Whale*, of which Bridie wrote two revisions, the best being the broadcast version entitled *Jonah 3*,[2] the approach is broadly speaking the same. Jonah is again a short, pompous, fat man with ginger hair, and the whale is a loquacious philosopher delighted with the opportunity of instructing his captive audience in the finer points of morphology, taxonomy and biological evolution. Even the most prolix lecturer must pause for a sip of water and, as the whale ships a few gallons, his captive audience is no more. Jonah, who has been muttering his interior monologue is cast ashore safe and sound. But behind the frivolity and flippancy lies a vein of seriousness not apparent in *Tobias*, which suggests that Bridie's choice of a biblical theme was not prompted by the desire to explode a myth. For Jonah emerges if not as a tragic hero then at least as

[1] Text from J. Bridie, *Tobias and the Angel* (London, 1952). 'James Bridie' is a pseudonym for O. H. Mavor.

[2] The two latter plays appear in Bridie's *Plays for Plain People* (London, 1944). In *It Should Happen to a Dog* (1956) – a brief one-act play on the theme of Jonah – Wolf Mankowitz adapted the 'modernizing' humour of A. P. Herbert and James Bridie to the idiom of the East End Yiddishist.

something very akin, and what began as comedy changes almost imperceptibly into a serious and sympathetic reappraisal of Jonah's spiritual odyssey and of the moral lessons in his final humiliation. From the moment he accepts his fate as a prophet, Jonah is no longer the ridiculous figure of Gittah-Hepher but the inspired man of God. To mark the transformation Bridie puts into his mouth at the moment of his delivery from the whale the entire thanksgiving prayer from the original text retained almost verbatim, and such direct quotation from the Bible has the immediate effect of dignifying Jonah, of restoring him to something of his traditional sanctity. The play itself continues its light-hearted treatment of the story, notably in its depiction of life at the royal court, but it is no longer at the expense of the central character. His impassioned condemnation of the evils of Nineveh and his solemn warning of its imminent destruction are dramatically powerful, and from that point the play moves inevitably towards Jonah's broken cry:

'O winds of the desert, blow the foolish, lying words I have spoken into nothing and less than nothing. All living things despise me, for I am utterly ashamed.'

Out of the humorous demythologization there has emerged a sympathetic and serious re-reading of the biblical account, a reappraisal of the prophet as a man.

In the last of his three biblical dramas, *Susannah and the Elders* (1937), Bridie took the further step, in common with so many of his contemporary dramatists, of inverting the moral values in the process of his reinterpretation of the story. In the Apocryphal narrative, the theme of justice is uppermost, and the lechery of the old men who attempt to seduce the innocent Susannah forms an abhorrent instance of the fallibility of man however highly respected he may be. But in the twentieth century, sex had become the new idol, its impulses had come to be regarded as irresistible, and the gratification of its passions at the expense of marital fidelity was increasingly condoned on stage and screen. In consequence the story takes on a different colouring in its twentieth-century version and the play opens with a prologue posing precisely this problem of moral reassessment:

'The old story says that these Judges who did this wickedness were false and evil to the bone; but who knows the heart of a man and what moves in that darkness? And is there any man living who has in him no tincture of goodness however unhappily he may do in his life? Tonight you are to be the judges of these old Judges. Search yourselves well that you may do justly.'

In itself the advice is salutary, but again like most of the contemporary reinterpreters, Bridie exerted the Procrustean prerogative of adjusting the story to fit the new interpretation. The modest and decorous Susannah of the Apocrypha is transformed into a 'fast' modern young girl, flirting with every casual acquaintance and playfully teasing her two adopted 'uncles', the Judges, whom she knows to be madly in love with her. Scorning the repeated warnings of Daniel and her old nurse, she learns too late the consequences of this immodesty. Although technically the Judges are condemned to death, dramatically they are exonerated and the guilt is laid at the door of Susannah. The Judges go nobly to their execution, accepting the court's decision, but the play concludes with Daniel's expression of doubt over the justice of his own intervention. The stern morality of the Old Testament is replaced by the modern tendency to absolve the guilty on the grounds of irresistible psychological impulse. Susannah has become more reprehensible for titillating the old men's passions than they for succumbing to them.

This demythologizing of the Bible by means of homely realism was closely paralleled on the continent by André Obey's *Noah* (1929). The product of a French experimental group interested in mime and in the simplicity of medieval dramatic techniques, it was translated into English in 1935 and produced on the London stage with John Gielgud in the leading role. The depiction of God sets the tone for this new interpretation of the story, for instead of the vengeful God of the Old Testament, remorselessly destroying all but a handful of his sinful creatures, he is portrayed as a fundamentally benevolent, if somewhat irritable, old man, wearily forced by the perversity, the greed, and the eternal rebelliousness of man to cleanse the world of its impurer elements. In accordance with the tradition only broken in such rare instances as *Green Pastures*, God himself never appears on the stage, nor is even his voice heard, but at crucial moments Noah holds a sort of telephonic conversation with him in which the audience listens in only at Noah's end. The device is extraordinarily effective in conveying a warmly anthropomorphic picture of God:

'*Noah* (*softly*): Lord . . . (*Louder*) Lord . . . (*Very loud*) Lord!
. . . Yes, Lord, it's me. Extremely sorry to bother You again,
but . . . What's that? Yes, I know You've other things to think
of, but after I've once shoved off, won't it be a little late? . . .
Oh, no, Lord, no, no, no . . . No, Lord, please don't think that . . .
Oh, but naturally, of course I trust You! You could tell me to set
sail on a plank – a branch – on just a cabbage leaf . . . Yes, You
could even tell me to put out to sea with nothing but my loincloth, even without my loincloth – completely – (*He has gone
down on his knees, but gets up immediately.*) Yes, yes, Lord, I beg
Your pardon. I know Your time is precious. Well, this is all
I wanted to ask You: Should I make a rudder? I say, a rudder . . .
No, no, Lord. R. for Robert; U for Una; D for . . . that's it, a
rudder. Good . . . very good, I never thought of that. Of course,
winds, currents, tides . . . What was that, Lord? Storms? Oh,
and while You're there, just one other little thing . . . Are You
listening, Lord? (*To the audience.*) Gone!! . . . He's in a bad
temper . . . Well, you can't blame Him; He has so much to
think of.'[1]

Theology has been left far behind and the obvious contradictions (a ubiquitous God who hasn't time to be in two places
simultaneously) provide that same charming *naïveté* and freshness of approach as had distinguished the work of Connelly and
Bridie. Noah himself is anything but sophisticated, and by a
reversal of the dictum that man is made in the image of God,
Noah's God becomes a projection of his own good-hearted,
bumbling self. Indeed, Noah undergoes the same tribulations as
God once he becomes the steersman and captain of a self-contained world. At the moment of the Flood, even the humble,
trusting Noah is momentarily horrified by the cruel and apparently indiscriminate slaughter; but by the end of the play his
own children mutiny against him, and as they step on to dry land
they quarrel for possession of a worthless boulder, symbolically
splitting into rival factions and shouting at each other the racial
insults: Nigger! Cissy! Chink! and Paleface! Noah's wife, in the
tradition of the mystery cycles and *Job*, rebels against the callousness of God, but Noah himself, who admits that he has given up
trying to understand God, pleads with the pathos of a lonely
old man:

[1] Translation by Arthur Wilmurt (London, 1935).

'Be up there a bit just now and again, will You? Just let me hear Your voice once in a while, or feel Your breath, just see Your light, even . . .'

At this moment the seven-coloured rainbow appears in the background. 'That's fine!' murmurs Noah as the curtains close, and the message of the play is complete. If there is evil in the world, if there are bloody wars and wholesale massacres, mankind is to blame and not God, who is doing his best to lead man in the right direction but is hampered at every step by human perversity and selfishness. It is a simple message, simply conveyed, and by its very simplicity is more effective than a theological treatise.

The comic touches enlivening the plays of this realistic school of biblical drama performed, as has been suggested, the important function of evoking a willing suspension of disbelief. The dramatist was automatically freed from the responsibility of explaining away miracle or of revitalizing the story by rewriting the plot. J. M. Barrie's *The Boy David* (1936) epitomizes the dangers of the more serious approach. His concern with the fantasy of childhood, the Peter Pan dream of eternal innocence, directed his interest to the story of David, and those scenes devoted to this theme possess an ingenuousness and candour sufficient to reawaken interest in the ancient tale. David's first meeting with Saul in a solitary glade, in which each is unaware of the other's identity, forges an instantaneous bond between the two ex-shepherds, delightedly comparing notes on sheep-rearing and farming. But in the following scene Barrie resorts to the tedious practice of revitalizing the story by means of fabrication. Samuel prophesies that a boy riding on an ass will usurp the throne; Saul's token found in David's possession is misinterpreted as a secret sign that he should be slain; and at this point we begin to wonder why Barrie troubled to use the biblical story in the first place. In a comedy, however serious the undertones, we are prepared to accept deviations from the traditional story. Bridie may invert the moral lessons of Susannah but he has been amusing and entertaining in the process, and Shaw's Bergsonian rewriting of *Genesis* is more than justified by its irreverent witticisms. Such sober rewritings as Barrie's produce the effect of a palimpsest in which the original script, now almost illegible, still serves to obscure the superimposed text.

Barrie himself gave up the struggle half-way, and substituted for a climactic final act a series of visions which merely retell the subsequent scenes of the biblical narrative. The performance of the play in 1936 with music especially composed by William Walton made little impression.[1]

A belated attempt to denigrate the biblical heroes, an attempt which forms in a sense the rearguard of those unsympathetic portrayals of Elijah and others in the Jezebel plays of Masefield and Dane, appeared in Laurence Housman's *Old Testament Plays* published individually during the forties, and together in 1950. These dramas are charged with a bitter antipathy to the biblical account in place of the more casual reinterpretations of his predecessors. At a time when the dramatic presentation of biblical miracle had long been discarded (except as part of deliberate fantasy), Housman attacked in his preface the 'extravagant taste for miraculous intervention' which obscured the truth of Old Testament history, and he insisted that these miraculous events were fabricated by the prophets in their attempt to win popular support. From the ardour with which he pushes at a wide open door, we may suspect that he was ridding himself of his own childhood frustrations rather than attempting to convert his contemporaries to a new appraisal of biblical 'mythology'. Housman, by this time in his eighties, had spent his childhood in the rigorously strict atmosphere of a Victorian household. Family prayers and scriptural readings before breakfast had, like church attendance, been obligatory, and Laurence, less pliable than his brother the poet, had kicked rebelliously against this pious discipline.[2] He did not break away from Christianity and, in fact, was throughout his life active in encouraging the use of the stage as a platform for religious teaching. In 1902 he wrote a brief and undistinguished verse-play, *Bethlehem*, in 1916 another short play entitled *Nazareth*, and then a succession of non-biblical religious plays mainly devoted to St. Francis, in all of which he offered an almost deistic view of Christianity with God apparently indifferent to mortal affairs and with human love and compassion as the fundament and coping-stone of the religion. The

[1] It was published in 1938 with a laudatory preface by 'H. G.-B.', who, I assume, was Harley Granville-Barker.

[2] Maude M. Hawkins, *A. E. Housman: Man Behind a Mask* (Chicago, 1958), p. 30.

Old Testament patriarchs and prophets he depicted in his final group of plays as Victorian father-figures, and he attacked them with a growing vehemence scarcely compatible with that love and compassion which he had preached. In *Abraham and Isaac*, the acrimony is confined to the preface, but the play itself transforms the command to sacrifice Isaac from a divine imperative to a self-imposed task. Abraham reasons that, since Isaac is the one possession he would unwillingly offer to God, his sacrifice alone will prove Abraham's faith, and he proceeds to convince himself that his reasoning is divinely inspired. The miraculous intervention of the angel is replaced by Isaac's cry of consent, and Housman has shown that the story never really moved outside the human sphere. *Jacob's Ladder*, produced at the Old Vic, indulged in a somewhat obvious exploitation of Jacob's duplicity –a duplicity recognized, of course, in the biblical text itself. Rachel claws Leah viciously for the marital substitution, Esau becomes a splendid figure of magnanimous forgiveness, and Jacob's promise to offer God one-tenth of all his future produce is dismissed as a miserly bribe. *The Burden of Nineveh*, a brief playlet devoted to the theme that Jonah was not tied to a whale but lashed to a beam, takes us back nearly a century to the nineteenth-century discussion of Cinderella's pumpkin. The reappraisal of the biblical account in a stage version is, after all, acceptable only on the condition that it provides good drama; but the obsession with demythologizing in Housman's plays left no room for comedy, dramatic tension, or even characterization outside these narrow exegetical bounds. Only the last of this group of plays achieves any dramatic power and that because of the novelty of the reappraisal; for the previous plays could not but appear dull to an audience by now conditioned to these naturalistic reinterpretations of the Bible.

His final play, *Samuel the Kingmaker*, provided the most extreme indictment of the biblical prophet yet to appear on the stage; for on the assumption that divine inspiration was a sham, the scripturally innocuous figure of Samuel emerged as (to use Housman's own phraseology) a prophet 'jealous in his own interests, greedy of power, vengeful, double-dealing and deceitful'. In the opening scene, Samuel admits to his sons that the childhood incident of a Voice in the night foretelling the death of Eli's sons was a deliberate fabrication; the choice of Saul by lot is prearranged; the rejection of Saul for his disobedience of divine law is merely Samuel's spiteful revenge for the latter's greater popularity; and the anointing of David, instead of preceding his selection as Saul's harpist, is made to follow it in order to form a personal blow at Saul himself. Indeed, there could be no clearer indication of Housman's treatment of the biblical text than the prologue of the play, in which the scribe Jasher declares that he was forced at Samuel's dictation to write falsehoods into the official history of the period, while his own truthful version was burnt. Moreover, Housman's obsessive desire to vilify the biblical account leads him into a strangely paradoxical position. For a while he rejects out of hand any possibility of divine inspiration or miraculous intervention, he has no hesitation in introducing the Witch of Endor as a weirdly omniscient creature, accurately divining the exact moment of a thunderclap and calling up Samuel's ghost from the dead. His antipathy towards the biblical prophet reaches its full force in the final words of the play addressed to Samuel: 'Dead rat! get back to your hole!' Samuel had joined Elijah and St. Francis on the rubbish-heap of discarded heroes.[1]

By now the Bible scarcely required demythologizing as Gordon Daviot's *Leith Sands* (1946) showed. For in this collection of playlets for the stage, two biblical pieces devoted to Rahab and Sara were casually inserted among a variety of vaguely feminist scenes set in Thebes, in Palestine, and in eighteenth-century England. There is no noticeable distinction in treatment between the sacred and the secular themes, and where Housman had indignantly denied miracle, the authoress here quietly assumes that the walls of Jericho were known by the spies to possess shaky foundations.[2] Again the biblical account is enlivened with touches of humour such as 'One of these

---

[1] In J. B. Priestley's *Desert Highway* (1944), the biblical scene, set in the days when the Assyrians were the Nazis of the day, forms only an interlude between acts, and I have therefore omitted it from this account. Similarly, the merits of Ann Ridler's *Cain* (London, 1943) seem to me to be poetic rather than dramatic. Although the lines are assigned to different speakers and a note at the beginning advises on staging, there is no effective characterization and the *dramatis personae* speak, with only occasional lapses, in the same highly sophisticated verse.

[2] 'Gordon Daviot' is a pseudonym for Elizabeth Mackintosh.

days, Lot, your wife's curiosity will be the death of her'. It is not brilliant wit, but it serves to treat the Bible with a mild flippancy helpful in humanizing its stories.

The iconoclasts had had their say, the vilifiers had torn down their heroes from their pedestals, and the moral reassessors had condemned the 'innocent' and acquitted the 'guilty' in rewriting the biblical stories. But that seriousness which had crept into the conclusion of Bridie's humorous play on Jonah betokened the inception of a less aggressive approach to the Bible, of a desire less to ridicule and distort the scriptural canon than to examine it with some reverence and even with some humility as a sacred body of literature which still possessed important lessons for mankind. And implicit in such a revaluation was the restoration of the biblical heroes to something of their pristine glory.

(vii) THE RELIGIOUS DRAMA SOCIETY

The drama of the western world had been reborn on the high altar of the cathedral at the most sacred moment of the liturgy, and the church had indulgently transferred it to the semi-religious guilds which were still under its authority. By the end of the sixteenth century, the church could no longer recognize its own offspring, and after publicly disinheriting it, ecclesiastical authorities either castigated or ignored the professional stage for the next three centuries. The only dramas it encouraged were those innocuous 'Sunday School' plays which acted out moral lessons for the young and simple-minded. In the twentieth century, however, a few far-sighted leaders of the church began to recognize that the new intellectual challenges to faith could no longer be countered by the cardboard wings of hymn-singing angels, and the Religious Drama Society was founded.

Between 1904 and 1922 the religious fare offered on the stage was typified by Miss A. M. Buckton's enormously popular Christmas pageant, *Eager Heart*, which drew packed houses at its seasonal performances. Young Eager Heart, resisting the blandishments of Eager Fame and Eager Sense while awaiting the coming of the King, hears a knock at the door. She finds a poor family seeking shelter and, to the accompaniment of traditional Christmas hymns, generously invites them in and offers them the food she has so carefully prepared for her royal guest. The poor family is, of course, suddenly transformed into the Holy Family of the Nativity, and the pageant concludes with the pointed question to the audience: 'Is *your* hearth ready?' By 1922, public interest in the pageant was flagging, and it was about then that the church began to seek a more sophisticated religious drama. William Poel's revival of *Everyman* and *Jacob and Esau* during the early years of the century had given some impetus to the staging of ancient religious plays, and the formation of the Morality Play Society by Mabel Dearmer in 1911 had furthered the interest.[1] The prime mover within the church was the then Dean of Canterbury, later Bishop of Chichester, George K. A. Bell, who in 1928 invited John Masefield to write a play for performance on the steps of Canterbury Cathedral. The play was his *Coming of Christ* which, like his earlier *Good Friday* (1917) and *The Trial of Jesus* (1925), was an uninspired series of biblical and morality scenes occasionally relieved by sparks of poetry. Characters introducing themselves 'I am a shepherd who keeps fold . . .' could scarcely stimulate an audience bred on Ibsen and Shaw, but at least the association with the Canterbury Festival of a well-known poet (soon to be appointed Poet Laureate) attracted the attention of more eminent writers to the potentialities of church drama – among them T. S. Eliot, whose *Murder in the Cathedral* was first performed at Canterbury in 1935. In the year following Masefield's play, the Canterbury Festival became an institution, and the Religious Drama Society was then formed under Bishop Bell's auspices to encourage the writing and performance of religious plays in co-operation with the church. E. Martin Browne was appointed a director of the Society and, with his experience on the professional stage and his contacts with professional writers, did much to encourage new dramatists and to raise the standards of church drama. As on the commercial stage, much of the writing was mediocre – perhaps rather more, since religious themes can so easily become mawkish in the hands of second-rate writers; but Dorothy L. Sayers and Christopher Fry, who are discussed in more detail later, wrote their first religious plays within this movement, as did Christopher Hassall, Charles Williams and Norman Nicholson.

[1] A detailed account of the church drama movement can be found in G. Weales, *Religion in Modern English Drama*, pp. 93 f.

The Religious Drama Society

Christopher Hassall, whose *Christ's Comet* was performed at the Canterbury Festival in 1938 and again in 1958, is the most conventional of the three. Avoiding any startling originality, he presents an oblique view of the Nativity by means of the Fourth Wise Man who misses the actual Birth. In a pleasantly colloquial verse enlivened by a quiet humour, he recaptures some of the oriental charm of James Elroy Flecker's *Hassan*—the beggar philosophizing in the market-place, the cruelty of the potentates, the star-studded heavens in which the comet suddenly appears to announce the birth of Christ. Uniting it all is Artaban's search. On hearing that he has missed the Nativity itself, he determines to search further:

> *Spirit of Beauty, whose impartial hand*
> *Uncolours Earth, and strews the way of sleep*
> *With listening silence and shut buds of flowers,*
> *Hallow this moment in my heart, make it*
> *A whetstone whereon after hours may grind*
> *Blunted resolve.*

By the time he discovers Bethlehem years later, Christ has already been crucified, but he is rewarded with a vision in which an angel appearing above the Cross assures him that his quest has not been in vain:

> *Here . . . is your haven, justly earned,*
> *With time to your first setting-out returned;*
> *For those who find truth, truth is born in them,*
> *And they are witnesses at Bethlehem.*

The play, like the verse itself, is unpretentious and by its very modesty is quietly convincing.

Charles Williams is a more controversial figure. A prolific writer—author of some forty books and primarily a novelist—he was as an editor of Oxford University Press closely in touch with current literary trends. His most ambitious play *Seed of Adam* (1936) offered a stimulating compression of human history into one brief act. Adam merges with the Caesars and is at the same time the father of the Virgin Mary, marrying her off to Joseph lest she go astray in her all-embracing love for mankind. This deliberate ignoring of chronology suggests with striking effectiveness the intimate relationship between the Fall and its partial rectification in the Nativity and Crucifixion, while the modernistic verse reminds the audience of the relevance of the theme for the twentieth century. The trouble is that the verse falls so far short of the subject-matter. It creates an impression of scintillating originality in its verbal juxtapositions and compressed imagery, but the effect remains superficial, and the banal internal rhymes betray the doggerel beneath the alliterative camouflage. Adam castigates the post-lapsarian sluggards:

> *Dullards of darkness, light's lazybones,*
> *poor primitives of our natural bareness,*
> *where's your awareness? will moans and groans*
> *for gold of brawn or brain regain*
> *the way to the entry of Paradise? up!*

With an eccentricity typical of his work, he presents the Annunciation in transliterated Hebrew (with a typographical error which neither editor has caught[1]) and one wonders what his audience was supposed to make of it. If stylistically he was straining after effects beyond his grasp, at least he avoided the archaisms of so much previous biblical drama and suggested the application of new poetic techniques to scriptural plays. His *House by the Stable* and its sequel *Grab and Grace* offer a mingling of a Nativity and a Morality play with Man befriended by Pride and Hell but reminded of his ethical obligations by his servant Gabriel. Man reluctantly offers his stable to the Holy Family and dismisses his friends, but they return a hundred years later for some slapstick with Faith and Grace. The verse once again gives an effect of sophistication but, that aside, the plays offer little advance over *Eager Heart*. His more recent *Terror of Light* moved into prose and the opening section has a simplicity and directness more effective than any of his verse drama. The disciples a few days after the Crucifixion come alive as troubled human beings unsure of their next move but convinced that the world has in some way been profoundly changed. But Simon Magus enters with Luna and the play disintegrates into scenes of ghosts and necromancy. Williams was by no means a neglig-

[1] Ann Ridler's edition of *Seed of Adam and Other Plays* (Oxford, 1948), and John Heath-Stubbs edition of the *Collected Plays* (Oxford, 1953), from which the quotation is taken.

ible writer, and numbered among his admirers such eminent critics as C. S. Lewis and Nevill Coghill;[1] but one suspects that their admiration for his verse was unconsciously coloured by their affection for the man and theologian who had composed it, and his plays will, I think, remain literary curios, provocatively novel in theme but stylistically ineffectual.

Norman Nicholson's *The Old Man of the Mountains*, a verse play on the theme of Elijah and Ahab set in modern Cumberland, was discovered by E. Martin Browne during the war and produced at the Mercury Theatre in 1946. Although like so many twentieth-century plays, it translated the biblical story into modern terms, it belonged to the new, more sympathetic school in taking the side of the prophet against the sinner. Elijah is not a pseudo-religious politician but rather the village Hampden insisting on the rights of the working class against the grasping land-owner Ahab. That Voice, so frequently used in the modern era as a symbol of God because it conveniently sidestepped the problem of miracle, is heard here too, but with a difference. It takes the form of a raven's croaking which Elijah repeatedly dismisses as a figment of his own imagination. Only at the conclusion of the play, when the audience's instinctive antipathy is lulled, does he recognize its divine origin. The verse here has a dignity sufficient to support the unsophisticated country setting and the delicacy with which the theme was handled suggested that a new era in biblical drama was beginning.

His later play, *A Match for the Devil*, first produced at the Edinburgh Festival in 1953, and published in 1955, reworks its Old Testament theme into a Christian message and does so with a smoothness and ease that almost makes one forget the original story. Hosea's denunciation of Israel in terms of his wife's harlotry and eventual re-acceptance into the household becomes in this play a lesson on the theme of love. Her harlotry here is prompted neither by licentiousness nor acquisitiveness, but by a longing to give of herself to others in the Temple precincts.

[1] The introduction to *Essays Presented to Charles Williams* (Oxford, 1947), published two years after his death, conveys very movingly the affection in which he was held by his circle of literary friends. Williams was greatly admired by W. H. Auden whose *For the Time Being* (1944) owed much to him. The latter work has not been examined here as it is dramatic only in isolated scenes.

She thus becomes the generous Canaanite in a corrupt Temple ritual, redeemed despite her moral laxity by her selflessness and love. Even her desertion of her illegitimate child, David, is purged away by her belated interest in him and her readiness to marry Hosea in order to establish a home. But Hosea's sin is that he spoils her, refusing to allow her to work lest she soil her delicate hands. Bored, she returns to her previous occupation and Hosea, in a burst of forgiveness, comes to reclaim her. But he must learn that love is a matter of giving, not of forgiving:

Hosea: *I spoke of forgiving when I ought to have asked*
　　　　　for forgiveness . . .
　　　For wanting you not what you are;
　　　For offering you the consciousness of guilt in
　　　part-exchange for love.

The Old Testament condemnation of sin with its hope of pardon for the penitent is here transformed into a plea for Christian love above all. In the process of transforming the message into contemporary terms, Nicholson suggests somewhat dangerously that Christianity condones sexual licence when it is prompted by the desire to give rather than to receive but that, apparently, was a risk he was prepared to take, and Gopher, the wife, emerges as the most attractive character in the play. The primary focus is, however, on Christian love rather than licence, and the pleasantly unpretentious verse once again helps to revitalize the story and to avoid any suspicion of sanctimonious moralizing.

(viii) 'THE MAN BORN TO BE KING'

After the cataclysmic devastation of a Second World War, beginning with the Nazi massacres and concluding with the annihilatory power of the atom bomb, mankind hesitated to declare with the same optimism as had the school of Thomas Huxley that the sole path to human progress lay in the direction of rationalist empiricism. Such farsighted thinkers as Joseph Wood Krutch, speaking from within the camp of the rationalists, sensed as early as the twenties a dissatisfaction with the amoral, aseptic world of science in which the human spirit cannot find a comfortable home. The human spirit

'. . . needs to believe, for instance, that right and wrong are real, that Love is more than a biological function, that the human mind is capable of reason rather than merely of rationalization, and that it has the power to will and to choose instead of being compelled merely to react in a fashion predetermined by its conditioning. Since science has proved that none of these beliefs is more than delusion, mankind will be compelled either to surrender what we call its humanity by adjusting to the real world or to live some kind of tragic existence in a universe alien to the deepest needs of its nature.'[1]

His analysis of the problem is excellent, but his prophecy of a continued dichotomy between man's spiritual needs and the new cosmogony rests upon an assumption proved false only too often in man's history. In almost every era, man has assumed that the temporary tendencies of his own age mark the direction of future progress, and that the unquestioned hypotheses of his century will remain unquestioned by his progeny. But history is always less linear than pendular, swinging back and forth in an unending series of action and reaction, of ebb and flow. The eighteenth-century Age of Reason was convinced that the Newtonian discoveries, the precise definition of aesthetic standards, and the enunciation of rules governing both macrocosm and microcosm, would inevitably lead within the foreseeable future to the establishment of a splendid orderliness and restraint in society, in art, and in life itself. Yet by the end of the century, Romanticism had contradicted the prophecy by idealizing the overflow of powerful feeling as the new criterion of literary excellence.

Perhaps we are guilty of the same fallacy in imagining that the rejection of biblical morality and even of biblical miracle in favour of scientific materialism is absolute and irrevocable. The so-called religious revival of recent years is, indeed, primarily a sociological phenomenon, a search for affiliation in an age of mass suburbanism.[2] But even this sociological phenomenon arises, at a deeper level, from the need to be recognized as an

[1] Joseph Wood Krutch, *The Modern Temper* (New York, 1956), p. xi; it was originally published in 1929.

[2] Cf. W. Herberg, *Protestant, Catholic, Jew* (New York, 1956), pp. 59 f.

individual rather than as a statistic; and it is a need which cannot be separated from man's instinctive dislike of being regarded, and of regarding himself, as a set of conditioned reflexes. Existentialism, even at its most nihilistic, is a search for human dignity in an alien world, and if the cold world of science cannot provide such human dignity, then man may well look back with a new interest and curiosity to the source-book of that spiritual world which he has rejected. He may approach it with more caution, with less propensity to confuse allegory with historicity; but if he has at last rid himself of his rebellion against the Victorian age, he may find in a less belligerent reappraisal of the biblical heroes a means of redignifying mankind and hence himself. Nor is this a vague hypothesis, for the bibilical drama of the last few years suggests that the move in this direction has already begun.

One of the most ambitious attempts to revitalize dramatically the spiritual message of the Gospels took place not on the stage but over the radio. In 1941, the religious deparment of the B.B.C. commissioned Dorothy L. Sayers to write a series of twelve plays in the form of a cycle relating the life, death and resurrection of Jesus, entitled *The Man Born to be King*. With the full approval of the church, all the tinsel and gilding of conventional piety were discarded in favour of a vigorous realism. The authoress deliberately circumvented the Authorized Version with its sanctified cadences and elevating archaisms, and by translating from the original Greek into a colloquial vernacular, she sought to lay stress on the *Man* of her title while yet preserving the mystery of a spiritual kingship. In effect, the Church was seizing the sword of its adversaries and beating it into a ploughshare. That vivid realism which had been used to expose the chicanery of the biblical heroes was now to be employed as a means of reimplanting belief. Despite advance cries of 'Blasphemy!' from the more conservative churchgoers, the plans were put into effect and the broadcasts made a deep impression even on those initially sceptical.[1]

[1] Published in London in 1943. The Foreword by Dr. J. W. Welch, director of religious broadcasts of the B.B.C., gives details of its reception and of its ecclesiastical support. Her broadcast play, *He that Should Come* (London, 1939), was realistic in comparison with previous treatments of the Nativity, but the lengthy verse prologue and the songs with which the play was interspersed tended to counterbalance the realism and to 'elevate' the sanctity.

Its performance over the radio rather than on the stage was not fortuitous. Legally the stage impersonation of any members of the Trinity was strictly forbidden by the Lord Chamberlain's office, and when consulted about the broadcast the Lord Chamberlain, who raised no objections in principle, nevertheless forbade the presence of any audience during the performance. Thus, however realistically Jesus himself was portrayed, the presentation was restricted to voice alone. Unlike most dramatists, Miss Sayers acknowledged the validity of the ban on the grounds that its lifting would open the door to commercialism and irreverence. She suggested, however, an easing of the law to allow individual licensing of particular productions which met with the approval of the censors. Moreover, Miss Sayers, in her introduction to the cycle, wisely noted the impossibility of regarding the Crucifixion as a tragedy in the fullest sense. Aristotle had demanded that the hero of a tragedy should be 'a mixed character, neither perfectly good nor perfectly bad', and Jesus was, by definition, the former. Her purpose, therefore, was less to present true tragedy than to evoke what she termed the 'exhilarating effect' which Christ's suffering produced upon believers. This she achieved brilliantly in her dramatic cycle, and what concerns us particularly closely in this study is that her use of realism succeeded, paradoxically, in reaffirming faith in the mystery. In other words, the assumption that realism and miracle were incompatible was being challenged. No attempt was made to rationalize the miracle, to ignore it, or even to tone it down. Today, some twenty-five years later, it has become the norm for preachers to speak of the Bible in colloquial terms in their attempt to impress their audiences with the relevance of its message for their own era; but in 1941 radio audiences were startled to hear the easy familiarity with which Jesus discoursed with his disciples:

Jesus: I will tell you what the Kingdom is like. You've watched your wife making bread. She takes a little piece of yeast and stirs it up into a mass of dough. Then she sets it aside and the buried yeast begins to work in silence and unseen, till the heavy lump rises and swells and becomes light and ready for baking. That is how the Kingdom will come.

Andrew: Like that?

   Jesus: Just like that. . . . Are you disappointed?

Andrew: I thought it would come with armies and banners, and a big procession riding into Jerusalem.

   Jesus: You may yet see the Messiah riding into Jerusalem.

 Simon: We rather expected signs and wonders and that sort of thing.

   Jesus: You *will* see signs and wonders. But you won't believe because you have seen wonders; you will see the wonders because you have believed.

The few traditionalists who were offended found it difficult to protest because the images and parables used by Christ in the New Testament were, in the tradition of the biblical prophets, taken from the familiar, everyday world, and it was only the varnish of successive generations which had dulled the vividness of the original colours. And the effect was all the greater since the plays not only acknowledged the incredulity of the watchers but exploited it positively by suggesting in such Pharisaical incredulity a parallel to the scepticism of the modern iconoclasts. The enthusiastic reception which the broadcasts received showed that Miss Sayers had not erred in suspecting that the public was ready to welcome the reinstatement of religious mystery so long exiled by scientific empiricism.

Such realistic presentation of miracle could be achieved more easily in a semi-dramatic version of the Gospels than in an Old Testament play. For throughout the debates of the nineteenth century the defenders of the faith, it will be recalled, had shied away from rationalist discussion of the central mysteries of Christianity. While the Old Testament miracles were at once discarded as superstitious elaboration, the Immaculate Conception was never subjected by them to close rationalist scrutiny, and even such peripheral miracles as the walking on the waves were staunchly defended. Their realistic presentation in vividly colloquial terms was, therefore, a reaffirmation of what had never been formally denied. Yet even the Old Testament miracle was gradually being reinstated, and a new reverence in the treatment of its stories was soon perceptible in their dramatization.

(ix) CHRISTOPHER FRY

Christopher Fry's *The Firstborn*, performed at the Edinburgh
Festival in 1948, appears superficially to conform to the traditions recently established on the biblical stage. The depiction of
Moses as a brilliant past general of the Egyptian army now
desperately needed by Pharaoh gives to Moses a powerful bargaining point lacking in the original story – a bargaining point
which reduces the miracle of the Exodus to the level of power
politics. Similarly, Moses is transformed from the humble, diffi-
dent servant of God into the Nietzschean superman, the driving
force behind a national liberation movement, greeting the miracle
of blood with the victorious cry:

> *We with our five bare fingers*
> *Have caused the strings of God to sound.*
> *Creation's mutehead is dissolving.*

Again the moral and religious intent of the biblical account is
replaced by the new concepts of willed survival.

Despite these changes, however, the ultimate purpose of the
play is neither authentic realism, nor even moral reassessment,
but an attempt to convey the very opposite – a sense of the
mystery of life, of the immense powers which lie behind the
trivial affairs of men; a search for meaning in a seemingly chaotic
world. The miracles, so far from being dismissed as superstitious
elaborations, are here reinstated to form the climax of the play,
and their acceptance as divine intervention presupposes the concept of an ordered universe. Thus Moses' Nietzschean qualities
are tempered by his recognition:

> *. . . Moses is now only a name and an obedience.*
> *It is the God of the Hebrews, springing out*
> *Of unknown ambush, a vigour moving*
> *In a great shadow, who draws the supple bow*
> *Of his mystery.*

If this constituted a rejection of the purely empirical world in
favour of a purposeful creation directed by a benevolent power,
it involved no pious, cloistered, and unquestioning acceptance of
that power. Indeed, the central theme of Fry's version of the

story is man's spiritual dilemma, the necessity of choosing between two evils in a world which is supposedly just. Like the protagonists of *A Phoenix Too Frequent* and of *The Lady's Not For Burning*, Moses must recognize the conflict between idealism and reality; he must descend from his utopian clouds in order to come to terms with the harsh cruelties of this earth. As a Quaker, Fry acknowledged the impossibility of achieving national liberty without the horror of bloodshed. Moses had thought of that bloodshed in abstract terms as retribution for the callousness of Egyptian persecution; but when the final plague is about to slay Ramases, Moses' spiritual son, his illusions of divine justice are temporarily shattered.[1]

> *I do not know why the necessity of God*
> *Should feed on grief; but it seems so. And to know it*
> *Is not to grieve less, but to see grief grow big*
> *With what has died.*

It appears that all great biblical tragedy must return to this central theme, the injustice of a supposedly just world, and for the twentieth century it arises from the search for meaningfulness. Milton's era required a justification of life within the framework of the Christian saga, Byron's a bulwarking of faith against the debilitating questionings of a growing science. But modern science had won so completely, had so laid waste the 'myth' of Christianity that the dramatist was now turning back to that 'myth' in the hope of rediscovering some more satisfying explanation of man's existence than the mere biological survival of the fittest. Anath echoes Moses' perplexity:

> *We are born too inexplicably out*
> *Of one night's pleasure, and have too little security:*
> *No more than a beating heart to keep us probable.*

Moses cries that he has 'followed light into a blindness', and this helpless groping towards some securer handhold in an incomprehensible existence provides the closing words of the play:

[1] In *An Experience of Critics*, ed. Kaye Webb (Oxford, 1953), Fry admitted that the main weakness of his play was the failure to prepare the audience for Moses' sense of personal loss at Ramases' death. For a general assessment of Fry, see Derek Stanford, *Christopher Fry: an Appreciation* (London/New York, 1951).

Christopher Fry

We must each find our separate meaning
In the persuasion of our days
Until we meet in the meaning of the world.

This perplexity, this dissatisfaction with the apparent point-lessness of existence contrasts vividly with the complacent piety of the Victorian bibliolater on the one hand and the optimistic confidence of the twentieth-century iconoclast on the other. If the nineteenth-century biblical drama had failed by portraying its characters as saints and sinners, the next generation of dramatists had grown tiresome by its inversion of the picture. To depict Naboth as a boorish fanatic abusing a noble and spotless Jezebel was, apart from its temporary novelty, scarcely better dramatically than the morally didactic presentation of the earlier tradition. Drama demands some inner struggle, some sense of the complexity of life; and the 'realistic' retelling of biblical narrative in the light of contemporary ethics, however refreshing and amusing, could not succeed as drama if the new ethical code was inversely as dogmatic and oversimplified as the Victorian. Fry's play, by conveying the paradoxes inherent in Moses' predicament, was, at the very least, restoring to the scriptural stage the prerequisites of tragedy, the framework within which the dramatist could succeed or fail by his own merits. And by turning to the Bible in his search for the meaning of life, he suggested a new reverence for its message, a convic-tion that concealed within its simple narrative lay truths valid for all ages.

His later play, *A Sleep of Prisoners*, performed inside the University Church at Oxford in 1951, not only added a new dimension to biblical drama but also suggested a fresh criterion for testing the validity of scriptural truth. The cluster of theories which at the turn of the century had seen man in terms of an organism motivated by primitive forces common to all folk-loristic traditions had detracted from his sense of individuality. If the initial implications of psychology had intensified this feeling by reducing man to an amalgam of conditioned reflexes, it had more recently suggested that the specific hereditary and environmental make-up of each individual served to differentiate him from the rest of mankind. The world of dreams was the meeting-place where the archetypal forces surged up to meet the specific world of the individual, and it was there that artists and writers were finding a reality and truth beyond the merely visible world. Fry's insight was to place within that archetypal dream-world the twentieth-century version of postfiguration. Where the early Protestants had elevated the biblical stories into archetypes by virtue of their scriptural sanctity and had looked for reworkings of those stories in their own lives in order to enjoy that sanctity vicariously, Fry saw the stories as almost Jungian archetypes—still sacred but working through the newly discovered psychological channels, and impinging upon the specific personality of each individual so that he act out in his own life the design suited to his own being. It constituted a return to the old concept of scriptural history as continuing cyclically beyond the Bible into the everyday world of man. It added, however, a new validation of scriptural truth no longer dependent upon irrational belief in miracle but rather upon a recognition that the biblical narrative exemplified within its stories the underlying patterns of human behaviour.

Four British prisoners of war, confined by the Germans in a church for lack of other available accommodation, move in and out of sleep during the long night, reliving the experiences of those Old Testament characters for whom they have a natural affinity. Peter Able, a projection of the pacifist author, irritates David King by his calm acceptance of his fate:

> *Any damn where he makes himself at home.*
> *The world blows up, there's Pete there in the festering*
> *Bomb-hole making cups of tea. I've had it*
> *Week after week till I'm sick. Don't let's mind*
> *What happens to anybody, don't let's object to anything,*
> *Let's give the dirty towzers a cigarette,*
> *There's nothing on earth worth getting warmed up about!*

King scuffles with the 'absent-fisted' Able and almost strangles him. They sleep and while a 'dream's dreaming him', King acts out his role as Cain in the first episode, for which Able has been named. This nocturnal vision adumbrates the twentieth-century dilemma, at the same time suggesting that it is not new—merely the eternal pattern working itself out in a slightly different form. While Cain is the traditional 'huskular strapling' indulging his animalistic passions, Abel has been transformed from the pious believer, meekly accepting the dictates of a benevolent God, into the seeker after spiritual truth, acknowledging the seeming emptiness of life but convinced despite all contrary evidence that Love must be the guiding force in Creation:

> *Here we are, we lean on our lives*
> *Expecting purpose to keep her date,*
> *Get cold waiting, watch the overworlds*
> *Come and go, question the need to stay*
> *But do, in an obstinate anticipation of love.*

It is a reversal of the Byronic picture. Where Byron's Cain symbolized the rebellion against conventional Christian belief, Fry's Abel typifies the rejection of contemporary disbelief. The latter's Cain utters the eternal cry of the self-justifying criminal, blaming everyone but himself for his own sin:

> *How was I expected to guess*
> *That what I am you didn't want?*
> *God the jailer, God the gun*
> *Watches me exercise in the yard,*
> *And all the good neighbourhood has gone.*

In the next episode David King is the eponym, and Peter plays Absalom. With a deft twist to the original story, Absalom is seen as the pacifist once again, rebelling as a Christ-figure against his father's bellicosity ('The window marked with a cross is where I sleep'), and in mime he is cut down by machine-gun fire as he hangs from the pulpit. The last full episode re-enacts the sacrifice of Isaac with Peter again as the victim. He is, as in the original story, saved by divine intervention but, though thankful to be spared, he feels the sorrow of the world in his vicarious sacrifice through the offering of a ram:

> *This would have been my death-time.*
> *The ram goes in my place, in a curious changing.*
> *Chance, as fine as a thread,*
> *Cares to keep me, and I go my way . . .*

> *There's a ram less in the world tonight.*
> *My heart, I could see, was thudding in its eyes.*
> *It was caught, and now it's dead.*

This is no superficial recital of biblical parallels nor a Procrustean adaptation of scriptural narrative to fit a contemporary mode. The very dream sequence allows the dramatist a certain flexibility, but he is here reliving those stories from within in search of the lessons they may have to offer his own age.

After a brief acting out of the Shadrac episode, Meadows summarizes the message of the play. There are no easy answers, no wonder-drugs of faith; but, returning to the old biblical concept of the birthpangs which will precede the messianic era, Fry sees in the coldness and cruelty of his world a sign that perhaps the springtime may be nigh, a springtime of which man must prove himself worthy by his love and compassion for his fellow man:

> *The frozen misery*
> *Of centuries breaks, cracks, begins to move;*
> *The thunder is the thunder of the floes,*
> *The thaw, the flood, the upstart Spring.*
> *Thank God our time is now when wrong*
> *Comes up to face us everywhere,*
> *Never to leave us till we take*
> *The longest stride of soul men ever took.*
> *Affairs are now soul size.*
> *The enterprise*
> *Is exploration into God.*

The play concludes with the reminder that we have been delving into that archetypal dream-world which contains, perhaps, a greater truth than our mundane existence:

> David (awake): *Did they fetch us up?*
> Meadows: *Out of a well. Where Truth was.*
> *They didn't like us fraternizing.*

One reason that this play so far outclasses Fry's earlier work is that he had at last disciplined that tendency to verbal pyrotechnics which had helped to win him fame but had soon so wearied audiences and critics.[1] It had dazzled with its surface wit, but lacked the deeper implications, the metaphysical ambi-

[1] Cf. Marius Bewley, 'The Verse of Christopher Fry', in *Scrutiny* xviii (1951), p. 78, and Denis Donoghue, *The Third Voice* (Princeton, 1959), pp. 180 f.

valence that all successful word-play must have. Here the word-play, toned down and rarely obtrusive, functions as an integral part of the play. In an attack on the meaningless jargon of war, the slogans supposedly justifying brutality, Peter cries:

> *What bastard language*
> *Is he talking? Are we supposed to guess?*
> *Police on earth. Aggression is the better*
> *Part of Allah. Liberating very high*
> *The dying and the dead. Freedoom, freedoom,*
> *Will he never clear his throat?*

On a naturalistic stage this would appear forced but, uttered by a man mumbling in his sleep, the broken phrases running through his mind, it is extraordinarily effective.

The contrast between the traditional depiction of Abel as the saintly figure of religious humility and Fry's spiritually disturbed truth-seeker aware of the tragic paradoxes of life is symptomatic of the religious anti-hero of the mid-twentieth century. It reflects, for example, a device used extensively in Graham Greene's novels. Although ultimately they preach a return to Catholicism, the word 'preach' is made singularly incongruous. In *The Power and the Glory*, instead of idealizing faith and salvation, of pointing to the comforts and security of membership in the spiritual church, Greene disarms objections by a merciless exposure of the hypocrisy and simony of the priests, the abuse of the confessional, the superstitious veneration of the Mass, and the veneer of piety thinly covering the moral depravity of the 'faithful'. Only then, having won the confidence of an initially antagonistic reader as well as having rid himself of his own reservations about the Church, does he disclose deep within the chicanery and self-deception of the broken-down priest the smouldering ashes of a faith which suddenly flames into martyrdom—a martyrdom which the priest himself is too humble to recognize as such. What might have been a nauseating tale of piety has emerged as a movingly human story of triumph within defeat. In the same way, Fry has taken us far from the credulous religiosity of the Sunday School play and, indeed, far from the confident iconoclasm of the anti-religious play to a serious and sophisticated exploration of man's internal dilemma in terms of the biblical archetype working through human dreams.

(x) MacLeish's 'J.B.'

Although this study is technically restricted to English drama, it will not, I believe, be out of place to conclude it with a glance across the Atlantic, particularly as the practice of simultaneous publication in England and the United States has made any sharp distinction between their mid-century works chimerical. Lionel Abel's *Absalom* performed in 1956 and first published in 1960 is an interesting, if ultimately unsuccessful, attempt to read the biblical story in existentialist terms, and it fails because of Abel's vacillation between existentialism and traditional Old Testament concepts.[1] By focusing the play on David's choice of a successor to the throne, he provides an ideal setting for an exploration of the central existentialist dilemma – the challenge to man in a mass-society that he take his life in his own hands and by means of a momentous decision escape the anonymity of passive surrender. The application of existentialist principles to the Bible was not, of course, original. Kirkegaard had unknowingly founded the school when he visualized the anguish of Abraham's struggle before the abortive sacrifice of Isaac – a struggle unrecorded in the Bible but eloquent in its silence. Here again was an opportunity for Abel to give voice to the biblical silence, or perhaps to rewrite the story as an existentialist might have experienced it.

The play begins promisingly. David, who prefers his more vigorous and handsome son Absalom, is hampered by an earlier oath to appoint Solomon his heir as a penance for his own sin with Bathsheba. Now is the time for him to 'transcend his situation', to renounce his vow and thus irrevocably to commit himself by a momentous decision. But he procrastinates until his inspired scribes reveal to him his future decision. It would seem that David has thereby been robbed of his choice, yet Abel continues the play as if the decision had been the king's. The paradox of a supernally dictated choice is repeated with Absalom,

[1] It was published in *Artists' Theatre: Four Plays*, ed. Herbert Machiz (New York/London, 1960).

who sees before the last battle a vision of his approaching death and then 'chooses' to die. Similarly, as if his father had not been a puppet of heaven throughout the play, Absalom informs him before his own death:

'Your acts from now on will be those of another. Nothing of you will remain to obscure, delay, or soften the extreme designs of God. You will be *His* plaything, *His* puppet even.'

If there is any denominator common to the variegated forms of modern existentialism, it is man's attempt to cope with the nothingness of his existence. Even within the school of religious existentialism, the I-Thou constitutes a desperate attempt to bridge the gulf of nothingness that appears to separate man from his God. By any standards, then, Abel's so-called existentialist play is in fact non-existentialist; for it accepts unquestioningly God's benign concern with human affairs and his direct intervention in those affairs by means of visions and personal inspiration.

A few years after the play was written, Abel formulated the dramatic theory which had prompted it. Tragedy, he argued, cannot operate without the assumption of an ultimate order, while what he terms 'metatheatre' (modern drama with its various ancient antecedents in which the inherent theatricality of the play is acknowledged) sees order as an entirely human improvisation. The only world existing there is that created by human striving and human imagination.[1] In such a world there is no room for the Old Testament God, at least as he is traditionally conceived, and to present the existentialist dilemma in this traditional setting as Abel has done is to strive for both worlds and achieve neither.

Paddy Chayefsky's *Gideon*, produced by Tyrone Guthrie in 1961, is a less ambitious play, aiming at little more than light amusement; and it is indeed a flimsy affair. Since Bridie's plays in the thirties, the novelty of presenting a biblical hero as an endearing simpleton had worn a little thin. By now the friendly Angel sitting cross-legged in the shade of a tree and gently reproving the unheroic hero for his cowardice, as well as the 'humorous' colloquialisms of the minor characters, had become mere stereotype.

[1] Lionel Abel, *Metatheatre: a New View of Dramatic Form* (New York, 1963), especially p. 113.

307

Joash: Now does anyone remember the ritual we followed last
year?

Helek: It didn't help much last year so I shouldn't worry too
much about repeating it exactly.

Such colloquial 'humour' depends for its effect on the contemporary prevalence of a pietistic reading, but such pietism had
long disappeared from the English and American scene. The
Angel at one point relieves the general banality of the play with
a sudden surge of eloquence and introduces a more serious note.
He recalls Moses affectionately as:

'. . . a hulking, hare-lipped, solitary man, quite unattractive
really, stammered, dour–nay, say sullen–lacking wit, one of
those over-earnest fellows. Yet I fancied Moses from the very
first. Gaunt he stood against the crags of Horeb, a monumentally
impassioned man. It is passion, Gideon, that carries man to God.
And passion is a balky beast. . . . Yet it inspirits man's sessile
soul above his own inadequate world and makes real such things
as beauty, fancy, love, and God and all those other things that
are not quite molecular but are.'

But this theme of a truth passionately conceived beyond the
scientific and molecular disintegrates into puerility. Gideon,
renouncing the Angel, describes his victory in battle as 'the
inevitable outgrowth of historico-economic, socio-psychological
and cultural forces prevailing in these regions', and the play ends
with the facile jingle:

> *Man believes the best he can,*
> *Which means, it seems, belief in man.*

Were these the only American contributions to recent biblical
drama, our digression would scarcely be justified. But from
across the Atlantic came Archibald MacLeish's moving play,
J.B., filling the theatres of America and Europe in its first
season, evoking a storm of protest and acclamation, and keeping
audiences hours after a performance immersed in discussions of
its problems and message.[1]

[1] For details of the play's reception in Europe, see the article by
Robert Downing in *Theatre Arts*, February, 1960, p. 29. The Broadway
production coincided with a national newspaper strike and hence its
immediate impact is not recorded in print. In Hanover, a local critic
noted that 'hours after the curtain had fallen, cafés in the vicinity of the

MacLeish's J.B.

In the course of this study, I have argued that biblical plays attracted the dramatist in inverse proportion to the current sanctity of the Bible; that such plays could only succeed dramatically if they acknowledged the inner doubts and struggles of the biblical protagonist by projecting into his characterization some of the dramatist's own unorthodoxies; and that the greatest of scriptural plays returned inevitably to some aspect of the Jobian theme – the search for order and purpose in an apparently haphazard world in which mankind is buffeted by the indiscriminate blows of a capricious fate. In the mid-twentieth century, the obliteration of Hiroshima provided the most glaring modern instance of such indiscriminate slaughter, the Bible had reached the nadir of its sanctity, and the time was ripe for a new surge of interest in its themes, and particularly in the Jobian quest translated into modern terms.

In fact, MacLeish had been anticipated by Robert Frost's dramatic poem *A Masque of Reason* (1945) which purported to be the missing forty-third chapter of *Job*. In this modern sequel to the book, Frost's sly humour, like Bridie's, serves to provide a screen for some serious exploration of the biblical story and of its implication. Job's wife, jealous of her feminist rights, insists on knowing why God is the Lord of Hosts but never the Lord of Hostesses; they both recognize God by his resemblance to Blake's painting; and scattered throughout the poem are gentle parodies of Yeats, Browning, Herrick and others. But beneath this genial flippancy lie some of the best summaries of *Job*'s message, couched in such deceptively simple terms that their elemental truth can easily be missed. Now that 'the audience / Has all gone home to bed', Job requests some fuller explanation of his ordeal, to which God responds:

> *My thanks are to you for releasing me*
> *From moral bondage to the human race.*
> *The only free will there at first was man's,*
> *Who could do good or evil as he chose.*
> *I had no choice but I must follow him*

theatre remained full of groups of people discussing untiringly the problems thrown up by MacLeish'. Downing also records that in Europe the successful play normally sees between five and ten performances during its first season; *J.B.* saw seventy-five.

The Modern Era

With forfeits and rewards he understood –
Unless I liked to suffer loss of worship.
I had to prosper good and punish evil.
You changed all that. You set me free to reign.

Despite some unresolved doubts about the justification for the trial, ultimately Frost's sympathies are with the Bible, and his tendency, as Eliot put it, to 'tease the orthodox Christian believer'[1] never leads him into a direct denial of faith. His humanistic need for free inquiry and the consequent antipathy to dogmatic formulae give an impression of heresy belied by his own assertions of belief, and in this masque the atmosphere he creates for the discussion reflects accurately his own approach to religious problems. For by placing the scene aeons after the event, he substitutes for the intense sufferings and urgent expostulations of Job a detached re-examination of the past crisis, an intimacy between God and Job as of two old friends who have fought and argued long ago in their youth, wholeheartedly forgiven each other, and are enjoying a nostalgic exchange of reminiscences about their earlier disagreements. God admits he was 'just showing off to the Devil' and Job magnanimously forgives him for being 'human'; but Frost has already established the real justification for God's actions and we are not prepared to take his later comments too seriously. In an amusingly inverted form which gives Job the credit rather than God, he acknowledges that Job's suffering did teach him and hence mankind the valuable lesson that God cannot be reduced to human proportions and compressed into the confines of human retaliatory justice. Although Frost has humanized the story, the warm sympathy which suffuses the brief work is far removed from the irritability apparent in such previous rewriters of the Bible as Laurence Housman. In the battle between religion and science,

[1] In a lecture at the University of Virginia in 1953 – quoted in L. Thompson, *Robert Frost* (Minn., 1959), p. 17. Hyatt H. Waggoner's *Heel of Elohim* (Univ. of Oklahoma, 1950), a stimulating study of science and religion in modern American poetry, discusses Frost and MacLeish, but was of course published before the appearance of *J.B.* Frost's *Masque of Mercy*, also a dramatic poem rather than a play (in which even the stage directions are set out as verse), modernizes the story of Jonah in terms of Christian forgiveness.

Frost accords the technical victory to science, but the spiritual victory remains with religion:

> *Look at how far we've left the current science*
> *Of Genesis behind. The wisdom there, though,*
> *Is just as good as when I uttered it.*

And the 'we've left' suggests that even the scientific victory took place under divine auspices.

MacLeish himself had explored the theme of creation as long ago as 1926 when he published his verse play *Nobodaddy*. The title offers a clue that he intended it partially as a refutation of Shaw's *Back to Methuselah* (1921) which had used the term in the Preface.[1] In MacLeish's play, one vital change is made in the traditional account of the Garden of Eden. On eating the forbidden fruit, Adam and Eve wait in trepidation for the divine thunderbolt to strike them, but instead are greeted with the deathly silence of God's indifference:

> *The trees*
> *Seem to have heard him, and the earth is sealed,*
> *Silenced against us, and the small white moon*
> *Looks down as though she feared us.*[2]

By transgressing divine commandment they have forfeited God's intimate concern with their welfare and his love and compassion towards them. Similarly, Cain, having slain Abel, challenges God to destroy him:

> *I have killed*
> *Your priest. I have profaned your sacrifice.*
> *I stand against you, cursing you. Lift up,*
> *Lift up your hand and slay me.*

But nothing happens. The immense indifference of heaven is the grimmest punishment of all.

The connection between this and Shaw's work is that the preface to *Back to Methuselah* contained the amusing passage on Bradlaugh's watch experiment. Relating the story at a party

---

[1] Blake, of course, had used the term as a jocular nickname for Urizen, the Father of Jealousy in *To Nobodaddy,* from the Rossetti MS.
[2] A. MacLeish, *Nobodaddy* (Cambridge, 1926), p. 43.

one day, Shaw found that his audience viewed with scepticism the tale that this atheist had once, taking out his watch, challenged God to strike him with a thunderbolt within five minutes if he disapproved of atheism. In the face of this incredulity, Shaw offered to repeat the experiment there and then – to the consternation of pious and atheistic alike:

'In vain did I urge the pious to trust in the accuracy of their deity's aim with a thunderbolt, and the justice of his discrimination between the innocent and the guilty. In vain did I appeal to the sceptics to accept the logical outcome of their scepticism: it soon appeared that when thunderbolts were in question there were no sceptics.'

At the urgent request of his host, who saw his party rapidly breaking up, Shaw was persuaded to forgo the experiment; but his point had been triumphantly made. Sheer superstition apart, it was obvious that God would not have accepted the challenge; *ergo* there was no God.

MacLeish's play reverses the argument. The very absence of divine manifestation in this world is, in a sense, God's means of manifesting himself; for the divine message is conveyed to the heart and not to the eye. When the universe is silent and cold, an empty nothingness, man has transformed the Somebodaddy into a Nobodaddy, and for him it is as though God does not exist. In the light of this thesis, it becomes apparent that MacLeish's famous sonnet *The End of the World* has been grossly misread as an affirmation of atheism, of a 'rank nihilism'.[1] It is really a pointer to the new direction taken by twentieth-century man. The octave describes man's absurd concern with trivialities, symbolized by the entertainment in the circus ring:

> *Quite unexpectedly, as Vasserot*
> *The armless ambidextrian was lighting*
> *A match between his great and second toe,*
> *And Ralph the lion was engaged in biting*
> *The neck of Madame Sossman while the drum*

[1] Thurston N. Davis, S.J. bases his Catholic summary of *J.B.* as 'an arid repudiation of religion' on this reading of the sonnet and on the connection he suggests between the two works. His article appeared in a symposium on *J.B.* in *Life* magazine, 18th May, 1959 and is reprinted in R. E. Hone, ed., *The Voice Out of the Whirlwind* (San Francisco, 1960), pp. 308 f.

MacLeish's J.B.

Pointed, and Teeny was about to cough
In waltz-time swinging Jocko by the thumb –
Quite unexpectedly the top blew off:

The sestet contains the warning:

And there, there overhead, there, there hung over
Those thousands of white faces, those dazed eyes,
There in the starless dark the poise, the hover,
There with vast wings across the cancelled skies,
There in the sudden blackness the black pall
Of nothing, nothing, nothing – nothing at all.

To interpret this as a manifesto of nihilism is to ignore the octave. Mankind is here not striving for spiritual union with God and disappointed by the hollow emptiness it finds. It is engaged in frivolity, in a perversion of life, and by its neglect of positive values has deserved the appalling neglect and emptiness of heaven. This fear of the dark void permeates MacLeish's poetry. It is central, for example, in *You, Andrew Marvell* and reaches its fullest force under the circus-top of *J.B.*

MacLeish was no pious fundamentalist. However boldly he defended God in *Nobodaddy*, he rewrote the biblical story in the process. Like Frost, he was searching in the Bible for the essential validity of its message, probing, scrutinizing, and cutting away what seemed extraneous in the conviction that within these ancient tales was concealed some almost ineffable truth. Nowhere is this better expressed than in an article which he wrote for the *New York Times* in which he defended his use of the biblical story in *J.B.*[1] Significantly, he entitled the article 'About a Trespass on a Monument', acknowledging the reverence with which he regarded the scriptural account – a reverence which again contrasts markedly with the cavalier treatment of the Bible in preceding dramatizations.

With picturesque humility he asks forgiveness for having 'constructed a modern play inside the ancient majesty of the Book of Job much as the Bedouins, thirty years ago, used to build within the towering ruins of Palmyra their shacks of gasoline tins roofed with falling stone'. He, like the Bedouin, is driven by necessity:

[1] *New York Times*, 7th December, 1959.

313

'Where you are dealing with ideas too large for you, which, nevertheless, will not leave you alone, you are obliged to house them somewhere – and an old wall helps.'

Job's search, he continues, was, like our own, for the meaning of affliction, and in our generation the hideous disasters of modern warfare have made the problem even more acute. Here MacLeish, with echoes of the almost forgotten Paley, categorically denies the theory that the cosmic watch winds itself, and he affirms his own faith in a divine Creator. This does not sound like the writing of a 'rank nihilist', but of a man seeking an answer, longing for confirmation of faith like Job himself. If his play does not toe the ecclesiastical line, neither does *Paradise Lost* nor, indeed, the original book of *Job*. The justification of God's ways, if it is to be anything more than a pusillanimous sermon, must be bold enough to transgress the bounds of orthodoxy in order to challenge belief. Only after the vigorous challenge can any mature reconciliation be achieved.

The play itself begins with the most effective device yet for avoiding the credulous dramatizations of the supernatural so distasteful to the twentieth century. The device consists of a gradual transition from the phenomenal world to the symbolic and, through the symbolic, to the supernatural – a move calculated to pacify the atheists within the audience and perhaps to satisfy MacLeish's own objection to complacent pietism. Had God and Satan begun conversing in the booming voices of a Sunday School play, the drama would disintegrate into mere religious propaganda. Instead, two broken-down actors, now reduced to selling balloons and popcorn, enter the huge circus tent, pathetic human failures dwarfed by their surroundings, yet betraying faint traces of their previous dignity. Their names, Mr. Zuss and Nickles, suggest their symbolic representation of God (Zeus) and Satan (Old Nick), but nothing in their speech or behaviour as yet confirms the suspicion. Curiously they examine the stage-setting for a performance of *Job* and casually finger the masks worn by their namesakes in the play. As each handles the mask, he seems to catch something of its quality, and their discussion of Job's courage or impertinence foreshadows the argument of the play. From a tersely colloquial dialogue they lapse into a more poetic, yet still colloquial, verse which creates an atmosphere more suited to symbolism.

MacLeish's J.B.

Nickles: *But this is God in* Job *you're playing:*
            God the Maker: God Himself!
            Remember what He says?—the hawk
            Flies by His wisdom! And the goats—
            Remember the goats?

They try on the masks and at once their voices are, as the stage
directions inform us, '*so magnified and hollowed by the masks that*
they scarcely seem their own'. The masks begin to speak as though
of their own volition, and as the actors tear them off, horrified
at what they have seen through the eye-holes, Nickles questions
whether he is really playing Satan. Zuss's answer marks the pen-
ultimate stage of the merger:

Maybe Satan's playing you.

They replace their masks in readiness to begin the play, but
the opening line is uttered by neither of them. A mysterious
Distant Voice intones the biblical lines, and from then on God
and Satan speak, as it were, through the mouths of Zuss and
Nickles. The transition from realism to the supernatural has
been achieved through the contemporary symbolist technique
of the stage so that the effect is one of dramatic sophistication
instead of pious gullibility. An equally valuable achievement is a
deliberate ambiguity which leaves us unsure throughout the play
when God is speaking through Zuss and when Zuss is interject-
ing his own human objections.

As his name J.B. suggests, MacLeish's Job is a successful
American executive, thankful in a slightly complacent way for
the blessings of life. He denies formally that the blessings are
deserved, but knows instinctively that God is with him. In this
twentieth-century form of postfiguration, MacLeish has injected
his own religious problems into the ancient story, adapting the
specific details of the original without altering the ultimate
lesson. As calamities overwhelm the modern Job—two children
killed in a crash, a toddler murdered by a sex-maniac, a daughter
crushed in the collapse of his own bank, a son destroyed by war—
J.B. is faced by the horror of an inexplicable and ruthless injustice. But at this stage, it is not J.B.'s answer which interests
us so much as the comments of Zuss and Nickles. For MacLeish
has still to work at removing the instinctive antipathy of a

315

predominantly disbelieving generation, and he achieves his purpose largely by forestalling these objections himself. Into Nickles'
mouth he puts all the cynicism of the nihilist, jeering at J.B.'s
'ham' acting, his 'insufferable' rich man's piety, the 'poisonous'
doctrines he instils into his children. Even Zuss is hesitant in
defending J.B. But Nickles' cynicism is just sufficiently over-
drawn to alienate the audience's sympathy.

> *Best thing you can teach your children*
> *Next to never drawing breath*
> *Is choking on it.*

This is too vicious a philosophy even for the iconoclast, and
Zuss dismisses it as a product of rancid intellectualism. The
same technique is effective in discrediting Nickles immediately
after the calamity. Where the biblical Job at once answers 'The
Lord giveth, the Lord taketh away. Blessed be the name of the
Lord', MacLeish's J.B. can only utter the first half. Zuss urgently
whispers:

> *Go on!*
> *Go on! Finish it! Finish it!*

but J.B. remains silent. Nickles exults in his victory; why should
J.B. go on, he asks:

> *To what? To where? He's got there, hasn't he?*
> *Now he's said it, now he knows.*
> *He knows Who gives, he knows Who takes now.*

At last J.B., mastering his rebelliousness, murmurs brokenly the
conclusion of the verse – 'Blessed be the name of the Lord'. It is,
perhaps, only a verbal affirmation of faith at this stage, but it is
sufficient to discredit Nickles who believed that no man in his
senses could even play the part of an accepting Job.

In effect, this is Graham Greene's technique once again. Every
charge, every objection of the iconoclast and doubter is admitted
as largely true; and this is not simply to disarm the atheist in
preparation for a final validation of faith. At a much deeper level
than the scoring of debating points, both writers are, like Job
himself, unorthodox questioners, ultimately accepting God despite their disbelief – or in the words of Tertullian, stubbornly
affirming *credo quia impossibile*. The formulation of the atheist's

objection is thus a formulation of their own inner doubts, a statement of the *impossible* despite which they believe.

By the time of the comforters' scene MacLeish can afford to be less generous to his inner atheist and to begin his rejection of that viewpoint; although even at this point the presence of the formal Church among the false comforters continues his rebellious unorthodoxy. The three comforters consist of Zophar the seedy cleric, Eliphaz the disillusioned scientist, and Bildad the communist. The first two are discredited on entry by their filthy clothing; and since the communist uses his rags as a badge of class-distinction, MacLeish takes care to denigrate him by means of the women's caustic comments. In a deliberate caricature of religious, scientific and communist jargon, MacLeish puts into their mouths the modern tendency to exonerate the criminal on the grounds of heredity, psychological impulse, class struggles, and original sin. The communist argues that historical necessity and the concept of the State make nonsense of the so-called sins of the individual:

> *Innocent! Innocent!*
> *Nations shall perish in their innocence.*
> *Classes shall perish in their innocence.*
> *Young men in slaughtered cities*
> *Offering their silly throats*
> *Against the tanks in innocence shall perish.*
> *What's your innocence to theirs?*
> *God is history. If you offend Him*
> *Will not History dispense with you?*
> *History has no time for innocence.*

Eliphaz offers the supposedly soothing explanation of the quack psychiatrist:

> *Come! Come! Come! Guilt is a*
> *Psychophenomenal situation —*
> *An illusion, a disease, a sickness:*
> *That filthy feeling at the fingers,*
> *Scent of dung beneath the nails . . .*

and Zophar, the cleric, insists categorically:

> *All mankind are guilty always!*

317

But in lone obstinacy, deserted even by his wife, J.B. proclaims as the corner-stone of his faith that without responsibility for his own actions man is a worthless statistic:

> *I'd rather suffer*
> *Every unspeakable suffering God sends,*
> *Knowing it was I that suffered,*
> *I that earned the need to suffer,*
> *I that acted, I that chose,*
> *Than wash my hands with yours in that*
> *Defiling innocence.*

To argue as some critics have that MacLeish has merely acted out Job in modern dress is to miss this central point. In fact, he has reoriented the story to meet an attack from the opposite direction. The biblical Job rejected the neat contemporary belief in a retaliatory God by insisting that his own punishment was undeserved, while the comforters, representing the conventional view, insisted on his guilt. In the twentieth century the roles are reversed: the comforters come to assure J.B. of his innocence, and it is he who insists on his guilt. Where Job and J.B. are at one is in their conviction of the individual's moral responsibility in a universe intimately concerned with his actions. But, in defending that position, the modern Job must of necessity redirect his defensive fire, and therein lay the basic originality of MacLeish's play.

With the climactic scene of J.B.'s insistence on his guilt, the *peripeteia* begins. The Distant Voice (not Zuss) speaks from the whirlwind in the original words of the Bible, intoning what MacLeish described elsewhere as some of the greatest lines in all literature, the recounting of the might, majesty, and magnificence of creation, whose immense workings puny men cannot begin to comprehend.[1]

> *Who is this that darkeneth counsel*
> *By words without knowledge? . . .*

> *Where wast thou*
> *When I laid the foundations of the earth . . .*

[1] In 'About a Trespass on a Monument', referred to above.

MacLeish's J.B.

*When the morning stars sang together
And all the sons of God shouted for
Joy? . . .*

*Wilt thou condemn
Me that thou mayest be righteous?*

J.B. is silenced not by logic, for the answer is meaningless to an atheist rejecting the existence of God. But for J.B., convinced that creation is purposive and ordered, the reply is fraught with meaning. It does not prove that justice exists; it questions whether man possesses sufficient knowledge of the master-plan and of its intricate workings to pronounce finally on its merits. As a Christian and perhaps also in response to existentialist parallels, MacLeish concludes with the theme of love. In a discussion of the biblical *Job* published in the *Christian Century* he argued that a primary message of the book is God's need to prove that man can love him for love's own sake and not as a *quid pro quo*.

'Without man's love God does not exist as God, only as creator, and love is the one thing no one, not even God himself, can command.'[1]

With this in mind, the close of his drama takes on a deeper meaning. J.B. submissively bows his head before the divine reproof, admits his error, and repents. At once both Nickles and Zuss tear off their masks and begin cynically to sneer at his 'arrogant, smiling, supercilious humility' in giving in to God. Again the author puts into their mouths the arguments of the sceptics, and having already discredited Nickles earlier in the play, now exploits Zuss in the part of the scoffer. The carpings and cavillings of Nickles and Zuss, despite their contrast with the stirring lines that have preceded them, are persuasive. Nickles, horrified to learn that God 'pays up' by restoring the wife and children, inquires cynically whether they are the same children or merely substitutes. Most of all, he cannot conceive how J.B. could be willing to accept life after such an experience. He attempts to persuade him to suicide, but J.B. turns away with humble dignity to welcome his wife back in love. In the midst of the darkness, resembling symbolically the desolation

[1] *Christian Century* (April, 1959), p. 419.

of Hiroshima and the empty blackness of MacLeish's earlier
sonnet, Sarah whispers the closing message of the play:

> *Blow on the coal of the heart.*
> *The candles in churches are out.*
> *The lights have gone out in the sky.*
> *Blow on the coal of the heart*
> *And we'll see by and by . . .*

For all the arid intellectualism of Satan, the environmental conditioning of psychology, the amorality of communism, and the
dogmas of the contemporary Church, it is in the mystery of Job's
non-empirical faith that the modern dramatist finds the most
valid pointer to the meaning of life. And unlike the writers of
earlier decades, he does not turn his back on modern thought in
a desperate attempt to shield his faith, but finds in his own dis-
satisfactions with current philosophies the confirmation of his
belief in the parallel of human and divine love.[1]

This play epitomizes the new sensitivity among biblical playwrights of the mid-century. There has not suddenly appeared in
our midst a Salvation Army of dramatists eager to lead an
evangelical revival. Even those most earnest in their religious
beliefs speak hesitantly from the midst of their own doubts
and perplexities—perplexities which by their very awareness
that religion offers no easy path to the intelligent believer
are all the more persuasive. Where at the turn of the century
the bastions of orthodox Christianity had been stormed by
the rationalists, the mid-twentieth century has seen a regroup-
ing of forces. The inhabitants of the citadel have grown rest-
less under the cold dictatorship of science, and in their search
for warmth are beginning to look back nostalgically, if not to
the stringent pietism of the Victorian, then at least to the dignity
of man in the biblical world. Evolution has depicted him as an
advanced organism justifying himself in the survival pattern

---

[1] I have discussed here the published text, used in the productions
at Yale and in Europe. During the Broadway production, MacLeish
was persuaded by his producer, Elia Kazan, to introduce changes in
the concluding section which merely confused audiences. The Broadway
text appears in *Theatre Arts* (February, 1960), and is discussed in
Burton M. Wheeler, 'Theology and the Theatre', *JBR xxviii* (July,
1960), 334. The correspondence between MacLeish and Kazan on
these changes can be found in *Esquire* (May, 1959).

solely by biological procreation; psychology as a complex of subtly preconditioned responses; and even democracy has left him with little but the infrequent use of a ballot box. Appalled by such cosmic alienation, the mid-century writer is less inclined airily to dismiss as outmoded the biblical world-picture in which the welfare and morality of each individual is of vital concern to his Creator.

In an era proclaiming the death of God, it is unlikely that a sudden religious revival is imminent; but there are signs that the cultural pendulum is slowly beginning to swing back. The existentialists are groping for meaning and for human contact in an otherwise empty world; the psychedelics have ostentatiously turned their backs on scientific progress in favour of mystical experience, taking love as their watchword in place of reason; Zen Buddhism and the myth of Sisyphus are no longer the absurd beliefs of ignorant forebears but are being seen anew as poetic projections of the human predicament. In each era biblical drama has responded to subtle fluctuations in the contemporary scene, and we may expect it to respond in our own generation to this growing respect for the mythic cycles of the past. The sudden lowering of biblical sanctity during the first half of this century produced an impressive list of dramatists interested in the Scriptures—Shaw, Yeats, D. H. Lawrence, Isaac Rosenberg, Laurence Housman, Bridie, Frost, Fry, MacLeish, and numerous others. Many of them exploited its themes with cynicism, some with deliberate iconoclasm. But by now the iconoclastic impulse has expended itself, the Bible remains below that degree of sacrosanctity which would preclude effective dramatization, and its archetypal themes await the modern playwright searching, like MacLeish, for the majesty of ancient walls in which to house his own spiritual problems.

ABBREVIATIONS

The following abbreviations have been used in the footnotes and bibliography:

CRAS	Centennial Review of Arts and Science
EETS e.s.	Publications of the Early English Text Society, extra series
ELH	Journal of English Literary History
Eng. Stud.	Englische Studien
ES	English Studies
HJ	Hibbert Journal
IJE	International Journal of Ethics
JBR	Journal of Bible and Religion
JEGP	Journal of English and Germanic Philology
MLN	Modern Language Notes
MLR	Modern Language Review
MP	Modern Philology
PMLA	Publications of the Modern Language Association of America
PQ	Philological Quarterly
RES	Review of English Studies
RN	Renaissance News
SEL	Studies in English Literature
SP	Studies in Philology
SQ	Shakespeare Quarterly
SR	Sewanee Review
SRen	Studies in the Renaissance
TLS	London Times Literary Supplement
TRSC	Transactions of the Royal Society of Canada
UTQ	University of Toronto Quarterly

SELECT LIST OF PLAYS

In this bibliography are listed only those plays examined in the text. Readers interested in further biblical dramas should consult E. D. Coleman, *The Bible in English Drama: an annotated list of plays* (New York, 1931); reissued 1968.

Anonymous. *The Chester Plays*, ed. Thomas Wright for the Shakespeare Society. London, 1843.

— *The Digby Plays*, ed. F. J. Furnivall. London, 1896, EETS e.s. 70.

— *The Drama of the Medieval Church*, ed. Karl Young. 2 vols. Oxford, 1933.

— *King Daryus* (1565?). Tudor Facsimile Text, 1907.

— *Ludus Coventriae or the Plaie Called Corpus Christi*, ed. K. S. Block. London, 1922, EETS e.s. 120.

— *The Non-Cycle Mystery Plays*, ed. O. Waterhouse. London, 1909, EETS e.s. 91.

— *Nebuchadnezzar's Fierie Furnace*, ed. Margaret Rösler. Louvain, 1936, Materials for the Study of the Old English Drama, xii.

— *New Enterlude of Godly Queene Hester* (1560/1), ed. W. W. Greg. Louvain, 1904. Materials for the Study of the Old English Drama, v.

Anonymous. *The Stonyhurst Pageants*, ed. Carleton Brown. Baltimore, 1920.

— *Terentius christianus*. 3 vols. Cologne, 1602–4.

— *The Towneley Plays*, ed. George England and Alfred W. Pollard. London, 1897, EETS e.s. 71.

Select List of Plays

Anonymous. *Two Coventry Corpus Christi Plays*, ed. Hardin Craig. London, 1957, EETS e.s. 87.

— *York Plays*, ed. Lucy Toulmin Smith. Oxford, 1885.

Abel, Lionel. *Absalom* (*1956*) in *Artists' Theatre: Four Plays*, ed. Herbert Machiz. New York/London, 1960.

Abercrombie, Lascelles. *Emblems of Love*. London/New York, 1912.

Austin, A. *The Tower of Babel*. Edinburgh/London, 1874.

Bale, John. *God's Promises* (*1538*). London/Edinburgh, 1908, Tudor Facsimile Texts.

— *Johan Baptystes* in *Dramatic Writings of John Bale,* ed. J. S. Farmer, London, 1907.

— *The Temptation of our Lord*. London/Edinburgh, 1909, Tudor Facsimile Texts.

Barnard, P. M. *Jezebel*. London, 1904.

Barrie, James M. *The Boy David*. New York, 1938.

Battine, William. *Another Cain, a Mystery*. London, 1822.

Bennett, Arnold. *Judith*. London, 1919.

Bèze, Theodore de. *A Tragedie of Abrahams Sacrifice*, orig. 1550, tr. Arthur Golding, 1577, ed. M. W. Wallace. Toronto, 1906.

Boyle, Roger. *Herod the Great* (*1694*) and *The Tragedy of King Saul* (*1703*) in *Dramatic Works*, ed. W. S. Clark. Cambridge, Mass., 1937.

Bridie, James (*alias* O. H. Mavor). *Plays for Plain People*. London, 1944.

— *Susannah and the Elders*. London, 1937.

— *Tobias and the Angel* (*1931*). London, 1952.

Browning, Elizabeth Barrett. *Drama of Exile* (*1844*) in *Complete Poetical Works*, ed. H. E. Scudder. Boston/New York, 1900.

Buchanan, George. *Jephthes* (*1554*) and *Baptistes* (*1578*), tr. Alexander Gibb. Edinburgh, 1870.

Byron, Lord George Gordon. *Cain* (*1821*) and *Heaven and Earth* (*1822*) in *Complete Poetical Works*, ed. P. E. More. Boston/New York, 1905.

Carew, Lady Elizabeth. *Tragedy of Mariam, the Faire Queene of Iewry* (*1613*), ed. A. C. Dunstan. London, 1914.

Chayefsky, Paddy. *Gideon*. New York, 1962.

Christopherson, John. *Jephthah* (*1544?*), ed. and tr. F. H. Forbes. Newark, 1928.

Select List of Plays

Connelly, Marc. *Green Pastures*. New York, 1930.

Crowne, J. *The Destruction of Jerusalem*. London, 1693.

Croxall, Samuel. *The Fair Circassian* (*1720*). London, 1743.

Dane, Clemence (*alias* Winifred Ashton). *Naboth's Vineyard* (*1925*). New York, 1926.

Daviot, Gordon (*alias* Elizabeth Mackintosh). *Leith Sands*. London, 1946.

Dryden, John. *The State of Innocence and Fall of Man* (*1677*) in *Dramatick Works*. London, 1725.

Ewing, Thomas. *Jonathan*. New York/London, 1902.

Fenton, Elijah. *Mariamne*. London, 1723.

Fry, Christopher. *The Firstborn* (*1948*). Oxford, 1954.

— *A Sleep of Prisoners* (*1951*). Oxford, 1954.

Garter, Thomas. *The Commody of the moste vertuous and Godlye Susanna* (*1568?*). London, 1936.

Giraudoux, Jean. *Judith*, tr. J. K. Savacol in *The Modern Theatre*, ed. Eric Bentley. New York, 1955.

Goldsmith, Oliver. *The Captivity* (*1764*) in *Works*, ed. P. Cunningham. New York, n.d.

Greene, Robert, and Lodge, Thomas. *A Looking Glasse for London and England* (*1594*) in *The Plays and Poems of Robert Greene*, ed. J. C. Collins, vol. i. Oxford, 1905.

Grimald, Nicholas. *Christus Redivivus* (*1541*) and *Archipropheta* (*1546*) in *The Life and Poems*, ed. and tr. L. R. Merrill. New Haven, 1925.

Hassall, Christopher. *Christ's Comet*. New York, 1938.

Heminge, William. *The Jewes Tragedy, or their Fatal and Final Overthrow by Vespasian and Titus*. London, 1662.

Herbert, A. P. *The Book of Jonah* (*As almost any modern Irishman would have written it*) in *The London Mercury iii* (*1921*).

Hill, Aaron. *Saul* in *Dramatic Works*. London, 1760.

Housman, Laurence. *Bethlehem*. London, 1902.

— *Nazareth*. New York, 1916.

— *Old Testament Plays*. London, 1950.

Howell, Owen. *Abel: written but with great humility in reply to Lord Byron's Cain*. London, 1843.

Lally, Gwen. *Jezebel* (*1912*). London, 1918.

Langner, Lawrence. *Moses*. New York, 1924.

Lawrence, David Herbert. *David* (*1926*). London, 1930.

Select List of Plays

MacLeish, Archibald. *J.B.* (*1956*). Cambridge, Mass., 1958.
— *Nobodaddy.* Cambridge, 1926.
Mankowitz, Wolf. *It Should Happen to a Dog* (1956) in *Religious Drama 3*, ed. Marvin Halverson. New York, 1959.
Markham, G., and Sampson, W. *Herod and Antipater.* London, 1622.
Masefield, John. *The Coming of Christ.* New York, 1928.
— *Esther.* New York, 1922.
— *Good Friday* (*1915*). London, 1917.
— *A King's Daughter.* New York, 1923.
— *The Trial of Jesus.* London, 1925.
Milman, Henry Hart. *Belshazzar* (*1822*) in *Poetical Works.* London, 1839.
— *The Fall of Jerusalem.* London, 1820.
Milton, John. *Samson Agonistes* (*n.d.*) in *Works* vol. i. Columbia University edition. 20 vols. New York, 1931–40.
Moore, Thomas Sturge. *Absalom.* London, 1903.
— *Judith.* London, 1911.
— *Mariamne.* London, 1911.
More, Hannah. *Sacred Dramas* in *Works*, vol. vi. New York, 1835.
Nicholson, Norman. *A Match for the Devil* (*1953*). London, 1955.
— *The Old Man of the Mountains.* London, 1946.
Obey, André. *Noah* (*1929*), tr. Arthur Wilmurt. London, 1935.
Otway, Thomas. *Titus and Berenice* (*1677*) in *Works*, ed. J. C. Ghosh, 2 vols. Oxford, 1932.
Parker, Louis N. *Joseph and his Brethren.* New York, 1913.
Peele, George. *The Love of King David and Fair Bethsabe* (*1599*), ed. W. W. Greg. London, 1912.
Phillips, Stephen. *Herod.* London/New York, 1901.
Polack, E. *Esther, the Royal Jewess* (*1835*). London, n.d.
Pordage, Samuel. *Herod and Mariamne.* London, 1673.
Reade, J. E. *Cain the Wanderer.* London, 1829.
Rosenberg, Isaac. *Moses* (*1916*) in *Collected Poems*, ed. Gordon Bottomley and Denys Harding. London, 1949.
Sayers, Dorothy L. *He That Should Come.* London, 1939.
— *The Man Born to be King.* London, 1943.
Shaw, George Bernard. *Back to Methuselah: a metabiological pentateuch.* New York, 1922.

Select List of Plays

Thorndike, A. R. *Saul.* London, 1906.

Udall, Nicholas (?). *Jacob and Esau* (*1557*), ed. J. Crow and F. P. Wilson. Oxford, 1956.

Wade, Thomas. *The Jew of Arragon.* London, 1830.

Wager, Lewis. *The Life and Repentaunce of Marie Magdalene* (*1566?*), ed. F. I. Carpenter. Chicago, 1902.

Watson, Thomas (?). *Absalon* (?), ed., tr. and with a critical study by J. H. Smith. Unpublished thesis at the University of Illinois, (1958).

Wells, Charles Jeremiah. *Joseph and his Brethren* (*1824*). Oxford, 1908.

Wilde, Oscar. *Salome* (*1893*), tr. Lord Alfred Douglas in *Complete Works*. New York, 1927.

Williams, Charles. *Seed of Adam, The House by the Stable, Grab and Grace, The Rite of the Passion,* and *Terror of Light* in *Collected Plays*, ed. John Heath-Stubbs. Oxford, 1953.

Yeats, William Butler. *Calvary* (*1920*) and *Resurrection* (*1931*) in *Collected Plays*. London, 1953.

INDEX

Apart from anonymous plays, dramas are indexed under the author's name.

Index

Bronzino, 89
Brooke, C. F. Tucker, 15
Brooke, H., 190
Brooke, Stopford, 204
Broughton, Hugh, 160
Brown, Carleton, 140
Brown, J., 189
Browne, E. Martin, 290, 293
Browning, Elizabeth B., 198, 216–18
Bryant, J. A., 129
Bucer, Martin, 79, 80
Buchan, A. W., 220
Buchanan, George, 79–82 86, 109
Buckton, A. M., 229, 289–90
Bullen, A. H., 101
Burney, Charles, 187
Burton, Robert, 154
Busher, Leonard, 158
Butcher, S. H., 131
Butler, Samuel, 265
Buxtorf, Johann, 104, 143, 160
Byron, 13, 192, 198–215, 221, 237, 259, 300, 303

Cain, 13, 19, 24, 27, 28, 31, 43–5, 125, 198–215, 302–3, 311
Calvin, 50–3, 76, 92, 109, 182
Campbell, Lily B., 53, 58, 68, 97–8
Carew, Elizabeth, 119, 173
Cargill, Oscar, 33
Carissimi, Giacomo, 185
Carmina Burana, 30
Carpenter, E., 220
Cary, *see* Carew
Casaubon, Isaac, 160
Celtes, Conrad, 58
Censorship, 52–3, 109–15, 139, 182, 226–32, 243
Chambers, E. K., 15, 21, 36, 53, 112
Chaucer, 26
Chayefsky, Paddy, 307–8
Cheffaud, P. H., 105
Chester, Mary, 158
Chester plays, 31–2, 37–8, 41, 43
Chettle, Henry, 118
Chew, S. C., 191, 200, 204, 210–11, 214
Christian Terence, *see* Terence
Christopherson, John, 79, 82–3, 86
Clark, E. M., 154
Clark, W. S., 174
Clarke, G. H., 249
Clough, Arthur H., 198
Coghill, Nevill, 293

Coleman, E. D., 142, 190, 196, 220, 230, 323
Coleridge, 200–3, 215, 218, 233–5
Colet, John, 50, 52
Collier, Jeremy, 133, 180
Colman, George (the younger), 227
Connelly, Marc, 263–4
Cook, A. S., 42
Corneille, 134
Cosbey, R. C., 42
Council of Arles, 110
Council of Carthage, 110
Council of Trent, 52
Covenant, 51, 62, 70
Coventry plays, 22, 25, 26, 118
Cowley, Abraham, 176
Craig, Hardin, 18, 32–3, 56, 93
Craig, James, 192
Creizenach, W., 84, 96, 101, 118
Crocus, Cornelius, 52, 56, 58
Cromwell, Oliver, 159
Cromwell, Thomas, 61
Crowne, John, 174–5
Croxall, Samuel, 192
Cunliffe, J. W., 105, 121
Cushman, L. W., 27

Daiches, David, 116, 160
Dalila, 154–73
Dane, Clemence, 250
Daniel, 34–5
Danielou, Jean, 27
Darwin, Charles, 233
D'Avenant, William, 139, 179, 182
David, 30, 34, 55, 56, 100–7, 176, 180, 189, 190, 193, 228, 252–4, 275–9, 285–6, 303, 306
Daviot, Gordon, 288
Davis, Thurston N., 312
Davy, C., 190
Dean, Winton, 184–7
Dearmer, Mabel, 290
Deborah, 56, 184–5
Dekker, Thomas, 118
De Mille, Cecil B., 226
Devil, *see* Satan
Digby plays, 30–1
Dixie, F. C. 198
Donne, John, 156
Donne, William, 227
Donoghue, Denis, 304
Doran, Madeleine, 127
Douai Bible, 50, 140

Index

Index

Index

Index